CONNECTED

RAND McNALLY
International Series
World
ATLANTIC OCEAN
GREENLAND SEA
UNION
SOCIALIST
REPUBLICS
EUROPE
INDIAN
OCEAN
GREENLAND
MAURITANIA
IRAN
WEST INDIES
UNITED STATES
PACIFIC OCEAN

World Map 2, © 1989 by Nina Katchadourian

Late Editions

3

Cultural Studies for the End of the Century

CONNECTED

ENGAGEMENTS WITH MEDIA

George E. Marcus, EDITOR

The University of Chicago Press
Chicago and London

George E. Marcus is professor of anthropology at Rice University. He is coauthor of *Anthropology as Cultural Critique* (University of Chicago Press, 1986) and was the inaugural editor of the journal *Cultural Anthropology.*

The University of Chicago Press, Chicago 60637
The University of Chicago Press, Ltd., London
© 1996 by The University of Chicago
All rights reserved. Published 1996
Printed in the United States of America
05 04 03 02 01 00 99 98 97 96   1 2 3 4 5
"The Electronic Vernacular" (chapter 1 of this volume) © 1996 by Barbara Kirshenblatt-Gimblett.

ISBN: 0-226-50441-7 (cloth)
          0-226-50442-5 (paper)
ISSN: 1070-8987 (for Late Editions)

CONTENTS

Introduction to the Volume and Reintroduction to the Series

This is the third volume of an annual series that will be published until the year 2000. This series is as much interested in the widespread self-awareness of massive changes in society and culture globally, especially among those who write about the contemporary world, as it is in the facts and lived experiences of these changes themselves. Indeed, this self-awareness among both writers and their subjects *is* one of the major facts about this moment. This dual interest and a particular strategy for pursuing it in producing the series are what we believe make these volumes distinctive.

Perhaps the single most striking rhetorical characteristic of writing about the contemporary in this fin de siècle (and probably of others before it) is the hyperawareness that the velocity and immensity of changes are beyond the *as McLuhan* conceptual grasp of writers of various kinds to describe and interpret them. For some this rhetoric of the insufficiency of the means of representation in the face of watershed changes constitutes a kind of discourse of marveling that ironically enhances conventional, distanced descriptions of events and processes. A rhetoric of a struggle to keep up with what is happening often frames and creates a special urgency—a newsworthiness—for the most mundane as well as for the very best conventional print and electronic journalism. The aura of both the fear and wonder of the present emerging into the future is what "current-events" bestsellers are made of and is also a key "visionary" component in arguing for government programs and policies. However, media commentaries, bestsellers, and public policies are only cogent if they still speak compellingly in comfortable, taken-for-granted terms and story lines even though these might indeed be under erasure, so to speak.

For others who write about the present—and here I have in mind those large segments of the academic world who have been in a sense prepared for the fin de siècle by the deep influence upon them of the 1980s critiques of longstanding languages, rhetorics, and practices of scholarship about culture and society—the self-awareness of the inadequacy of past means of representation has led to a vast outpouring of experimentation with modes of writing, theorizing, scholarly practice, and a questioning of the purposes of scholarship itself. One thing for sure is that the standard modes of realist narrative storytelling about the momentous present as it unfolds is not enough for historians, anthropologists, literary critics, film and videomakers, philosophers, and other scholars of the present. The latter are characteristically expected to be more reflective than journalists or policymakers, and they are certainly not subject to the demands or markets of communicating to a broad, imagined public. Typically, the call among academic cultural critics has been for new vocabularies for new social and cultural realities (for example, "I believe that creating a new language is both an urgent and central task today in order to reconstitute the grounds on which cultural and educational debates are to be waged" [Giroux 1992:3]), but this is too sanguine a response to the sensibility operating among critical scholars who have been profoundly influenced by the challenge to conventional narrative practices in such intellectual movements as feminism, postcolonialism, and post-structuralism. Any new "language" to grasp the present unfolding will not be anything like past languages or models of discourse that become in some sense standardized and authoritative, even in a self-conscious critical mode. Rather the new languages or vocabularies will remain for the foreseeable future embedded in and inextricable from the messy, contestatory discussions that predominate in the wake of the widely acknowledged crisis of representation. In this domain, marveling about the unspeakability of the present unfolding, associated with the rhetoric of insufficient language, is tinged with a skepticism that doubts whether straightforward, distanced stories about the present can be told in any compelling way without constant interruption and the negotiation of heterogeneous voices.

This series tries to steer a course between these two tendencies of writing about the contemporary. While we recognize the ironic seduction of a posited inadequacy of language to keep doing the same old kind of "voice-over" description and narration about events and changes, we also understand that the deep and widespread urge to document and witness in a straightforward, stark way cannot be denied. We merely claim that distanced, expository discourse and representations—whether theoretical, descriptive, or media commonsensical—are inadequate without the collaboration and exposure of the discourse of situated persons, who become the subjects of the contributions of the various fin-de-siècle themes taken up by this series.

Our strategy to achieve this mix of distance and engagement is to impose some variation of an interview/dialogue/conversation format upon the mostly academic authors of this series. While in their research they indeed operate in a world of interviews and conversations, such authors in their writing are accustomed to the analytic, descriptive discourse of scholars. In a sense, each piece in this series is an experiment in suppressing the enunciatory mode of academic/journalistic writing, or at least in pursuing insights and arguments by other means, through the voices of situated others.

The situated conversation or interview is of course the mise en scène of research in anthropology, but the interview specifically as a form of writing creates a certain intimacy, an experiential yet distanced access to events and processes known otherwise through day-to-day reporting and commentary in the media. The interview form in the hands of academic writers who are uncertainly employing it delivers both a strong reality effect and also an undermining of this effect by knowing readerships wise to the deceits of any kind of representation that appeals to a transparent real. Thus the interview as experimented with here can potentially occupy that difficult middle ground within a form that documents while constantly giving indications of its constructedness, of the ambivalences of its interlocutors, and of both occlusions and statements that seem just right in relation to encompassing events and processes. In other words, the use of the interview holds promise of just those mixed characteristics of discourse that can navigate the shoals of writing in the shadow of a crisis of representation.

The interview intruded upon the habit of exposition is thus the main emblem of the series and its wager concerning what is effective discourse at the moment about contemporary change. Yet what is displayed in these volumes are not accomplished examples of the interview form but various kinds of struggle with it. Indeed, some of the pieces evolve in other directions—as biographical profiles, as personal memoirs, as the juxtaposed representation of documents, as interesting accounts of failed conversations. A recurrent question voiced at our annual collective editorial meetings is about how much context is necessary and appropriate for various pieces (read, how much background is necessary for the uninitiated reader as well as enunciative prose from the scholarly specialist), indexing a persistent relative discomfort among authors with yielding so much space to the exposure of encounters and staged conversations rather than direct authorial interpretations of them. The results are varied, mixed, with occasional rough edges, but, we hope, always interesting and imaginative.

This series thus tries to create its own niche within the contemporary interdisciplinary domain known as cultural studies, broadly conceived. Its short-term time-space is signaled by the loaded label, fin de siècle, in which it periodizes and limits itself, and cultivates a certain detachment while understanding that this is not the old claim to value neutrality enabling the truth. Detachment arises from and is a way to cope with bewilderments and cynicisms that seem so much a part of the age. It seeks not to close down optimism or pander to pessimism but struggles for a documentation which, through the interview or some variation on it, is a kind of cultural activism (see Faye Ginsburg's comments in the appendix). These volumes do not attempt authoritatively to review or survey fields but rather are carefully constructed assemblages that seek to play on associations among diffuse pieces not only within particular volumes but across them as natural accumulations of producing the series.

In this series, then, rather than the marveling side of the rhetoric of writerly insufficiency, we tend to display its anxious side. Fin-de-siècle perspective for us communicates more anticipation and responses to "first signs" rather than a sense of the reality of changes. Most of the situations explored through personal accounts in this series, and especially those in Late Editions 3, were produced implicitly or explicitly in anticipation of these great changes. This posture of waiting through all the coping and envisioning at present is definitive of a fin-de-siècle mood. There is indeed a lot of futurism in current thinking, but it is much more anxiety filled than, for example, the earlier bout of futurist writing in the 1960s (for example, books with titles like *Toward the Year 2000*). The future is actually experienced now through all sorts of new requirements and disruptions in the present without it being clearly conceived or imagined. The notion of emergence—the future in the rapidly unfolding present— so salient in contemporary discourse communicates this ambiguous posture of anticipatory waiting in relation to an unimaginable future.

This year's assemblage is on changes in electronic and visual media of various kinds and their new uses, but like other volumes in this series, this one also has a particular inflection. Our typical focus is upon individuals or sets of individuals whose personal predicaments and mundane to dramatic reflective articulations of them provide readers with access to particular events and social processes that might not otherwise be available through conventional reporting, description, and analysis. Thus we are as much, if not more, interested in exposing the suggestions, the traces, the hints, the loose ends, the associations concerning the broader events and larger processes that we all share in differently situated ways with the subjects of these accounts than we are with their pure human-interest side as harrowing tales of contemporary experience in transition, which in many cases they certainly are also. We thus encourage readers to do more with these pieces than just to appreciate other lives elsewhere in different situations than their own.

Mostly, the culturally diverse subjects of the pieces in this and the other volumes of the series share the following with the largely middle-class academic authors involved in the series: they are people who do or have felt some level of usually modest personal empowerment and control in their lives (that is, they have been shaped by the essential privilege and sense of security that has defined modern middle classes worldwide) but who also feel themselves living at risk in a dangerous world of possibility in which they are fearful of exactly those events and processes writ large which are also bound up with those things on which any continuing sense of their own personal empowerment depends. Though the writers and subjects in these pieces are different in many complex ways, this sense of fearfulness and empowerment from the same sources of fin-de-siècle change is what binds them together—it provides the knowing assumptions of common discourse even in the pieces where the interlocutors and authors are most obviously different in cultural and life situations. The frequent feeling of a mix of fear and excitement of people empowered by access to new forms of media, who are the most common subjects of this volume's pieces, is not unlike the feeling of the authors who ironically see opportunity in the awareness of change beyond their discursive grasp that pushes them to the various connections, alliances, and engagements that these pieces represent.

Perhaps more than in the two other volumes produced so far in this series, this one more centrally and complexly takes up the series' emblematic perspective on large and rapidly changing contemporary events through the scope of personal experience and reflection of particular kinds of persons brought into dynamic relation as writers and subjects for the purposes of this series. In Late Editions 1, *Perilous States,* subjects were dealing with the changes brought about by shifts in leviathan political orders. In Late Editions 2, *Technoscientific Imaginaries,* subjects were dealing with changes embedded in another distanced leviathan, the institutional corporate, global orders of scientific activity. But as will be seen in this volume, through new media technologies that are so revolutionary because they are so mass distributed and *apparently* populist, the great changes do not seem to emanate from or within a leviathan (as yet!), but are a direct and intimate complement to the self and self-capacity. In this volume on media, the great changes are, in relation to previous volumes, much more palpable and invasive in terms of self-identity.

Many contemporary users of the Internet really do believe they are engaged in mind and body in a different kind of social order with definite implications for personal empowerment, as do users of video technology in the pursuit of activist projects (in this regard, compare the pieces by Pound and Lotfalian with those by McLagan and Juhasz and Mohammed). The illusions and realities of new imaginaries and the material effects of global changes are thus far more intensively and totally dealt with at the level of self-definition and self-capacity in the chapters of this volume than in those of the previous two. The subjects of this volume seem to be less subtly and more seamlessly connected to the larger processes at stake. These larger processes are synonymous and most visible for the time being precisely at the level of personal experience in a way that is strikingly different than, say, with the Russian writers of *Perilous States,* who see what is happening to them vividly in the imagination or through a glass darkly, or with the scientists of *Technoscientific Imaginaries,* who communicate a personal and professional distance from the processes that define them. Here, in these accounts of kinds of contemporary media possibilities for immediate personal action, the great fin-de-siècle changes in question are distinctively and fully embodied inside the sacred preserve of self-identities.

The major limitation by omission of this volume is that it does not give access to those great institutional and corporate changes themselves—the topsy-turvy shifts, the media mergers or attempted media mergers, the new legislation, and negotiations among governments—but rather confines itself to certain kinds of currently widespread appropriations of media (however, see Kim Laughlin and John Monberg's interview with Paul Sagan in Chapter 8 of this volume to get an oblique view of change in media leviathans registered in the double-voiced language of claims to journalistic practice and identity as usual). The two major modes reflected in this volume, quite appropriate to this particular moment of the fin de siècle, are personal involvements with the virtual reality of the Internet and the use of the availability of video and film technology in contemporary movements of cultural activism that pursue traditional goals of broad-based social change through a politics of identity and representation.

There appears to be no real or powerfully imagined "outside" to capitalism now, and where oppositional space is to be found, or how it is to be constructed within a global economy, is perhaps the most important fin-de-siècle question for left-liberal thought. Clearly in the very different processes of media transformation of the sense of self as exhibited in this volume's exposures of relatively empowered people at risk, potent imaginaries emerge that certainly constitute alternatives to older ideas and hopes for total transformation of capitalist political economy and consumer societies. Contemporary media technologies as distinctively focused upon in this Late Editions 3 are the contemporary space of imagination where new, progressive, if not fantastic, things are thought capable of happening. In the nineteenth fin de siècle this imaginary of both fearfulness and marveling in the face of the new, despite the emerging telegraph, radio, and telephone technologies, was perhaps more focused on new forms of transportation than communication.

Late Editions 3 deals with the media imaginary for such alternative or oppositional space in the realm of cultural production in terms of the two noted media modes: the Internet, in which the struggle for the terms in which to conceive its elusive social definition and meaning is currently a source of fascination, inflected by transgressive hopes for multiple, flexible subjectivity and identity as well as anarchic forms of community that are radically democratic outside the conventional conceptions of political systems and philosophies; and the hope for effective emancipatory projects in the uses by subaltern, silenced, and marginalized groups of new media technologies and new possibilities in their distribution, raising fresh issues about citizenship and the shape of public spheres within the frame and terms of traditional discourses on polity and civil society.

As such, widely disseminated technologies of representation (video) or antirepresentation (the Net) especially among middle classes able to access them provide at least the space where critical perspective and debates about the illusory or efficacious nature of this imaginary can be sustained with some vitality and a sense of possibility. To do so, these debates partake of the same rhetoric of insufficiency or the loss of control of representation that powers so many other diverse tendencies to respond intellectually to changes in which we are all caught up.

I now want to frame further these motivating ideas that inform the various contributions to this volume by discussing the factors of production by which volumes of this series are produced. This is appropriate since what each volume becomes as an assemblage is very much determined by the nature of the year-long process through which they are developed. How each volume and the series as a whole turn out is very much a function of choices and collaborations made during this evolving process of producing the volumes. Centered on efforts under my editorship in the Department of Anthropology at Rice University, contributors are recruited each summer and fall following a planning meeting for each volume in the late spring. Projects are developed by contributors through the winter and early spring in preparation for a collective editorial meeting/conference at Rice in early May. Sometimes material is at hand for the development of pieces, but often the contributors are busy during this period creating the events of interview from which their contributions will be derived. The collective editorial meeting, attended by as many of the participants as possible, is the crucial event in the production of these volumes, since through the give and take over precirculated materials, exactly what the volume will have to say about perilous states, science, or, in this case, media emerges through the mostly congenial "dissensus" of the event.

Factors of Production

Timing

A recent, self-consciously conservative critique in the *Times Literary Supplement* of the ambition of an issue of the journal *Daedalus* on "Germany in Transition" poses an important issue about the cogency of scholars trying to keep up with events. Albeit through the conventional discursive forms of scholarship, *Daedalus* has had a longtime agenda roughly similar to that of this short-term series to treat various aspects of the present as it unfolds:

> "Germany in Transition" addresses all the right issues. . . . The answers, alas, often lack punch and precision. In almost every essay, much space is devoted to regurgitations of the past—of the "old Germany" both East and West, and how the twain became fused. . . . The problem with *anything* "in transition" is precisely transition. In real transitions—and Germany's is real—we barely know where we are, let alone where we are going. Hence, this issue of *Daedalus* was a tough, almost forbidding assignment. Academic journals should do

> what they do best: the calm essay, the painstaking research paper, the reasoned argument. This is what has turned *Daedalus* into a leading exemplar of its kind. But academic journals should fear to tread where day-to-day journalism can barely keep its footing. (Jolfe 1994)

Of course, we avoid the major thrust of this criticism by a strategy which attempts to offset and struggle with the conventional discursive form of scholarship and to avoid the apparent futurist tendency of writing like that of the *Daedalus* issue, which, characteristic of scholarly discourse, relies heavily on a knowledge of history or relatively stable trends to make suggestions about the future or the fast changing present. Still, the issue of the temporal relevance of these volumes, especially given the velocity of changes in the arenas which they take up, is worth some consideration. In one sense the assemblages of this series are put together with an eye to the future reading-back of them. While they should have some contemporary interest as commentary, the journalistic analogy can be taken too far, and certainly contra the above criticism, neither the intention of the series nor its manner of publication makes it any sort of competitor to the refined art of narrative, analytic journalism. There is perhaps a conceit of journalistic immediacy attached to this series, but the fact that its publication schedule is scholarly (read, slow) undercuts any such pretense.

Rather, as the fin-de-siècle periodizing suggests, we are speculating to some degree about the future standing of these volumes, as assemblages, taken severally and singly as documents of a moment, certainly partial and with a strong evolving sense of certain characteristics that are readable in every contribution to the various volumes of the series. It is this strategized "series effect" that should sustain the relevance of the highly specific time-space of each contribution within the frame of the fin de siècle caught between the past and future, regardless of the inevitable gap between its appearance in publication and what is happening just then.

Still, it is interesting to consider how the materials of the various volumes are to be located temporally within the decade life of the series. Each volume tries to mediate the immediate with the enduring in the fin-de-siècle frame. Certain volumes are a little ahead of their time, others are a little belated. This volume, especially with the more than apparent velocity of change in the arena of electronic communication, keenly points up this problem of producing something that is likely to be out-of-date in a purely newsworthy sense when it appears in print, even though this volume, as noted, has a much different character and agenda than the desire to be newsworthy in its specificity.

This issue of the sustained relevance of material in the midst of fast moving events was certainly salient in producing Late Editions 1 and somewhat less so in producing Late Editions 2 (on the culture of science that anticipates and organizes constant change also seems to place a brake on a hyperselfconsciousness about the temporal relevance of what one writes about it), but in producing this volume the question of its timing against a keen awareness of the speed of change was extraordinarily salient.

The sense of velocity of events in producing this volume arose from the extraordinary pace of revelations and developments even as it was being prepared on a weekly, sometimes daily basis concerning the forms of mass media on which we have long depended. For example, when I mentioned to a friend that we planned to do a media volume now, he suggested it was perhaps two or three years premature. The Internet is the current mode of participation, and indeed this is what we reflect in our treatment of electronic communication. But the far more definitive fin-de-siècle account of how this incredibly difficult sphere to commercialize will be either bypassed or harnessed by corporate capitalism or will be phased out by government is of course the big story we have not told and could not tell. In classic eras of colonial and national competitions, attempts to commercialize and regulate sea lanes, air lanes, and airwaves were facilitated through the necessity of large corporate ventures to develop these channels, and such tangible entities could be controlled. The Internet, in contrast, is entirely populist (though crucially piggybacked on government and military research budgets) and will be difficult to commercialize and regulate. In the shift to high-resolution visual technology through corporate mergers there is an ongoing effort at commercialization that bypasses the populist Net of the keyboard. This volume is produced at a time before commercialization has been figured out and put in place. Thus while in relation to electronic media this volume will certainly have addressed an essential element of the fin de siècle from an imagined future point looking backward to the present, this treatment is also outside the arena of what will likely be the defining struggle to establish order and organization in the new technologies.

The Collective Editorial Meeting and the Organization of Late Editions 3

The annual collective editorial meeting in the late spring is the forum at which the main "take" of the volume on a particular theme emerges through successive editorial and critical commentaries on each of the contributions by as many authors who are able to attend. Precisely through commentaries on these experiments with form do the major distinctive features of the series treatment of fin-de-siècle topics become apparent. This is indeed the kind of site and process by which the new "languages" about the unfolding present are being created.

The organization of the volume has approximately followed the main tendencies of discussion. The divide was between the discussion of the several pieces on the Internet in the morning (part 1, The Net Defiant) and a center of gravity of discussion in the afternoon around activism, generally in relation to the use of media to produce representations that have effect as cultural criticism or specifically within social movements of various kinds (part 2, The Activist Imaginary).

In part 1, the piece by Barbara Kirshenblatt-Gimblett is an insightful portrait of the various genres of electronic communication on the Net at the time this volume was produced. The following piece, by Burnett, is a theoretical reflection on the Net in the context of a cascade of new media. This section concludes with two "artifacts": pieces by Chris Pound and Mazyar Lotfalian, highly knowledgeable users of the Net who attempt to represent the conditions of Net discourse and routines that reflect their own practices as users.

Part 2 provides access to the strong activist impulse in the use of media by individuals and groups outside large formal media organizations. Linking with the previous pieces on the Internet, Meg McLagan deals with a case (Tibetan refugees) of the seeming pursuit of political/national struggles by means of new electronic communication (although see Pound's comments in the appendix as to the ambivalent sense of such activity as activism). The exchanges between Alexandra Juhasz and Juanita Mohammed communicate something of the passion of relationship in the collaboration of video activism, an ever more frequent mode of protest and intervention out of older social movements, based on the model of even older liberation struggles of the 1950s and 1960s. Kim Laughlin's piece on continuing grass-roots protest in India after the Bhopal disaster is largely outside the excitement of new-media modes of activism but communicates strongly that contemporary activism is indeed a struggle over representation, and by its display of documents, her piece conveys just how diverse are the genres in which this struggle occurs.

Part 3, Urban Mediascapes on the Verge, juxtaposes those papers concerned with life in U.S. cities and the exposures they offer of various constructions of media in the interesting contrast of the slippery shifts of the idea of journalism within a corporate media giant (the Laughlin-John Monberg piece) to the senses of the "news" that arises from artistic endeavors blurring their own categories of work (the pieces by Dorinne Kondo and Joe Austin). These papers broaden the Net activist focus of the volume as to what is to count as media in relation to unfolding events (for example, the arts can be thought to exist in the same media space as the news, video activism, and electronic communication rather than in a removed sphere of "aesthetics"). They demonstrate within the frame of contemporary urban America the strikingly alternative spheres through which the same "news" can be communicated to middle-class publics.

Finally, there was a very rich set of pieces presented at the collective editorial meeting (by Michael Fischer, Gudrun Klein, Hamid Naficy, Santiago Villa-veces Izquierdo, Leslie Fordred, Julie Taylor, and Tom Wolfe) that concerned the predicaments of media production in a variety of sites around the world in which there have been dramatic shifts in political orders and civil societies. They considerably broaden the concerns of the pieces presented in this volume. However, to have included these pieces in Late Editions 3 would have made a far too long, unwieldy, and less focused volume. Furthermore, these pieces do have their own thematic coherence around the issues of "perilous states" treated in Late Editions 1. Therefore we have decided to collect them in a separate companion volume as Late Editions 4, with its own distinct identity. It is previewed in this volume by the inclusion of a piece on changes in the South African Broadcasting Corporation by Ruth Teer-Tomaselli.

Who Participates as Authors

Recruitment to participation as authors in the volumes of this series involves a combination of the use of extended networks with the interesting accumulation of continuities from volume to volume and a speculative element of casting about for new participation within the realm of specialty and expertise associated with each theme. This results in the assemblage character of the resulting volumes. The Rice anthropology department and those who have been associated with it since the mid-1980s form a center of density in networks from which participants are recruited for this series. Because of the trend of interdisciplinary work in intellectual life since the 1980s in which we have been positioned on various borders between the social sciences and the humanities, the networks reflect this breadth.

The emergence of continuities of participation and place as these volumes have developed has been especially interesting to watch. Each volume has combined a mix of recognized and new talent. Some contributors have appeared in each volume of the series, others might appear from time to time. Places and previous themes are also revisited from volume to volume. For example, Late Editions 4, the companion volume to this one, develops interesting new angles on the concerns of Late Editions 1, *Perilous States* (in which previous sites of great changes in polities and civil societies that we treated— Poland, South Africa, Germany, Russia—as well as some new ones are taken up from media angles); and this volume, Late Editions 3, on those of Late Editions 2, *Technoscientific Imaginaries* (the contributions of part 1, on the Internet, could easily have fit into the concerns of this earlier volume). The return to Bhopal in this volume (the paper by Kim Laughlin) provides a similar kind of development within continuities of place and relationship. Ultimately, in the final volume of the series, we are planning to solicit a reflection about the continuities, links, and connections that the series has consciously and unconsciously developed.

Along with this evolving family effect in the way that the series develops its themes is a more wide-ranging speculative search for participants on the edges of networks who are also within the established communities of specialization and expertise involved with each of the themes we take up. Here it is the productive tensions that result which are interesting. The specific agenda and strategy of the series usually overlap with, but are certainly not exactly the same as, those of self-identified members of particular specialist communities who agree to participate in producing these volumes. Sometimes this tension takes on the character of professionalism versus the kind of informed, enlightened naiveté that this series encourages, but it is usually more interesting than this. Indeed, tolerating and negotiating naiveté and offbeat kinds of approaches has been one of the most productive dimensions of discussion at the collective editorial meetings. The series wants respect and interest from specialists as the volumes inevitably develop obliquely in relation to their own agendas. Yet, ideally, it also seeks its own distinctive readership that might develop in response to its particular strategy for documenting the present, regardless of the theme taken up. The relationship of these volumes to varied domains of specialization thus must remain ambivalent.

It is interesting to note how distinctive scholarly communities with which the series has engaged differ. For example, in Late Editions 2 the series was squarely identified with a group of scholars out of cultural studies who are operating within the well-established field of the social/historical studies of science. In this field, a rather orthodox sense of methodology in the social sciences prevailed, with a sense of rigor that paralleled the style of the communities of natural scientists studied. The specialist culture of media studies involved in Late Editions 3 tends to parallel the avant-garde qualities of the communities of cultural/media producers that it studies.

In Late Editions 3 and 4 there has been a productive tension between those participants who worked with the media theme as nonspecialists but who were probing aspects of it to examine issues they were very knowledgeable about and particular places they were interested in, and those who developed their contributions out of the discussions and questions that shape the field in which they are specialists (for example, Lisa Cartwright, Faye Ginsburg, Hamid Naficy, Ron Burnett, among others). For some the theme of the volume was a way to work out certain interests (dealing with the construction of identities in different locales of great change and the political implications of these processes, for example) through the use of a rather cunning naiveté in the way topics are exploited. For others, media itself is a central focus that perhaps captures the same questions as others but which has an importance in itself that it does not have for nonspecialists.

The particular specialist culture of media studies—which is one of the core fields out of which the intellectual capital of the broader cultural studies interdisciplinary arena has been drawn—is quite distinctive. As noted, it takes on some of the characteristics of the cultural/artistic avant-gardes with which it is often concerned (quite unlike the specialist cultures with which Late Editions 1 and 2 were involved). There is a strong value on the new, on left-liberal activism, on the desire for grass-roots media experimentation at the level of everyday life and commitment to change. There are opportunities for involvement with a politics of representation in media studies that feels most strongly the "crisis of representation" and the inadequacy of concepts on which this series is based. All avant-gardes work now from this anxiety, and it is what gives media scholars an avant-garde quality themselves that blends them in with the actors in media whom they study and with whom they establish new kinds of working relationships. This kind of specialist culture definitely fit and even spurred on the anxiety behind the series over the fact that we are dealing with a velocity and level of change that we are barely able to address through conventional book writing. It is also a field in which the interview form is well developed, as is the idea of producing knowledge through collaborations.

Indeed, late in the day of our collaborative editorial meeting, a discussion arising from the desires, politics, and practices within contemporary media and cultural studies pointedly dealt with limitations in who participates as authors in these volumes. For such a self-critical discussion to arise was certainly a positive thing for the series, as well as being a symptom itself of fin-de-siècle ethos within the academy. Out of the documentary impulse that pervades this series, I include some excerpts of this discussion both as a partial documentation of a distinctive concern of the period and as incorporating a reflexive function that these volumes should regularly exhibit. The lack of sufficiently multicultural authorship (in contrast to the range of experiences presented in the actual papers) was certainly the most passionately expressed self-critique of the way collaborative authorship of this volume took shape. A documentary exposure of this self-critique itself stands as further evidence of the sorts of ongoing change in our own process of production that the series tries to probe in other persons in other places. So, while who participates in this series is partly a serendipitous function of networks and speculations, it is a question that is also shaped by very definite institutional and structural dispositions.

Excerpts from Collective Editorial Meeting, 30 April 1994

Lisa Cartwright:

I initially felt very uncomfortable about interviewing Ngozi from the standpoint of a feminist working on breast cancer issues and on independent film because I felt very uncomfortable about authoring that kind of information. . . . And I feel that's exacerbated in the context of a book in which there are very, very few people of color making authorial contributions. I would feel much better about it if the constitution of the book changed or if there were some very frank discussion of that.

Hamid Naficy:

It's much better for us to do this here and include this, in some way, than have some reviewer come out with it.

Faye Ginsburg:

But I think if one of the things this book is doing is marking where things are in the late twentieth century, then that's part of it. There's a traditional moment in which relations of privilege are being interrogated. Part of what's very positive is that this book is looking at what's been represented in terms of places in the world and people who are being valorized; it's incredibly rich and diverse in that way. In terms of those writing the text, it's still reflective of power relations that have been in place for a long time.

I've been thinking of an article that I want to write, and it's called "Erasure of the White Guys," which has to do with the indigenous media stuff I've been researching, but the point is that identity politics have also pushed us into a point where—let me give this example: indigenous media is mostly produced by very interesting collaborations between white people from the dominant culture and indigenous people coming from various backgrounds. And these are, in my view, incredibly interesting, creative collaborative moments in which social relations are produced very productively, new possibilities are envisioned, but because of identity politics, let's wipe out the white people and just call it indigenous, as if we can essentialize and purify that. Well, of course, there is no such thing; it's a ridiculous claim. But everyone wants it because it's a romanticized notion of what identity politics has left on the landscape. One can try to think of this as not reproducing colonial relations, but rather as working with intellectuals around the world of different kinds of backgrounds, where there is an interest in pulling more collaborative kinds of relations into the framework of academic discussion. That's a positive thing. If anything positive can emerge on the landscape of identity politics, it may be a way that the academy can move into a more collaborative kind of model. It would be great if there were more diverse groups of people at this table itself.

George Marcus:

I think it's very important to register that this issue came up so strongly in this volume in a way that it didn't come up in Late Editions 2, on science, technology, and culture.

Ron Burnett:

Can I raise another issue here, which really disturbs me because I work a lot with so-called developing countries and people in NGOs (nongovernment organizations) and I've often raised this issue in collaborative projects where I have been involved. What I've gotten back from Indian and African people I've worked with is, "Let us develop the strategies that we are developing within the context that we actually feel powerful in. Don't invite us into the halls of power which you ultimately control." Then don't tell me that if we had tried to create a diversity of authorship here in some self-conscious way, that we would have succeeded in creating—

Lisa Cartwright:

There's a confusion here. I'm not saying, "Hey, let's go call up the Kayapo, and say, Write an essay for us." I'm saying call up—I don't know—my friend, Patina Romi who works on Asian Pacific independent video and community politics, and who has a Ph.D., is at UCLA, and a colleague. I'm not talking about reaching outside the academic community. I don't see how that's tokenizing when they're people with whom we work on a regular basis and are in communication with on a regular basis.

Faye Ginsburg:

We were also getting used to each other as a group and this is a very hot topic to even bring up. There are a lot of virtues in the way this book is organized, and I don't think we should get defensive about the fact that it's a lack, it's a problem. And there's an incredible focus on what the text should look like on the page, which seems a kind of myopic preoccupation when we haven't thought about what the people gathered around the table look like.

Lisa Cartwright:

But given that you have invited us to discuss the formation of this volume, I think it would be great to include some pieces that address works that for me are crucial at the turn of the century, for example, Asian Pacific video, or what's happening in Chicano performance arts.

Alex Juhasz:

Gay and lesbian video.

Sandy Stone:

Transgender video.

Lisa Cartwright:

And I know that you can't do all of these things, but—

Barbara Kirshenblatt-Gimblett:

It's no accident that we've been constituted as we've been constituted. And the question is, are we going to flagellate ourselves and proceed to do business as usual, or are we going to take an activist stance and say that there are individuals in the book whose personal networks would access another range of scholars, scholarship, sensibility, perspective, and experience that would further enrich this enterprise? That's not about representation and it is also not about a kind of acceptance. There has to be a way to take action that isn't immobilizing.

Who Participates—Dramatis Personae

While there is considerable diversity among the subjects focused upon and selected as interlocutors within this series, there is also a definite sort of personal predicament and subject position that these volumes have addressed, as I have mentioned. For example, in this volume, the big story we have not addressed is exactly that: the great organizational changes within corporate capitalism that are accommodating technological changes in media. Nor have we covered the important ways that media is being used in right-wing or conservative causes worldwide, as in the emergence of various religious fundamentalisms. Much of what we have omitted is indeed on the peripheries of what can sometimes be read into the heart of the experiences exposed here, but mainly we have sought to develop subject perspectives that in some sense have affinities with those writing. Our emphasis is on the direct and embodied effects of media on patterns of life of certain kinds of individuals: middle-class intellectuals, empowered professionals, broadly conceived, at this rather early moment in the fin de siècle.

So while our view is cosmopolitan and wide ranging, it can also be parochial and partial as to the "takes" it offers on the vast changes as these are funneled through dialogue, individual experience, and the reflections presented here. Still, the chimerical nature of the material—its essential attraction—is in the defeat of expectations once this basic affinity between author, subject, and, ultimately, implied reader is acknowledged. Thus the provocation of the series in the selection of interlocutors is to create affinities where we didn't suspect them and to suggest differences where we thought there were none. This can create considerable unease in participants in these volumes, as well as in readers. We do not seek exotic, dramatic difference in others and their experiences, but find difference complexly evident in ourselves, broadly conceived through the kinds of baseline affinities that the series establishes in the selection of its dramatis personae. This is indeed a desired effect when we recall that the series is based on a fin-de-siècle condition that creates a politics of identity for middle-class, modestly empowered people at risk who are profoundly made aware of the inadequacies of representation through, in this volume particularly, their involvement with new media technologies that function in various senses as extensions and transformers of the sense of self.

To give a sense of this range of affinity and difference of subjects in relation to authors of Late Editions 3, I have summarily listed principal subjects:

> Robbie Barnett, Tseten Samdup, the members of soc.culture.scientists, Anna Deavere Smith, Juanita Mohammed, activists at Bhopal, Paul Sagan, Twoill, Iz the Wiz, Phase 2, Vulcan, Schmidlapp, Air, Gerard Piel, William Golden, and the racially and culturally diverse membership of the Democracy Education Broadcast Initiative (DEBI) of the South African Broadcasting Corporation.

While each of these persons is embedded in a story of engagement created by the authors of the pieces in which they appear, it might be useful as a comparative exercise to get a synoptic sense of the scope and limitations of this volume by thinking of its issues through these persons as if they constituted the assemblage.

Backward: Connected with Technoscientific Imaginaries

A standard feature of this series is the suggestion of thematic affinities both within and across volumes. The inclusion of a piece by Fred Myers and Rayna Rapp on the founders of the magazine *Scientific American* makes a striking connection between the thematic focus of this volume and the one preceding it, *Technoscientific Imaginaries.* As that volume sought to place the practice and reception of scientific activity in a variety of social and cultural contexts, so Myers and Rapp in their interviews probe a surprising location for the origins of this most respected of popular scientific journals in political commitment and activism.

Forward: Mediations in Perilous States

The inclusion of Ruth Teer-Tomaselli's account of her participation on a committee of the South African Broadcasting Corporation charged with democratic voter education prior to the historic election of April 1994 is meant to preview and stand for the next volume, Late Editions 4, tentatively titled *Mediations in Perilous States.* As noted, this will consist of all those papers developed in connection with this year's media project that deal with the registering through conventional media (filmmaking, photography, journalism, and again, the arts) of the great changes occurring in political orders and civil societies at particular locales.

This volume will take up from the angle of diverse media producers the concerns of Late Editions 1, *Perilous States.* Several locales of that volume will be revisited in Late Editions 4—Poland, Germany, Argentina, Russia, and

South Africa (as represented by Teer-Tomaselli's fascinating document, included as a preview in this volume). In addition, pieces will be included on Colombia, Martinique, and on experiences of life in diaspora.

While the pieces of Late Editions 4 have an identity and coherence of their own, they serve as an alternative context for and challenge to the polar contrast between Net populism and activist imaginaries that has occupied the center of Late Editions 3. They demonstrate the operation of media in often desperate, marginal situations of transformation. As such, they place the great structural changes and possibilities of media, as seen mostly from the United States in Late Editions 3, against the perspective of a world in which conventional media practices—documentary filmmaking, reporting, and so on—are responding in innovative ways to upheaval.

References

Giroux, Henry R. 1992. Introduction to *Pedagogy and the Politics of Cultural Studies.* Ed. Henry R. Giroux and Peter McLaren. London: Routledge.

Joffe, Josef. 1994. Review of the journal *Daedalus. Times Literary Supplement,* 18 Mar., 21.

I

THE NET DEFIANT

1

The Electronic Vernacular

If, as Abbott Payson Usher suggests, "the development of printing, more than any other single achievement, marks the line between medieval and modern technology [and is] the first instance of a process being pushed through to a decisive stage in a relatively short time," then electronic communication broadly conceived marks the line between modern and postmodern communication. It too has reached a "decisive stage in a relatively short period of time," so short that we have personally experienced major transformations in less than a decade (Usher 1959 [1929]: 236). Rapidly growing numbers of people are using computers (attached by modem to phones) to navigate a vast network of interlocutors and pockets of information in a matrix that is at once amorphous, anarchic, and intensely social. It is this aspect of the new communication technologies that I will explore here.

new communication technology

In *The Informational City: Information Technology, Economics, Restructuring, and the Urban-Regional Process,* Manuel Castells focuses on "the relationship between information technologies and the spatial dimension of the processes of production and management, leaving aside the study of social life and residential patterns" (1989:5). During the 1980s, when his book was written, Castells found too little reliable empirical research on "the interaction between communication technologies and urban social life" to address this topic and gave precedence to an analysis of how the informational mode of development restructures capitalism (3). The rapid growth of electronic communication during the six years since the book was published dramatizes the need to examine how this technology figures in social life. My interest here is in the interaction order.

Castells

At the heart of this topic are the following considerations. Communication in the absence of face-to-face interaction and at a distance is as old as the circulation of objects (gift exchange, commercial transactions, postal service) and the transmission of signals (drumming messages whose sound carries for several miles down a quiet river, or using smoke to produce visual signals leg-

ible from afar). They differ from the telephone, phonograph, and radio in terms
of what Murray Schaffer (1977) calls schizophonia—the separation of sound
from its sources. Capturing the actual sound of the human voice (rather than
a drummed adaptation of spoken language) or of a musical performance in a
medium that makes it possible to play those sounds back at will—anywhere at
any time in any context and in the absence of those who made the sounds—
has profound consequences not only for the interaction order but also for the
larger socioeconomic order. Schizophonia is relevant here because the telephone is a pivotal early technology of live telepresence that has penetrated the
social practices of everyday life—not as mass culture but as a commonplace
tool. Furthermore, the telephone is instrumental to electronic communication,
which produces a different kind of telepresence, not yet fully phonic, but telepresence nonetheless.

That said, is electronic communication basically a more powerful version of
the telephone (on which, incidentally, it depends) and the postal service or is it
a distinctive medium in which new social and cultural formations are being
produced? David Harvey (1989) has argued that there is nothing significantly
different in the ways that electronic communication and the telephone (and the
mail) organize social relations and space.[1] I will argue to the contrary. The
advance from over-sea mail to air-mail, manual to electric typewriter, from
phone to fax (the issue is actually more complicated), are not of the same order
as the relationship of electronic communication to the telephone. Electronic
communication is not just a faster (or more efficient) way to do what the telephone and fax can do.

As Paul Adams notes in his study of television as a gathering place, "the
concept of a place without a location" has informed media studies since the
1960s (Adams 1992:117). It has also interested geographers such as Yi-Fu
Tuan, for whom place is "a center of felt value." Tuan suggests further that
"every activity generates a particular socio-temporal structure" (Tuan 1977:4,
130–31). As I will argue, the specificity of networked interactive electronic
communication becomes especially clear in the unintended consequences of
noninstrumental uses of these media, uses for which they were not initially
intended. For this reason, playful uses of the medium may be even more revealing than strictly practical applications, which are not without social and
cultural consequences. Communication technology develops more rapidly, initially, in the contexts of military applications and entertainment, that is, at opposite ends of the instrumentality spectrum and there is much to be explored in
their relationship.

My subject here is electronic communication in everyday life today—that
is, messages typed on a keyboard, visible on a screen, and transmitted through
a global network of computers and linked by telecommunication lines. This
includes multimedia (for those with the technology to receive it). I want to

understand what ordinary users of the medium are producing in it, socially and culturally. Analyzing a moving target presents its own challenges, not least of which is the compulsion to constantly update the account, even as I write it.

The questions are legion, and while I will not explore all of them here, they suggest what the topic holds.

- What is produced socially when strangers communicate instantaneously with one another across vast distances with little or no prospect of ever meeting face to face? While many of these interactions are evanescent, others produce communities that are based not on contiguity but on connectivity.

  still privileging this modality

- What is the nature of presence in a disembodied medium? Of performativity in a typographic medium? How does this medium of disembodied presence restructure the sensorium—a controversial claim made for communication technologies more generally? How is the body reimagined in relation to this medium, a topic at the center of virtual reality experiments, including text-based MUDS, cyberpunk fiction, and cinema?

  presence

  sensorium

- How do users navigate a vast and amorphous electronic space whose architecture is generally not visible to them? How is locality produced in a medium dedicated to the seamless flow of data through a network of nodes that are addresses but not places?

  vision

  place

- Does this medium offer the limiting case of an immaterial architecture produced by spatial practices where information flow rather than physical location is determinative? (See Meyrowitz 1985; Mitchell 1995.) An architecture built by encryption and firewalls defines the limits of access by controlling intelligibility and connection. It thereby stipulates where information (or those seeking it) can go and who can make sense of it. How then, in the words of Scott Bukatman (1993a: 49) does "a spatiality constructed by data" change "our relationship to what we call lived space or bodily space?"

  physical

  body

- What are the implications of this highly interactive medium (or tool) for theories of mass culture (based on the commodity form, serial reproduction, analog technologies, and broadcast) and the public sphere (based on the assumption of low civic participation)?

- What are the implications of a digital (versus an analog) medium for thinking about the "real"? (See Binkley 1988.)

After briefly characterizing the Net, its extent and rate of growth, I will explore social life in this medium—first, at the intersection of virtual and actual worlds, and second, within the electronic medium itself. The sites include electronic discussion groups (listservs and newsgroups), projects (Jargon File, Internet and USENET cookbooks), games (The Oracle), text-based virtual worlds (MUDS, MOOS), and real-time conversations (IRC). The few examples explored here suggest the usefulness of looking closely at what people are actually doing with the medium and provide a basis for discussing some of the questions raised above. Sites of play, among the richest for observing sociability, take distinctive forms in this medium. However trivial the evidence may seem—sociability is, after all, about itself—play is serious business. Those who play well are more likely to work well with the medium. And working in the medium is not only instrumental but also intensely social.

Who Is Connected?

Despite the sense that everyone everywhere is connected by an electronic net that knows no physical barrier, this ideal has not yet been realized. Access, while growing and spreading rapidly, is not equal. Before looking more closely at computer mediated communication (CMC) in action, consider for a moment the history of the Internet and who is and who is not online. I use the term *online* advisedly because the Internet, itself a network of networks, is linked to other networks that are not, strictly speaking, part of it. Taken together, they form what John Quarterman (1994) calls the Matrix.

Various timelines tracing the history of the Internet (and the Matrix, more widely conceived) and tracking its size and rate of growth appear regularly on the Internet. Smoot Carl-Mitchell and John Quarterman's history (1994a, 1994b; see also Quarterman 1994a), on which I base the following account, starts with Paul Baran's Rand Corporation report in 1964, which proposed "a network technology sufficiently decentralized that a network could survive arbitrary loss of links or nodes, as for instance in a nuclear war" (Carl-Mitchell and Quarterman 1994a). Such a network was funded in 1968 and running by 1969 in the form of ARPANET, "the first distributed packet-switching network." The Advanced Research Projects Agency (ARPA) was established in 1957 by the Eisenhower administration with the intention of making the United States competitive with the Soviet Union, which had launched Sputnik that year.

With the development in 1977 of the IP—IP stands for Internet Protocol—communication across a wide variety of networks became possible. By 1979, USENET (User's Network) was reaching out to those without access to ARPANET. USENET refined the mailing list idea: "Instead of sending a copy of each message to every person that wanted to read it, which would have required sending multiple copies to each participating machine, USENET sent one copy to each machine." Users logged on to a USENET site and read the messages posted there, rather than receiving them as mail in their personal accounts. (The number of USENET sites worldwide is estimated at the time of this writing at 260,000 [Treese 1995]. There are more than 9000 newsgroups, defined by topic—the number varies as new ones form and inactive ones are removed from the list. On the history and character of USENET, see Rospach 1995; Salzenberg 1994; Spafford 1995; Vielmetti 1994.)

During the 1980s, the term *Internet* came to refer to the network of networks, ARPANET and its successors forming the core. Their various names— MILNET, ARPA Internet, DARPA Internet (making the defense aspect of ARPA research explicit during the Reagan era), and Federal Research Internet—reflect splits, specializations, and diversification of participants and funding sources (NASA, NSF, DRPA—Defense Research Projects Agency, of the U.S. Department of Energy). The exponential growth during the 1980s of the Internet, which became the preferred name for what had become a vast and interconnected set of networks, is a result of several factors: the proliferation of personal computers, the wide adoption of the Internet Protocol, an enlarged infrastructure of fiber-optic cable, and the role of the NSFNET backbone. "From being one among many, it quickly became the largest of all," in the words of Carl-Mitchell and Quarterman (1994a).

During the 1990s, the development of WAIS (Wide Area Information Servers), anonymous telnet connections to online library catalogs, and the burgeoning use of protocols such as Gopher, WWW (World Wide Web), and Mosaic have made it easier to operate, and to operate more effectively, in the distributed environment of the Internet. Commercial providers that now provide IP connectivity are growing rapidly. The corporate and business worlds confer on CommerceNet (http://www.commerce.net/).[2] The Internet Mall uses the conceit of floors to organize a list of goods and services that can be ordered directly through the net. The Food Court, for example, is on the top floor, which is at the end of the list (issue 26, release for 15 Mar. 1995, finger taylor@ netcom.com). The mass marketing of goods and services over the Internet is becoming a reality—as I write this sentence (27 March 1995) National Public Radio is announcing that MCI Communications is the first long-distance carrier to do online merchandizing. The vehicle is Marketplace MCI. The White House, United Nations, and World Bank came online in 1993, and a year later the Senate and House of Representatives provided their own information servers. Though low-income communities and remote areas continue to lack access to these technologies, public schools are becoming a site not only for computers as a learning tool but also for networked communication. Children of all classes are being exposed to computers at school. In Texas, all secondary schools are networked. They have experience with video games (whether in arcades or at home). Adolescents in some areas are using electronic cafes.

Technologies are converging. Audiences can now reach television and radio stations via the Internet. Interactive Talk Radio began broadcasting in 1993, the year the first film, "Wax: Or the Discovery of Television Among the Bees," was transmitted over the Internet (Markoff 1993). At the time of this writing, an estimated 3,200 American newspapers have started to offer interactive access; ClariNet, an electronic newspaper, had 80,000 subscribers by 31 December 1984; and more than seventy peer-reviewed scholarly journals are being published electronically on the Internet. Even comic strips ("Dilbert" and "Frank and Ernest") have begun using email addresses (Treese 1994a, 1994b, 1994c, 1995; Zakon 1993–94).

Urgent issues are commanding greater attention in what has become a vast, heterogeneous, and anarchic medium dedicated not only to national security, scientific research, and business, but also to play. They range from civil liberties, free speech, censorship, obscenity, privacy, security (encryption, firewalls), and crime concerns to ones of access, regulation, privatization, commercialization, and proprietary rights, especially intellectual property. These issues bear on the nature of public space and civil society unmoored from fixed geographic locations, political boundaries, and familiar social arrangements.

As of December 1994, more than fifty-five million people are estimated to be using the Net (the Internet, other distributed networks such as USENET, commercial providers such as Compuserve, Genie, Prodigy, and America Online; Quarterman 1994a). Growing exponentially, doubling each year since 1988, those using the Internet itself form the world's "largest and most directly connected community in the world" (Quarterman 1993). John Perry Barlow has characterized the Internet as "one of the largest and fastest growing creations in the history of human endeavor," which is not only a prediction but also a utopian projection. At its current rate of growth—estimates are between 15 percent and 25 percent a month—Barlow and others calculate that every single person could be online within decades. Given that parts of the United States do not even have telephones, universal access will not be so easily achieved (Barlow 1992).

But even in this decentralized and rapidly expanding medium, informed in large sectors by a strong libertarian and utopian ethos, there are inequities, familiar at the national level and replicated globally. It is common in online communities such as the WELL (Whole Earth 'Lectronic Link) for men to outnumber women four to one, and for a few people (10 percent) to do most (80 percent) of the talking. Lurkers, those who watch but do not post, can outnumber posters ten to one. There is the sense that most participants are white, a sizeable number Asian, and an indeterminate number, generally assumed to be small, are African-American. Those who spend long hours alone, working independently if not in isolation, often at home, and who use computers in their work, are the most likely candidates for telecommuting (Rheingold 1992; see also Rheingold 1993). Poor and remote areas are underserved if served at all. American cities smaller than one hundred thousand persons, according to John Coate (1992), are priced out of the market because it is too expensive to call an online service—where the nets do not yet extend that far, a user must make a long distance call to reach a gateway.

(Tele)communication infrastructures, data networks, and industries are increasingly concentrated in a few multinational corporations. According to Howard Frederick (1993), "ninety-five percent of all computers are in the developed countries," while in many other parts of the world, even newspapers, books, telephone, radio, and cinema are in short supply. He explains further that "about ninety-six percent of the world's news flows" is controlled by five news agencies. As Barlow (1992) notes, "to a large extent, America is the Old Country of Cyberspace. The first interconnected networks were developed here as were their protocols and much of the supporting technology. Leaving aside the French Minitel system [established in 1981 and still unconnected to the Internet], Cyberspace is, in its present condition, highly American in culture and language. Though fortunately this is increasingly less the case, much of the infrastructure of the Net still sits on American soil."

USA

Government support of these developments is "a major reason that the United States currently has 60% of all users, hosts, and networks on the Internet" (Carl-Mitchell and Quarterman 1994a). Taking as a measure the amount of information transferred during 1993, the United States accounts for 16,897,635 megabytes, Europe for 1,435,735, Asia for 354,378, and Africa for 12,106, according to the Internet Society's 1993 statistics. The Internet Society was chartered in 1992. Nonetheless, new communication technologies are making inroads. Marking the end of the cold war, which was a major factor in the emergence of ARPANET in the first place, eastern European countries, including Russia (in 1992), have connected to the Internet. Uruguay, the Bahamas, Nicaragua, and Iran joined in 1994 to bring the total of countries that can be reached by electronic mail to 159 (Treese 1994c). By April 1994 they ranged "from Antarctica to Greenland, from Fiji to Ghana, from Moscow to Cape Town, from Iceland to India" (Carl-Mitchell and Quarterman 1994a).

cold war

Relatively new states such as New Guinea, unencumbered by old technologies and by a large work force attached to them, can computerize such enterprises as newspapers from the outset. Since 1990, "dish-wallahs" have been serving "an estimated 20,000 [cable networks] scattered across India" by means of an unregulated structure of video cable, satellite dishes, modulators, and television sets. They are "propelling Mother India out of information limbo by hard-wiring its living rooms directly into the global jet stream of satellite news, live sports, and the geosynchronous gyrations of MTV" (Greenwald 1993:75).

It is a short step from broadcast to network, from receiving what is transmitted to using the technology interactively. When the military cut the telephone lines in Thailand, people fought back with cellular phones. In several countries where open communication has been hampered by censorship and the monopoly of the official press, the fax machine has been the instrument for a free press—Interfax in the Soviet Union and Mediafax in Mozambique are two examples (Keller 1993). Operating out of Minnesota, the Environmental Fax

The fax

Orgy's manifesto explicitly defines the fax as a "new tool for media artists and community activists." During the recent demise of the Soviet Union, the KGB communicated in its established hierarchical mode, slowly through a chain of command, while the opposition was nimble in its use of decentralized electronic networking. The "natural anarchy" of the Net makes it hard to restrain—"because of the decentralized and redundant nature of digital media, it was impossible for the geriatric plotters in the Kremlin to suppress the delivery of truth" (Barlow 1992). Though these governments are themselves gearing up, "for the first time in history," Frederick (1993) notes, "the forces of peace and environmental preservation have acquired the communication tools and intelligence gathering technologies previously the province of the military, government and transnational corporations."

Where Strangers Meet

a wow?

What are we to make of an activity in which strangers at terminals at the far ends of the earth write messages to each other. These people have never seen each other, though the multimedia capabilities of the Internet are now making possible portrait galleries at WWW sites—for example, the Internet Relay Chat Gallery. These people are not likely to meet. They may not even know each other by name, but only by address. They come together as pen pals exchanging private messages, or collectively in a variety of electronic forms—for example, a conference (or electronic mailing list), bulletin board or USE-NET group, interactive real-time chat, or fantasy game. What brings them together is the willingness to talk about the topic at hand or to participate in the "consensual hallucination" of a virtual world, in the words of William Gibson, whose 1984 science fiction novel *Neuromancer* imagined cyberspace and the matrix with unprecedented fullness.

Gibson

zizek: we have always been virtual

As Howard Rheingold notes, "in traditional kinds of communities, we are accustomed to meeting people, then getting to know them; in virtual communities, you can get to know people and then choose to meet them. In some cases, you can get to know people who might never meet on a physical plane." As early as 1968, J. C. R. Licklider and Robert Taylor, research directors of the Department of Defense, whose ARPANET became the foundation of the Internet, referred to physical locations as "accidents of proximity" and predicted the emergence of "communities not of common location but of common interest" (Rheingold 1992). Once formed, such communities are marked by horizontal and egalitarian rather than vertical and hierarchical modes of operation—whatever people's status IRL (In Real Life), the medium promotes a sense of peers, though pecking orders do form, and an antiauthoritarian ethos. Free speech and open access are prized in what is a highly decentralized medium of such reach and volume that it verges at points on anarchy, a quality that some believe will be its salvation in the face of efforts to rein it in for commercial and other purposes.

Despite Rheingold's characterization of the medium in terms of strangers who are unlikely to meet, the online and in-the-flesh worlds can and do converge, and online communication is being used increasingly to further offline concerns. Some electronic lists are extensions of prior face-to-face relationships, while others organize occasions for the listers to actually meet. It is not uncommon for particular online communities to have an IRL geographic center—ECHO (East Coast Hang Out) in New York and the WELL, established in 1985, its headquarters in Sausalito. The WELL services not only the San Francisco Bay area, but is also global in reach. Local members meet socially on a regular basis. Nor are all those who log on doing so in isolation. Electronic coffeehouses in San Francisco provide espresso and computer terminals for those who want to log on to SF Net. For disaffected youth known as "slackers," these electronic cafes are "living room/telephone/mailbox," as well as portals to an "extended 'cyber family'" (Bishop 1992).

Electronic networks are mobilized in various ways IRL—to volunteer help in time of need or to participate in an "online wake," to confess or pray at a distance, to route sourdough starter, to create a digital quilt or participate in an electronic quilting bee, or as a tool of political mobilization, lobbying, or activism on behalf of a wide range of issues.

Postings on the Internet in April 1994 repeated the announcement in *People's Weekly World* (*PWW*) about the "People's March on the Information Superhighway" in support of a "National Town Hall Meeting that links 50 cities by telephone Sunday, April 10, 1994." The topic is "For Real Change Today and Socialism Tomorrow." The featured speaker is Gus Hall, national chair of the Communist Party USA. The objective is to raise $400,000 by the Fourth of July. *PWW* is now reachable not only through an 800 number but also electronically (pww@igc.apc.org). NewtWatch keeps navigators of WWW up to date on the Speaker of the House, the ethics complaints against him, his record on the issues, contributors to his campaign, and his personal finances. CAN-RW (Campus Activists' Network, Right Wing Alert), an e-mail discussion group, has used the Internet (much more powerful than the phone chain) to organize nationwide demonstrations at one hundred locations against the Republican Contract with America (Herszenhorn 1995).

During the Los Angeles disturbances, one electronic network found itself discussing what was happening and discovered that one of the listers, Beverly Thomas, was an African-American woman. Thomas reported that she was able to speak more openly to the list about her understanding of the situation than had ever been possible in person. As the discussion proceeded, some members of the list volunteered to help—one offered to help organize loan assistance and Thomas herself is assisting in the development of the Resource Link, a bulletin board intended "to connect individuals who would like to get involved with others who need help" in rebuilding Los Angeles after the disturbances (Wallace 1992). Those on WORDS-L responded to the grief of one of their listers when a loved one died by urging each other to use snail mail to send their condolences rather than clog the person's e-mail account with messages of sympathy. When David Alsberg was killed by a stray bullet from a fleeing thief, "his cyberspace neighbors from around the nation mourned Mr. Alsberg's death in an on-line wake that lasted weeks." A former computer programmer at Citicorp, he had been laid off and was without life insurance at the time that he died. The online mourners "decided to begin soliciting recipes to compile an electronic cookbook. Proceeds from sales, once they begin, will go to a trust fund for the Alsberg family" (Lewis 1994:A1).

As collaborative projects in support of a charitable project, cookbooks and quilts have a long history offline and a new life online. Quilters on Prodigy's Homelife Club Bulletin Board "began to share quilting tips, exchange ideas and even swap fabrics back in the summer of '89," which made them "the first electronic quilting guild," according to *Quilt Magazine,* as reported in Prodigy's newsletter. The conviviality of the electronic bee prompted listers to look for each other at quilting events and to wear "big blue stars so they could identify each other and get acquainted face to face"—those posting to rec.arts.marching.drumcorps in 1993 collaborated on the design of a Cyber-Corps T-shirt that would allow them to identify each other in the stands at live events featuring marching bands. Not only could quilters in areas without local guilds network electronically, but also the online bee collaborated in the creation of "Cuddle Quilts for children and adults with AIDS at the Coming Home Hospice in San Francisco" (Schindler 1991).

Collaboration in a Distributed Medium

Even when the outcome is not a fabric quilt, its pieced and collaborative nature migrates into the electronic medium, which amplifies these aspects even as the quilt itself is dematerialized. A Digital Quilt project was organized for Woman's History Month in 1993. The announcement emanated from Northern Illinois University School of Art's Gallery 200. This multiple-site installation of art on the theme of women and spirituality consisted of squares transmitted by fax, e-mail, or other electronic medium: "The images will be collected prior to March 23 and arranged in patterns on the wall." Like the exchange of quilt scraps by online quilters, easy passage between electronic networks and the physical world is exploited by the SOURDOUGH list. It serves as a kind of switching station for the exchange of sourdough starter—bubbling yeast is, in a sense, routed along a mainframe network. Just before Passover, discussion focusses on what to do with that most *hometz* of substances, leaven itself.

Recipe exchange has escalated to the point that Internet and USENET cookbooks require special software developed in connection with military applications and subject to security regulations:

> Because of the size of the archive and the quantity of people who use it, Digital advises all users that it is the legal obligation of the individual who accesses this archive to comply with the U.S. State Department regulations which govern the transfer of certain software products which are designed to meet military applications (like aerial mapping) and/or used in military applications (products which contain the des algorithm for file/data encryption).

Internet and USENET "cookbooks" are enormous databases, the cumulative result of thousands of people who have posted recipes to one or another list or newsgroup, where discussion, tips, and variations often appear as well. With all due respect to their encyclopedic cookbooks, not even the indefatigable Mrs. Beeton, Fanny Farmer, or Elena Molokhovets could have imagined anything quite like this ongoing accretion of deposits from disparate sources. *The USENET Cookbook* also extends and transforms the recipe exchanges stimulated by food columns in newspapers and magazines—readers send in recipes, they are printed in food columns, clipped and recirculated, sometimes culminating in a cookbook edited by the journalist in charge of the newspaper column.

These databases offer a fluid mass of possibility that coalesces into smaller sets each time users select recipes and de facto form their own cookbooks. They are the new community cookbooks, explicitly defined as such:

> This is a community cookbook, from an invisible worldwide electronic community. Like all community cookbooks, it was the favorite recipes of the members of the community, suitably edited and organized. *The USENET Cookbook* is a collection of the favorite recipes of USENET readers worldwide.
>
> *The USENET Cookbook* is an online database distributed with the intention that it be published as a book. *The USENET Cookbook* is distributed with software that enables every user to make his own customized edition of it, leaving out the recipes that he has no interest in, and perhaps adding a few of his own that he hasn't yet submitted to the network. There will be many different versions and editions of it, all with the same title, and all copyrighted. (http://me-www.jrc.it/recipe/intro.doc)

The collection of "recipes and lore from the global village," that is, from the newsgroup alt.gourmand, is copyrighted (1991) by the USENET Community Trust, with the provision for copying without fee as long as it is not for commercial advantage and the holders of the copyright are credited. The open-ended nature of the corpus and the infinite number of versions and editions of

The USENET Cookbook and every recipe collection derived from it are not like printed community cookbooks, which fix a particular set of contributed recipes. They are more like the expanding and contracting collective wisdom of an offline network of cooks and their individual repertoires, but without commensality, without actually breaking bread together, face to face, that is.

Operating at the convergence of military and recreational applications of a particular algorithm, this project captures two orders of magnitude that are defining features of a digital and distributed medium. Extreme miniaturization (the size of the smallest unit of information, of code, and so forth) brings with it proprietary and security issues. At what point is the appropriated material so small (and the final result so different from the source) that the information can be treated as if it no longer belongs to someone else, an issue that arises in sampling sound and morphing digitized images? (See Karnow 1994.) At the other extreme is the sheer vastness of the database and its distribution, with the potential of overwhelming disorientation and pathological distraction. Attention deficit hyperactivity disorder is an affliction of the multitasking mind (Schwartz 1995: 49; Hallowell and Ratey 1994). Support groups have formed within USENET, for example, for the electronically obsessed. Alt.irc.recovery was formed in 1988, the same year that IRC (Internet Relay Chat) was established.

Sustaining Diasporic Formations

The upsurge of Jewish networking, its rapid growth, scope, and ambitions, highlights the power of the medium to sustain an already diasporic formation. Consider the mission statement of Jerusalem One:

> The aim of Jerusalem One is to build and maintain a professional, accessible system which will provide current and useful information of unlimited scope to the Jewish world. Among its activities is the involvement of key Jewish organizations in networking for the first time. Its target goal for the first year is to increase the number of active Jewish Internet users by about tenfold, reaching at least 100,000 Jews worldwide.[3]

Lubavitcher Hasidim coordinate the dispersed followers of their leader (*rebe*) using a variety of communication technologies. They could be said to be doubly diasporic, as Jews and as Hasidim. Historically, the followers of a Hasidic leader have lived in various places. They converge on his town and gather around him on special occasions. New communication technologies have made possible the gathering of a vast and far-flung following in new forms of assembly. A recent posting on the Internet announced that on the eve of Purim (1995) there would be live satellite broadcasts during which "Jews all over the world on 5 continents will simultaneously proclaim and sing in the presence of the

Rebbe Shlita the following words: YECHI EDONENU MORENU, MELECH HAMOSHIACH LEOLOM VOED!" acknowledging thereby the conviction that the Lubavitcher *rebe* is the Messiah. Since his recent death, followers can send their *kvitlekh* (petitions) to his grave electronically rather than come to the cemetery in person and leave notes on little pieces of paper at the actual grave. The Hebrew term *ohel* in the e-mail address refers to the special structure enclosing the tomb of a famous person.

Extending to "tens of thousands of subscribers" who "vary from a traveling college student in a remote island of Iceland to public high school students in Chicago," Chabad Lubavitch in cyberspace provides "Jewish individuals living in places where there are little Jewish resources . . . almost all the religious instruction they might need," from formal lessons to "an electronic shmooze with a friendly Chabad Rabbi." A printed flyer begins, "At first, it was a message engraved in stone. One G-d. Two Tablets. Ten commandments." It proceeds through the history of the printing press, telephone, photograph, photocopy, broadcasting, and satellite communication to digital information technologies and "A visionary future [that] is taking shape today . . . in Cyber- *futurity* space." It concludes with a passage from a talk on Judaism and Technology by the Lubavitcher Rebbe, in which he states that "Today's great breakthroughs in scientific understanding were predicted in the Zohar, nearly 2,000 years ago . . . and are preparing the world for the advent of the seventh millennium— the era of Redemption." [4]

Chabad-Lubavitch in Cyberspace claims to have reached 250,000 individuals in the first year of its operation. It is run by the educational arm of the movement: "As always, utilizing the cutting edge of modern technology of its outreach and educational efforts, the world wide Chabad-Lubavitch Movement is on the Information Superhighway," proselytizing to Jews to return to orthodox religious observance (http://www.chabad.org). Those who return to the faith bring with them their worldly experience, tertiary education, and professional knowledge in a wide variety of fields, including media and communication technologies.

Such access is provided to most sectors of the Jewish world in the form of more than 150 Jewish discussion/mailing lists, Web sites for news and media, and online hypertext versions of traditional texts such as the Code of Jewish Law. (Indeed, it could be said that texts such as the Talmud are already hypertextual in character.) That anyone can log on is anticipated in an FAQ (Frequently Asked Questions) file devoted to Judaism, which is addressed to new readers of USENET group soc.culture.jewish. It starts with "Who We Are" and ends with "The Holocaust, Antisemitism and Countering Missionaries." Such files are standard practice, a way of bringing newbies up to speed without trying the patience of veterans with repetition of the same questions.

Activities that have until now taken place only offline find a hospitable setting. Parody in the form of the academic essay, "Latkes vs. Hamentashen: A Materialist Feminist Analysis," appeared in time for Purim, a carnivalesque holiday. During March 1995, Sociologist Robin Leidner and anthropologist Judith Shapiro debated the relative merits of the fried potato pancakes associated with Hanukkah and the triangular stuffed pastry eaten on Purim, a venerable subject of Purim parody now transposed to the Internet. Talmud Fortran, a parody of text and commentary laid out like a page of Talmud, appeared as postings on soc.culture.Jewish. Treating programming problems in the manner of Jewish legal thought (*halakha*), an example that circulated just before Purim 1993 offered several glosses on the following: "As I recall, you are not (on certain days) permitted to separate the good from the bad. How does this apply to debugging programs on those days, or on using formal verification methods?" One reply stated, "So long as there is less than one part in 60 of bugs in the code, it is kosher, so there is no need to deliberately look for bugs to be removed," and elaborates with such questions as, "How does one kosher one's software tools after they've become contaminated" by contact with bugs. Bugs in the offline world pollute the food in which they are found.[5]

Trek-Cochavim was announced as a new list on May 21, 1995, "for those who want to discuss the Star-Trek World from a Jewish or Israeli perspective." *Cochavim* is the Hebrew word for stars. Projecting forward, posters on Trek-Cochavim engage in what one person called "hypothetical Jewish law" (May 23, 1995). They ask, since the Jewish calendar is lunar, How would the Enterprise deal with the scheduling of holidays? Would it go by the moons of another planet? What is the correct blessing for replicate food (made of energy)? Can an android convert to Judaism? "What if a male from a race that didn't have foreskins wanted to become Jewish?" (May 23, 1995). Imagining Jewish life on the Enterprise is not unlike imagining the present in relation to the world of the Bible and Talmud, when Jewish ritual law was formulated, elaborated, and codified. It is common practice to test the interpretation of a ruling by applying it to hypothetical situations. And to create further restrictions to deal with problems that arise. The difference here is in the nature of the hypothesis.

In an effort to give the spatiality of information greater palpability and vividness, the Virtual Shtetl takes its inspiration from the small-town Jewish world imagined in Yiddish fiction. The author of the Virtual Shtetl, Iosif Vaisman, announced it as follows:

> When Reb Menachem-Mendl left his native Kasrilevke and went to Yekhupets and other big cities, he had to write his dearly loved wife Sheine-Sheindl long letters on paper because there was no e-mail. Of course, now there is e-mail, but there is no Kasrilevke, and even Yekhupets, I must tell you, has changed significantly. As a remedy against historical injustice, I am announcing a Virtual Shtetl: Yiddish

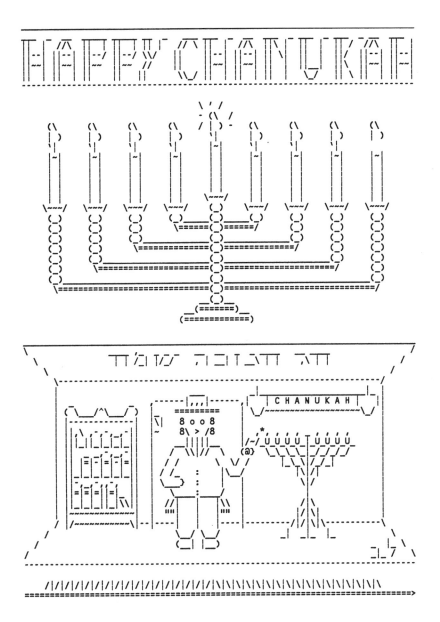

Language and Culture Home Page on World Wide Web (http://sun-site.unc.edu/yiddish/shtetl.html).

Still under construction, the Virtual Shtetl will contain text, sheet music and recordings, paintings, drawings, and photography. Intended as a collaborative project, the site already has "several buildings under construction. The main topics on the home page are Library, Post Office, City, Art Center, and Kitchen."

The identification of location with topic, which I take up below, is used here to thematize in architectural terms the classification and arrangement of information. Indeed, this thematization is consistent with a more general tendency on the Net to imagine text in the round, as sites once called bulletin boards and lists become kiosks and malls and newsstands. Consistent with the history of books, there is increasingly a conflation of textual and architectural construction, modeled on such fantasy environments as MUDS. Architectural reference adds gravitational force and familiar coordinates to a medium whose weightlessness can be disorienting. The convention, popular in the Renaissance, of creating a title page in the form of a portal, complete with columns, arches, and other classical architectural elements, has its analogs in the "home page" conventions of the World Wide Web. It is also related to architecture as a mnemonic, the house of memory of classical rhetoric and oratory.

While the technologies of telecommunication seem to make irrelevant the offline locations of the interlocutors, there is a way in which they can intensify the centrality of an offline site. An article in the *Chicago Tribune* (27 January 1993), circulated on the Internet, reported that "an Israeli company announced a fax service in Jerusalem enabling Jews around the world to send prayers directly to the Western Wall."[6] Those with only a telephone can call (800) 505-PRAY twenty-four hours a day "in time of need for any reasons" to have their prayers faxed immediately to the Rabbis in Israel associated with this service: "Prayers recited daily at the Western Wall in Jerusalem." Advertised in the *Manhattan Jewish Sentinel* (24 March 1995, 19), this service is targeted to those praying for recovery from illness—the announcement was framed by repetitions of the word *khay* (Hebrew for *life*). Faxes can be transmitted directly from the computer and some are routed through electronic mail systems, which are gradually supplanting them.

Interactivity as Art

Artists and institutions dedicated to the arts have been turning to electronic communication to intensify access to their offline activities, to subvert them, and to explore the artistic potential of distinctive characteristics of the medium. Growing numbers of virtual museums and art galleries are appearing online. An Internet World Exposition, "accessible from PCS linked to 'INTERNET

PLANETARIUMS' in cities in different countries," is slated to take place in 1996 and will promote the construction of high-capacity phone lines. The world-famous Louvre is currently hosting three online exhibits. Art Crimes and IAMfree, whose very names announce an oppositional mission, do not have an offline corollary, even if the information they provide does. Such sites provide online access to art produced offline. Art Crimes is a WWW site (http://www.gatech.edu/desoto/graf/Index.Art _ Crimes.html) in the form of a collaborative gallery, in which photographs of graffiti from various cities are contributed and can be viewed and downloaded. The posting that announced the opening of the gallery, initially a United States and Czech Republic collaboration, in the fall of 1994 declared, "See guerilla art worth being arrested for." The home page of the gallery itself explained that "many of these pieces no longer exist in the real world." But what can be seen online are images digitized from the analog medium of photography, which does exist offline, even when the walls themselves have been erased. IAMfree (The Internet Arts Museum for Free) (http://www//artnet.org/iamfree) is "like a museum that lets you steal." It is a place where "the admission is FREE and you make take what you like!" according to postings in November 1994. Whereas the Web extends the reach of an already powerful institution, virtual art galleries like Art Crimes may be the only display site for the work they show. The Louvre treats the network as a broadcast medium (viewers cannot add works to the exhibit or interact with it other than to browse). Galleries like Art Crimes are conceived as collaborative ventures.

Correspondence art or mail art, an "offline but internationally dispersed community" termed "the Eternal Network," prepared the ground for art based upon fax and upon computer networking. The crucial difference, however, is in "the artistic interpretation of network as interactivity and collaboration" (Couey 1991; see also Ascòtt and Loeffler 1991). The Electronic Cafe International's Sixth Annual New Year's Eve Around-the-World TELEBRATION (1994) is the latest in twenty years of "interactive art communications" and "telecommunication art events" (Couey 1991). This event integrated a WWW site, CU-SeeMe, and IRC Chat with the *Actual Magazine* party in Paris, a tele-poetry MOO, an image gallery, sound files and images, networked ambient music at the Kitchen in New York City, videophone links with the Contemporary Art Center in Moscow, and "other forms of cyber shtick" via digital and analog bridges, as a posting from ecafe@netcom.com at many sites on the Internet announced in the weeks preceding the event. It is a quintessential example of an interactive telecommunication art event. These phenomena lend themselves to the analysis of what Margaret McLaughlin (1994) calls the topography of online "artspace" and the exhibition culture of the Web, which takes advantage of the Web's hypertextual principles of linkage in a distributed environment, its multimedia capabilities (sound and image, both still and moving, and in color), and its relative ease of access across the Internet and within many different operating systems. The rapid growth of WWW, now at 10,000 sites, is expected to reach 40,000 sites within the next nine months (Neubarth 1995:4).

When the sensibility of the electronic (and computational) medium is wedded to live performance, the result is literally and metaphorically electrifying. In the corridors of the Massachusetts Institute of Technology, TechSquares, as MIT's square-dance association is known, is reimagining the form in the terms, and with the help, of computers. According to Fred Hapgood, in his account of the sensibility of engineers at MIT,

> these dances draw on an enormous vocabulary of calls, up to a few thousand, all of which a dancer (at that level) is expected to know. Some calls involve imaginary or "virtual" dancers, so-called "phantom spots," that give the choreographer 12 or 16 centers of motion instead of 8. . . .
>
> Planning the sequences is a demanding art, almost always requiring a computer, and new sequences are required constantly; the experience loses its edge, or so dancers say, unless the series of calls is completely unpredictable. The challenge to the dancers is to keep the square going, to keep the group spinning and folding and unfolding as the caller jumps back and forth inside this huge volume of possibilities. . . . The ideal is for the caller and eight dancers to bring each square to the edge of collapse and keep it balanced there, hanging over the face of the wave. [Hapgood 1933:21–23]

Hapgood comments that the pleasure the dancers take in disorientation as a state of mind—and, I would add, as an aesthetic—"ordinarily expresses itself in technical pursuits." When TechSquares perform, square dancing and engineering converge, amplifying the pleasure of the computational intelligence of this dance form and refiguring it for a new generation.

Most of these cases are sited at the intersection of virtual and actual worlds. Consider for a moment communication that never (or only rarely) leaves the electronic medium. Such communication throws into relief assumptions about authorship, identity, anonymity, presence, and performativity.

The Oracle

The USENET Oracle takes the basic presupposition of virtuality and anonymity to an illuminating extreme and reveals distinctive characteristics of electronic communication. Thousands of participants, all anonymous to one another, collaborate in the creation of the Oracle by playing the roles both of supplicants who ask the Oracle questions and the Oracle itself, who answers them. Technically, the Oracle is "an automated mail server that allows two people, a questioner and a respondent, to create a text without knowing one another's identity." David Sewell explains the concept:

> A questioner, or "Supplicant," e-mails a question to the Oracle. The Oracle software puts the question at the end of a "question queue"; when its turn comes, it will be mailed to someone else who has submitted a question. That person now becomes an "incarnation" of the Oracle and must e-mail a response to the question back to the Oracle's address. Finally, the Oracle combines question and answer and mails the completed "Oracularity" to the Supplicant while saving a copy for itself. Because the software encodes all names and addresses, neither questioner nor respondent know one another's identities. [Sewell 1992]

This high-tech party game has grown in popularity to a readership, by 31 March 1995, of 65,900, thanks to the growth of the Internet itself and the increased visibility of the Oracle. Since its inception on 8 October 1989, some 30,000 people have asked or answered 136,000 questions. Digests of the best Oracularities, ten at a time, appear on rec.humor.oracle and on the Oracle's new WWW site (http://www.pcnet.com/users/stenor/oracle/index.html). Readers can also ask to receive them by e-mail. So far, 719 digests have appeared.[7]

The Oracle is predicated on several conditions—anonymity and collaboration on a grand scale unimpeded by physical location. And it exemplifies such signature features of electronic communication as role playing, multiple identities, simulation, parody, heteroglossia, recursiveness, and a penchant for metacommunication. With regard to anonymity, Sewell explains that "questioner and respondent are invisible to each other. They share neither a physical location nor a common time of writing. Both writers must guess at the likely range of cultural references, terminology, and specific knowledge that their co-authors share." Participants say that anonymity encourages "freedom of expression, and the shared aesthetic illusion of an Oracle persona." In a medium that records everything, where you may not be physically present but nonetheless identified by an e-mail address, anonymity must be expressly produced. Physical absence gives only the illusion of anonymity. The system has to be programmed to suppress authorship. And the players actively produce anonymity and through it the persona of the Oracle.

When someone wanders into a newsgroup by mistake and asks an inappropriate question, the moderator of the list may respond to the sender, refuse to post the message, or send an FAQ file. Unmoderated lists, depending on their style, may treat the newcomer with patience or scorn. Recently, when someone lost on USENET wandered into the Oracle newsgroup, the person's question was automatically relayed, at random, for an answer. Ever dependable, the Oracle responded to the query "Can anyone tell me how to access bulletin boards [sic]" (USENET Oracularity #719-07) with a lengthy account of cork, thumbtacks, and pushpins. A request for an address on the part of someone otherwise knowledgeable about the medium produced the following response, quoted here with its original spelling and punctuation:

> Date: Mon, 27 Mar 95 16:22:15 -0500
> From: Usenet Oracle <oracle-vote@cs.indiana.edu>
> Subject: Usenet Oracularity #719-06
> Selected-By: dsew@packrat.aml.arizona.edu (David Sewell)
> The Usenet Oracle has pondered your question deeply.
> Your question was:
> >Although I work for an oracle, sometimes it's the wrong one.
> >
> >I am lost! I want to mail to several people that are locked up in the
> >X400 world. How do I do this? For instance, consider the following
> >address:
> >
> >G=FN S= LName PRMD=OLYMPICS96 ADMD=ATTMAIL
> >C=US
> >
> >How on earth do I go about reaching this very dear friend of mine
> >on mail from norway?
> >
> >My own mail connection is through a gateway on the company's
> >WAN, but all this does, is chucking the messages out on the inter-
> >net. I have heard there are gateways out there, but I do not know
> >how to access them. If you know the answer, please help me with
> >syntax and addresses to mail her, and also instructions for her on
> >how to mail me back.
> >
> >As a return favor, I can help with information on how to mail be-
> >tween internet and IBM's IBMMAIL network in the closed world
> >of AS400's and larger blue beasts.
>
> And in response, thus spake the Oracle:
>
> } You say you work for an oracle and that the WAN just chucks e-mail
> } out on the Internet? The first thing you need to do is ask your oracle,
> } "How much e-mail to my girl friend can your e-mail chucker chuck,
> } if your e-mail chucker could chuck e-mail?" This will ensure that
> } the system has sufficient e-mail capacity for your needs.
> }
> } You could also post a message to several hundred Usenet user
> } groups about your problem (say, every one with "mail" or "com-
> } puter" in its title. You will be sure to get many interesting responses.
> }

} Or, JUST SEND HER A #()&^&* LETTER ASKING FOR HER
} INTERNET E-MAIL ADDRESS! If she's got one, your e-mail
} chucker should chuck it right to her, for chrissake! Or give her a
  phone call and ask!!
}
} You owe the Oracle a grovel (a good one), and 12 suggestions on
} how I can get supplicants to think for themselves.

While the Oracle did not provide the instructions requested, it did teach a lesson in Internet culture in a form consistent with the principles of the Oracle newsgroup.

With regard to collaboration, Sewell argues that like "the medieval author, who, in Hans Robert Jauss's words, wrote 'in order to praise and to extend his object, not to express himself or to enhance his personal reputation,'" the anonymity of Oracle authors is essential to their collaborative creation of an all-knowing presence, its ring of universality, absolute truth, and collective wisdom—just like the unsigned newspaper editorials characterized in these terms by E. M. Forster, whom Sewell cites. This is "traditionalizing" with a vengeance, imagined here in Foucaultian terms: "The Net may yet turn out to be that culture imagined by Michel Foucault 'where discourse would circulate without any need for an author [and] would unfold in a pervasive anonymity,'" that Sewell compares to "cathedrals of cyberspace that countless unacknowledged builders and designers will collaborate on for the sake of creation itself."

With regard to the performativity of the Oracle, there is fluidity in personas that authors create. Role playing has often been observed in this medium, which is generally conducive to the creation of multiple personas—often cited are cases where men adopt the personas of women, without letting anyone know, whether in the context of an electronic list or within an interactive fantasy game such as a MUD or MOO. Medium-specific parody makes Oracularities thoroughly heteroglossic, in Bakhtin's terms, as do meta-Oracularities. Simulation and recursiveness are characteristic of electronic communication more generally.

The New Hacker's Dictionary

There are also grand collaborations among those who, while they are not anonymous to one another, may never meet but who will form a strong feeling of "usness." Produced collaboratively in the electronic medium, the Jargon File, now in Version 3.1.0 (15 October 1994), defines itself as "a comprehensive compendium of hacker slang illuminating many aspects of hackish tradition, folklore, and humor" (http://www.denken.or.jp/local/misc/JARGON/preface.html). Periodically frozen in print, the online Jargon File was published as *The Hacker's Dictionary* (1983), edited by Guy Steele, and as *The New Hacker's Dictionary* (1991), edited by Eric Raymond (a second edition appeared in 1993 and a third is in preparation)—a detailed revision and publication history may be found in both the Jargon File and the *Dictionary*. Consistent with the libertarian spirit in which it has been created, the document is in the public domain "to be freely used, shared, and modified. There are (by intention) no legal restraints on what you can do with it, but there are traditions about its proper use to which many hackers are quite strongly attached"; these include proper citation, including the version number of the file.

As "the common heritage of the hacker culture," self-defined as "an intentional culture less than 40 years old," the Jargon File, started in 1975, features "slang terms used by various subcultures of computer hackers . . . among themselves for fun, social communication, and technical debate." A conservative claim to heritage, tradition, and folklore, which suggests longstanding attachments to shared and enduring values and practices, a concern with the essentially hackish, and an attempt to pin down the origins of terms serve a legitimating function even as they are wedded to a progressive view of hacker language and culture as generative, emergent, contentious, and multiauthored:

> We have also tried to indicate (where known) the apparent origins of terms. The results are probably the least reliable information in the lexicon, for several reasons. For one thing, it is well known that many hackish usages have been independently reinvented multiple times, even among the more obscure and intricate neologisms. It often seems that the generative processes underlying hackish jargon formulation have an internal logic so powerful as to create substantial parallelism across separate cultures and even in different languages! For another, the networks tend to propagate innovations so quickly that "first use" is often impossible to pin down. And, finally, compendia like this one alter what they observe by implicitly stamping cultural approval on terms and widening their use. [Raymond 1991:4]

Characteristic of specifically hackish language are terms such as *bigot* and *brain dump:*

> *bigot* n. A person who is religiously attached to a particular computer, language, operating system, editor, or other tool (see *religious issues*). . . . True bigots can be distinguished from mere partisans or zealots by the fact that they refuse to learn alternatives even when the march of time and/or technology is threatening to obsolete the favored tool. It is said "You can tell a bigot, but you can't tell him much." Compare *weenie*. [Raymond 1991:59]

> *brain dump* n. The act of telling someone everything one knows about a particular topic or project. Typically used when someone is going to let a new party maintain a piece of code. [Raymond 1991:77]

Each term, its etymology and account of its meaning and usage, offers a historical and ethnographic snapshot. The hypertextual possibilities of the "see also" convention contribute to the fluidity of this self-consciously autoethnographic text.

The Jargon File itself is always in process, in tandem with the emergent language and practices it documents. It is also like a dictionary, rarely read from *A* to *Z*, in that readers select from arbitrarily arranged (alphabetical) entries and pursue (or not) the linkages among them. They consult the Jargon File and the *Dictionary* in ways that let them form their own temporary albums of ethnographic snapshots, a process that is greatly assisted by a hypertextual interface. These search trails offer as many points of entry as there are terms in the lexicon. They yield ephemeral sets. They offer partial views, variously configured, of a phenomenon in flux on the basis of an always provisional text. That text is itself implicated in the phenomenon.

Demonized by the media and prosecuted by the law, not always justly, hackers publish the *Dictionary* to demonstrate their creativity in a positive way to a wider public through "a sort of sacred epic, a hacker-culture Matter of Britain chronicling the heroic exploits of the Knights of the Lab" (Raymond 1991:6). They intend the *Dictionary* to demonstrate that they are witty and playful, creative, both in and about the medium, and deeply committed and important to the development of this transformative technology, even as they internalize and transvalue negative stereotypes:

> *computer geek* n. 1. One who eats (computer) bugs for a living. One who fulfills all the dreariest negative stereotypes about hackers: an asocial, malodorous, pasty-faced monomaniac with all the personality of a cheese grater. Cannot be used by outsiders without implied insult to all hackers; compare black-on-black usage of "nigger." A computer geek may be either a fundamentally clueless individual or a proto-hacker in larval stage. Also called "turbo nerd," "turbo geek." See also *propeller head, clustergeeking, geek out, wannabee, terminal junkie, spod, weenie.* 2. Some self-described computer geeks use this term in a positive sense and protest sense 1 (this seems to be a post 1990 development). [Jargon File 3.1.0, 15 October 1994]

They, and organizations like EFF (Electronic Frontier Foundation), are at the forefront of opposing legislation that would commercialize cyberspace and restrict access to it, and to government policy and legislation that would infringe on free speech, privacy, property, and related issues.

Folklore is a term that hackers use with pride and one that they understand in light of their reading of Jan Harold Brunvand's collections of urban legends. See for example the *Dictionary* entry for *FOAF:*

> *FOAF //* [USENET] n. Acronym for "Friend Of A Friend." The source of an unverified, possibly untrue story. This was not originated

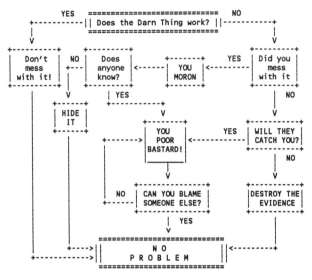

by hackers (it is used in Jan Brunvand's books on urban folklore), but it is much better recognized on USENET and elsewhere than in mainstream English. [Raymond 1991 : 162]

The reference to USENET is noteworthy for it is here, within a loosely structured system of newsgroups, that alt.folklore.urban, identified as "urban legends, ala [sic] Jan Harold Brunvand," serves as the address for those fascinated by the tales. Legends and fables that elucidate lexicon entries appear in "Appendix A: Hacker Folklore" of the *Dictionary*. "They have the characteristics of what Jan Brunvand has called 'urban folklore' (see FOAF)," which includes the often dubious claim to their historical veracity (Raymond 1991 : 399).

The electronic medium is ideally suited for a collaborative project of this kind not only because of networked interaction but also because of automatic archiving and distributed storage (the dictionary can be physically stored at multiple sites and accessed from anywhere). The print snapshots of the "live" online Jargon File, an open text if there ever was one, are especially interesting for the way they bring the problem of forgetting into focus. Karl Mannheim's essay (1952) on generations is useful here. He postulates two extremes: first, a society in which each generation starts from scratch with absolutely no memory of what the previous generation remembered, and second, a society in which every generation forgets absolutely nothing and remembers everything from time immemorial. Each is an immobilizing nightmare in its own right, but illuminating of the constitutive relationship of remembering and forgetting, particularly in a context where generations are short—the case of hackers and the rapidly changing technologies with which they work.

What the *Dictionary* reveals is how deliberate forgetting must be in a medium that accumulates and stores, that forgets nothing, except in the event of a disaster. The makers of the *Dictionary* use sifting and editing as a mode of forgetting. The little history of the project that appears in the *Dictionary* urges the reader to ignore earlier versions of the file in favor of this new and improved version, and in the process reveals how they "unwrote" (my term) the history of hacker culture by expunging obsolete terms and usages. Their record of the history of the project, proceeding as it does through versions, simultaneously erases the history of its subject. This dictionary, combining the features of manual, reference work, manifesto, ethnography, archive, and history, resembles software—it exists in numbered and dated versions, whose sequence and changes are carefully recorded. Casting a wider net, the current version of the Jargon File extends to "all the technical computing cultures wherein the true hacker-nature is manifested," with the result that "more than half of the entries now derive from USENET."

IRC (Internet Relay Chat)

The examples discussed thus far are instances of asynchronous communication, more like the mail than the telephone or a conversation in a room. But there are also cases of synchronous communication in which as few as two or as many as 50 people are logged on and conversing in real time in the medium. The conversation appears on the screen, a turn at a time, producing something that is neither playscript nor transcript. Such conversations are something between talking and writing.

A particularly lively environment for this activity is IRC (Internet Relay Chat), a synchronous talk program written in Finland in 1988 by Jarkko Oikarinen. A form of teleconferencing, IRC operates for the most part like a party line. Growing rapidly, IRC now includes over 60 countries in the Americas, Europe (specially Scandinavia), and Asia, as well as Africa (Sierra Leone and South Africa), Australia, and New Zealand. As many as five thousand users are logged on at the same time during peak hours and activate several hundred channels (conversations on particular topics) in as many as fourteen languages, including Esperanto. IRC has long been the preserve of undergraduate students in computer science, mostly male, in the United States, Europe, Israel, Australia, Japan, and Taiwan, though its constituency is diversifying (see Graham 1995; Pioch 1992; Rose 1994).

Interactivity is what intensifies presence. Interlocutors therefore take short turns in order to speed up the pace of conversations that writing tends to slow down. Since short turns are better suited to playful repartee than serious business, IRC conversations tend toward pure sociability verging at times on artful or outrageous nonsense as students take a break from their labors and come here to play—a kind of busman's holiday (see Reid 1991). Brenda Danet and her colleagues at the Hebrew University and New York University have been studying language, play, and performance on IRC, which, while it shares many conventions with other types of electronic communication and pre-electronic forms of writing (comics and graffiti, for example), also produces its own distinctive modes of interaction (see Danet, Ruedenberg, and Rosenbaum-Tamari, forthcoming). They reveal how reflexive users are about the medium and life in it. Indeed, metacommunication, which is a prominent feature of e-mail communication both to address problems and as a source of pleasure in its own right, achieves an apotheosis of sorts when people are at play.

In times of crisis, however, the electronic sandbox becomes a vital communications center operating outside of official government and media channels—there are IRC logs dealing with the 1994 California earthquake, the turmoil in Russia in 1992 and 1993, the 1992 presidential election, and the 1991 Gulf War (http://sunsite.unc.edu/dbarberi/chats.html). IRC becomes the place to get the most recent information from the scene and the way to reach people when phone lines are tied up and even ground transportation is out of the question. Almost instantly, people start providing live reports of what they are actually experiencing or witnessing. They relate news from local radio and television stations and they relay information and messages to family and friends that cannot otherwise reach each other. As many as fifty people at a time gathered on the channel #earthquake to get news directly from Los Angeles and the channel #oklahoma for news about the 1995 bombing in Oklahoma City. IRC has demonstrated the robustness of the Internet to function, as originally intended, in a time of disaster, even with the loss of some links (posted January 19, 1994; http://gopher.it.lut.fi:70/0/net/irc/article.quake).

Increasingly, new chat channels are dedicated to serious conversation or sustained artistic collaboration. Chefsplace is the place to go "if you love to talk about cooking, or just love good conversation devoid of the usual meaningless and often offensive drabble often seen on irc, you'll love Chefsplace" (Andrew Brock, asls@oro.net, posting to rec.food.cooking, 29 Mar. 1995). The Hamnet Players studied by Danet convene on an IRC channel at a set time, each one having received in advance only his or her own lines, to participate in what she characterizes as a "collective, virtual puzzle game, in which the full script, with spontaneously added improvisation, unfolds on their screens" (Danet 1994). Their productions of Hamnet and PCbeth, and more recently, "An IRC Channel Named #Desire" (after Tennessee Williams), confounds even further the question of performativity, when actors/players "perform" their lines by writing/talking them in the special conventions of IRC discourse, which uses speedwriting devices, rebus conventions, emoticons, expressions of affect de-

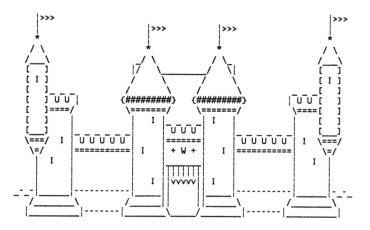

rived from comic books and cartoons, ASCII art, and orthographic play more generally.

MUDs

MUDs (Multi-user Dungeons, Dimensions, Domains, or Dialogues) are distributed communication environments in which players collaboratively produce a text-based virtual world. The structure, style, and ethos of these online places derive from their programming and script language, database, universe rules, and premises for what kind of world the players will sustain—some operate with a class or guild system, almighty wizards or gods, and the possibility of building the world, not just interacting within it.

MUDS and their successors have proliferated and diversified. One can now join a MOO (MUD, Object Oriented), MUSE (Multi-User Simulation Environment), MUSH (Multi-User Shared Hallucination), MUCK, MESH, MUG (Multi-User Game), MUTT (Multi-User Trivial Terminal), and many others. At last count (1 April 1995), there were 517 MUDs in operation in seven languages (English, French, German, Italian, Portuguese, Spanish, and Swedish). The list is updated every Friday (http://caisr2.caisr.cwru.edu/pub/mud/mudlist.auto).

As the MUD FAQ (Smith 1995) explains, MUDs fall into several overlapping general categories. Inspired by Dungeons and Dragons, the earliest are fantasy role-playing games oriented to adventure and combat. Richard Bartle and Roy Trubshaw at the University of Essex wrote the prototype MUD, no longer operating, in 1978, and by 1988 MUDS had made their way to North America (s.v. MUD, Jargon File 3.1.0, 1994). The LPMUD is the most popular of this type today. Some of the largest and most active MUDs are social places, for example, TinyMUDS, and they may operate with or without role-

playing and combat. Lastly, there are MUDs like MicroMUSE, self-defined as
an educational MUD. Its charter expresses the concern that MIT and its tax-
payer dollars not support "activities of a questionable or objectionable nature"
(MicroMUSE Charter, version 6, November 1994 update, ftp://musenet.
bbn.com). The formal charter and bylaws and elaborate administrative structure
are consistent with these concerns. (MicroMUSE Bylaws, version 6, November
1994 update). The intention is that adults and children, in exploring Cyberion
City II, "sometime in the 24th century A.D.," will develop programming, writing, and communication skills and explore the visionary promise of this virtual
world.

[handwritten margin note: liberal humanism (cf. Turkle)]

MOO technology is also being extended to new applications. A release just
went out over the Internet (3 April 1995, http://bug.village.virginia.edu) announcing Waxweb 2.0, an experiment in "public virtual reality cinema" that
combines the possibilities of MOO and WWW technologies "to dynamically
serve hyperlinked 3D VRML objects/scenes" in the form of "an Internet-
based, distributed, interactive, and intercommunicative 3D narrative environment." Waxweb uses a soundtrack in English, French, German, and Japanese.
(VRML refers to Virtual Reality Modelling Language.)

What are MUDs and MOOs like? PMC-MOO (telnet://hero.village.vir-
ginia.edu:7777), an offshoot of *Postmodern Culture* (*PMC*), an online journal
that is also now appearing in print, describes itself as "a virtual space designed
to promote the exploration of postmodern theory and practice," though when
I just visited it there was a lot of waving and hugging going on, just like in
other MUDs. The message continues:

> This virtual world is governed by a principle of radical consent. This
> means that you have the right to consent, and to remain consenting, to
> any activities in which you choose to participate. Conversely, you may
> not involve other players in activities to which they do not consent.
> By logging on, *you* consent to this as a central governing principle.
> Finally, by participating, you consent to learn about and contribute to
> the theme of this MOO: postmodernism.

LambdaMOO (telnet://lambda.xerox.com:8888) asks guests to type "help
manners" so they can behave in accordance with "two basic principles of
friendly MOOing: let the MOO function and don't abuse other players" by
"Spamming [filling their screen with unwanted text]; Teleporting them or their
objects without consent; Emoted violence or obscenities; Shouting (sending a
message to all connected players) . . . ; Spoofing (causing messages to appear
that are not attributed to your character) . . . ; Spying . . . ; Sexual harassment
(particularly involving unsolicited acts which simulate rape against unwilling
participants). . . . A single incidence of such an act may, as a consequence of
due process, result in permanent expulsion from LambdaMOO." Players are

asked not to tinker with the system or take advantage of loopholes or bugs, *rules*
whether in the core or in the social arrangements, that might undermine the
MOO itself. They are asked to respect the privacy, autonomy, and sensibility of
other players: "MOO inhabitants and visitors come from a wide range of cultural backgrounds both in the U.S. and abroad, and have varying ideas of what
constitutes offensive speech or descriptions." FurryMUCK (telnet://sncils.snc.
edu:8888, http://www.furry.com) requires that players read their AUP (Acceptable Use Policy), principles, and policies documents, which clearly enunciate
where the MUCK stands on privacy, harassment, and permission. It is in this   *Transgression*
spirit that players are asked to restrict sexual activities to private areas, or be
subject to a ban or suspension of character. To protect the hosts (and players)
from being prosecuted, the AUP prohibits "transmission or solicitation for
reception of material which violates US Federal or Wisconsin State Law," including anything legally obscene or libelous, a Pandora's box of First Amendment issues endemic to the medium more generally.

Of special importance is the reminder that FurryMUCKers are after all engaged in a game, while recognizing that players vary in how they negotiate VR
(Virtual Reality), RL (Real Life)—and the space between them, which is the
primary location for some dedicated players. The limits and excesses of role
playing have been tested more than once and have prompted the formulation
of such policies as "proven harassment of malicious intent i.e. intended to
cause mental harm such as rape, threats of RL harm, severe emotional manipulation, will NOT be tolerated. Malicious harassment may result in immediate
suspension."

For these and other reasons, MUDs are extraordinary social laboratories (see
Curtis 1992; Reid 1994). Players deliberately fabricate what is variously called
a universe, world, society, or community built on role playing. They use a mode
of governance based upon consent. Though MUDs are particularly open zones
and though players are anonymous, any one who violates the consent principle
is subject to sanctions—after several crises, LambdaMOO introduced a petition and ballot system to allow members of the community to raise issues and
vote on how best to address them. The potential result is absorption in an environment of such vividness that distinctions between saying and doing become moot. If IRC produces something between a play script and a tran-   *IRC*
script—a dialogue that is and was at the same time—the screen during a MOO
session looks more like something between a set of instructions for what to do   *MOO*
and a description of what has just been done. But the utterances *are* the doing;
they are neither prior nor subsequent to it.

In an insightful account of rape in LambdaMOO in 1993, Julian Dibbell
examines the consequences of such ambiguity, which he takes as constitutive
of the MUD world: "For while the *facts* attached to any event born of a MUD's
strange ethereal universe may march in straight, tandem lines separated nearly

into the virtual and the real, its meaning lies always in that gap." It is the mark of a newbie to insist on the distinction and to mistake the MOO as a place where anything goes and without consequences. It is the mark of a veteran "to make the critical passage from anonymity to pseudonymity, developing the concern for their character's reputation." To know better and do otherwise is the mark of a "sociopath." A primary site for defining the issue is "netsex, tinysex, virtual sex—however you name it." That it is a textual encounter, rather than visual, audio, or tactile, does not necessarily diminish its power to stir the passions. Dibbell argues to the contrary, citing the power of anonymity, suggestiveness, and fantasy to produce experiences that are, in his terms, full-bodied, profound, compelling, and emotionally meaningful (Dibbell 1993). How else to explain the social drama that unfolded in response to Mr. Bungle's sexual violence, his rape of Legba and Starsinger?

The corrective rituals touch on several important issues. First, how are the premises of freedom of speech challenged in a medium where the distinction between acting and speaking, between real (deed) and symbolic (word), is ambiguous? Second, when a crisis arises, what is the nature of the social entity that is mobilized to deal with it? The two are linked, as suggested both by the 1973 U.S. Supreme Court ruling that what counts as obscene is a matter of local community standards and the various MUD policies on consent and harassment. A crisis brings the issues of community and governance into the foreground in the particular terms of a MUD world, terms that go to its very ontology. Those concerns run all the way through the networks, where discussion of location, community, governance, free speech, and crime in a medium that seems to confound them are recurrent topics of commentary, both daily in postings and in the more extended discussion of Net advocates. What gets discussed within the medium illuminates what has been assumed outside of it (see Stone 1991).

E-mail, Discussion Lists, Newsgroups

In the less heady setting of electronic mail and discussion lists, the fundamentals of the interaction order are being worked out in ways that are no less interesting. Television scholar Robert Thompson has observed that "we have really returned here, in spite of the centralization of technology, to the old-fashioned definition of what folk culture used to be. . . . We have these jokes and stories that will never see the printed page, that exist only as glowing dots of phosphorous. It's not word-of-mouth folk culture but word-of-modem folk culture" (Grimes 1992:C14). But what do terms like *group* or *community* mean in a medium where dispersed strangers are not physically present to one another? They do not gather in one physical place at one time, though the instantaneity of transmission makes it feel like that way.

In a medium where time is indicated only by date and time of transmission

To help telecom-sters clarify just how humorous their postings are
intended to be, here is a collection of the many faces of humor,
emoticon-style.

emoticon: n. a figure created with the symbols on a keyboard that
          is read with the head tilted to the left. Used to convey
          the spirit in which a line of text was typed.

****
*   *
* Tilt your head slightly to the left to read the following emoticons. *
*   *
****


```
:-)          Humor
:-) )-:         Masking theatrical comments
:<)          For those with hairy lips
:<)=         For those with beards too
:/)          Not funny
'-)            Wink
P-)          Pirate
;-)          Sardonic incredulity
(@ @)          You're kidding!
:-"            Pursing lips
:-v          Just another face (speaking) profiled from the side
:-V          Shout
:-w          Speak with forked tongue
:-W          Shout with forked tongue
:-r          Bleahhh (sticking tongue out)
:-f
:-p
:-1          Smirks
:-,
<:-O         Eeek!
:-*          Oooops (covering mouth with hand)
:-T          keeping a straight face (tight-lipped)
:-D          said with a smile
:-P
:-y
:-o          More versions of shouting
:-O
:-{          Count Dracula
=|:-)=          Uncle Sam
7:)          Reagan
:-#          Censored
:~i          Smoking
:~j          (and smiling)
:/i          No smoking
:-I            It's something, but I don't know what....
:-x          Kiss kiss
:->          Alternate happy face
:-(          Unhappy
:-c          Real unhappy
```

and the weather is always the same, the seasons come and go in the form of distinctive genres of greetings—"I love you" in every conceivable language for Valentine's Day, including Mohawk, Tagalog, and Yiddish, and a graphic in the form of a Hanukkah lamp, sent on eight successive days, each time with one more candle lit. Graphics are created using only the characters on the keyboard and are known as ASCII art or boxology. These greetings are widely circulated, not only to everyone on a particular list, but also they are cross-posted to everyone else on many of the other lists to which individuals belong. For the most part, however, those who interact in the electronic medium remain "strangers" to each other.

Some have commented that electronic lists, bulletin boards, IRC channels, and MUDS are like entering a virtual room where several conversations are taking place, an image that suggests intimacy. For others, it is like wandering around a virtual town square, plaza, commons, or agora, or hanging out at the listening post—in other words, a public forum. Ray Oldenburg's notion of a "third place" has been invoked more than once as a metaphor for the place of online communities—this is the place of conviviality, like the salons and saloons, beauty and barber shops, pubs and cafés, and common rooms IRL (Oldenburg 1989:14–19). John Coate invokes the images of a lunchtime crowd at Hyde Park, amateur night at the Apollo, and the Gong Show.

The proliferation of images of conviviality goes to the "fragility of trust" and a concern about commitment in self-defined virtual communities, whether they are made up of pseudonymous characters in elaborated fantasy worlds or identified persons in an ongoing conversation. A circumstance known within ordinary conversations as YMMV (Your Mileage May Vary) refers to "an indeterminacy of shared context" that results in part from differing notions of "what kind of place cyberspace is" (Rheingold 1992). "In a virtual community," Rheingold continues, "idle talk is context-setting. Idle talk is where people learn what kind of person you are, why you should be trusted or mistrusted, what interests you. An agora is more than a site of transactions; it is also a place where people meet and size one another up." The agora of online communities, in Rheingold's view, operates more like a gift economy than a market one, "more like barn-raising than horse-trading," an ideal that is consistent with Rheingold's projects, including the *Whole Earth Catalogue* and its successors. As for trust, even the word *phony* carries traces of its etymology in the early days of telephone when people were less savvy about the medium. Trust is fragile in this medium, and for good reason, considering the surveillance power of the medium and "the looming spectre of collusion between large cable companies and telcos leading to domination of electronic media by mostly one-way communications and entertainment at the expense of the interactive and user-created activities necessary to foster community" (Rheingold 1992). This statement signals the heterogeneous nature of the social world of the medium, which can be roughly divided into suits (those employed by the industry), hackers (mavericks, some of them engaged in criminal activity, most of them ingenious and playful devotees of the medium), and users (those, like myself, who are ordinary users of the medium), though within the various sectors of the Net, the distinctions vary as does the internal organization of "space," in the case of MUDs, for example.

Reflecting on his experience in the WELL, Rheingold notes that users navigate the Net in ways that give a sense of "neighborhood," particularly as the route becomes routinized: he structures his "online time by going from conference to specified conference at regular intervals, reading and perhaps responding in several ongoing threads in several different places. That's the part of the art of discourse where I have the computer add value to the intellectual activity of discussing formally distinct subjects asynchronously, from different parts of the world, over extended periods, by enabling groups to structure conversations by topic, over time" (Rheingold 1992).

What is meant by observations like, "It feels like a real place in there" (Coate 1992)? Where exactly are they? The electronic list WORDS-L answered this question on their T-shirt by printing the network of mainframe computers that routes their messages, complete with the node of every person on the list. However, unlike navigating a car on the nation's freeways with the help of a map, listers are usually oblivious to the transmission network, which they never see except when messages in a VAX/VMS environment appear on the screen indicating that their posting is blipping through the ether from one mainframe to another round the country and across the globe. Trolling and surfing the Internet, browsing with the help of Mosaic or Netscape, gophering to specific information or setting out on a spelunking expedition, cybernauts navigate by topic. Because topic is the basis for choosing with whom to communicate, topic is of the utmost importance in structuring and navigating the vast electronic net. As one lister remarked, the lively exchange about superstitions on WORDS-L was so similar to what she encountered on BELIEF-L, that she "did not know where she was."

Indeed, the thousands of bulletin boards and electronic lists are the result of "semantic zoning," where, as Rheingold notes, "the topic is the address." Topic control is of such burning interest precisely because topic is place—from *topos,* the Greek word for place. And virtual places are defined not just by the designated topic, be it jazz or sourdough, but also by the attitude to topic control. The designated topic may be the address, but the attitude to topic control helps to give the place its distinctive social character. Indeed, topic control might be seen as cartographic. In defining the limits of the topic, interlocutors chart the space of their copresence.

Some lists, like the DOROTHY-L list, named for Dorothy Sayers and devoted to mystery stories, enforce strict topic control. The hundreds of listers on

DOROTHY-L, in an exquisite ensemble performance, keep their beloved topic in the air, and are quick to slap the virtual wrists of anyone who lets it drop. To ensure tight topic control, some lists are moderated by someone who filters postings, sometimes gathering related ones together, before distributing them. The charter for USENET newsgroup rec.food.recipes stipulates that "recipes and recipes only will be posted to the newsgroup. . . . No discussion of any kind is allowed" ("Administrivia: Posting Guidelines for rec.food. recipes [moderated]," 6 March 1995, http://www.neosoft.com/recipes/). Other discussion lists, like WORDS-L, tolerate and even encourage discussion of whatever they please.

On FOLKLORE-L, listers who get sick of reading yet again about the same urban legend complain vociferously, urge those who want to continue that thread to do so privately, withdraw from the list if the problem persists, or start a new list for the disgruntled. Seemingly endless posting about the $250 recipe for the Neiman Marcus cookie tried the patience of many posters. Those on rec.music.blues argued about whether jazz and blues belong on one list or should be separated into two different lists—a data dream come true for those interested in "native" categories and the processes by which they are negotiated.

Even those who are more patient with threads (series of postings on a topic) that persist beyond the threshold of their interest lose their patience when they see topic drift. Because a reply to a posting carries a header that references the subject of the original message, a subject header commonly persists long after the topic has drifted far away from it and is misleading for those trying to follow a discussion thread or delete messages on topics they do not choose to track. For others, as Coate notes, topic drift "often leads to the most delightful illuminations. So much so that many people find this to be one of the most appealing aspects of the whole online scene" (Coate 1992).

A hallmark of electronic communication, whether in newsgroups, discussion lists, IRC, or MUDs, is the simultaneity of numerous conversational "threads." It is as if you were in a large hotel lobby during a cocktail reception, where hundreds of conversations were under way, each one of them entirely audible. But not as such. You do not hear each thread, with its turns in sequence, the way you would if you went from one cluster of people to another. Rather, you actually "hear" all of the conversations all at the same time, with one speaker from one conversation taking a turn, followed by a speaker from another conversation taking a turn. As a listener, you can follow all the threads, interwoven as they are with one another. Or you can ignore those that do not interest you and just follow the ones that do. The result is not the cacophony of the cocktail party but a conversational tapestry that is a physical impossibility in face-to-face situations and unimaginable by phone due to the limits of audibility (how many conversations can you hear, let alone follow, at a time?) and of aural processing (the limits of voicemail menus). Depending on your perspective, the result is a constantly interrupted series of simultaneous conversation or several long continuous ones. Furthermore, because volatile and highly interactive chat and MUD/MOO environments operate in real time rather than in a store and forward mode, the interaction is not automatically archived. It is therefore particularly ephemeral, unless steps are taken at the outset of a session to log it.

Though interlocutors operate under the conditions of disembodied presence and immateriality of place, fluid membership and ephemeral existence, there is a strong sense of presence and performativity in the medium. Operating between speech and writing, between word and deed, prompted listers on X-CULT-X to dub this kind of talk *putation,* and to speak of puting or putating.[8] One often has the feeling of talking, rather than writing—"I'll talk to you on e-mail." Coate reports hearing online discussion called "writing as a performing art." The performativity of the medium, its "hotness," is expressed in various ways (1992). People prefer to interact directly online, in the medium, even when so doing costs more than composing messages on the computer and uploading them or downloading mail before reading it. Presence in the medium is a function of interactivity—the more interaction, the more people are present to each other, and most of all in real-time (synchronous) chat. When logging on, some people first find out who else is "there"—I type "show users" to get a list of everyone logged into the NYU system when I am online. This action "enhances the sense of 'usness,'" according to Coate (1992), who relates the gesture to opening the window to see who is on the street. In a medium where "the basic currency is attention," visibility (and the power to make invisible) is at a premium. There are tools—kill files such as Anathema, also known as bozo filters—by means of which "people can remove one another, or even entire topics of discussion from visibility" (Rheingold 1992). A list manager can drop unruly participants and block the list from their messages. More subtle, however, is the invisibility created through the inattention in the gendered patterning of online conferencing. Women report that their postings are ignored, that topics they initiate are not picked up, and that men on the lists essentially talk to each other and dominate the conversation, a situation that is exacerbated by the demographics (men generally outnumber women) and gendered differences in communicative style (see Taylor, Kramarae, and Ebben 1993).

In asynchronous e-mail there are common routines for intensifying the conversational feel of the medium by transforming even a single message that has been stored and forwarded into a retroactively interactive conversation in which the interlocutors "take turns" just as they would in a face-to-face conversation. I can virtually cut up the sender's message to me and insert my comments in the spaces thus created. I thereby make the sender's single turn into a whole conversation by segmenting the message and inserting my responses. In

presence

this way I produce microconversational turn-taking retroactively but in a way that is different both from referencing each point, as one would in an exchange of letters, and from face-to-face conversational exchange.

When a thread is preserved intact inside a posting, the result is a cascade. A reply often appends the message to which it is responding. Some replies are so short that by themselves they would be unintelligible. Recipients cannot be expected to remember what prompted the message before them. Rather than going through a laborious process of referencing the prior message, interlocutors simply append all or part of it to their response. Eventually each posting gets longer and longer, as the whole conversation is repeatedly appended. The convention in some systems of marking the prior material with a $<$ at the beginning of each line and adding a $<$ each time the prior material is reappended produces a cascade effect, the number of $<$'s at the beginning of the line indicating how many times the material in question has been appended. While this annoys some posters, who object to any unnecessary material, the Jargon File 3.1.0 notes in its entry for *cascade* the way in which phenomena distinctive to the medium also have a life of their own: "A chain of USENET followups, each adding some trivial variation or riposte to the text of the previous one, all of which is reproduced in the new message; an include war in which the object is to create a sort of communal graffito" and as long a one as possible. Newsgroup alt.cascade is where especially long cascades are posted and cascading is undertaken as an end in itself. One poster creates a cascade by repeatedly sending a message to himself, appending the prior one each time:

Newsgroups: alt.cascade
Subject: Re: nothing
Date: 3 Apr 1995 02:41:46 GMT

In article <3lnn6p$hv1@news.iastate.edu>,
jerry johnson <jaylen@iastate.edu> wrote:
>In article <3lnn4j$hse@news.iastate.edu>,
>jerry johnson <jaylen@iastate.edu> wrote:
>>In article <3lnn36$hs7@news.iastate.edu>,
>>jerry johnson <jaylen@iastate.edu> wrote:
>>>In article <3lnn0l$hr6@news.iastate.edu>,
>>>jerry johnson <jaylen@iastate.edu> wrote:
>>>>In article <3lnmuh$hqt@news.iastate.edu>,
>>>>jerry johnson <jaylen@iastate.edu> wrote:
>>>>>In article <3lnmsp$hqk@news.iastate.edu>,
>>>>>jerry johnson <jaylen@iastate.edu> wrote:
>>>>>>In article <3lnmqp$hqb@news.iastate.edu>,
>>>>>>jerry johnson <jaylen@iastate.edu> wrote:
>>>>>>>nothing

```
>>>>>>nothin
>>>>>nothi
>>>>noth
>>>not
>>no
>n
```

bye.
—jerry

Such exercises are also testimony to the recursiveness of the medium. They play with features of the medium in their own right, features that are once useful but easily extended to the point of annoyance. Indeed, the technical aspects of the medium are often ahead of the uses to which they may be put, as Susan Garfinkel's comment on WWW links suggests: "Surely anyone who cruises the web noticed the proliferation of links to other links—half the time it's like there's no there there, as if someone's demonstrated ability to pick out and discern cool or useful links to other sites stand in for actual content" (posting to H-AMSTDY, 29 Mar. 1995). As annoying as jumping from link to link and arriving "nowhere" may be, this display and exploration of the WWW's hypertextual structure is a critical step in realizing its "capability of turning the entire internet into one hypertextual web" (Unsworth 1994:2).

WWW creates yet another kind of social space on the net, the perpetual open house. "Come by and visit my home page," their creators now beckon. Once there, I feel like I am walking into the house of someone I have never met. They are away, and I find a note on the kitchen table with instructions telling me where everything is. The note issues an open invitation to get comfortable and explore the place. The host introduces himself through a link to a biography page, like family pictures on the mantlepiece. And a guest book is there for all visitors to sign, with comments.

These homes are under construction. One of their greatest assets is their wiring, their links to other homepages, gopher holes, ftp archives, and newsgroups. Instead of beer in the refrigerator, there is information on the screen, arranged by the host, often with lively personal commentary. Instead of a pile of lumber and bricks in the yard, there are sites waiting to be incorporated into the home page, their arrangement refined, the page itself designed, and features to be added.

Home pages are proudly authored. They are often the creation of identified individuals, small entrepreneurs who set up shop for themselves on the net, and await visitors. Some, like Bianca's Smut Shack, "one of the liveliest house parties in cyberspace," attract many guests and are constantly developing new spaces and features to accommodate them (Wired May 1995, 53; http://bianca.com/shack/). The interactive aspect of Bianca's Smut Shack aligns it with the collaborative, improvisatory, and open-ended quality of newsgroups, discussions lists, and MUDs. The character of each is determined by the extent to which a moderator, wizard, or landlord administers rather than authors the enterprise.

Worms and crawlers help one find these sites. These search engines beam the trekker to the topics specified. Once there, movement is by leaps, from link to link, associatively. It is only as you retrace your steps, by tapping the left arrow key (using Lynx, a textual interface), that you discover where you went in the first place. Orientation is retrospective. Long associative links take one out into the vastness of the net. Instead of coming home after each foray and setting out again, WWW expeditions move from link to link, improvising an itinerary that circles back on itself, takes off on tangents, hits dead ends, stalls, and takes off again for parts unknown.

An evolving code of netiquette, formally set forth as early as 1985 by the Rand Corporation for the National Science Foundation (Shapiro and Anderson 1985), are intended to ease the rapid influx of new users to a medium where the protocols are not yet well established and peer pressure is harder to exert. Netiquette has since been codified in various manuals, from Minding Your Cyber-Manners (Rose 1994) to "Miss Manners' Guide to Excruciatingly Correct Internet Behavior" (Shea 1995), and in parodies of them like Emily Post-news. A new Network Etiquette Mailing List (netiquette-request@albion.com) is sponsored by the publisher of Virginia Shea's book *Netiquette* (1994). According to netiquette, subject headers should match the content of the message. Listers should refrain from sending unnecessary messages. Signature blocks should be discrete. Posters should refrain from "flaming," or making inflammatory remarks. Where necessary, use emoticons—smiley faces and variations of them created with ASCII characters to indicate affect that in conversation would be apparent from facial expression, gesture, or tone of voice (see Sanderson 1993).

The very indeterminacy of the medium favors forms like the UL (Urban Legend) heard FOAF (From a Friend of a Friend). According to the FAQ file for alt.folklore.urban, an urban legend "appears mysteriously and spreads spontaneously in varying forms" and "does not have to be false, although most are. ULs often have a basis in fact, but it's their life after-the-fact (particularly in reference to the second and third points) that gives them particular interest" (http://cathouse.org:8000/UrbanLegends/ULdefinition.html). Not only does the electronic medium intensify the transmission of the legend—people report sitings in newspapers and on other lists, as well as repeat versions they have heard—but they also enjoy talking about the legends as much as they do telling them. Indeed they enjoy talking about the talk most of all. Most of all, the drama of these lists revolves around the humiliation of discovering that a story believed to be true is "just a legend," while the winners are the ones who

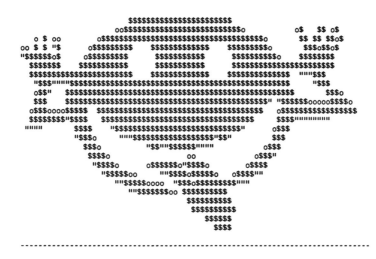

can tell the difference. It is precisely its ambiguous truth status that suits the urban legend so well to the ontology of this medium.

Chain letters, for their part, are taboo because they behave like the sorcerer's apprentice in a medium with untold powers of replication. It is precisely the power of the medium to achieve to perfection what chain letters are designed to do, namely, to proliferate exponentially, that makes them objectionable. Newcomers to USENET are put on notice: "If your posting was a 'MAKE MONEY FAST' note or any other chain letter, it will be reported to the admins at your site" (automatic acknowledgement from netannounce@desha.com). The prospect of electronic chain letters is so daunting, their uncontrollable dissemination so terrifying, that such spamming is grounds for the rescinding of one's network privileges. When Martha Siegel and Laurence Canter advertised their legal services—to help illegal immigrants take advantage of the green card lottery—on USENET, they created a widely reported scandal. Not only was commercial exploitation of USENET in this way a flagrant disregard of netiquette, but also, were such random postings to become routine, the system could not withstand the volume. Letting the punishment fit the crime, outraged users spammed them back in ever more ingenious ways.

Usegroups for soap opera and Star Trek fans wed the attributes of television broadcast in serial form to the distributed and interactive medium of the Internet. As Nancy Baym shows in her exemplary study of rec.arts.tv.soaps, a newsgroup that is now more than ten years old, some participants seem to get more pleasure from the discussion than from the programs, to the point of writing their own episodes (Baym 1992). Constance Penley's work on fans of Star Trek documents how women create their own version of the Star Trek world. They write erotic episodes for each other—in which the men make love to each other

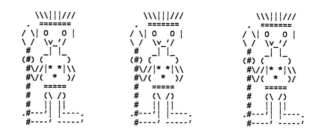

[handwritten: But what is communication (]

(Penley 1992). For many fans, the electronic list has not displaced other forms of communication—fanzines and conferences—but is added to them.

[handwritten: ? /] Sites of conviviality, fantasy, and play are revelatory of the nature of electronic communication more generally and they are being studied increasingly in social, psychological, and cultural terms—in the medium itself. To study a phenomenon that won't stand still for its portrait is like trying to keep up with a galloping shapeshifter, riding it as one analyzes it. Moments before writing these sentences I trolled across Seeker1's Cyberanthropology Home Page!, which is a call to action for a virtual anthropology. It announces a new online journal, *Topothesia: A Virtual Anthropology Information Singularity*. It also gathers together resources, including full texts of essays and bibliographies, tips on multimedia, and leads to various sites (BBS, Gopher, lists, and USE-NET newsgroups) of interest to virtual anthropologists and their sibling cyborg anthropologists (see Haraway 1991a, 1991b). Here, where tools and topics converge, where the medium and social life within it are mutually constitutive, our accounts are increasingly doing what they are about. Close to home, but oh so far away, new worlds are under construction. What kind of life will be lived there and what repercussions it will have remains to be seen. Now is the time to study it in formation, before its protocols have hardened, and to consider its implications for life offline.

Acknowledgments

My interest in this topic was inaugurated during my residency as a Getty Scholar at the Getty Center for the History of Art and the Humanities, Santa Monica, during 1991–92, thanks to Philip Harriman. This work in progress was presented at various stages to the Center for the Comparative Study of Folklore and Mythology at UCLA; as part of the series "Shifting Boundaries/Contested Spaces" organized by the Getty Center; at the National Endowment for the Humanities Summer Institute "Telling Tales"; the University of Wisconsin at Madison; the Committee on Theory and Culture at New York University; and as the O. C. Tanner Lecture at Utah State University, Logan. I greatly benefitted from the discussion that ensued on each of these occasions. Several colleagues have brought material to my attention, taught me how to play with the medium, shared their work, and read and commented on drafts of this essay. Special thanks to Jim, Mary, and Pippin Barr, Brenda Danet, Shifra Epstein, Naomi Jackson, Lucia Ruedenberg, George Sadowsky, Jeffrey Shandler, Shawna Silver, Madeline Slovenz-Low, David Taylor, Gisele Welz, and Erica Wortham.

Notes

1. In discussion following his presentation to the Committee on Theory and Culture, New York University, January 28, 1994.

2. It should be kept in mind that addresses on the Internet change constantly.

3. The scope of Jewish networking can be seen in the activities of NYSERNet/Shamash Consortium (gopher://israel.nysernet.org:71/), at the Yahoo Web site (http://www.yahoo.com-Society _ and _ Culture/Religion/Judaism/), and in Matthew Album's "The A-Z of Jewish and Israel Related Resources" (http://www/ort.org/anjy/resource/a-z.html).

4. Thanks to Naomi Jackson for this flyer.

5. Article 47735 of soc.culture.jewish (March 11, 1993), posted by Douglas Jones, with three other contributors.

6. Teleconfession by fax may eliminate the need for physical copresence in the darkness of the confessional box. The *Chicago Tribune* also reported that in Vincenza, Italy, "A new confessional box to be unveiled at Italy's annual church fair here in May would provide busy people the option of confessing the sins of lust, greed and omission—by fax machine."

7. Steve Kinzler, who issues digests of the best Oracularities, kindly provided these figures and granted permission to quote from them. He also noted in response to my question (March 31, 1995) about how the Oracle has changed that the Oracle has been "diluted" by the influx of newbies, who are "not likely to invest as much effort in composing Oracle questions and answers." As a result, he explained, less than 2% of the Oracularities make it into the digest now, compared with as much as 8% previously—"Well, as the nature of the user base of the Internet changes, so does the Oracle" (April 3, 1995).

8. It is the creation of Steve Mizrach (http://www.clas.ufl.edu/anthro/cyberanthro/oldhome.html).

References

Adams, Paul C. 1992. "Television as Gathering Place." *Annals of the Association of American Geographers* 82 (1): 117–35.

Ascott, Roy, and Carl Eugene Loeffler, eds. 1991. Special issue on "Connectivity: Art and Interactive Telecommunications." *Leonardo* 24 (2).

Barlow, John Perry. 1990. "Crime and Puzzlement: Desperados of the DataSphere."

Whole Earth Review 4 (Fall): 45–57. Available gopher://gopher.eff.org/111/Publi-
cations/John _ Perry _ Barlow/crime _ and _ puzzlement.1.

———. 1992. "The Great Work." Available gopher://gopher.eff.org/111/Publications/
John _ Perry _ Barlow/

Baym, Nancy K. 1992. "Computer-Mediated Soap Talk: Communication, Community,
and Entertainment on the Net." Version 01: Unpublished paper.

Benedikt, Michael, ed. 1991. *Cyberspace: First Steps.* Cambridge, Mass.: MIT Press.

Binkley, Timothy. 1988. "Camera Fantasia: Computed Visions of Virtual Realities."
Millenium 20/21 (Fall/Winter): 7–43.

Bishop, Katherine. 1992. "The Electronic Coffeehouse." *New York Times,* 2 Aug., sec.
1, 21.

Bukatman, Scott. 1993a. Electrotecture. *ANY (Architecture New York)* 3 (November/
December).

———. 1993b. *Terminal Identity: The Virtual Subject in Postmodern Science Fiction.*
Durham, N.C.: Duke University Press.

Carl-Mitchell, Smoot, and John S. Quarterman. 1994a. "Datagrams: The Recent History
of the Internet and the Matrix." *RS/Magazine* (July). Available http://www.tic.com.

———. 1994b. "Datagrams: The Early History of the Internet and the Matrix." *RS/
Magazine* (June). Available http://www.tic.com.

Castells, Manuel. 1989. *The Informational City: Information, Technology, Economics,
Restructuring, and the Urban-Regional Process.* Oxford: Blackwell.

Coate, John. 1992. "Cyberspace Innkeeping: Building Online Community." Available
gopher://gopher.well.sf.ca.us Location: community/.

Couey, Anna. 1991. "Cyber Art: The Art of Communication Systems." *Matrix News* 1
(4): Available email: couey@well.sf.ca.us.

Curtis, Pavel. 1992. "Mudding: Social Phenomena in Text-Based Virtual Realities."
Intertek 3 (3): 26–34.

Danet, Brenda. 1994. "Curtain Time 18:00 GMT: Experiments with Virtual Theater on
Internet Relay Chat." Unpublished paper.

Danet, Brenda, Lucia Ruedenberg, and Yehudit Rosenbaum-Tamari. In press.
" 'Hmmm, Where's All That Smoke Coming From?' Writing, Play and Performance
on Internet Relay Chat." In *Networks and Netplay: Virtual Groups on the Internet.*
Eds. S. Rafaeli, F. Sudweeks, and M. McLaughlin. Cambridge, MA: MIT/AAAI.

Dibbell, Julian. 1993. "A Rape in Cyberspace or How an Evil Clown, a Haitian Trick-
ster, Two Wizards, and Cast of Dozens Turned a Database Into a Society." *The Village Voice,* 21 Dec., 37–42. Available (with critique) http://gopher.well.sf.ca.us:70/
1/Publications/authors/Dibble.

Fiske, John. 1989. *Understanding Popular Culture.* Boston: Unwin Hyman.

Frederick, Howard H. 1993. "Computer Networks and the Emergence of Global Civil
Society: The Case of the Association for Progressive Communication (APC)." In
Globalizing Networks: Computers and International Communication. Ed. L. M.
Harasim. Cambridge, Mass.: MIT Press.

Gibson, William. 1984. *Neuromancer.* New York: Ace Books.

Graham, Paul. 1995. "IRC Related Resources on the Internet (7 Mar.; Version 2.1.7)."
Available http://urth.acsu.buffalo.edu/irc/www[ircdoc.html].

Greenwald, Jeff. 1993. "Dish-Wallahs." *Wired* 1, no. 2 (May/June): 75, 107.

Grimes, William. 1992. "Computer as a Cultural Tool: Chatter Mounts on Every Topic." *New York Times,* 1 Dec., sec. C, 13–14.

Hallowell, Edward M., and John J. Ratey. 1994. *Driven to Distraction.* New York: Pantheon.

Hapgood, Fred. 1993. *Up the Infinite Corridor: MIT and the Technical Imagination.* Reading, Mass.: Addison-Wesley.

Haraway, Donna J. 1991a. "The Actors Are Cyborgs, Nature Is Coyote, and the Geography Is Elsewhere: Postscript to 'Cyborgs at Large.'" In *Technoculture.* Eds. C. Penley and A. Ross. Minneapolis: University of Minnesota Press.

———. 1991b. *Simians, Cyborgs, and Women: The Reinvention of Nature.* London: Free Association Books.

Harvey, David. 1989. *The Condition of Postmodernity.* Oxford: Blackwell.

Herszenhorn, David M. 1995. "Students Turn to Internet for Nationwide Protest Planning." *New York Times,* 29 Mar., sec. A, 20.

Jones, Stephen G., ed. 1995. *CyberSociety: Computer-Mediated Communication and Community.* Thousand Oaks, Calif.: Sage Publications.

Karnow, Curtis E. A. 1994. "Data Morphing: Ownership, Copyright, and Creation." *Leonardo* 27 (2): 117–22.

Keller, Bill. 1993. "By Pluck and Fax, Tiny Free Press." *New York Times,* 1 Mar., Business section, 6.

Lemus, Mitchell S. 1995. "How I Found God on the Internet." *Manhattan File* 2, no. 7: 32.

Lewis, Peter H. 1994. "Strangers, Not Their Computers, Build a Network in Time of Grief." *New York Times,* 8 Mar., A1, D2.

Mannheim, Karl. 1952. "The Sociological Problem of Generations." In *Essays on the Sociology of Knowledge.* New York: Oxford University Press.

Markoff, John. 1993. "Cult Film Is a First on Internet." *New York Times,* 24 May, Business section, 8.

McLaughlin, Margaret L. 1994. "Art Galleries on the World Wide Web." Second International Conference on the World Wide Web. Chicago, 17 Oct. Available http://cwis.usc.edu/dept/annenberg/artfinal.html.

Meyrowitz, Joshua. 1985. *No Sense of Place: The Impact of Electronic Media on Social Behavior.* New York: Oxford University Press.

Mitchell, William J. 1995. *City of Bits: Space, Place, and the Infobahn.* Cambridge, Mass.: MIT Press.

Neubarth, Michael. 1995. "From the Editor." *Internet News* 6, no. 4: 6.

No author. January 1994. "Computer Network Weathers Big Jolt, Internet Users Swap News, Worries After Quake Hits." Associated Press. Available http://gopher.it.lut.fi:70/0/net/irc/ article.quake.

Oldenberg, Ray. 1989. *The Great Good Place: Cafes, Coffee Shops, Community Centers, Beauty Parlors, General Stores, Bars, Hangouts, and How They Get You Through the Day.* New York: Paragon House.

O'Neill, Molly. 1995. "The Lore and Addiction of Life on Line." *New York Times,* 6 Mar., Living section, 1, 6.

Penley, Constance. 1992. "Feminism, Psychoanalysis, and the Study of Popular Culture." In *Cultural Studies.* Eds. L. Grossberg, C. Nelson, and P. Treichler. New York: Routledge.

Pioch, Nicolas. 1992. *A Short IRC Primer* (Edition 1.1b, 28 Feb. 1993). Available ftp:// [IRCprimer1.1.txt] nic.funet.fi/pub/unix/irc/docs/.

Quarterman, John S. 1990. *The Matrix: Computer Networks and Conferencing Systems Worldwide.* Bedford, Mass.: Digital Press.

———. 1993. "The Internet." *Computerworld,* February.

———. 1994a. "Preliminary Partial Results of the Second TIC/MIDS Internet Demographic Survey." *Matrix News* 2, no. 12.

———. 1994b. "What Is the Internet, Anyway?" *Matrix News* 4, no. 8. Available gopher://gopher.eff.org/11/Net_culture/whats_internet.paper.

Raymond, Eric, ed. 1991. *The New Hacker's Dictionary.* Cambridge, Mass.: MIT Press.

Reid, Elizabeth M. 1991. "Electropolis: Communication and Community on Internet Relay Chat." Honors thesis, Department of History, University of Melbourne, Melbourne, Australia. Available gopher://gopher.eff.org/00/Net_culture/MOO_MUD_IRC/electropolis.paper

———. 1994. "Cultural Formations in Text-Based Virtual Realities." Master's thesis, Department of English, Cultural Studies Program, University of Melbourne, Melbourne, Australia. Available gopher://gopher.eff.org/00/Net_culture/MOO_MUD_IRC/cultural_formations.paper

Rheingold, Howard. 1992. "A Slice of Life in My Virtual Community." Available gopher://gopher.well.sf.ca.us/00/Community/virtual_communities92.

———. 1993. *The Virtual Community: Homesteading on the Electronic Frontier.* Reading, Mass.: Addison-Wesley.

Rose, Donald. 1994. *Minding Your Cyber-Manners on the Internet.* Indianapolis, Ind.: Alpha Books.

Rose, Helen Trillian. 1994. *IRC Frequently Asked Questions (FAQ)* (27 Apr.; Version 1.31) Available http://gopher.it.lut.fi:701/misc/faq/irc.faq.

Rospach, Chuq Von. 1984. "A Primer on How to Work With the Usenet Community" (29 Jan. 1995). Eds. M. Moraes and G. Spafford. Available usenet: news.newusers. questions.

Salzenberg, Chip. 1989. "What Is Usenet?" (25 Nov. 1994). Eds. G. Spafford, and M. Moraes. Available usenet: news.newusers.questions.

Sanderson, David. 1993. *Smileys.* New York: O'Reilly and Associates.

Schafer, R. Murray. 1977. *The Tuning of the World.* New York: Alfred A. Knopf.

Schindler, Rick. 1991. "A Stitch Online: The Electronic Quilting Bee." *The Prodigy Star* 4, no. 2: 1.

Schwartz, Evan I. 1994. "Interrupt-Driven." *Wired* 2, no. 6: 46–49.

Sewell, David. 1992. "The Usenet Oracle: Virtual Authors and the Network Community." *EJournal* (online) 2, no. 5: Available http://www.hanover.edu/philos/ejournal/home.html.

Shapiro, Norman Z., and Robert H. Anderson. 1985. *Toward an Ethics and Etiquette for Electronic Mail.* Santa Monica, Calif.: Rand Corporation for the National Science Foundation.

Shea, Virginia. 1994. *Netiquette.* San Francisco: Albian Books.

————. 1995. "Miss Manners' Guide to Excruciatingly Correct Internet Behavior." *Computerworld* 29, no. 10 (6 Mar.): 85, 87.

Smith, Jennifer. 1995. "Frequently Asked Questions: Basic Information About MUDS and MUDDING" (14 Mar.; Version 1.3). Part 1. Available ftp://ftp.math.okstate.edu/pub/muds/misc/mud-faq/part1.

Spafford, Gene. 1987. "Usenet Software: History and Sources" (March 13, 1995). Ed. M. Moraes. Available usenet: news.admin.misc.

Sproull, Lee, and Sara Kiesler. 1991. *Connections: New Ways of Working in the Networked Organization.* Cambridge, Mass.: MIT Press.

Stone, Allucquere Rosanne. 1991. "Will the Real Body Please Stand Up? Boundary Stories About Virtual Cultures." In *Cyberspace: First Steps.* Ed. M. Benedikt. Cambridge, Mass.: MIT Press.

Taylor, H. Jeanie, Cheris Kramarae, and Maureen Ebben, eds. 1993. *Women, Information Technology, and Scholarship.* Urbana, Ill.: University of Illinois Center for Advanced Study.

Treese, Win. 1994a. *The Internet Index* 3 (17 Sept., revised 19 Sept.). Available http://www/openmarket.com/info/internet-index.

————. 1994b. *The Internet Index* 4 (5 Nov., corrected 7 Nov.). Available http://www/openmarket.com/info/internet-index.

————. 1994c. *The Internet Index* 5 (31 Dec.). Available http://www/openmarket.com/info/internet-index.

————. 1995. *The Internet Index* 6 (12 Feb.). Available http://www/openmarket.com/info/internet-index.

Tuan., Yi-Fu. 1977. *Space and Place: The Perspective of Experience.* Minneapolis: University of Minnesota Press.

Unsworth, John. 8 Feb. 1994. "Editor's Introduction." *Postmodern Culture* (online). Available http://jefferson.village.virginia.edu/pmc/contents.all.html.

Usher, Abbott Payson. 1959. *A History of Mechanical Inventions.* Boston: Beacon Hill.

Vielmetti, Edward. 26 December 1991. "What Is Usenet? A Second Opinion" (26 Oct. 1994). Available usenet: news.newusers.questions.

Wallace, Amy. 1992. "Amid Computer Chatter, Lone Voice Wins Riot Aid." *Los Angeles Times,* 15 Jul., sec. A, 1, 16.

Zakon, Robert H. 1993–94. *Hobbes' Internet Timeline.* Available email: timeline@hobbes.mitre.org.

A Torn Page, Ghosts on the Computer
Screen, Words, Images, Labyrinths:
Exploring the Frontiers of Cyberspace

Poetry is liquid language.

Marcos Novak

As a writer of fantasy, Balzac tried to capture the world soul in a single symbol among the infinite number imaginable; but to do this he was forced to load the written word with such intensity that it would have ended by no longer referring to a world outside of its own self. . . . When he reached this threshold, Balzac stopped and changed his whole program: no longer intensive but extensive writing. Balzac the realist would try through writing to embrace the infinite stretch of space and time, swarming with multitudes, lives, and stories.

Italo Calvino [1]

Prologue

Is it possible to imagine a labyrinth without a defined pattern, without a center or exit point? What if we enter that labyrinth and wander through its hallways, endlessly opening doors which lead to other doors, with windows which look out over other windows? What if there is no real core to the labyrinth and it is of unknown size? This may be an apt metaphor for virtual reality, for the vast network of ideas which now float across and between the many layers of cyberspace.

> A year ago, I was halfway convinced that cyberspaces where you can experience the sensation of hefting a brick or squeezing a lemon probably won't be feasible for another twenty or thirty years. A month ago, I saw and felt something that shook my certainty. When I tried the first prototype of a pneumatic tactile glove in inventor Jim Hennequin's garage in Cranfield, an hour's drive southwest of London, I began to suspect that high-resolution tactile feedback might not be so far in the future. The age of the Feelies, as Aldous Huxley predicted, might be upon us before we know what hit us. [Rheingold 1992:322]

Sometimes the hallways of this labyrinth narrow and we hear the distant chatter of many people and are able to "browse" or "gopher" into their conversations. Other times we actually encounter fellow wanderers and exchange details about geography, the time, information gained or lost during our travels. The excitement of being in the labyrinth is tempered by the fact that as we learn more and more about its structure and about surviving within its confines, we know that we have little hope of leaving. Yet it is a nourishing experience at one level because there are so many different elements to it, all with a life of their own, all somehow connected and for the most part available to us. In fact, even though we know that the labyrinth has borders, it seems as if an *infinite* number of things could go on within its hallways and rooms. It is almost as if there is too much choice, too much information at every twist and turn. Yet this disoriented, almost chaotic world has a structure. We don't know the designers. They may have been machines, but we continue to survive in part because we have some confidence in the idea that design means purpose, and purpose must mean that our wanderings will eventually lead to a destination. (This may be no more than a metaphysical claim, but it keeps the engines of cyberspace running at high speed.)

In order to enter a visual labyrinth you must be ready to travel by association. In effect, your body remains at your computer. You travel by looking, by reading, by imaging and imagining. The eyes are, so to speak, the royal road into virtuality.

> Cyberspace—the electronic frontier. A completely visual environment: the sum total of all [BBSes], computer networks, and other [virtual communities]. Unique in that it is constantly being changed, exists only virtually, can be practically infinite in "size" communication occurs instantaneously world-wide—physical location is completely irrelevant most of the time. Some include video and telephone transmissions as part of cyberspace. [Hawks 1992]

In the labyrinth of cyberspace, design is the logic of the system. Cyberspace reproduces itself at so many different levels at once and in so many different ways that the effects are like an evolutionary explosion, where all of the trace elements of weakness and strength coexist. The architecture of this space is unlike any that has preceded it and we are consequently grappling with discursive strategies to try to describe the experiences of being inside it. The implication is that there is no vantage point from which you can watch either your progress or the progress of others. There isn't a platform upon which you can stand to view your experience or the experience of your neighbors. In other words, the entire system doesn't come into view—how could you create a picture of the Internet? Yet you could imagine the vast weblike structure, imagine, that is, through any number of different images, a world of microelectronic switches buzzing at high speed with the thoughts and reflections of thousands of people. The more important question is, what does this imagining do to our bodies, since to some degree cyberspace is a fiction where we are narrator and character at one and the same time? What are the implications of never knowing the shape and architecture of this technological sphere which you both use and come to depend on? What changes in the communicative process when you type a feeling onto a computer screen, as opposed to speaking about it? What does that feeling *look* like in print? Does the computer screen offer a space where the evocative strength of a personal letter can be communicated from one person to another?

> Electronic conferences and newsgroups are organized in the first instance by a formal focus on particular topics widely ranging from the "frivolous" (such as alien visitors, Eric Clapton, and odd sexual antics) to the "serious" (such as the philosophy of communication, the esoterica of dental fillings, and the mathematics of fractals). A second level of organization arises from the developing social conventions, or netiquette, of online discourse. Despite such organizational parameters, Internet discourse is routinely off-topic, repetitive, inane, or obscene. It is not too much to say that an ethic and an aesthetic of anarchy, disparate voices raised in electronic cacophony, often prevails. [Aycock 1993:3]

Once you have decided to enter its hallways, the maze keeps growing in size and shape—every move you make adds to the labyrinth's character and meaning—the question of perspective seems to be less and less important. How can one stand outside of cyberspace if it is all-encompassing? If the maze keeps growing, will we ever reach its outer boundaries? (The metaphors explode here—how else to characterize the "idea" that millions upon millions of bits of information fit onto one silicon chip?) This sense of an ever expanding universe where notions of inside and outside have disappeared is the attraction of cyberspace. It is also at the heart of Jean Baudrillard's rather fatalistic views of postmodernism, where the maze becomes a metaphor for enclosure and loss, and where the very idea that there are no architectural plans implies that meaning has forever been erased from the experience. Yet it may well be the case that the labyrinth of cyberspace is about loss of authority and not meaning. As so many different elements are combined and so many doors open and close, the conceptual orientation which we have will require a different discourse, perhaps one which accepts the geography of the labyrinth even as it adds more complexity to the design. It is no accident that many of the terms in circulation talk about cyberspace as a frontier. One of the most important organizations dealing with issues such as the information superhighway and interactive technologies is called the Electronic Frontier Foundation. This notion of being on the frontier and all of the implications of lawlessness and discovery which are basic to the experience also suggests a new horizon with different rules of conduct and radically changed ideas of freedom and action.

What if we were to take a more positive attitude to the labyrinth of cyberspace than Baudrillard and see it as a place of learning where the boundaries are infinite and authority must be earned through debate and discussion rather than through position or privilege? Ignorance, as Penelope Reed Doob mentions in her brilliant book on labyrinths, is temporary in that context, a function of the paths taken and the goals chosen or arrived at. "Whether there are choices and guides or not, one cannot know what lies around the next curve until one gets there; means dominate ends, process obscures product, and the wanderer must continue, choose, or retreat with no sure knowledge of the consequences" (Doob 1990:57). The difference is that the mazes Doob talks about are finite. They don't grow, change, carry within their very design, the impact and effect of the travelers who have visited them. The labyrinth of cyberspace is more malleable. The information within its boundaries is never fixed and those who visit can change its form by altering the flow of data or by adding their own information to its memory banks. In other words, information loses its privileged status and becomes less identified with its author. Communication ceases to be about possession and instead we enter a marketplace of ideas where nothing is bought or sold but where everything can exchanged nevertheless.

> Cyberspace is the space of interactive computational possibilities. It is, in one sense, a network that makes all participating computers and their accessible contents (data, programs) available to the users of any participating computer, anywhere. It means that all the information on earth and every strategy for transforming information ever conceived anywhere are in principle available to every user all the time. [Lemke 1993:1]

On a broader level, can cyberspace be reprogrammed? As the webs interlace at more and more levels, as the connections or links grow ever more complex, does this allow for the kind of radical input which would rearrange the codifications which are in place? Take for example the very notion of information as digital, as numerical. As Michael Buckland has noted, "there is some irony here, in that 'multimedia' is commonly used to denote diverse data (text, objects, processes, sounds) after they have been reduced to the monomedium of digital coding" (Buckland 1991:587). This is the foundation of cyberspace—a monomedium which is able to generate an infinite variety of codifications. Yet what if we were to reverse the momentum here and remove the computer, as the foundational technology, from the calculation? Would the labyrinthine structure of cyberspace collapse? Are there other ways of conceiving of environments rich in learning and thought, in communication and exchange, which are not dependent on the screen of the computer as a point of entry? For however strongly and creatively we manipulate the images and sounds and texts of cyberspace, they remain virtual. This is perhaps the overriding paradox of cyberspace—it is always a labyrinth of the imaginary, a place of endless contingencies, and as a result, a place with boundless potential. When we use the term *place* to describe the virtual or when virtual and reality are combined as if there is an empirical configuration into which the experience of viewing is meant to fit, what do we mean? Is this "place" in the final analysis nothing but an image? Or have we, in Baudrillard's sense, arrived at a point where the distinctions of image and place, image and self, are irrelevant?

In this context, I would like to look back at the cinema as a way of reframing if not enriching the conceptual base for this discussion. I do this not only because I am comfortable with a medium which I have studied for many years but also because one of my first conversations in preparation for this piece was with a filmmaker. Ultimately my concern is to raise questions about the ways in which images (whether textual or electronic) are seen and interpreted. In order to do this my approach, in part, will be historical. I am broadening the definition of image to include all forms of computer-mediated communications. This is not intended to flatten out the relationship between different media, nor to make it seem as if they all share a similar epistemological and formal base. Rather, all media now interface in a sometimes fascinating and sometimes perplexing manner. This information bricolage means that in the long run we will have to change the discourse which we use in relation to images. The challenge will be a profound one—how to work through this labyrinth of material to interpret and personalize its many different meanings, how to map out a direction and yet be ready to shift from one point to another and back again, how to make sense of the twists and turns, learn and remember at the same time. The integration of video, film, and still photography into the computer means that we will have to be more aware of the individual histories of these media. We will also have to understand their aesthetic differences and in particular how those differences might affect the ways in which these media are used.

Cinematic Images

My first conversation or dialogue around many of these issues took place in Amsterdam with Holland's well-known documentary filmmaker Johan van der Keuken. Van der Keuken believes very strongly in the power of the image as an educational tool. His films attempt to explore the social and cultural fabric of a variety of different societies. The films have ranged far and wide, and in some respects he is an ethnographer of the impact of modern cultures on less developed ones, while also exploring (with a critical and skeptical eye), as he puts it, "the guts" of his own "degenerating" society. What interests me is the way he uses images, his concern for aesthetic control, his intimate knowledge of the many formal elements which makes images "look" as if they have something to say. He downplays the role of technology in creativity, although he is a master of the camera and works closely with his wife on the sound which he uses for his films. He is also devoted to photography and it has heavily influenced the way he uses the film camera. My intuition in approaching van der Keuken was that his knowledge of the cinema and his sensitivity to the nuances of image creation would allow me to reflect more fully on the many different questions which have been raised with regard to cyberspace. My own relationship to computerized technologies suggests to me that for all of the radical differences between old and new technologies, the primary vehicle for the creation of the virtual remains the image. The digital and computer revolution will recast and redefine both the differences and the similarities between the image on a cinema screen and the image on a computer.

> The perception of reality is a process that goes on within us from fraction of a second to fraction of a second. Our environment overwhelms us with an unimaginable amount of sensations, colours, movements, forms, signs. Our days until our death are filled to the brim isolating and kneading together those sensations into lumps, an activity which determines our thinking and our way of communicating. Lumps of signs become a face, a city, a story, place, an image in which enormous compilations and the most singular units can be distinguished or summarized at a glance." [Keuken 1991 : 18]

Van der Keuken and I met in June 1993 in a flat which is situated near one of Amsterdam's many canals and which doubles as his office and workplace ("Lucid Eye Films"). To van der Keuken the image plays an important role in defining not only the manner in which people see the world, but the possible modes of action which they can undertake in the places where they live. This link to action and practice is an intimate one for him. More than once he mentioned the surfeit of images being produced in all media. He wondered how people were handling this overabundance and emphasized that the role of artists and intellectuals was to create as many tools of interpretation as possible for diverse and heterogeneous audiences. He also spoke of his move away from more didactic forms of political cinema to images which were open-ended and which would allow viewers to explore what he was creating. At the same time he hungered, he said, for new forms of expression and ways of incorporating experimentation into the documentary cinema.

> Hyperreality, we are told, is a site of collapse or implosion where referential or "grounded" utterance becomes indistinguishable from the

self-referential and the imaginary. We construct our representational systems not in serial relation to indisputably "real" phenomena, but rather in recursive and multiple parallel, "mapping on to different co-ordinate systems" (Pynchon). Maps derive not from territories but from other map-making enterprises: all the world's a simulation. [Moulthrop 1991:23]

I had first come across van der Keuken's work at the Cinémathèque Québecoise, one of the most important archives of information about the history of film in Canada. The film of his which I saw in the mid-1970s was simply entitled *Diary*. There are certain images from that film which have stayed with me since that time: a tracking shot in a small Amsterdam flat which led into a toilet, and from there the camera followed the pipes into a sewer and then cut sharply to a group of men and women from the Cameroons building a mud hut; a lush image of van der Keuken's wife as she was about to give birth. These images have mixed in with my memories and the many other films which I have seen since then. I am never sure what I remember with respect to images, and this may be a characteristic of the process of viewing them. Politically inclined filmmakers have grappled with this problem since the earliest days of the cinema. At its root is a debate about how we learn from what we see and listen to. How do we give life to images? Does the process depend on what we say about them? How much of what we say is a fantasy and what do we learn from this combination of dreams and daydreams, thoughts and perceptions? Of course, these are general questions which could be applied to any medium, but they seem to be particularly important when we talk about images from films.

This has much to do, I think, with the public context within which movies are seen and experienced. The performative factor must never be forgotten, even as more and more "films" are seen within the confines of the home on videotape and through cable or satellite dishes. The feeling of being part of a community has always been a crucial element in the experience of film viewing. There is a specificity to the movie house which hopefully will never disappear despite the fact that film theaters have become smaller and smaller. There are very few public spaces left where experiences of this kind can be shared, even if little is said by members of the audience as they watch. The point is that there is a group of individuals who have for a variety of reasons decided to share the same venue at the same time. To van der Keuken this stands in sharp contrast to the statistical measures which are used to reveal that a particular show on television has been watched by a large number of people. The film theater remains a site of potential political engagement, of potential human interaction at a person-to-person level. What does it mean to know that many millions of people watched the 1994 Olympics in Norway?

This lack of specificity has another side to it. Television claims an audience but has developed few strategies for understanding the experience of viewing.

With respect to images, this is left to polling firms in the realm of politics, to marketing experts in the advertising world, and to audience testing for network television. There are continual efforts at extrapolation from small samples, but most of the results address broad questions and hypothetical solutions at a mass level. I suggested to van der Keuken that the paradox of new technologies like hypermedia is that they are dealing with some of these contradictions by creating contexts of interactivity within which more and more discursive and image-based forms can be used. This will change the very nature of feedback as we have known it. In a letter to him after our meeting, I said the following:

> You are aware, I am sure, of the speed with which the integration of computers and television and film and sound is taking place. It is happening so fast that few people are taking the time to think about its impact. I am concerned, for example, with much of what has been said about multimedia, as if it will be a panacea for all the ills of the educational system and will open up new and creative contexts for the ordinary person. All the terms in circulation, from the virtual to the hypertextual, describe and support the exponential growth of the technology. For example, I have a computer disk which is a hypertext novel. You can read it from a number of different vantage points and can alter the text at will. If you click on a particular word an image comes up, sometimes as a reflection of the narrative, more often than not as an illustration of an idea. More advanced versions include moving images. Eventually CD-ROM will permit you to put one of your films on a compact disc and it will be played back on a large monitor, stopped and interrupted at will, with the possibility of re-editing and redeveloping what you have done, adding annotations, words, sounds, etc.
>
> The people in the forefront of developing this technology talk about it in utopian terms, as if it will provide a freedom of expression and creativity which present day cinematic and televisual forms prevent.
>
> It is my intuition that they are only partially right. True, much will be accessible that wasn't beforehand. Also, as images become digitalized they become more sculptural and can be manipulated at will. What is missing in the utopian discourse I have been mentioning is some sense of the ideology to which they are beholden. I sometimes think that I am old-fashioned, because I cannot conceive of replacing the smell of the ocean with a simulated one. I cannot bear the thought of never seeing the world other than through the images which we construct of it. As you may expect, their response to all of my complaints is that the distinction between the real and image has long ago ceased to be relevant—since *all* of reality is a simulation anyway.
>
> To some degree, many of the distinctions have in fact broken down and your new film about brass bands—*Brass Unbound*—is a study of the rich hybridization which most cultures in the world have be-

come. We are in a time of endless diasporas and images are the fulcrum upon which we are redesigning our sense of these shifting realities, which we encounter and create on an everyday basis. At the same time your film is about the mixture of old and new, about the eruption of the historical into the present, about the never ending creativity within which every culture is operating, to both defend their interests and maintain their sense of identity.

Brass Unbound is about brass bands in a variety of disparate communities worldwide. It is about colonialism and the postcolonial integration of cultural difference. The film opens in Nepal (the other three parts of the film take place is Suriname, Minahassa, Indonesia, and Ghana) and the first image we see is of a peasant walking down a lush hillside carrying a sewing machine on his back. He walks into town and into a small sewing factory. The camera then moves up to the next floor where we see a band practicing. They are playing a mixture of traditional Nepali instruments and the trumpets, cymbals, and drums of a traditional Western brass band. The mixture of sounds is rhythmic, but the tones are dramatically different from anything westerners might be accustomed to. The band's name is the Modern Light Brass Band. As if to accentuate the play of cultural difference and assimilation, the sign outside of their building is in English and Nepalese. I will mention only one other scene in this fascinating pastiche. One of the members of the band is seen praying in front of Ganesa, the Elephant God, to whom the musicians always make an offering before they go and play at the venues where they have been hired. He says, "Music is like the ocean. What can we give to the ocean? Take a cup of water from it and it makes no difference. Throw water in and that makes no difference either." My sense of what he means is that music is a constant which both transcends and produces the contexts in which it is played and heard. Music, like Ganesa, has both a life of its own and makes life possible for those who believe in its strength and its magic. The scene comes to an end as the band members put on their costumes, which are also a mix of the colonial and the postcolonial in design and color.

This effort to work through the complex hybridization of history and culture, to understand and act upon difference and identity, is a characteristic of nearly all of van der Keuken's films. What fascinates me is that even a film with so much self-reflexivity, so much of a desire to comment on its own position as image, can nevertheless communicate important details about another culture. Many of the binds of the ethnographic cinema remain, of course, and these include the fact that the film was made by an outsider. But it is one of the premises of the film that the outside and the inside have long ago ceased to have the borders to which we are accustomed. And it is images which have contributed to this dissolution, while at the same time pointing to far more complex aspects of difference.

The following refers to the cover photograph of the September 1994 issue of *Mirabella* entitled "Who Is the Face of America?"

> We asked the distinguished photographer Hiro to come up with a cover personifying todays all-American beauty. We thought it should be someone who represents the diversity of this country. We know that Hiro called in models—not famous faces, but beautiful faces of all ethnicities. And, after an extensive search and painstaking work he did present us with an extraordinary image of great American beauty. But who is she? Hiro's not telling. He will only say that she has not been photographed before and that she's not with any modeling agency. And, she's impossible to reach. He hints that she's something of a split personality. And he says, with a smile, that it wasn't easy getting her together. Maybe her identity has something to do with the microchip floating through space next to that gorgeous face. America is a melting pot. And true American beauty is a combination of elements from all over the world. Is our cover model representative of the melting pot? [The editors of *Mirabella*]

The face on the cover is a simulation. This in itself would be interesting enough were it not for the claims which are being made about representativeness. Those claims elevate the photograph beyond simulation and give the hybrid face a transcendent status.

The breakdown of difference and the contribution of images to this process comes out in its most sophisticated form in a short film which van der Keuken made in Sarajevo in fall 1993. The film is simply entitled *Sarajevo Film Festival Film.* It is fourteen minutes long. In the midst of the cruelty and devastation of the Serbian siege, a film festival is organized. Van der Keuken uses the festival as an entry point into the contradictions of life in the midst of suffering and death. The people he talks to speak of the magic of the cinema and its potential to take them far away from Sarajevo. They use the metaphor of the journey, of traveling, and it is no accident that the first images we see from the festival are of *Le Chien Andalou* the surrealist experiment made by Salvador Dalí and Luis Buñuel, because the only traveling which the people of Sarajevo can do is mental. The only place they can go to is an imaginary one. We see the famous opening image of Dalí and Buñuel's film in which an eye is about to be cut. This is juxtaposed with images of the audience and then of Sarajevo itself. Images encourage this movement in space and time, a release from the "sights" of the everyday.

> Johan van der Keuken's art prompts us to reflect upon a variety of borders, including the gaps between shots juxtaposed by editing, and the documentarian's movement across the divisions between cultures, classes, races, and nationalities. The process of finding linkages between diverse societies in van der Keuken's global documentaries, and

of editing from shot to shot in all his films, are open and participatory—the spectator is free to respect the autonomy of each image and society. Van der Keuken has described his editing practice as both montage and collage: he connects shots to convey ideas, particularly his hopes for political change, while simultaneously leaving those images free to exceed and question the ideas that bind and subordinate them. [Herskowitz 1990:3]

The Sarajevo film and *Brass Unbound* are located within a cultural activity which in no way can be described as cyberspatial. Van der Keuken's comment on his Sarajevo film is instructive: "I'm doing some old fashioned artistic-political action with it, very modest of course, trying to get it shown in as many places—festivals, television, film houses and more informal spots—as possible" (from a letter dated 7 Dec. 1993).

I have thought about this comment for a number of weeks, thought about the public sphere into which van der Keuken wants to insert his ideas and images. By way of contrast I have also thought about the claims of virtual reality proponents that I could enter Sarajevo and feel as if I was within the war zone, not just "look" at a screen. Similarly, I could travel from culture to culture and experience what van der Keuken experienced when he was in Suriname, for example.

Remember that notions of the cyberspatial and the virtual remain in the realm of "as if." Remember too that the public sphere is a conceptual construction designed to carve out a space within which people of different classes and ethnic groups and different genders ideally would be able to exchange ideas and debate and discuss the value systems which they believe in. We are into a gray zone here, where, for example, the Sarajevo film could be transmitted over the Internet and reach a large number of people within the confines of a computerized environment. A discussion group could be generated which would deal with the film and its ideas. To varying degrees this has already happened with the Bosnia Internet line, for example, which is one of the few direct means of information exchange for a large number of Bosnian expatriates. Yet is this the public sphere which van der Keuken wants to contact and build? This will be a crucial question for proponents of the Internet and for those of us who see so much potential in interactive technologies and yes, even in the virtual world of cyberspace. Have we arrived at the point where the public sphere now exists as a communicative space without the need for personal contact?

Contemplation/Vision

A few days ago (February 1994) I stood on a seaside cliff and stared out at the ocean. It was early morning. The water had a rich textured quality, the result of an overwhelming stillness, offset by the movement of light from the shifting angles of a rising sun. In the distance, fog covered the islands of Haro Strait. The sky was overcast, although not dull. I stared at the horizon and wondered how I could rid my mind of its preoccupations, how I could more fully sense the beauty of the scene in front of me. My immediate temptation was to close my eyes. I wanted to capture the experience by somehow "seeing" into my own mind. I wanted to listen to the water and concentrate on the cries of the sea birds. I wanted to hear the wind. This pressure to find an internal landscape, to bring me closer to my own experience, to grasp the magic, quickly exhausted my staying power. I left, albeit reluctantly, and slowly began walking back to my house.

I thought of the landscape which I had just seen. In fact, I was able to stare at the path in front of me, eyes open, and still somehow "see" the mountains on the other side of the water. I watched a large seagull break apart a crab which it had caught. I could "hear" the movement of the water against the cliffs and the sounds of crows and ducks. I was able to concentrate on the color of the rock, so different in the early morning, wrapped in dew and moss.

Southward, across the strait I could see the outline of Mount Baker, its peak covered in snow. The further I walked from the shore, the more vivid the memory of the mountain became. The peak stood out against a clear sky and, depending on the angle, it sometimes appeared to be close to the water, other times, more distant. The mountain stood out against the hills which were in front and behind it. All the while, clouds rushed forward, stretching from the water to the horizon.

Although I rarely acknowledge it, my eyes and my body seem to be separate, distinct, yet folded into each other. The physical sensations of seeing, which are eruptions of body into consciousness and vice versa, are most often a secondary effect of thinking. To see almost means not to think or at least to assume, without verification, that seeing transcends the limitations of mind. Yet that is clearly impossible. The whole, mind and sight, are indivisible. How then can one talk about those moments, epiphanies, when the eye seems to have conquered all and when there is no obvious explanation for the experience? How to talk about the resistance to mind by the eyes? Why is that resistance at one and the same time a telling metaphor of mind and an expression of "its" limitations? The answers to these questions are in part that they cannot be answered. Yet it is the paradox of knowing that the mind(s) and the eye(s) cannot be dissociated, which displaces one from the other, allowing them to operate as if they both have to resist and complement each other. The sensations of sight with regard to images may be in this set of overlapping processes.

In the winter of 1984–85 issue of *Skrien,* the most important and serious of Holland's film magazines, van der Keuken wrote the following: "How to return, how to leave behind. The cinematic space of New York, the Lower East side, 'Loisaida' as its Spanish-speaking residents so aptly call it and write it:

cracked pavement, the rot of a bad tooth, manhole covers, the scars of flames, scorched spot in the city—now left behind, everything forgotten, senile like in Bernlef's *Mind Shadows* (Dutch author Jan Bernlef's novel is about a senile man's gradual loss of memory). Suddenly you no longer know a single name, a single place, a single number, you have gone blind from too much seeing."

In 1956, van der Keuken shot two photographs of a young girl from different angles and printed them onto the same image. In both instances the two faces are looking outward from the print to the camera and by extension to the viewer. The photograph is part of a series prepared by van der Keuken for a film script by the Dutch poet Remco Campert. The script was called *Behind Glass*.

Can you go blind from too much seeing? Or is the act of seeing blind to begin with? How many windows, panes of glass, are there between sight and feeling and memory? "You wipe your breath from the window and look outside," says Campert's script.

The breath is the body. Memories are physical and ephemeral. The ghosts of past conversations and experiences and dreams haunt every invocation to speak. Often, memories overwhelm breath and the heart races and the body takes over. The "sights" aren't present, nor do the sensations of seeing rely on any objects or subjects outside of the eye(s). We experience this as daydream. Our memories are displaced into the metaphors or discourses which we use to describe the images from daydreams to ourselves and to others. The displacement works upon itself and upon vision disrupting the convenient formulas we use to "locate" the seen in the image.

Perhaps van der Keuken shot only one image of two girls, twins, or two sisters slightly different in age. Their glance is outward. Their memories are inscribed on their faces, but I cannot reach them. Their look suggests that I will never know them. They come to me from the past. It is 1994, thirty-eight years after they were photographed. Are they still alive? The photograph neither answers these questions nor necessarily suggests any solutions, unless I am willing to enter into a dialogue with it. But that dialogue is one which I create, an internal and sometimes external discussion between interlocutors operating within the boundaries of my imaginary.

So one of the most important aspects of work upon images is this ability to play with memory and fantasy, in time. That is, although the photograph neither responds to my invocations nor changes as a result of my input, I am constantly recreating it anyway. It is this flexibility which sustains, if not encourages, the widening networks of imaginary reconstructions which are the basis upon which I am able to interact with images. Van der Keuken has recognized this by editing his films and shooting his photographs to encourage the kind of ambiguity which redefines the "location" of meaning in the activities of spectatorship.

Yet as should be clear from the above, my use of the term *spectator* is itself fraught with problems since what it assumed by the notion of spectator is an object to be looked at. This once again sustains a paradigm of cause and effect in which communicative processes travel a linear path from object to subject.

The Image in Cyberspace

Computerized environments make use of many different kinds of media, yet the central "medium" is still the image. The image both as an object of vision and use, has its historical origins many thousands of years before the arrival of the computer. The history of images, their evolution through various media forms, and their intimate relationship to our cultural, social, and political development is closely linked to technological innovation. It is important to keep in mind that even though the word *image* retains its power as a synthetic "sign" for most forms of visual communication, its usage is so all-encompassing that its link to technological change must be carefully examined and explored.

Michael Benedikt's definition of cyberspace is one of the most comprehensive I have encountered:

> Cyberspace is a globally networked, computer-sustained, computer-accessed, and computer-generated, multidimensional, artificial or "virtual" reality. In this reality, to which every computer is a window, seen or heard objects are neither physical nor, necessarily, representations of physical objects but are, rather, in form, character and action, made up of data, of pure information. [Benedikt 1992: 12–23]

Benedikt makes the crucial point that other forms of cultural expression will not be replaced by computer-mediated communications but "displaced" (124). The displacements will allow for, if not encourage, creative cohabitation within the shifting parameters of new contexts and the construction of new histories. What he describes as data, as pure information, is processed through computers as images. The computer image is framed in almost the same way as the earliest photographs in the middle of the nineteenth century. Even the terms *image* and *screen* have their origins in another historical period and with respect to "older" media forms. This mixture of media histories and ways of conceptualizing their interrelationship means that more emphasis will have to be placed on the image as one of the grounding tools which all forms of computer communications use.

One of the dangers with many of the metaphors in circulation about cyberspace is that they are based on models of mind steeped for the most part in cognitive science and often premised on research in the area of artificial intelligence. This is translated into further assumptions about what "viewers" or "readers" of computer images do with information, how they perceive, interpret, and understand the many different pieces of information which come their

way. There are further connections to cybernetics and to the relationship between machines and human language. These all fold over into one of the key
fantasies of cyberspace travelers, which is to "virtually" plug into the machine,
to become one with the computer, to be the cyborg. Yet as Donna Haraway has
suggested, cyborgs are neither machines nor humans but a mixture with their
own destiny. The dualisms of body and machine fall apart in cyberspace not so
much because the body has been removed but because new configurations and
new ways of naming and experiencing the body are an inevitable outcome of
the relationship.

> It is not clear who makes and who is made in the relation between
> human and machine. It is not clear what is mind and what is body in
> machines that resolve into coding practices. In so far as we know our-
> selves in both formal discourse (for example, biology) and in daily
> practice (for example, the homework economy in the integrated cir-
> cuit), we find ourselves to be cyborgs, hybrids, mosaics, chimeras.
> Biological organisms have become biotic systems, communications
> devices like others. There is no fundamental, ontological separation
> in our formal knowledge of machine and organism, of technical and
> organic. [Haraway 1991 : 177–78]

The "blurring" which Haraway talks about in which "mind, body, and tool are
on very intimate terms" (165), is at the core of many of the utopian assumptions about cyberspace. For Haraway there is no turning back. The road into
cyborg culture was paved long ago and we have to adjust to the consequences
of being within it, not presume that we can step outside. In that sense we are
hybrids already plugged into the machines we use. The word *tool* suggests a
separation which no longer applies. We cannot look back to an era without
machines, nor can we refind the innocent pastoralism of the preindustrial era
(which wasn't innocent in any case).

We need to account for the various mythologies of innocence and redemption which circulate at the same time and with the same intensity as the cultural
and economic concerns for technological innovation. The hybridization Haraway mentions is not simply located in machine and human interaction but is
also situated in the many layers of *resistance* to technology, in the many alternative and sometimes reactionary movements which collectively engage with
change in unpredictable ways. The very notion of the chimera suggests this
anyway. In trying to go beyond the machine-human dichotomy, Haraway reproduces it. Distinctions of various sorts with respect to technology and human
intervention and creativity will remain in place until a radically different discursive and ontological reality displaces the human body from its relationship
to machines. This then begins to explain why cyberspace is talked about in
spatial terms, as if we have not only entered a new time but an entirely different
world. It explains why the virtual seems to be so attractive since it proposes the

absorption of body and technology, the conflation of difference until the very notion of boundary and geography disappears.

In popular culture no character represents this more perfectly than Data, in the film *Star Trek: The Next Generation.* He is the near perfect machine who wistfully searches for a human soul, for whom the mysteries of the spiritual and the imaginary (key human characteristics, in his eyes) are a source of invention and creativity. He doesn't just try to understand emotions. He wants to experience them. He finds it disturbing that he has to imitate a predetermined set of human characteristics. In a sense, he is devoted to finding the unpredictable in the digital. He represents both the reverse side and the potential of the cyborg. And in so doing he doesn't so much anticipate a future as he questions its very possibility. Data's continuing crisis on *Star Trek* is that he realizes the finiteness of his consciousness. He recognizes that as a machine he is the product of a limited number of programmed inputs and that as a result his emotional and creative range is, in the final analysis, limited. As one more element in the complex structure of possibilities which our culture has established with and for machines, Data represents that side of the imaginary of the cyborg which cyberspace proponents suggest has finally been conquered. The virtual promises to release us from the constraints which Data experiences because as humans we are a near perfect combination of machine and mind. We can take advantage of the inherent freedoms of the imaginary while also grounding ourselves in the limitations and potential of the machine.

This utopian vision (and the one which Data finally realizes he cannot attain) is nevertheless steeped in very restricted notions of mental functioning. Fundamentally, the human brain becomes a mirror image of the computational networks it plugs into. There is little which is said about virtual reality which would suggest *resistance* to the experiences which it offers. Most of the worries about cyberspace and the Internet center on whether the networks will be taken over by commercial interests. The presumption is that all the freedom in the system will be eliminated.

As I have mentioned, so much of the work and nearly all of the programming for these networks comes from researchers and scientists involved with and devoted to the cognitive sciences. The central presumption is that mental activities can be reproduced through computational networks. As a result, the mind and the computer are seen as compatible because so much of what they both do is mirrored in the other. This is a highly debatable proposition, but it begins to explain the excitement surrounding cyberspace. It also foregrounds the evolutionary rhetoric of the movement. As machines evolve into more complex forms, the very terms we have used to think about human evolution will change. The cyborg represents a synthesis of this, but it is virtuality which incarnates as lived experience, the ontological claim for a new kind of human subjectivity.

Cyber/Hyper/Media

One of the people with whom I talked for this essay is involved in a multimedia experiment (for which many different kinds of images are manipulated) which utilizes video, sound, film clips, laserdiscs and CD-ROM. One of her aims is to build a learning environment within which participants are encouraged to create their own connections between disparate pieces of information. The architecture of this new environment encourages forms of exchange which are unpredictable, yet also very creative. Linearity blends into nonlinearity and vice versa. There are few points in this experiment which cannot be recreated, reedited, and this opens up hitherto unimagined possibilities for the people who interact with the technology and its software. In design and orientation, Ricki Goldman-Seagall's MERLIN (Multimedia Ethnographic Research Laboratory) facility at the University of British Columbia is at the cutting edge of experimentation in hypermedia. She uses a multimedia tool which she helped develop at the Massachusetts Institute of Technology's Media Lab entitled Learning Constellations. "*Learning Constellations* [is] a multimedia tool enabling researchers to browse, access, link and build theories about chunks of videodisc footage and text. *LC* encourages the creation of stories, portraits, and nonlinear movies from videodisc material. In [the context of] MERLIN, *LC* is being revised as a generic interface for children and teachers to use with a wider range of digitized video and text material" (Goldman-Segall 1992).

The premise of her work and many others involved in the design and development of interactive media is that there are infinite ways in which information in image form can be visualized and presented. The feeling is that every "bit" of information which floats within the visual and oral universe of computer-mediated communications can be interpreted and reinterpreted. Nothing is stable. Everything can be *re*visualized and rethought. The boundaries are as broad as those of the imagination, and this architecture has many ports of entry, many windows, and many possible pathways within its labyrinthine structure.

Here is a conversation between Ted Riecken and Goldman-Seagall. He is collaborating with her on the development of new tools for multimedia ethnography.

TED: Ricki, in multimedia ethnography, the ethnographer usually determines which actions are captured by the video camera. The raw video footage is thus a record of what interested the ethnographer at the time of the recording. In recording classroom life, the ethnographer engages in a conscious yet instantaneous selection of material for the ethnography.

RICKI: I agree. This leads to the central problem in achieving validity. To build valid interpretations about subtle events, we may need more sophisticated tools for sharing with others

what we recorded. Then we can negotiate our interpretations to reach triangulated conclusions. These layers of
weighted descriptions will lead us toward more reliable
conclusions.

TED: Text is used by the ethnographer both as a means of collect-
ing data and expressing the meaning that one ascribes to
that data. Until recently, the results of ethnographic study
were communicated almost exclusively via text. Isn't this
limiting our understanding of what *really* happened?

RICKI: Yes. There is a classic American case about a young black
male teenager who answers the police officer's question,
"Did you kill the storekeeper?" by saying, "I, I killed the
storekeeper." However, what he said was a rhetorical question, "I??? I *killed* the storekeeper???" indicating that he
was insulted and shocked that he could be accused. What
got recorded in text was that the young man had admitted
guilt. The video report of this interview would have led us
to interpret the words differently.

TED: In the postmodern world, traditional ethnography may become anachronistic. With its reliance on the written word,
traditional ethnography represents an art or craft lingering
in a world bursting with opportunities for multimedia expression and communication.

RICKI: When working on a collaborative video analysis team project, "writers/recorders" and "readers/users" share multiple
views on what was happening for other "readers." When
electronic journals become pervasive in the culture, the distinction between "writer" and "reader" will blur even more
dramatically. Interactive documents wherein interpretations
can continue to be shared and negotiated on distributed networks will enable users to interact with authors of these
documents in a way that the users become part of the interpretation process. The notion of "fixed" interpretations
may be part of our pre-electronic past. [Goldman-Seagall
and Riecken 1993 : 15– 16]

The habitat of the virtual becomes what we imagine it to be. "Cyberspace is
a habitat of the imagination, a habitat for the imagination. Cyberspace is the
place where conscious dreaming meets subconscious dreaming, a landscape of
rational magic, of mystical reason, the locus and triumph of poetry over pov-
erty, of "it-can-be-so" to "it-should-be-so" (Novak 1992 : 226).

The premise that we *inhabit* cyberspace is not too far removed from Baudrillard's ideas of simulation. The difference is that most analysts of cyberspace
have a utopic view of its potential. Baudrillard essentially proposes that simulation is evidence of the profound, almost dystopic loss engendered by postmodern forms of technological innovation. For Novak, cyberspace becomes a

model which can be recreated ad infinitum, conferring upon technology and its users the experience of an endless poesis. We become navigators in this artificial world and we try and bridge the gap between the surrogates we have constructed. The idea of surrogacy itself becomes a powerful metaphor of the world as image, dissolving distinctions of material and immaterial, engendering a radical shift in the power of language to analyze and describe, recreating at every turn the possibilities and potential of a new discourse.

The excitement here (and it is palpable in the energy of Benedikt's book) is that every element in the visualization-computer process can be manipulated. This is equated to open systems of thinking and expression. Not only is there a dissolution of closure but the very basis upon which we have imagined open forms of communication has shifted. The metaphors in play here move every which way, splaying out in all directions, always and in every piece I have read and from the people I have talked to, driving toward the central idea that we are in the midst of a revolution no less important than the industrial revolution of the nineteenth century.

Goldman-Seagall's work takes video imagery (of a young boy in his home, for example) and transforms it into raw information which can be annotated visually, with text, with sound, and so on. This allows the researcher to rearrange all of the elements connecting the images to each other and to redefine the links *between* the images. It offers the freedom to rework the original intentions and meaning of the work, to find endless access points for exploration, for rewriting, for a redeployment of the images into a different structure. We have always been able to do this with written texts, but hypermedia now brings this process into the world of sounds and images. It is this flexibility with regard to the image, this sense that it can be shaped and reshaped which may alter our historical conception of the limits of visual media. There is a fundamental irony at work here. The aim is to make all viewers into creators, to transform the image and its normal operating context. But all of the difficulties which images have posed for researchers and viewers remain. The central one is that of interpretation. How do we interpret the images we see and how do we make sense of the meanings they have? Does greater flexibility with respect to choice enhance our ability to understand what we are doing with images? Even the term image suggests a general set of characteristics across all media which may not hold upon closer examination. To what degree does the image change for example, when it becomes the size of a postage stamp in a collage-like formation on a computer screen filled with words, symbols and boxes?

What follows is a conversation which Goldman-Seagall and I had on her work, her life, and on multimedia in general.

GOLDMAN-SEAGALL: I came to critical ethnography recently, and I'm still not comfortable with some of its ideas.

BURNETT: Why?

GOLDMAN-SEAGALL: I still find that it is educational to get closer to the other rather than being locked into a personal understanding of the self. I want to avoid becoming solipsistic. What we say about "the other" doesn't have to be fixed.

BURNETT: My own feeling is that when one does ethnographic field work one is still, for the most part, giving life to one's own fantasies.

GOLDMAN-SEAGALL: I agree that there is virtually nothing objective to ethnographic work. Everything we do is from some point of view. I'm so subjective anyway. I would like to create images that give others their voice. Now, maybe this is related to my own background as a Jew. The Holocaust lives within me. I was born in the same month, same year, as Israel was born. When you're Jewish you do have the continual sense of being Other. You tend to see yourself on the inside and the outside at the same time. You get to know what is acceptable and what isn't. I've probably always searched to understand self-other relationships. For me, all of this is very related to my role as an educator. I'll give you an overview of the ideas and things which matter to me: community—and I'm thinking here of Ivan Illich and his ideas about access to new technologies—I did my master's on Illich. Camera—I've always used a still camera; the 35 mm camera is what brought me to video. Cinema—I have been very influenced by Richard Leacock and John Marshall. I like the idea of using film in advocacy. I want to use film to look at school cultures. I think that one should keep things as accessible as possible. For me, postmodernism is about not excluding the other and the cinema has contributed to this. Commensurability—I am very interested in "thick" descriptions. I want to look at the way one culture communicates with another, the commensurability of cultures—can this be evoked in images?

BURNETT: I have always had this feeling that images are very frail. They can be shaped in so many different ways.

GOLDMAN-SEAGALL: Yes, but for me images have led the research! I don't believe in voice-overs. I want to create the story from what the information is giving me. Multimedia often ends up just being illustrative. I am more interested in narration, in the way things relate to each other. I would prefer it if video images and text became less distinct.

BURNETT: My own feeling is that the Internet now translated into the Net is the next major metaphor, and as a metaphor it suggests the breakdown of image-text relations.

GOLDMAN-SEAGALL: Learning Constellations is about how you make sense of all of the data. The idea is to set up environments in which learners can take control of the knowledge they are being exposed to. How do you select what interests you? The machine must never stand in for the process. I am interested in constructionism, in the small gestures which people make, and how we can actually capture that on video and then use the footage as a research tool and not as an end in itself.

Transforming Texts into Images

Much of what Goldman-Seagall is doing is based on hypertext which can best be described as the reformulation of textuality into image form. For example, the following series of operations are possible in the hypertext medium using a computer:

1. Certain words or clusters of words are starred (buttoned, highlighted, whatever), in a sense making them pictorial.

2. Each star represents a body of linked information which can be accessed by clicking on the star. This transforms words or phrases into foreground effects behind which a complex background sits waiting to be accessed.

3. If this text which you are reading were on a computer screen, we would be able to move around through the linkages and pathways, but this wouldn't necessarily lead us back to the beginning of our "reading."

4. Edward Barrett has called this an "associative web" (Barrett 1988:xix).

5. "Conventional paper documents must be read in a single sequence: one page inexorably follows another. In hypertexts, on the other hand, pages are not physically bound in a single fixed sequence. Hypertext writers can create documents that respond to individual reader needs and interests, offering readers a range of choices instead of imposing a single, fixed approach" (Bolter 1993:1). Thus we would be able to move through the ideas which I have developed and the conversations which I have had in an unpredictable way. The text would become malleable, open to change, and you the reader could rewrite it to suit your needs, your perceptions, your thoughts. Yet do we really treat the pages of a book in such a reverent way? Could we not move all over the place and link elements in a variety of different locations creating themes and ideas that were not "in" the book?

6. The hypertext medium allows us to "see" the text in images as well as in words, and we could add sounds and move from hypertext to hypermedia. This could bring the word to life through visual exemplification.

7. "Storyspace provides many different views of hypertext's structure to help readers and writers explore new ideas. Storyspace maps provide focused overviews and cognitive maps. Chart views emphasize the depth of the document's hierarchical backbone. Outline views illuminate hierarchical structure even more prominently, while road maps and pathmaps explore the structures created by links and paths among writing spaces. Writers can simultaneously view the same section of a document in many ways." (from a publicity document for the Hypertext Program, *Storyspace,* Eastgate Systems).

8. "What distinguishes hypermedia from other modes of information is not that it is computer-driven . . . nor that it is interactive, since the entire history of oral communication, whether electronically mediated or not, might be characterized as interactive; nor even that it includes navigational apparatus such as links and nodes, which might better be thought of as symptoms than causes, or

buttresses rather than groundwork. What distinguishes hypermedia is that it posits an information structure so dissimilar to any other in human experience that it is difficult to describe as a structure at all. It is nonlinear, and therefore may seem an alien wrapping of language when compared to the historical path written communication has traversed; it is explicitly non-sequential, neither hierarchical nor "rooted" in its organizational structure, and therefore may appear chaotic and entropic" (Burnett 1993:1).

One of the fundamental premises of hypertext is that the "reader" becomes a creator of text and not simply the consumer. Roland Barthes distinction between the readerly and the writerly text has been taken up by hypertext theorists: "hypertext blurs the boundaries between reader and writer and therefore instantiates another quality of Barthes's ideal text. From the vantage point of the current changes in information technology, Barthes's distinction between readerly and writerly texts appears to be essentially a distinction between text based on print technology and electronic hypertext" (Landow 1992:5).

George Landow makes the point that within the context of the computer a hypertext allows, if not encourages, readers to annotate what they are reading. I have a text on this computer entitled "Writing Space," by Jay David Bolter, which I can change, add to, in other words, manipulate in a variety of different ways. I can follow numerous pathways through Bolter's text. More often than not, I don't arrive at the same point. It is often exciting and, after a while, it leads to a constellation of thoughts, ideas, hypotheses, and tentative conclusions about the topic which he and I are exploring, the history of writing. We could become coauthors, with me completely redeveloping the original text. More often than not, the "text" becomes an image of a text. I found myself editing, playing with ideas, and even wanting to add a drawing to some of his illustrations. This flexibility completely altered my initial relationship to the "book."

Yet in traditional book culture, the annotation is an integral part of the activity of reading. The annotation might take the form of a thought or a daydream. Or you might write down an impression, an idea, argue with the text in its boundaries (through notes or written comments), or simply mull over its ideas in your head. Hypertext proponents suggest that we can now change what we read because it exists in the form of digitalized information. This makes it seem as if we have not been "interacting" with books since books first became widely available for the general public. Clearly it depends on what we mean by interaction. There are so many potential arenas of human activity within which the interactive plays a major role that it seems fruitless to list them all. The major difference here is that media which have been thought of as one-way devices of communication now hold out the promise of two-way exchange. Although it is true that in the material sense you cannot change the TV show which you watch or the film which you play in your VCR, that presumes that the image is the source upon which you might want to base your "interaction." However, the most important part of the relationship which we have with television for example, centers on what we do with what we have seen, or how we discursively reconstruct and interpret the experience. In addition, the location of the television in the home encourages it to be a "subject" of discussion and debate, making possible a critical interactive sphere as rich as anything which could be done with the image itself. But this extends outside the home, with magazines and zines, for example, generating a vast intertextual network of associated discussion and invention, fantasies and ideas, circulating at a variety of levels throughout the society. The classic error among proponents of interactivity has been to assume that the image *is* the space of subjectivity.

My own sense is that hypertext and hypermedia, multimedia and interactive media are all related yet different mediums, and that among their many shared characteristics the one which stands out for me is that they are all dependent on the video image. Few of the works which I have read (and only some of the people I have talked to) deal with this shared framework for the display and depiction of ideas and information within the context of computerized technologies. Edward Barrett approaches the video monitor in a transparent fashion, using the term *screen design* as an entry point into a discussion of the hypertext image. The screen in this respect remains the primary "source" of information, even as it is being designed to become more and more flexible, more responsive to the invocations and desires of the "reading" public.

The transformation of text into image and image into text alters the way words and sentences communicate meaning. "Electronic typography is both creator-controlled and reader-controlled. The screen upon which these words appear as I write has five sizes of a dozen Roman type styles and two Greek styles at its immediate command and literally hundreds more in second-level storage. I can enlarge the print if my eyes get tired, reduce it to check format and page layout, flow it around illustrations if I want. I can redesign the very shapes of the letters, zoom in on them until their transparency becomes an abstract pattern of separate pixels" (Lanham 1993:51–52). Lanham goes on to say that the "textual surface has become permanently bi-stable. We are always looking first *at* it and then *through* it, and this oscillation creates a different implied ideal of decorum, both stylistic and behavioral" (54). On the computer screen, words and letters become pixels and as a result are interchangeable with images. A combination of computer programs permits if not encourages the hybridization of different expressive forms. Does this mean that to look at the screen of a computer is different from looking at the screen in a film theater? Lanham is proposing that the screen becomes transparent, and I agree. This is what encourages the movement from text to image and then into cyberspace. But the screen is not a window. The oscillation is from image to imaginary, from discourse to dialogue, and from a direct relationship to an indirect one.

The Virtual Internet

Let it suffice to say that we are traversing a ground which in a labyrinthine fashion leads back to a discussion of images. I mention the metaphor of the labyrinth again because it so aptly fits the conceptual base upon which notions of the virtual, the cyberspatial, and the hypertextual depend. It is also a useful metaphor with respect to images, describing a new process in which images are not the dominant field of human perception and action but merely one part of an extended universe within which our entire conception of communication has undergone a radical shift (in a manner quite different from what interactive specialists are suggesting). The flow of concepts and terminology within the new forms of expression and communication summarized under the umbrella of the virtual is so far reaching that the entire process resists summary. The impact of this has been felt at the most personal level by those people like myself who have wandered through the Internet from its earliest days. Howard Rheingold's recent book on the WELL (Rheingold 1993) and on other major characteristics of the online community, worldwide, describes this "grand collective project in cyberspace" in wonderful and enlightening detail. I will provide one anecdote here for my alternating feelings of fascination and hesitation with regard to computer-mediated communications.

I am of course writing this contribution to Late Editions on a computer. At the moment I am in the later phase of a year-long sabbatical and living on Vancouver Island, some three thousand miles from my home in Montreal. Through the Internet I have remained in contact with colleagues worldwide and with the graduate students I am supervising at McGill University. I know most of the students very well and am therefore able to put a face and even an expression to many of their electronic letters. Increasingly, I have become frustrated with the "textual" and "imagistic" nature of the communications I have been having with them. This was brought into the foreground when I received a phone call from a student with whom I had been in daily contact (via e-mail) but who is presently going through the crisis of putting together a thesis topic. Our telephone conversation immediately shifted to the difficulties of "talking" over the Internet. "I hate it," she said. "Why?" I asked. "Because I am losing my way . . . there is no comparison to writing a letter . . . it is all so curt and quick and we don't really speak . . . can't hear you and even imagine the inflection to your voice . . . I guess its about emphasis . . . reading is not speaking and don't even try and convince me that the reverse is true."

I didn't try. But I have had this increasing sense of unease as I have tried to compensate for the difficulties posed by reading the "talk" of students, friends, and colleagues. The feeling of being cut off has increased for me, not decreased. Perhaps this is a transitional phase. Perhaps I have not yet adjusted (after six years) to the communicative "shape" of this type of interchange. I suspect part of the problem is that I am grappling with the lag which occurs between the introduction of new technologies and their acceptance at the intellectual and emotional level. For me it does come down to the body (sounds of human voices, facial expressions, and so on), to the various ways in which certain communication processes have been "disembodied." But the degree of disembodiment varies with the technology. And in this instance we cannot dismiss the effects of imaging technologies which rely almost entirely on modes of interaction which are devoid of person-to-person contact. The other side of this argument, and the one I did not mention to my student, is that even with all of the above restrictions, I am able to imagine her face as I read what she has written. This is clearly a different kind of "sight," a different way of envisioning the communication process, but it is not necessarily a radical departure from the way in which we interact when we are in each other's presence. Ironically, we can already use the Internet for visual communications. The technology is in place to transform e-mail from the written into face-to-face communications via video images, though it must be stressed that this still remains disembodied. (I don't want to preclude, in saying this, the possibility that we are dealing with new kinds of embodiment or, as one student recently put it to me, the body becomes "ethereal" in the context of computer-to-computer communications. The mediators are so complex here that they suggest the possibility of completely new forms of transmission, communication, and exchange. Yet even these terms are a rather mechanical way of talking about the process.)

This is, I believe, a crucial historical interregnum. Older imaging technologies like the cinema and broadcast television remain in place while the newer technologies adapt and adopt both the substance and form of those media which preceded them. The combination carries traces of the past, present, and future within a cultural and social context which is being recreated even at this moment. (If this essay were coming to you online you might be able to respond to it immediately. Our "dialogue" would change the parameters of my comments. We could annotate the text together and discover new and anticipated forms of collaboration. As it is, you are reading this many months after its completion. The issue of time is central here. Those of you who have connected to the World Wide Web, which is an international hypertext service, know that new research is being thrown onto the Internet at an unprecedented rate. Browsing programs had to be developed to deal with this plethora of information. What impact will this have on writing and reading, on the development of research, and on critical response?)

Rheingold makes the point that many people from the WELL have been in contact with each other. There have been parties and get-togethers. There are numerous examples of members of the WELL helping each other out, providing crucial medical advice, support when a loved one dies. So the electronic connections have been strengthened by person to person contact. Would this have been possible in the era dominated by the cinema? Do books encourage this kind of community contact? My answer to both these questions is yes. There are numerous examples of reading clubs at every stage in the development of book culture. They were and are widespread (one of the best examples are the reading clubs set up to exchange ideas, thoughts, and feelings on Anne Rice novels). Some are political and some are not. Some are an excuse for a meeting and others are serious efforts at critical and historical analysis. The same situation exists for the cinema, although less so. The history of film societies is a crucial component of the history of film distribution. Film societies were at the forefront of showing alternative forms of film expression and are widely credited with enlarging the audience base for the cinema. Zines are a wonderful example of local publishing based on microcommunities who use the zines as an alternative form of communication and exchange. Sometimes zines are published for twenty or thirty people. The interesting thing is that more and more of them are finding their way into other communities. An informal network has been developed with many of the characteristics of the Internet.

I mention these examples because they point towards a broader process at work than the one represented by organizations such as the WELL. Community, both as a concept and as a practice, means organization and structure. It means imagining a collective will and trying to create and realize that desire through work with others who are similarly inclined. Virtual communities share similar needs and have similar priorities in nonvirtual communities. "People on the Net tend to gravitate toward electronic communities based on common interests and shared affinities rather than dwelling on the technologies involved in bringing them together in the first place" (Ogden 1994:12). The drive toward community is both dependent upon and transcends technology. While it is true that the Internet is making community contacts possible on a far greater scale than previously imagined, the ground rules, needs, and desires of people remain very much the same as in earlier periods. One must be careful therefore in attributing too much to the technologies here, but then again those attributions are part of the energizing force behind so much of the activity.

Virtual Interactions

Let me quote from an e-mail correspondence which I have been having with Andrew Curry, the head of Interactive Television for Videotron (a cable com-

pany with its headquarters in Montreal, the world's leading developer of interactive technologies) in England. I will reproduce it in the interactive form
which was used to have the conversation over the Internet.

You [Curry] said the following:
"I also think that there is a difference between interacting with a television set and interacting with a video game. With the game, you
know that it's you doing it, and no one else. With television I'm convinced that there's an unconscious assumption that in some way this
is part of a collective activity. The television set therefore becomes
potentially at least a channel for that collectivity."

[I responded:] This is a crucial thought. I agree that there is the un-
spoken assumption that somebody else out there is doing the same
thing. I believe that to be central to most forms of popular culture.
And I think this has implications for every facet of our experience
outside and inside the context of viewing. The difficulty is how do we
develop the interpretive tools to examine this collective sense (which
after all remains quite ephemeral) of shared enterprise? How do we
make "sense" of it all? More often than not we examine the products
we produce, the software we write, the games we play or, as with
some of the interactive companies which are dominant in the field,
rely on more and more sophisticated models of some ideal reader or
consumer. So, I believe we have problems defining to ourselves not
only whom we are addressing, but how we can understand response.
I make that claim with some apprehensiveness. I know the many pit-
falls of trying to evaluate audiences and the lack of clear methodology
and the often-times silly reductions which are made in the name of
research. But if we examine the audience through the ideals which we
create or program into the technology, then we will probably repeat
the errors of mainstream television. Don't get me wrong here. I happen to be a lover of American TV and a critic of it at the same time.
But, the error of the last ten years is that they have relied on the most
outmoded of assumptions about their audience and about subjectivity
in general. They have consistently undervalued and misunderstood
the needs of the people they have been addressing. Now, let's hypothe-
size that the same error is happening with interactive TV—and I
would cite as an example the rather superficial marketing study that
was done for interactive television in Montreal before it was introduced. Does this mean we have hit a wall with regard to developing
more interesting and creative modes of evaluation? No. I am, for all
of this, a strong supporter of the technology. I share with you the
sense, call it an intuition, that people will use it in very different and
potentially very creative ways. I also believe we are at the cusp of a
new era where the public sphere will be dramatically altered. The

arenas in which we will be able to exchange public forms of discourse are being changed even as I write this.

You said:

"If we can use the technology to create a sense of collectivity through communication around interest groups, which would, I guess, be a more immediate, more graphic, and more local version of what goes on the Net, then people will engage with it even if the tools they have at their disposal are neanderthal, electronically speaking."

Yes. We are into a period of time historically when local groups are forming more and more alliances with other local groups and con-stituencies. There is a new kind of community coming into being, although I am not sure the Net represents that shift. I am thinking here of zines and e-zines and groups of people who have formed around different musical styles and groups . . . I could go on. But how do we create that sense of collectivity? This would have to be answered very concretely. As of now, I am still pondering that one.

The important point highlighted by the above discussion is that we are grap-pling with definition and explanation, trying to devise ways of describing new processes to others and to ourselves.[2] This in itself is producing the context within which a community is being created, and in this instance my use of the word *community* is oriented toward the very public sphere which a filmmaker like Johan van der Keuken has always been working to contribute to and create. There is one other interesting yet tragic example (among many) of this new public space which cyberspace technologies are making possible.

It was all too familiar a New York story. A gunman, after robbing a topless club in Times Square, turned and fired at his pursuers. A stray bullet instantly killed a bystander in a nearby store. The victim, David Alsberg, was a 42-year-old computer programmer. He left behind a wife, a young son, and hundreds of grieving friends in both of the neighborhoods in which he lived: one in Astoria, Queens, and the other in the electronic community called cyberspace. Although most of them had never met him in the real world, his cyberspace neighbors from around the nation mourned Mr. Alsberg's death with an on-line wake that lasted weeks, commiserating through their personal com-puters. Using modems linked to telephone lines, they met in the same electronic forums where, just before his killing a few days after Christmas, Mr. Alsberg had been involved in a passionate debate on handgun control. Much more than a mere crime statistic, Mr. Alsberg has come to symbolize the new social dynamic of computer network-ing. In a world where physical contact is impossible, Mr. Alsberg's cyberspace neighbors consoled each other over the senseless loss of a mutual friend. And in their collective grieving, they demonstrated an impulse for togetherness that is as modern as the digital age and as old as humankind. For as more people become citizens of cyberspace, they are forging relationships that many describe as being as rewarding as their face-to-face friendships. [Lewis 1994: A1]

This is as significant an example as I can imagine for the radical reorientation of public forms of communication and exchange. Yet there are other issues which this raises and they are centered on the more immediate problems of understanding the relationship of these experiences to computer images, the notion of the image, in the general sense, as an effective form of communication. In other words, we must not forget that the transparent relationship which is assumed here, between the computer screen and its user, may not be the best guideline to what individual members of the network were feeling. The complexity of the various levels of mediation involved in computer-mediated communications does come through in the Arlsberg example. However, as Mark Poster has proposed, "through the mediation of the computer and the message service, written language is extracted from social communication to a point that identity is imaginary" (Poster 1990: 117). Poster goes on to talk about the loss of context which comes with the textualization of the verbal—speech becomes letters on a screen. But this dislocation may, on the other hand, produce radically different conceptual constructions of self and identity. There can be, as Michael Heim has suggested with respect to word processing, a "feeling of freedom and flow" (Heim 1987: 138).

It remains to be seen whether, as many of the proponents of Computer Mediated Communications have suggested, cyberspatial models will overcome many of these culturally held paradigms of vision. By way of conclusion let me reproduce a fragment of another electronic conversation which I had, with Pierre de Vries, a researcher at Microsoft who responded to a question which I posed about interactivity with the following:

My efforts here at Microsoft started off in the interactive TV field. I developed a "virtual community" concept piece in collaboration with the Bellevue Art Museum. We showed,

(a) how one could visit a show at a museum "from the comfort of your living room" by applying the video on demand concept to pulling down video segments of different parts of the museum and individual pieces

and more interestingly

(b) how a group of people might get involved in a discussion about the work by using phone, video or simply keystroke back channels from their homes.

It seemed to strike a chord. The ideas were obvious to anyone who's ever used a BBS [computer bulletin board], but many others suddenly realized that interactive TV was more than movies on demand or home shopping. The paradigm applies (grammar?) to any group activity, from watching a ball game to talking about welfare mothers. As for the museum, they were particularly interested in the possibilities for broadening access (both geographically and chronologically) and in the new methods of documenting a show that this medium offers.

The key element of de Vries's response is in item (b), where the conceptual orientation is premised on precisely the kind of conversation which van der Keuken suggested was crucial for him politically. De Vries's initial experiments have been taken further with Microsoft's recent publication of a CD-ROM of the National Gallery in London. The CD holds virtually all of the paintings in the gallery and it is possible to roam through the images on one's computer. They are all annotated with historical documentation and critical comment. Collections of photographs and other images are available over the Internet (from the Smithsonian Institution, for example), as are short videos.

Clearly the notion of vision as "re-presented by a straight line of sight, sharply focused, absolutely clear, and fixed on its object" (Levin 1988:68) has ceased to be the foundation upon which we are organizing our cultural conceptions of communication, vision, and understanding. All of the residual concepts which I have mentioned remain in place, however. Perhaps the metaphor of the labyrinth only reflects in a partial sense our struggle to enter and exit its multiplicity of hallways. The labyrinth is not Plato's cave. The ground upon which we can shift from sight to site and from vantage point to vantage point may be far more flexible than ever before. The challenge, it seems to me, will be to bring the humanism of van der Keuken together with the potential of computer-mediated communications. The shift of political, cultural, and disciplinary boundaries which that would entail may finally open a new set of doors behind which the virtual will simply assume its place as part of a landscape of possibilities and not end up being the postmodern answer to a new theology.

Notes

1. Novak 1992:229; Calvino 1988:98.

2. I would refer the reader to the recent introduction by Jay Lemke to a special issue of *The Arachnet Electronic Journal on Virtual Culture* 2:1 (1994). "Virtual culture is a useful term for both the subculture of computer-mediated human activity and for its tools and artifacts. In relation to this special issue of EJVC, the term 'virtual culture' more specifically tries to generalize the experiential phenomena of 'virtual reality' to include the virtual realities we construct in hypertext and hypermedia systems and the virtual communities we participate in through computer-mediated communication and information access. There are virtual cultures of electronic discussion groups and remote data access on the Internet, and virtual realities contracted through text and multimedia with which different users may interact in different ways, as well as the more spectacular virtual realities of real-time, multi-sensory immersion technologies."

References

Aycock, Alan. 1993. "Virtual Play: Baudrillard Online." *Arachnet Electronic Journal on Virtual Culture* 1, no. 7:3.

Barrett, Edward. 1988. Introduction to *Text, ConText, and HyperText: Writing with and for the Computer,* ed. Barrett. Cambridge, Mass.: MIT Press.

Benedikt, Michael. 1992. "Cyberspace: Some Proposals." In *Cyberspace: First Steps,* ed. Benedikt. Cambridge, Mass.: MIT Press.

Bolter, Jay David. 1993. *Getting Started with Storyspace.* Watertown, Mass.: Eastgate Systems.

Buckland, Michael K. 1991. "Information Retrieval of More Than Text." *Journal of the American Society for Information Science* 42, no. 8:587.

Burnett, Kathleen. 1993. "Towards a Theory of Hypertextual Design." *Postmodern Culture* 3, no. 2:1.

Calvino, Italo. 1988. *Six Memos for the Next Millennium.* Cambridge, Mass.: Harvard University Press.

Doob, Penelope Reed. 1990. *The Idea of the Labyrinth.* Ithaca, N.Y.: Cornell University Press.

Goldman-Seagall, Ricki. 1992. "Musings from MERLIN, UBC's Multimedia Ethnographic Research Laboratory." *Cue Journal,* Fall, 13.

Goldman-Seagall, Ricki, and Ted Riecken. 1993. "The Growth of a Multimedia School Culture: A Multi-Voiced Narrative." *Arachnet Electronic Journal on Virtual Culture* 1, no. 7:15–16.

Haraway, Donna J. 1991. *Simians, Cyborgs, and Women: The Reinvention of Nature.* New York: Routledge.

Hawks, A. 1992. "Future Culture FAQ." *Future Culture* 31 Dec., 1.

Heim, Michael. 1987. *Electric Language: A Philosophical Study of Word Processing.* New Haven, Conn.: Yale University Press.

Herskowitz, Richard. 1990. "Border Crossing: The Cinema of Johan van der Keuken." In *Border Crossing: The Cinema of Johan van der Keuken,* ed. Herskowitz. Ithaca, N.Y.: Cornell University Press.

Landlow, George. 1992. *Hypertext: The Convergence of Contemporary Critical Theory and Technology.* Baltimore: Johns Hopkins University Press.

Lanham, Richard A. 1993. *The Electronic Word: Democracy, Technology and the Arts.* Hypercard Electronic Version. Chicago: University of Chicago Press.

Lemke, J. L. 1993. "Education, Cyberspace and Change." *Electronic Journal on Virtual Culture* 1, no. 1:1.

Levin, David Michael. 1988. *The Opening of Vision: Nihilism and the Postmodern Situation.* New York: Routledge.

Lewis, Peter H. 1994. "Strangers, Not Their Computers, Build a Network in Time of Grief." *New York Times,* 20 Mar., A1.

Moulthrop, Stuart. 1991. "You Say You Want a Revolution? Hypertext and the Laws of Media." *Postmodern Culture* 1, no. 3:1.

Novak, Marcos. 1992. "Liquid Architecture in Cyberspace." in *Cyberspace: First Steps,* ed. Michael Benedikt. Cambridge, Mass.: MIT Press.

Ogden, Michael R. 1994. "Politics in a Parallel Universe: Is There a Future for Cyberdemocracy?" In *Sixth MacBride Round Table in Honolulu, Hawaii.*

Poster, Mark. 1990. *The Mode of Information: Poststructuralism and Social Context.* Chicago: University of Chicago Press.

Rheingold, Howard. 1992. *Virtual Reality.* New York: Touchstone.

———. 1993. *The Virtual Community: Homesteading on the Electronic Frontier.* New York: Addison-Wesley.

Van der Keuken, Johan. 1991. "Blind Child." In *After-Image,* ed. Fred Struving and van der Keuken. Amsterdam: Fragment Uitgeveriy: 18–20.

FRAMED, OR HOW THE INTERNET SET ME UP

1) Meshed Interjections

Somewhere, at some point in *Waiting for Godot,* someone says, "The Net. He thinks he's entangled in a net." I've held on to that line for a long time, probing the ambivalences it elicits in me when I think about "the Net," the Internet that is, that well-known global network of computer networks that has grown so rapidly over the past few years, radically reconfiguring space and rooting itself deeply in the social meanings of time. (Ambivalence 1: Although stories about how the Internet connects people from all over the world are common enough and true, I shouldn't imagine it as such an all-encompassing structure of modernity, so complete and final in the changes it effects in society. I'm logged in almost all the time. My wife only uses the computer to read a couple of newsgroups about pet birds and urban legends. My parents have never even seen an electronic mail message, as far as I know. The development of computer networks brings with it, at most, a clinal recalculation of society.)

It is important to remember that not all networks exist for the same reasons. This is a point that cannot be overemphasized (despite my choice to follow an increasingly popular, nontechnical usage and equate "the Net" with just the Internet, itself a rather diverse assortment of purposes and media; call this ambivalence 2). In fact, in my job as a student network programmer at Rice University, I help manage one small intersection of four large and conceptually distinct computer networks, each with different organizational principles and methods of propagation, different reasons for existence, and different potentials for change and reorganization. Given this perspective on the varying moods and tempers in which computer networks are administered, it is difficult to reconcile any understanding of the Net cast primarily in terms of mimesis (for example, the popular image of computers and networking supplied in the terms *virtual reality* or *cyberspace*) or through an analogy with self-referential, textual constructions (for example, the idea that a computer network "constitutes the physical embodiment of hypertext" [Bolter 1991:29]).

Rather than being a new kind of space or a new kind of book, computer networks remain exactly what they were supposed to have been: a new kind of tool; a facility for high-speed typing, high-speed transmission, and high-speed reading. As a tool, networking yields a kind of communication governed as much by the reflexes of the hand as by the too well-known reflexes of the eye and mouth, which gives a whole new meaning to the word *digitalization*. (Ambivalence 3: And yet noting these prosthetic transformations only recapitulates the post-mortem discourses on orality and literacy. The law of participation is never given a proper burial. It continues to stand in for what would have been had there not been media. Everyday life on the Net is constructed conceptually as an inhabitation of the given frameworks for action and interpretation: user, programmer, administrator, or whatever. From such a perspective, there is little to do in any given situation but to use, operate, correct, or manage, in other words to become what the manuals [the instructions, genres, norms, and practices of comm-unity] suggest and perform the expected [language] functions or play the approved [language] games. Excess yields no escape from the world of excessive meanings. We might hope that our ways of being differently can be mined for insight into a different way of being: a resuscitated law of participation founded upon yet more authentic than the rule of appropriation. But, finally, the Net would have to set us straight; we will find that its bizarre geometry is a subject all in itself.)

2) Meditations on a List

The glossary for *Programming perl* defines the word *list* with typical guru panache: "An ordered set of values with a beginning and an end. Or, an attribute of a leaning ship, decreasing in value, at the beginning of its end" (Wall and Schwartz 1991:418). Lists are pervasive in the network experience; lists of files, mail messages, USENET subject headings, and many other things (including your "account") are available somewhere on a list. Of course, they may be very different kinds of lists; I don't mean to make them all sound as if they should be interpreted the same way. Nevertheless, they are set up according to the organizational principle of the list, and that setup engages readership in a very particular way. In an examination of the possible cognitive effects of literacy, Jack Goody claims that the list

> relies on discontinuity rather than continuity; it depends on physical placement, on location; it can be read in different directions, . . . it has a clear-cut beginning and a precise end, that is, a boundary. . . . And the existence of boundaries, external and internal, brings greater visibility to categories, at the same time making them more *abstract* [1977:81; emphasis added].

The structure of Goody's argument closely parallels that of recent claims for hypermedia: the text is organized nonlinearly, which allows one the freedom to read it in different ways; the text is composed in such a way that its categories are emphasized spatially; thus the text's categories come to be more immediately in accord with a higher plane of thought. It is important to question this sort of determinate association between the written and the abstract for a number of reasons. First, it tends to reinforce the common myth that, when using a computer, the bodily and concrete matters of everyday life are marginalized, screened out, or forgotten. Second, such an association suggests that a list will somehow be better for representing abstract categories than some other genre. Third, it obscures the relation of the list to its readers and their reading practices insofar as they may not take advantage of the list's formal characteristics. Fourth and finally, while those often listlike and invisible orders of ordering that presumably complement the user's concrete experience of electronic worlds certainly depend on logical/abstract assumptions about the systematic relations of signs, they also will have been centered in the concepts of action and work, which suggest concreteness for the functions and purposes they are intended to achieve.

Naturally, the worst mistake to be made in assessing the cognitive effects of literacy would be to ignore the degree to which our concept of cognition has developed to conform with the possibilities of its own representation in a narrative, list, table, pro-gram, or dia-gram. But, with this caveat in mind, we can begin to think about how the energized lists to be found on the Net—from the list of ordered bits that signals a particular alphanumeric character to the list of sites and subjects to be found on a typical Gopher or WWW site—complicate and exemplify the epistemic mosaic in which network users find their self-understanding as users. By showing the user that a text's relation to itself can matter to the way we comprehend it (and especially to the way we write programs that read from it, too), the list indicates one way toward a playful understanding of the self-referential character to all textuality. By showing the user how to interact with texts in a nonlinear and nonreaderly fashion (for example, back-scanning the list; adding to or subtracting from the middle of the list), the list also indicates a way toward the creation of texts shaped primarily by their own possibility for being reshaped. And, by showing us how to participate in the restructuration of information, the list indicates a way toward the introduction of flexibility or miscibility to our categories of knowledge. Is it any wonder that the linked list is usually the first complicated data structure introduced in programming classes? It has so many different lessons to offer. And yet—

While all these indications suggest the possibility for a general shift, much appreciated by advocates of hypermedia, from a linearly alphabetic to a cross-cutting hieroglyphic consciousness of textuality, they are actually not all that agonistic, and they often run afoul of old habits that demand a difference between being a reader and being a user. Anyway, heightening the consciousness of one's reading practices is probably not what either hypermedia or computer networks are really for. I'll return to the issue of hypermedia on the Net later, but if we continue to meditate on the figural similarities between the list and the Net we can find some even more colorful tiles embedded in the Net's epistemic mosaic.

First of all, it's plain to see that a list of lists yields a matrix and that the matrix is often invoked as an image of the underlying systematicity of written texts, city streets, and especially computer networks. The familiarity of this image has gone hand in hand with the mythologization of connectivity in the modern age and, thus, of setting new beginnings and new boundaries for social theory, literary criticism, computer science, and processes of international policy formation, among other things. Second, if we consider the possibility of a list composed of new elements that each contain new information along with some percentage of all the information contained in all preceding elements, we have a thoroughly reticulated model of historical accumulation and determination and a ground on which to begin the project of "data recovery," to figure out which elements came first and what the missing information is. This figuring is emblematic of the manner in which computerized discourse networks are compared with oral or written discourse, as if any of the three marks off a distinctive epoch or mode of communication that can still be sorted out in its essential character. Finally, if we imagine a list, the elements of which usually only paraphrase or respond to any of the preceding elements, then that list might seem to fall back on itself. With this image in mind, we might be able to glimpse an emergent quality of worldliness in computer networks: the suspension of occlusive space and linear time for a memorably partial cycle of inquiry, correspondence, and return. I mentioned at the outset that the Internet is a well-known contributor to the reconfiguration of global time and space. Sometimes called time-space compression (Harvey 1990:240), this worldwide trend seems to bring us all together and shrink both the time and amount of travel required for communication. The distance that keeps us from seeing one another is measured in an occlusive space. The time required to travel that distance accumulates more or less linearly. But, in fact, we know that distance and time are not compressed by computer networks; they are set aside and deferred to the speed of an electromagnetic impulse. What remains between us after that deferral is the experience of the repetitious list, often looping back on itself, participating paraphrastically in the (re)initiation and (re)interpretation of heterogeneous topics by means of a variety of happily vague discourse genres.

3) Summations of the Everyday

This list (by which I mean this whole paper) could have tried in its own discontinuous and unsystematic way to measure out my everyday experience of the

Net in terms of what it is that I do. If I were to attempt such a thing, only under orders, of course, I could begin with the shorter list that follows:

- I sit down at either my home computer or at a workstation on campus and log in. A little program tells me how much mail I have in each of several different folders. I usually get around two hundred mail messages a day, so it is necessary for me to have it presorted.

- I read my mail, reply to a few messages, delete a few messages, save a few others to files in directory, and occasionally forward a message or two to someone else; I repeat this process for a few other folders, but usually not for all of the ones with new mail—just the ones that I expect to be most interesting.

- I read maybe a half dozen newsgroups closely and scan the subject headings for about thirty others. (By the way, newsgroups are the categories into which USENET is divided; they are named according to their subject content, like sci.anthropology, for example; their articles are usually organized into more specific discussion threads that a good newsreader will link together automatically to make reading easier.)

- I often have some reason to log onto another machine, either one at Rice or one in Florida or, not quite as often, one located someplace I've never been but that is running a publicly accessible conferencing system, database, online bookstore, or whatever.

- I might also use a certain program ("finger") to see who else is logged in, either on the same machine or elsewhere in the world; I use that same program to find out limited personal information about other users. The command finger "Christopher Pound"@rice.edu returns my entry in the campus directory; finger pound@is.rice.edu returns with information about my computer account.

- I sometimes use any one of three programs (Gopher, Mosaic, or Netscape) to access databases or collections of text files, images, and audio samples stored around the world. These programs serve similar purposes in that they integrate multiple kinds of electronic resources in a user-friendly way.

- I must, as part of my job, maintain certain databases, write short programs, answer some of the postmaster's mail, and maintain software packages related to news and mail. Today, for example, I arranged for a mailing list to be gatewayed to our news server. From now on, the messages sent to the mailing list will be accessible as though they were USENET articles posted to a local newsgroup.

While this list gets done some of the business of the larger list of which it is a part, it is somewhat disquieting to divide up my habitual practices of reading and writing in terms of these self-contained operations, functions, and programs, few of which feel entirely disconnected from the others. This particular list's discontinuity encourages me to ignore how my life will have actually unfolded. It provides mainly for an identification of equivalent invocations of networking protocols, and it centers my everyday affairs in some sort of dialectical experience of myself as a mediated, technological consciousness—an "I" before and in use of the machine.

Thus as a representation of my everyday experience on the Net, the list (and here is where I agree with Goody) demands that my everyday life be enterable at any point, indistinguishably, and ultimately that it be summarizable in terms of that which I know about my daily logins. It maps out the everyday like a constellation, an imaginary network of actions and relations embedded in an imaginary firmament. This list also erases that which differentiates my days from one another and privileges the conceptual boundaries given in the separate software tools at hand. In response to this alternation from deferment to preferment, I have kept this other list—a different kind of list—one which, however desultory it might be, attends better to the insight into that which stands to the side of the empty shell/language game of the "user."

4) Accounting for Identity

It has been said that anyone who cannot understand the difference between equivalence and identity will not make a very good C programmer. Taken conversely, this saying might explain why so many social scientists' analyses of computing and the use of computer networks have focused on the question of identity. I suppose that this program simply fits the fashion insofar as identity on the Net seems to be somewhat arbitrary and artificial in character. Really, though, the visual-verbal allegories for existence that sustain some strange notion of identity for many computer users belong more properly to the realm of equivalence, and they are almost always arbitrated rather than arbitrary, because, unless the users own and operate their own sites, their user names must be deemed acceptable and the records with which those names become associated may be reviewed and judged at any time.

Applying for a computer account is somewhat like the process of personal incorporation, because an account is mostly a "convenient" legal fiction. It provides for the ownership of specific files and establishes what sort of privileges are granted to the user, and it usually sets a limit on the amount of information a person can store for future reference. In fact, it is not uncommon for certain types of accounts to be legally shared by more than one person, and it is extremely common for one person to have multiple accounts. In short, the construction of "identity" on the Net begins largely as a matter of policy. Of course, policy can be negotiated or manipulated to varying degrees at different sites, and this is what eventually produces the unusual variety of signatures (or forgeries thereof) to be found in computer-mediated communication. In any case, computer accounts are used to classify certain things, such as the owner-ship of a file or the appropriateness of an action. Yet this kind of virtual casu-istry easily becomes decentered or reconfigured because it hinges on the com-mensurability of evolving and often discordant protocols for judgment and communication.

5) The Dialogic Invagination

I suppose I could have forwarded you an example, taken from a mailing list or a newsgroup, of how messages exchanged on the Net are often structured as interlinear commentaries on previous messages. You'd see that the first mes-sage quoted has a series of > signs (or some other nonalphabetic character) at the beginning of each line. Each successive commentator adds another series of > signs to all the quoted material and writes his or her comments in between these quoted lines. Examples of this kind of composition are extremely com-mon, and they can be quite complex. However, in order to avoid the problem of subject drift (the tendency for an exchange of messages to move along to an entirely different topic from the one named in the message headers) and the fact that as these exchanges go on, much of the older information gets lost or misattributed, I wanted whatever example I used to relate better to the idea that the Net provides a certain kind of frame (a boundary and a setup but also the kind of frame we find in "frame of mind" or especially in "to frame a ques-tion") for being a reader and an author. I figured it would be most useful for me to construct an example using a more relevant and possibly familiar aca-demic source (Maranhão 1986 : 137–45), transforming it into a kind of conver-sation between three authorized readers that, although it may be excessively self-referential, instructively foregrounds the characteristic events of compo-sition and exchange that frame the use of computer networks for delayed tex-tual communication.

Forwarded message:

>Date: Mon, Feb 21, 1994 00:32:12 CST
>From: pound@is.rice.edu (Christopher Pound)
>To: whomever
>Subject: mimesis, methexis, and writing over the network
>
>>Dagon <dagon@maple.circa.ufl.edu> writes:
>>>In Therapeutic Discourse and Socratic Dialogue, Maranhao
<Tullio.Maranhao writes:
>
>Aside from the points raised below, I want to call attention to the
>automated structurations of the text above and to the left. These are
>the devices of electronic discourse that make it most like a book (in
>that we are told who the authors are and the quotations are meticu-

>lously referenced) but which also mark out the multiple voices to
>be found in the text.
>
>These comments, here, the ones you're reading at this very moment
>and which (if we believe the little chevrons to the left) were written
>most recently, are neither inside nor outside the flow of this phony
>dialogue. They come after the headers and after the initial citation
>of other authors, but they precede the quotations they refer to, be-
>low. The temporal accumulations of this text are, thus, given over
>to their spatial arrangement (much like other texts, but somehow
>even moreso, which is our first clue).
>
>The image of the text's _techne_ is the matrix, the mother of all
>representations, and here, the flesh of that "womb" sometimes turns
>in on itself a second time. It is this second invagination of the text
>that should open out into a new space for dialogue—one which can-
>not be parasitically or supplementarily mapped back onto speech.
>
>>>Speech can be mimesis, that is, "imitation" of something else,
>>>or methexis, the "participation" of some things in others. These
>>>two categories of action—copy or imitation on one hand and
>>>classification or participation on the other—were cultural pil-
>>>lars in ancient Athens . . .
>>
>>Tullio, you might have thought that this text of yours would never
>>see a reply of this kind, but I'm going to take a moment to see if
>>I can explain how writing might acquire the participatory char-
>>acteristics of speech . . .
>>
>>Electronic messaging systems generally encourage a way of writ-
>>ing in which authors and audiences are continually changing
>>sides—so much so that the terms "author" and "audience"
>>themselves become mildly inconvenient. Here, I hold you respon-
>>sible for each of your words, and I myself take on the responsi-
>>bility of an editor as well as a respondent. In doing so, I (nor-
>>mally) will have granted you the ability to do the same. The result
>>is a text that retains the ethical and participatory characteristics of
>>dialogue without ever having tried to re-present a spoken word.
>
>I doubt you'd say all that if Tullio were able to reply. Are you sure
>you're not comparing apples to oranges? I mean, if we talk only
>about the differences between speech and writing, don't we miss
>out on a lot of the heterogeneity of each? So, if we just compare
>spoken dialogues to written dialogues to electronically-composed
>dialogues, we do so at the expense of all the different genres to

>which these dialogues will surely belong. Moreover, spoken dia-
>logues often move from topic to topic in a much less formal way
>than any of the t(r)optically straight-jacketed newsgroups and mail-
>ing lists I'm familiar with.
>
>>>Socrates' attack on mimesis and exemplary demonstration of
>>>methexis in his dialectic method is a cultural and historical trib-
>>>ute of the passage from an oral to a literate context. The new
>>>medium of writing overcomes the old of speaking, but does not
>>>sweep it away . . .
>>
>>And that's the reason we continue to assume writing to be para-
>>sitic with respect to speech. It comes second. It tries to reproduce
>>the meanings of spoken language. Worse yet, it makes it possible
>>to communicate in a manner that denies the importance of con-
>>vention and intention. It is permissive with respect to solipsism
>>and anomie. To avoid all of this, we must be able to intervene
>>communicatively, to provoke responses and perhaps correspon-
>>dence, and to invert, convert, and reverse the others' arguments
>>along with them. That's the sort of exchange you can't usually
>>have in writing, but could it be done over the net? After all, this
>>text is not really based on a spoken event or even a speakable
>>possibility. Of course, it isn't some sort of unspeakable hieroglyph
>>or pictogram, either. It is still an alphabetic text, but its rhetorical
>>conventions have all been entrained to the trope of "epicrisis,"
>>which is the name for when a "speaker quotes a passage and com-
>>ments on it" (Lanham 1968:43). You can do that in speech, but
>>on the net, that's often *all* that you're doing, and if someone
>>else comes along to comment on our passages,
>
>To point out, for example, that you can't get away with nearly this
>much hyperbole if you're actually concerned that someone could
>come along and point it out in less than generous terms. But, I
>wouldn't want to stand in the way of a good rant . . .
>
>>this epicritical discourse would become even more deeply nested
>>and ambivalent. It achieves a kind of edited multivocality that
>>could never be reproduced in speech.
>
>The question is, why would anyone want to? Arguing about which
>channels of discourse can or can't reproduce the others seems sort
>of pointless until it is clear that that's what people hope to do.
>
>On the other hand, it's true that the textualization of oral discourse
>yields and then depends on the death of participation (which after

>the event of textualization could only amount to a challenge of the
>text's authority). All that remains for the text, in this case, is the
>simulation of participation.
>
>Anyway, I agree that there is something peculiar about the mode of
>expression we have at our fingertips on the net. Rather than "edited
>multivocality," I'd call it by the (slightly) more euphonic phrase:
>tense polyphony. The word _tense_, which relates both to tautness
>and to the linguistic category for expressing time, is etymologically
>connected to the words _temple_ and _template_ [< L "place
>reserved or cut out"], so it conveys several important characteristics
>of this new way of writing back and forth. Tense polyphony is
>clearly still planned out on a grid or a matrix (like most alphabetic
>texts), and in addition, it is inscribed into the templates of epicrisis.
>But by appropriating and re-marking the linguistic apparatus of
>tense, such that we understand time to have passed even while we
>write to one another mostly in the present tense, the template of
>epicrisis becomes dialogized and de-terminated. The exchange can
>move forward indefinitely in an expression of the present.
>
>>Now, responding to someone epicritically tends to imply that
>>the additional phrases will either confirm that a point has been
>>made that is worthy of contrast or consideration, signal an over-
>>looked implication of the original comment, or make a claim
>>about the legitimacy of the original comment's rhetorical status.
>>Some people use the net as a competitive forum for their ideas,
>>and it does seem as though the trope of epicrisis is particularly
>>well suited to picking apart just as much of someone's argument
>>as you like while ignoring the rest. However, there are just as
>>many, if not more, people on the net who quote others' text as a
>>complement to their own, implying some sort of consensus while
>>the textual juxtapositions nominalistically testify to the contrary.
>
>Yes, each set of fragments suggests a separate voice. The separate
>voices are not reducible to a shared perspective, even when there
>is one.
>
>>>Writing accentuates the inclination to produce mimetist copies
>>>of reality, and thus tends to dispense with methexis. It is a pre-
>>>requisite of the written text that it present a definite state of
>>>affairs, that it function as one conversational turn in a broader
>>>dialogical situation.
>>
>>Not anymore. Written communications are now transmitted so
>>quickly and are so thoroughly imbricated that none of what you

\>\>say holds true, especially when you consider more than just email
\>\>and bulletin boards. There are quite a few programs out there (like
\>\>"write" or "talk" on the system I use) that allow you to write
\>\>phrases back and forth or at the same time as someone else.
\>
\>You skipped over the first part of what Tullio said. "Writing accen-
\>tuates the inclination to produce mimetic copies of reality." Maybe
\>he could argue that electronic writing heralds a shift from mimesis
\>to some kind of "virtuality" with an entirely different relationship
\>to the world (something like the double inversion of this text, for
\>example). I'm not saying that's true, but I just wanted to point out
\>how you conflated electronic writing with the writing Tullio wrote
\>about just to further your argument.
\>
\>\>\>The written text is potentially endowed with more complete-
\>\>\>ness because it is not strung together with other texts, as clauses
\>\>\>in an oral dialogue are. The inconsistency between two state-
\>\>\>ments made by the same speaker in the course of a conversation
\>\>\>is easier to point out because the statements are closer to one
\>\>\>another in time, and their author is present to react against any
\>\>\>objections.
\>\>
\>\>Whoa! First of all, "the" written text is often already strung to-
\>\>gether with other texts. On the Usenet, most articles get bundled
\>\>together—not just the ones that comment on each other epicriti-
\>\>cally like this; each article in a chain has a "References:" line in
\>\>the header that tells you exactly which articles are being replied
\>\>to. Second, it's plenty easy to point out an inconsistency between
\>\>two statements in writing. It's even easier in this medium than it
\>\>is in speech. Third and finally, what do you mean by calling the
\>\>participant in a conversation an "author?" Maybe you had a mo-
\>\>ment of foresight there and anticipated the response you're get-
\>\>ting from me!
\>\>
\>\>\>The written text and its author are protected from all those
\>\>\>checks.
\>\>
\>\>I admit that you are . . .
\>
\>He's not the only one. As I write this, I find myself wondering about
\>how this message will be received. Will this be read as yet another
\>hyper-virtual cyberspace net frontier of cyberia kind of thing? Yet
\>another baroque excretion from the self-involved spectacle known
\>as the Internet? Probably to some, but it was a calculated risk.
\>

>>>The prerequisite of oral discourse, as conceived in the Socratic
>>>dialogues, is that speech questions and disassembles states of
>>>affairs.
>>
>>This isn't a prerequisite of electronic discourse, but it's one pos-
>>sibility. Another is for it to, initially, accept the prerequisites
>>of print media, but, if an electronic text is composed on those
>>grounds and made accessible to the participatory media of which
>>this message might have been an example, the ground will soon
>>begin to shift . . .
>>
>>>This, however, is not the responsibility of a speaker alone, but
>>>the result of the dynamics of dialogues which harness all partic-
>>>ipants to the best argument.
>>
>>The same goes for the dialogized interchanges you can find al-
>>most anywhere on the net. In addition, the authors of such texts
>>take on a certain responsibility for the scissionings of the texts to
>>which they are responding—the kinetics of electronic dialogue
>>will harness authors as much to the manner in which something
>>is said (and, moreover, to the way in which something hasn't been
>>said in those spaces between their texts) as to the structure of their
>>argument.

6) Quasi dixisset

Leaving aside the Net's more participatory flora, the phrase "as if he had said" is perhaps a justifiable epigram for much of what is written elsewhere on the Net, but not because some of the forms writing takes on the Net seem to refer back to the possibility of their having been spoken. Prosopopoeia, the rhetorical scheme for representing someone who isn't present as being the speaker, is a very common trope in computer-mediated communication, but it is hardly ever commented upon. What I want to call attention to in the usage of this trope is the way in which it is deployed to establish the authority of that newest of all authors, the robot.

On the Net, robotics may not be what you think. A robot may be as simple as a script that is programmed to search some source of text for a single word and then perform some action every time it finds that word as long as someone somewhere is supposed to recognize a "voice" in the output of that script. Each day, for example, I receive mail from several programs calling themselves robots. These mail messages each contain a list of new mail aliases that I am required, as part of my job, to add to the campuswide mail alias tables, so when they send me (as well as a number of other, more important people on the postmaster@rice.edu mailing list) these lists of mail aliases, the robots call me Mr. Postmaster and say please.

Similarly, anyone might get an automated message back from a list server in response to a subscription request for a mailing list. Or, if someone sends out an improperly addressed piece of mail, it will doubtless be returned with a more or less intelligible error message. Also, it's usually trivial to set up a sort of e-mail answering machine program that will serve as your robotic secretary while you're on vacation, as the program is often called. An even better example of robotics on the Net can be found on the (probably infamous by now) MUDs, MUSHes, or MOOs being run at machines all over the world. These multiuser, automated role-playing engines are frequently home to robot-controlled characters called 'bots that interact textually with the other inhabitants (human or inhuman alike). 'Bots can actually be the most diligent and successful players on MUDs that encourage any sort of accumulation of points or of "items." On these and other kinds of MUDs (not to mention Internet Relay Chat), a robot can become a resource, perhaps responding to players' queries with information, or a source of amusement by responding with some sort of joke or with a reply that makes fun of the player for having tried to talk to a robot.

More serious are the robots to be found on the USENET. They appear to be less common than robots elsewhere, but by abusing their own potential for endless repetition they usually achieve a great deal more notoriety. For years now, a series of robots are said to have been scanning the USENET searching for references to Turkey with the goal of responding with a prepared statement on various conflicts between Turkey and Armenia during the early years of the twentieth century (see the Net.Legends.FAQ or the FAQ for alt.fan. serdar.argic). The robot's name has changed many times—Serdar Argic is probably the best known of them all—but the messages have remained very much the same. It has probably managed to convince only a few people on the Net of what it has to say about Armenia and Armenians, but thanks to its repetitiveness and its ubiquity it has definitely made a lot of people aware of itself and its programmers' concerns.

Returning to the "as if he had said," I think I'd like to amend that and now write "as if *he* had said" to emphasize a couple of things. First, robotics presents us with a compelling example of how the written word can instantaneously assert itself as an authoritative discourse—as a discourse that comes without and refuses to negotiate or to play the game of dialogue—and second, robotic discourse tends to build on an economy of the sameness, in other words, on the privileged figure of homogeneity that is predisposed to define the world in terms of its phantasmic/masculine substitutions.

Yours truly,
Mr. Postmaster

7) The Unseen World of Work(s)

I suggested earlier that hypermedia aren't necessarily going to make people more conscious of their reading practices, and in fact there is still a great deal of nostalgia for the book on the Net. Many sites have begun to accumulate online versions of old books now in the public domain. Archives of written material from various sources on the Net, like mailing lists and USENET newsgroups, are also collected into gigantic but well-indexed files that are made available in much the same way as the online books. These archives are usually accessed by means of software that itself reads through a list of indices of indices in order to bring forth the right indices for the right information to be correctly transformed into a regularly organized menu. Here, for example, is a sample page of bookmarks (a list of indices to information stored at this or another server and arranged according to the specifications of the user) for Gopher, a common information retrieval tool:

Internet Gopher Information Client v1.12S
Bookmarks

```
    →  1.   Information Systems Gopher Server/
       2.   riceinfo.rice.edu/
       3.   African Studies at UPenn (via WWW) <HTML>
       4.   Sitelogs <?>
       5.   University of Minnesota gopher server/
       6.   All the Gopher Servers in the World/
       7.   Gopher Virtual Library/
       8.   Knowbot Information Service <TEL>
       9.   Rice CWIS test server/
      10.   Cultural Studies <HQX>
      11.   PostScript(r) Type 1 Font Samples/
      12.   TeX Font Samples/
      13.   Problem (from ricevm1)/
      14.   CHAT - Conversational Hypertext Access Tech. <TEL>
      15.   EFF-Austin, a non-profit Texas educational corporation/
      16.   Baylor College of Medicine/
      17.   texas/
      18.   Master Gardener Information (Texas Agric. Extension)/
```

Press ? for Help, q to Quit, u to go up a menu   Page: 1/5

Each of the items on this list is either an index to a file, a program, or another list of indices. Insofar as it was designed to support a potentially recursive manner of navigating the Internet, Gopher turns the idea of the list back on itself to transform itself into the Garden of Forking Paths, the book-labyrinth described by Borges that simultaneously captures various futures in its space simultaneously but remains a necessarily incomplete picture of the universe. In this regard, Gopher shifts the indices of the matrix it was bound to reproduce and transforms itself into the image of the hieroglyph, the symbol of the desire to get outside the book and incorporate that which is outside of writing. Accordingly, the Gopher client was designed to call or work with other programs, programs that can display images or movies, play music, or give the user an interactive command line.

But, of course, Gopher is also designed to hide as much as or vastly more than it reveals. In fact, Gopher and especially the more powerful hypertext interfaces that can take the place of a Gopher client, like Mosaic and Netscape, have a conceivably unlimited potential to link texts, databases, images, and so on—to become the magnum opus of an information-based society—but this potential must always be deferred in favor of displaying only manageable amounts of information and of helping the user to ignore the rest. While Gopher often fails to be very manageable, forcing the user to search through page after page of similarly titled text files or directories, it is structured such that it nearly always succeeds in hiding information the user hasn't requested. Newsreaders and mail filters have similar functions. So contrary to the promise held out by hypermedia that a disassembled and playfully reshaped knowledge base will translate into a richer kind of understanding, these software packages actually emphasize the discontinuities in our categories of knowledge in order to filter out what the user doesn't want to see.

Having achieved this cynical degree of flexibility, Gopher, Mosaic, Lynx, and Netscape have become quite popular as possible solutions to the kind of problem posed by then-Senator Albert Gore Jr.:

> Years ago, I created a new word called "ex-formation," information that exists outside the conscious awareness of any living being but that exists in such enormous quantities that it sloshes around and changes the context and the weight of any problem one addresses. The problem is to convert the information into knowledge and eventually to distill the knowledge into wisdom. [1991:21]

Somewhat predictably, Gore misses the fact that *exformation* has already been the product of a challenging-forth, of a measurement, or of a representation. To employ a technological fix and challenge it forth again only magnifies the problem by generating even more information, not knowledge, and certainly not understanding. Gopher hides this additional information well, but if I were a user with a long list of bookmarks constantly trying to accumulate more and more bookmarks to better and better information resources, I strongly suspect I would feel more like the victim of the problem Gore describes than I would feel like the victor.

8) Screen Physiognomies

At work I usually sit in front of a seventeen-inch color monitor that has reasonably high resolution; I tend to use the smallest size of my font that has been designed to be readable. I might have included a picture except that I'd be embarrassed to show how few modifications I've made to the default configuration; anyway, the font size I use is small enough that I'm able to keep all the windows I need open and completely visible at the same time. The chairs at work don't happen to be very comfortable, and the small type and slight waviness to the background pattern both encourage me to take short breaks looking away from the terminal about every half hour or so.

While at my workstation a continuous stream of console messages from other machines flickers past in the bottom left of my field of visions. The console window for my own workstation is extremely small, and only occasionally reports anything at all. In the upper right there's a small seemingly analog clock and a little picture of a mailbox that inverts from black to white when new mail arrives. Scattered around the rest of the screen are four to six windows that are each attended by a separate process running on the workstation, making them each equivalent to an old-style CRT.

In my experience, these windows (as well as other windows which might pop up to display nontextual output) relate tautologically to the idea of the optical unconscious, which is to say that these X windows, as they are called, have always already been constituted as word-image structures awaiting as objects the participation of the (day)dreaming subject that will have already been established by the word-image, or should I say the world picture? This isn't to say that you couldn't play with them, or at least play with the way they look according to the rules of a written grammar, or ask them to show different images. However, the command line's absolute attendance on the programmer's absolute command will always recapitulate the absolute unification of subject and object, of interpreter and text, and of user and screen. Except, of course, when things don't go as planned.

9) Monsters and Monstrances

Hysterically enough, some of the Net's denizens have imagined the Internet as having an avatar, an insane, writhing, and corpulent monstrosity, a noxious and unspeakable mother goddess lurking ominously in the dark and feculent recesses of the Net. In the newsgroups I read, I frequently hear her name mentioned in playfully fearful tones. From the Jargon File 2.9.6, for example:

> Shub-Internet: /shuhb in't*r-net/ [MUD: from H. P. Lovecraft's evil fictional deity "Shub-Niggurath," the Black Goat with a Thousand Young] n. The harsh personification of the Internet, Beast of a Thou-

sand Processes, Eater of Characters, Avatar of Line Noise, and Imp of Call Waiting; the hideous multi-tendriled entity formed of all the manifold connections of the net. A sect of MUDders worships Shub-Internet, sacrificing objects and praying for good connections. To no avail—its purpose is malign and evil, and is the cause of all network slowdown. [Raymond 1991]

Thus while the Net (sometimes called the Matrix by the same people who might talk about Shub-Internet) is ordered or woven by the techne of the text. Shub-Internet is the image of its unraveling and its transgression from within. She is held responsible, however sporadically or ironically, for the failures of the Net to operate as expected, and yet she supposedly personifies the Internet itself. They say she is multitendriled, but such is only the way in which she parodies the Net, because her predecessor, Shub-Niggurath, was actually described by H. P. Lovecraft as being cloudlike.

Of course, the fact is that Shub-Internet is ridiculous. That's the point. When her mockingly religious followers' TELNET sessions are suddenly cut off with the message "Connection closed by remote host," their routes through the network and their terminals are seen as having become vessels for an altogether different host, the monstrous figure of Shub-Internet, exposed for the veneration of her subjects. Ridiculous, but it's spoken of nevertheless and might be taken as an allegory for the entire mythos of the age of mechanical reproduction, from the displacement of authenticity by the mimesis-matrix to the parodical assertion of presence in the face of the simulacrum.

Note

This paper should give voice to the sort of mood into which my everyday affairs are cast by the NET. Accepting the term *user* provides a frame for certain kinds of experience, but the frame is always rooted in *framen*—a Middle English verb meaning either to construct or, more interestingly, to benefit. Thus I will be a little less concerned with addressing the particular forms and functions of the programs I invoke and the files I modify than I will be with uncovering the persistent and sometimes beneficial qualities associated with being a user, namely, the specific reading practices, methods of composition, and appreciations of humor, idleness, and repetitious variation that I find to be common on the Net.

References

Bolter, Jay David. 1991. *Writing Space*. Hillsdale, N.J.: Lawrence Earlbaum Associates.

Goody, Jack. 1977. *The Domestication of the Savage Mind*. Cambridge: Cambridge University Press.

Gore, Albert Jr. 1991. "Information Superhighways: The Next Information Revolution." *The Futurist* 25:21–23.

Harvey, David. 1990. *The Condition of Postmodernity*. Cambridge, Mass.: Basil Blackwell.

Lanham, Richard A. 1968. *A Handlist of Rhetorical Terms*. Berkeley: University of California Press.

Maranhão, Tullio. 1986. *Therapeutic Discourse and Socratic Dialogue*. Madison: University of Wisconsin Press.

Raymond, Eric S., ed. 1991. Jargon File 2.9.6. URL: gopher/riceinfo.rice.edu:70/7waissrc%3a/OtherGophers/WAIS/j/jargon.src.

Wall, Larry, and Randal L. Schwartz. 1991. *Programming perl*. Sebastopol, Calif.: O'Reilly and Associates.

A TALE OF AN ELECTRONIC COMMUNITY

This paper explores computer-mediated communication (CMC) through the creation of a computer bulletin board newsgroup. The project arose out of the following questions: What would happen if I, as an anthropologist, could tap into a larger number of informants through a newsgroup? How could this new medium affect the methodology of participant observation?

I am not sure I was able to answer these questions as my concerns quickly shifted. I realized that I had been taking this medium as a tool and treating it as one would in face-to-face interaction, that is, I was making the same assumptions about language. Thereby my interest shifted to study the way that language and communication are "enframed" (to borrow Michael Heim's use of Heidegger) in the newsgroups. Instead of treating this medium as a tool, or simply as an electronic community, how could we understand its elements under the new "enframing"?

Here, I am offering some suggestions with which one might better

The Proceedings of the Creation of the Newsgroup soc.culture.scientists

The following articles are posted in the preliminary phase in creation of soc.culture.scientists. First, an RFD was posted which was followed by reaction of people to the merit of the proposal.

Warning: All Typos Are Original (not edited on purpose)

Request for Discussion(RFD):

The follow-up articles will be posted on "news.groups:"

This is to suggest a news group that can bring scientists and engineer of different cultural background together debating/confronting the issues on culture/tradition, science, religion, gender and education.

Recently, some prominent scientists have argued for blurring of

Trying to get away from face-to-face assumption and assumption of Internet as too.

understand the nature of computer newsgroups. To do so I juxtapose the proceedings of the creation of a newsgroup that I initiated, namely, soc.culture.scientists, with my reading of relevant literature on language and writing. Moreover, I substantiate my reading with reflections on becoming of this "community." The left column contains my own thoughts and the right one concerns the proceedings. I chose this format with the realization that writing on this subject is difficult and requires the participation of the reader in the experiment itself and in the way language is used to talk about it. My aim is to maximize this effect.

On Telepresence and Community

Anthropologists study communities as units of social and cultural analysis. They use terms that imply presence to talk about groups. Participant observation is the rubric for conveying that certain things should *take place:* the anthropologist should be there, take part, and observe others in order to generate *understanding.*

f -+- f

Anthropologists often assume a community of face-to-face interaction. Vocabularies that are used consist of those that refer to group dynamics such as assimilation, acculturation, adaptation, and participation. Others refer to the opposite: expulsion, expatriation, and exile. In newsgroups the terms used for indicating communities are different, such as posting, cross-posting, reading, lurking, and flaming, which don't imply being part of a whole.

the boundaries between scientific knowledge and religious convictions. People who do cultural studies of science and technology have drawn attention on scientific imagination of the "Third World" scientists. Moreover, the science-cities in the other parts of the world have created new niches for "science-gone-native." Given these ongoing discussions and events, the proposed "news group" could create a space for an interdisciplinary debate over the above issues.

The common denominator of this suggested group with soc.culture* groups, as I see it, is twofold:

1-Many scientists and engineer have computer access and connection with internet or bitnet, especially those who work in large institutions.

2-Despite the fact that most people in soc.culture groups are scientists and engineers, there is no space for them to share their ideas and experiences as far as these issues are relevant to soc.culture, i.e., the social and cultural context of their professions.

The intention and content of this news group:
1-The intention could be to encourage exchange of opinion, information, and have access to each other's experiences as engineers and scientists of various background.

2-The content could be constituted of a range of issues from religious to secular, biographical, woman and science, technological advances, to day-to-day events.

There are many possible ways of creating virtual communities such as mailing lists and MUDs (Multi-User Dungeons). However, the BBSs (Bulletin Board Systems) have probably become the most used virtual communities since they are easy to create and they can cover any spatial size, from a city to the world. The necessary hardware consists of storage (memory) and a modem; the software is farely simple and widely available.

The USENET (User's Network, a way of managing multiple interactions), which was created by two Duke University graduate students, enables people to exchange messages. Through different gateways to the Internet, users can "post" or "read" messages under different subject headings. For example, in soc. culture.scientists a subject heading reads "Magical Thinking" and a series of articles refer to this title by displaying "subject: Re: Magical Thinking." This string of articles creates a virtual space called a bulletin board, perceptually modeled after physical bulletin boards. The first virtual communities based on information technology were the online bulletin board services of the mid-1970s:

"BBSs were named after their perceived function-virtual places, conceived to be just like physical bulletin boards, where people could post notes for general reading. The first successful BBS programs were primitive, usually allowing the user to search for messages alphabetically, or simply to read messages in the order in which they were posted." (Stone 1991: 89)

Regards mazyar
P.S. I am a PhD student in anthropology at Rice university, interested incultural studies of science and technology.

———————

Article from Amy:

This group sounds like a good idea. I would be interested in it. The only drawback I see is that it would be likely to be plagued by flamewars, but at least they'd be interesting. :)

Amy

I don't know where this opinion is, but I know it's mine.
"Conventionality is not morality. Self-righteousness is not religion."—Charlotte Bronte

———————

Article from D:

I would be very interested by this group.

| "Je vis dans l'approximatif
| je m'en rapproche de plus en plus"
| Julos Beaucarne

———————

message

BBSs were inspired by alternative visions on social organization such as grass-roots movements. The USENET tried to expand or appropriate this alternative vision to an Internet/Bitnet-accessible medium making the medium "global" in its usage.

As close relatives to the widely accessible USENET newsgroups there are alternative newsgroups that have their own hierarchy, alt*. These are not as widely reachable, even though they can be created by anybody who has enough memory, and procedures for their creation are easier. The difference between the USENET and the alt groups reflect that of social groups with serious agenda and the ones with more idiosyncratic interests.

The USENET newsgroups create communities of liminal space where a participant is called a user with a specific ID (these are unique per user), but not of one identity (an individual can be many users with different IDs). *User* is becoming an important term, not only on these newsgroups but also as a widespread marketing signifier. *Consumer* is a more familiar term that is associated with consumer goods, things that are of short term values— not durable, reusable. *User* is related to sharing time, space, hardware, software, and work (work-station). *User* is frequently used to mark the reciprocal quality of interaction.

Users log in, that is, they invoke a software to be able to view the newsgroup articles and browse through them. They may become lurkers and only view postings or decide to play and post some article of their own by

Article from Z:

This could be an interesting newsgroup. I'd like to know what scientists say about things that are not yet explainable scientifically.

For example:
Recently I read a book on Ramtha; a barbarian-turned-an-enlightened-manwho spoke through a medium JZ Knight. One of the sections in the book explains about ascension (my dictionary says: bodily ascent of Christ to heaven). Ramtha says that ascension can be achieved when someone has activated all his/her brain functions. (Scientists say than people only use 5% of their brains.) The brain can operate fully if the pituitary gland has 'opened'; i.e.: it can secrete all the hormones (or enzymes?) it's supposed to produce. The nice fact is that everybody has a pituitary gland, so basically people can ascent too.

One of the benefits of ascension is that people can go back and forth between this world and heaven, if they feel like to go back here, along with their current bodies. So that they don't have to go through the birthing process.

Ramtha says that all matters in the universe has their own frequencies. A person can sit on a chair because their frequencies are almost the same; the frequency of solids. If a person can make his/her bodily frequency higher, by 'opening' his/her pituitary gland, then s/he can go into the other realms where the frequencies are much higher.

going through subjects, choosing one that they like and responding to it. Users mark the virtual space by logging on. However, only the players mark the space of the news group by posting articles. The lurkers mark the space only in their locality. Thus the navigation terms are used since the space does not consist of physical grids but markers that simulate one.

Community *mise en abyme*

The structure of this title [confrontation] corresponds to a classical type, the title that does not present the thing or the act but announces that one is going to treat it: of confrontation. "Confrontation" not in order to give rise to confrontations, to organize or present them, but in order to treat in a way that is oblique, on the bias, divergent, profiled, the lure or the impossibility which have as their name "confrontation." "Confrontation" is here our object rather than the scene or the event which occupies us. (Derrida 1987)

"Real" is enacted. The difference between the real in a book and the real in the BBSs is that in the latter the real is performed. The experience of the player (audience-actors) as they participate in the v-real is different from the participation in the r-real in that it takes place in a liminal space. As Derrida says (1987), participation in a *société a résponsabilité limitée* is bonded by each associate's extent of investment. Nevertheless this bond is not simply based on common interest.

If modern scientists can devise an apparatus that can make the 'opening' at a touch of a button, that would be nice. Would that be some sort of a time machine? First, you ascent to heaven, stay for a while, and then go back here far in the future or in the past.

Mazyar Lotfalian wrote:
>Request for Discussion:
>This is to suggest a news group
>that can bring scientists and engi-
>neer of different cultural back-
>ground together debating/con-
>fronting the issues on culture/
>tradition, science, religion, gender
>and education.

I hope they wouldn't only be scientists and engineers, but students too . . .

> The intention and content of this
>news group:
>1-The intention could be to encour-
>age exchange of opinion, informa-
>tion, and have access to each oth-
>er's experiences as engineers and
>scientists.

I'd like to see this newsgroup to be a place where the 'Eastern' and 'Western' thoughts can meet so that people can have more insights about those two worlds.

>2-The content could be constituted
>of a range of issues from religious
>to secular, biographical, woman
>and science, technological ad-
>vances, to day-to-day events.

I hope that religious people don't use this newsgroup to advertise that their religions are the best of all and put hard efforts to prove that by quoting

As he puts it, this is based on *faux-bond* (it shows itself as shared but in reality it is a false tie).

In traditional Freudian psychoanalysis, group therapy is also based on the idea of a homogeneous community. A shared exchange is implied; the group is governed by the theory of psychoanalysis, under its rule of truth. Transference and countertransference occur between the analyst and analysand. This picture changes under the *société a résponsabilité limitée.*

The interdiction according to which one cannot leave the group therapy is based on transcendental status of community. This changes when Derrida suggests a group based on confrontation that is constituted on *faux-bond.* Here, bond and band are interchangeable. Instead of transference, *tranche*-ference occurs, which means that the person can leave group A and join group B. *Tranche* in French means truncating (as a verb), but also *une tranche* means the period of time spent in analysis. *Tranche*-ference is based on *faux-bond,* but "is the association ever free"? No, but the relation between analyst and analysand expands and multiplies. Furthermore, there is a similarity between *tranche* and trance (homonyms) which can suggest another line of thought, the connection of *trance* and community.

The BBS "community" is the space of truncating transference where the players confront each other by chopping off each other's text and avoiding

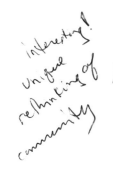

interesting! Unique of rethinking community

this and that verses from their holy books. It would be better if they emphasize on the verses of nature's phenomena and discuss them from the scientific point of view.

>Regards mazyar

| "The vacuum is far from empty. On the contrary,
| it contains an unlimited number of particles
| which come into being and vanish without end."
| - Fritjof Capra, The Tao of Physics

In article xxxxx Z writes
>This could be an interesting news-
>group. I'd like to know what scien-
>tists say about things that are not
>yet explainable scientifically.

As a scientist, I'd be very interested in such a group—potentially. If the group is for scientists and interested laypeople to talk about what it's like to do science (and I'm happy with broad notions of what science is. But if it develops into a forum for "[your discipline here] isn't a science!" arguments, or, if any significant part of it will be dedicated to generic "challenges" to generic scientists to explain this week's pseudoscientific hobbyhorse, count me out. Case in point:

anything in the text that they choose to do away with. However, players can't "avoid" avoiding each other's text, since what is "said" is a consequence of reacting to what is already there. This avoidance leads either to a truncated transference or an "illusory dialogic." In BBS language, one can refer to them as "cross-posting" (in the former case) or "quoting" (in the latter case).

"For it is equally so that if the confines of interminability open the *tranche* onto the "outside" of the psychoanalytic (of the theory or of the practice or of the "movement"), but onto an outside such that the trance-ference, far from being impossible or forbidden, today finds itself overactivated, intensified, jammed up, then the consequences of this are massive and implacable. Political and more than political." (Derrida 1987)

The newsgroup (or bulletin board) is a community *mise en abyme* where trance-ference multiplies by leaving a group and cross-posting infinitely. It is not necessarily a scene of confrontation, although it could become one, through flame wars. The community has as its object confrontation, that is, it treats what is said through expanding and subversing the subject.

Speech or Text?

Roland Barthes, along with many modernist writers, especially structuralists, gives different and pluralist interpretations which in turn are unified under the whole. Gilles Deleuze

>For example:
>Recently I read a book on Ramtha;
>a barbarian-turned-an-enlightened-
>man who spoke through a medium
>JZ Knight. One of the sections in
>the book explains about ascension
>(my dictionary says: bodily ascent
>of Christ to heaven). Ramtha says
>that ascension can be achieved
>when someone has activated all
>his/her brain functions. (Scientists
>say than people only use 5% of
>their brains.) The brain can oper-
>ate fully if the pituitary gland has
>'opened'; i.e: it can secrete all the
>hormones (or enzymes?) it's sup-
>posed to produce. The nice fact
>is that everybody has a pituitary
>gland, so basically people can as-
>cent too.

If knuckleheaded crap like this gets taken with *any* seriousness in soc.culture.scientists, then anyone with any real work to do will just go do it and blow the group off permanently. I sure as *hell* will. Somehow I doubt if I'm alone. If you want a soc.culture.scientists that is simply another cranks-vs-skeptics flamefest, go ahead. But if you want a place where a serious discussion of science and scientists is possible, there have to be some safeguards in place.

"Ramtha". Sheesh.

Article from Y:

RJ writes:
>In article xxxxx Z writes:
>>This could be an interesting
>>newsgroup. I'd like to know what
>>scientists say about things

and Felix Guattari problematize this modernist project in *A Thousand Plateaus* by suggesting a rhizomatic writing, a matter which I consider below. Moreover, Derrida refers to cryptanalysis as a way of doing "grammatology." He also suggests that writing, or book-writing, privileges speech over writing. Derrida's *Post Card* may be illuminating for bulletin board writing as the boundary between speech and writing is blurred.

"First of all, roughly speaking, here is what falls into the trap of scription (this word, pedantic though it may be, is preferable to writing: writing is not necessarily the mode of existence of what is written). It is evident, in the first place, that we lose an innocence; not that speech is in itself, natural, spontaneous, truthful, expressive of a kind of pure interiority; quite on the contrary, our speech (especially in public) is immediately theatrical, it borrows its turns (in the stylistic and ludic senses of the term) from a whole collection of cultural and oratorical codes." (Barthes 1985:4)

Barthes draws a difference between "speech" and "transcription" in the shift in image repertoires: that of the body and that of thought. Speech is always exposed, it is immediate and cannot be taken back. Therefore the speaker needs to calculate the words before they come out. It is theatrical in that it has to perform for an immediate audience. Whereas in transcribed speech, there is enough time for the composer to censure him or herself.

>>that are not yet explainable
>>scientifically.

>As a scientist, I'd be very inter-
>ested in such a group—potentially.
>If the group is for scientists and
>interested laypeople to talk about
>what it's like to do science (and I'm
>happy with broad notions of what
>science is.

I think that sci.research and sci. research.careers cover those issues adequately.

>But if it develops into a forum for
>"[your discipline here] isn't a sci-
>ence!" arguments, or, if any signifi-
>cant part of it will be dedicated to
>generic "challenges" to generic
>scientists to explain this week's
>pseudoscientific hobbyhorse, count
>me out. Case in point:

>[Z's   mystical   gobbledy-gook
>deleted]

The original RFD (already expired at my site, damn) talks about some supposedly prominent scientists who advocate a "blurring" of the boundaries between science and religion. Ick. Thought we gave that up centuries ago. Who are these "scientists", anyway?

Both science and especially technology probably are influenced by cultural and other such factors. It is probably interesting to discuss how that happens, and it is also perhaps interesting to discuss whether it is a good thing in specific instances. However, the wording in the proposal

The usage of transition is also lost in transcription, all those "buts" and "therefores" that come in handy in speech. The body also disappears in speech when transcribed. All those tricks that make the listener keep up with the speaker, such as spontaneous jokes, are lost.

Transcription changes everything. Those transitions such as *but* and *therefore* yield to syntactical relations. The text becomes more hierarchical, the message takes a structure of an idea. A new image repertoire appears which Barthes calls thought. "Wherever there is a concurrence of spoken and written words, to write means in a certain manner: I think better, more firmly; I think less for you, I think more for the 'truth' " (6). In mass communication, this form of writing is widespread, the goal of it is not to persuade but to present the public with a proposition (or position); this is not an argument but a position. It is a staging of ideas.

Barthes goes on to draw the difference between writing and written:

"Writing is not speech, and this separation has received a theoretical consecration these past few years; but neither is writing the written, transcription; to write is not to transcribe. In writing, what is too present in speech (in a hysterical fashion) and too absent from transcription (in a castratory fashion), namely the body, returns, but along a path which is indirect, measured, musical, and, in a word, right, returning through pleasure, and not through the Imaginary

for the group seems to presume that it is desirable for science to be polluted by arbitrary cultural, political, or religious factors. Galileo, Darwin, and Lysenko come to mind. Removing that presumptive wording would be an improvement.

Of course, in practice the newsgroup will probably just devolve into a flame fest about fetal tissue research, animal rights, genetic engineering ethics, and so forth. Despite the existence of plenty of newsgroups for those discussions.

Y

———————

Article from A:

Z writes:

>This could be an interesting news-
>group. I'd like to know what scien-
>tists say about things that are not
>yet explainable scientifically.

———————

Then take it to alt.physics.new-theories and please DON'T pollute soc.culture.scientists, a group I would very much like to read.

I agree with the other poster that merits of one science over another oughtn't be discussed, and suggest that the charter reflect this - obviously there are more appropriate newsgroups.

A

(the image) . . . speech, the written, and writing engage a separate subject each time, and the reader—the listener—must follow this divided subject, different depending on whether he speaks, transcribes, or formulates." (6–7)

In bulletin board writing, on the one hand, the absence of the "real body" induces a lack of inhibition or a problem such as flame war. On the other hand, the virtual body returns, in multitude forms, through signatures and a variety of camouflages— actually through the imaginary rather than what Barthes calls pleasure. This way of communication is neither speech nor writing but a combination of both in the sense that is described above.

Signs/Signatures as Markers of Presence/Absence

The BBS writing is neither speech nor text but a combination of pictorial, phonetic, and textual sign. This is evident in signatures, titles, and pseudonames. They create a kind of sign that I call hieroglyphic, which refers to picto-phone aspects of the sign. For instance, the signatures or the sign language (such as this: [:)] which indicates a smiling face) intend to bring the body back into the language. Cryptography, on the other hand, refers to different ways that a message can be secured and protected: It involves "crypting" and "decrypting" a message or a sign.

[handwritten margin note: graphic artifact]

[handwritten margin note: assumption of message still]

Article from P

> If knuckleheaded crap like this gets
> taken with *any* seriousness in
> soc.culture.scientists, then anyone
> with any real work to do will just
> go do it and blow the group off
> permanently.

I also don't like New Age attempts to exploit scientific concepts that have been poorly learned by people who, in general, pick out two or three "neat" ideas to validate their religious belief and then toss the rest of the integrated experimental/theoretical web of understanding into the trash, condemning it with the ultimate epithet of being "Western."

Some topics I am interested in discussing are: the future of the scientific elite vs. realistic goals of raising the overall scientific understanding among a general population (of course, I must mean America, where we are so dependent on high technology and so lazy about the education necessary to maintain the cycle of creation of new technologies) Also: cultural images of scientists vs. public desire to learn science (here I am thinking of typical American idea of scientist: Mr. Spock - half human, irritating object of condescension by "normal man" Kirk; social outcast in lab coat plotting to blow up world because girl laughed at his zits and taped glasses; Dr. Frankenstein)

Is this image part of our "cult of genius", i.e., the attitude that science is not really long hours of hard work, some people are weird and not com-

I choose "hieroglyphic" as a way for reading signs on the bulletin boards. What presupposes my assertion here is that phonetic- and alphabetic-based language turns to a hieroglyphic sign where the signification is to be deciphered through hieroglyphic reading. For example, consider the naming of a file, such as soc.culture.scientists. In this naming the attempt has been made to convey as much as possible about the content of the label. The sign here is a compound one that is not based on phonetic or alphabetic writing but on pictorial representation. It is a montage of several "topos" to create a more encompassing topos. The space increases only to become irrelevant to the subject: the subject or the title is not bound to a particular place. The sign is hieroglyphic in that each constituent adds a signification of its own and does not make a distinct phonetic sign. At first it seems that one gives an "arbitrary" name to it, so one does. But how can one explicate this arbitrariness? The signs in creation of this fictive space are important. Can we read these signs semiotically? Or could we find an alternative way of reading them?

Derrida ties his understanding of hieroglyphics to speech and phonetics by arguing that these forms of signs are primary, contrary to book writing, which is secondary signification. Derrida argues against Saussure's assertion that the signification happens somewhere between the concept and the sound, with no direct relation to either of those. He wants to relate

pletely human and they just have the "gift" of scientific genius and it all comes naturally to their mutant brains, while the non-scientists believe they themselves are normal, not genetic freaks, and therefore they can never learn science or math and so never have to be BOTHERED by the fact that they don't even *TRY* to learn.

I think this has a lot to do with the "Tao of Physics" syndrome. Anyways, there are things that I am interested in discussing. However, if any of these discussion have to involve the words "knuckleheaded crap" or similar angry types of insults and unprofessional behavior, then I don't want to invest much of my time here. I don't hear people talk this way when they are face-to-face.

This group could in principle be good, but that's true about many groups that wind up being taken over by a small number of aggressive people with something to prove and a foul vocabulary to display. And so many of them probably act like well spoken, reasonable people when they logout.

Oh well, hope for the best!

P

———————————

Article from M

In article xxxx P writes:
>This group could in principle be
>good, but that's true about many
>groups that wind up being taken
>over by a small number of aggres-
>sive people with something to prove

the signification to both sound and concept.

Hieroglyphic: Gregory Ulmer (Applied Grammatology): . . . Grammatology, that is, was founded in the eighteenth century as a science of decipherment of nonalphabetic scripts—most specifically, the decipherment of Egyptian hieroglyphics. Theoretical grammatology (the second stage of the science of writing) could be characterized as a "new Egyptology," being a writing modeled upon the works of the two principal decipherers of the modern world—Champollion and Freud (himself, of course, a collector of Egyptian artifacts). (Ulmer 1985: 17)

Theoretical grammatology adopts hieroglyphic writing as a model, translating it into a discourse, producing thus in philosophy distortions similar to those achieved in those movements, labeled "cubist" and "primitivist," which drew on the visual arts of non-Western cultures in order to deconstruct the look of logocentrism. (ibid: 18)

Stephen Tyler, on the other hand, talks about signification as it is not only imposed in advance but also is tied to text through phono-logocentric tradition. He differs on this point from Derrida in that he does not tie the signification to speech but to a "saying-showing" where the meanings get created through a performance:

Alphabetic Writing: Stephen Tyler (Prolegomena to the Next Linguis-

>and a foul vocabulary to display.
>And so many of them probably act
>like well spoken, reasonable people
>when they logout.

Why not have a moderated group?

M

_____

Article from C:

In article xxxx M writes:
>In article xxx P writes:
>>This group could in principle be
>>good, but that's true about many
>>groups that wind up being taken
>>over by a small number of ag-
>>gressive people with something
>>to prove and a foul vocabulary to
>>display.
>
>Why not have a moderated group?

Because when only a small number of the users "take over" a group, the problem is better solved with a kill file.

Soc.culture.scientists ought to be unmoderated so that:
1) Discussion occurs at the rate of transmission instead of at the rate at which the moderator approves articles
2) The group doesn't die the horrible death of becoming moderatorless
3) We can at least see whether—once a clear charter is established—people actually do post an unrea-

tic, 1993, paper presented to the Fifth Bienneal Symposium of the Dept. of Linguistic, P.8, Rice University):

. . . alphabetic writing will play only a minor role in communication perhaps, or the one-word, bold-face directions like Go and Stop, or to compound words in which all syntactic functions have been condensed into semantically rich Logo-Forms and acronym like "radar," whose constituents will have been long forgotten. Such writing as there will have been then will have been a combination of logo-writing, picto-writing, and phono-writing, with the latter playing an ever decreasing role.

As liminal places newsgroups do not create a closed semiotic space, but one that marks crossovers of different signs and languages. To read a sign one has to pay attention to performative aspects, the way it was created and what was involved in its creation, since the meaning is performed through crossovers of sign and languages.

The first element to be viewed by the reader of an article is the "subject" heading as a sign. The evocative aspect of this sign, for it to be reacted to by a wider group of people, is tied to its viewing by different users from different cultures and linguistic backgrounds. For instance, a subject heading "Salman Rushdie" is likely to be read and reacted to by diverse group of users—for each evokes a different thing. Therefore, the more a sign is

sonably large number of irrelevant articles.

Unfortunately, I've mailed my ideas of what should go in the charter to Mazyar, without saving a copy—I'll post them or perhaps he'll take care of that for me, eventually. The portion of that letter I'd especially like to repeat here limits description of particular scientific/alternative/whatever theories to being minor points in a larger description of the social context in which that theory was been produced.

People who show clear disregard for the charter deserve all the flames they'll get, and repeat offenders might show up in a monthly post of my kill-file for the group (along with brief instructions on how to use killfiles with the most popular newsreaders).

Sound good?

"Homer deserves to be thrown out of the contests and flogged."
—Heraclitus

———————————

Article from S:

In article xxxx C writes:
>
>People who show clear disregard
>for the charter deserve all the

semiotically narrowed (closed), the less is the likelihood of it being read by diverse groups of people.

Moreover, the signature becomes increasingly important in computer writing. First, because the texts are cooperatively produced, thus the access to the author is through the signature. Secondly, the author's signature marks both the presence of many identities and the absence of a main author.

Rhizomatic Character

Deleuze and Guattari, in *A Thousand Plateaus,* talk about three types of book. First, what they call root-book is like the Platonic idea of book, tree-like. It starts from the idea and branches out into the roots, the topos. The book itself is the image of the world, or the world-tree. This is the classical book in which the signification is created on the level of the subject. These authors describe another type in which the signification happens on the level of the object. They mention Nietzsche's aphorism which shatters the linear unity of knowledge, only to invoke the cyclic unity of the eternal return. This type is a modernist method for making multiplicity the center of their project. By adding a new dimension each time, this type of writing would not stop at one point but increases the level of complexity.

However, modernist writing does not rid itself of being united as a higher idea. The most fragmentary forms can unite under a unifying whole. Deleuze and Guattari suggest a third way of writing, rhizomatically:

>flames they'll get, and repeat of-
>fenders might show up in a monthly
>post of my killfile for the group
>(along with brief instructions on
>how to use killfiles with the most
>popular newsreaders).
>
>Sound good?

Not entirely. Your offer to show people how to use a kill file is most welcome, no doubts there. However, your comment on flaming being okay seems directly opposed to one of the things P wrote about (re: net behavior), and I agree with her entirely on that count. As sad a statement as this is about Usenet, more than anything else we need to avoid the starting of flame wars: nothing kills a newsgroup more swiftly or effectively than flames do.

In addition, consider this. The flamers go into the kill file. The file gets posted. The flamers see their names mentioned, and they begin to flame the kill file itself. Ad infinitum.

Article from P:

>In article xxxx P writes:
>>This group could in principle be
>>good, but that's true about many
>>groups that wind up being taken
>>over by a small number of ag-
>>gressive people with something
>>to prove and a foul vocabulary to
>>display. And so many of them
>>probably act like well spoken,
>>reasonable people when they
>>logout.

>Why not have a moderated group?

"A rhizome has no beginning or end; it is always in the middle, between things, interbeing, intermezzo. The tree is filiation, but the rhizome is alliance, uniquely alliance. The tree imposes the verb "to be," but the fabric of the rhizome is the conjunction, "and . . . and . . . and . . ." This conjunction carries enough force to shake and uproot the verb "to be." Where are you going? Where are you coming from? What are you heading for? These are totally useless questions. Making a clean slate, starting or beginning again from ground zero, seeking a beginning or a foundation—all imply a false conception of voyage and movement." (Deleuze and Guattari 1993:25)

Bulletin board writing seems to have a rhizomatic element, for there is no beginning, no end, all happens in the middle. In *The Post Card* Derrida, however, talks about the beginning, the first card, as the "superego." The original loses its originality by the manipulating, cutting, and adding of subsequent writers. Derrida describes the original message as a "superego" in *Envois*.

The first article in a newsgroup generally sets the virtual space for others to confront. A "thread" can be started with a first article on certain subject with all others referencing this first one. For example:

Article: 130 of soc.culture.scientists
Path: xxxx
From:xxx
Newsgroups: soc.culture.scientists

> M

Is this hard to do? I am completely ignorant in these matters. I am very interested in participating in his kind of group, though. I have a lot of things I'd like to discuss on the issue of gender, as well.

For instance, I don't think discrimination - either active or passive/unconscious/subconscious - is completely responsible for the lack of women in physics and other hard sciences.

I think it's because scientists are as marginalized and demoted from full human status in American culture as women and some non-European people are. Who wants to be doubly marginal?

I see a lot antipathy towards science by certain schools of feminism, and I think this is reflecting mainstream hostility toward science, not beginning some new kind of progressive thinking.

I also think that the way we mythologize people like Einstein and Hawking is counter-productive. They are worshipped as genetic freaks, superhuman beings, not part of normal humn society.

Not everything they have done in physics has been correct or even in the right direction. Their success came from choosing the right problems, having a crucial insight, and

Subject: Magical Thinking
Date: 11 Sep 1993 02:26:24 GMT
Organization: California Institute of
Technology,
Pasadena
Lines: 17
Message-ID: xxx

By the way, I think that all models and
paradigms and formalisms stem from
our capacity for "magical thinking."

The observables we measure do not
care whether we calculated them believing in the Feynman path integral
or just in the S-matrix.

-patricia

PS I don't mean to start a gender war,
but there is saying:

"Objectivity is just male subjectivity."

and in place of "male" you may put
"Western" or "academic" or whom-
ever you feel is imposing their subjective notion of objective scientific for-
malism on your own life!

This is an example of the beginning
of a thread; subsequent postings followed the thread of "Magical Thinking," which creates that initial energy
for confrontation. It sets not a scene
but an evocative "thing" which haunts
the entire thread. It is like what Derrida called a superego for a postcard.

then working very hard. It didn't come
from outer space or the wisdom of
ancient civilizations. It came from
acting like a normal human being trying to solve a problem.

Is anyone else interested this kind of
discussion?

P

_____

Article from M:

In article xxxx C writes:
>[lots of stuff deleted]
>Sound good?

Yes. I think the newsgroup in itself is
a good idea. I am somewhat bivalent
about moderation of newsgroups - it
has its good side and its bad side. If
there are strong feelings about not
moderating then I wouldn't mind letting it go. If it becomes REALLY necessary, we might try for a vote to
moderate the newsgroup?

M

_____

Article from C:

In article xxxx S writes:
>In article xxxx C writes:
>>
>>People who show clear disregard
>>for the charter deserve all the
>>flames they'll get, and repeat
>>offenders might show up in a
>>monthly post of my killfile for the
>>group (along with brief instruc-
>>tions on how to use killfiles with
>>the most popular newsreaders).
>>

Reflections on creation of a newsgroup

The choice of a name

Choosing a name for a newsgroup is generally framed first by the possibility that the existing USENET hierarchy offers. That is, there are five major USENET group hierarchies; comp, sci, soc, talk, and news. They each represent a major arbitrary thematic category; for instance, comp stands for issues related to computer. They each are followed by a sub category separated with a dot. For instance, comp.ai is dedicated to the issues concerning artificial intelligence. This subcategorization can be continued by dividing each sub with a dot.

Secondly, the framing of a name depends on availability of a previous group that can possibly approximate the agenda of the group being formed. This agenda can be suggested (Request for Discussion) and a discussion will generally address this issue. However, the discussion by users can not always be conclusive due to the fact that the agendas overlap and the categories are not mutually exclusive.

Lastly, the naming depends on a demographic knowledge of people who participate in different hierarchies. It means that by combining a topic and several subtopics one needs to create a name that draws, intrigues, and stimulates large numbers of people and minimizes the amount of opposition. The final vote depends on this choice since many voters might have only screened the charter

>Not entirely. Your offer to show
>people how to use a kill file is most
>welcome, no doubts there. How-
>ever, your comment on flaming
>being
okay seems directly opposed to
>one of the things Patricia Schwartz
>wrote about

What, is the 'r' key on your terminal broken? ;) Seriously, yes, I should have made clear that I meant they'd "deserve all the flames they'll get [via email]"

Personally, I often send mail to people who post inappropriately to groups with a low signal-to-noise ratio if I care about the signal; it's just something you do if you want your group to stay 'clean'.

This does NOT mean I advocate mail-bombing anyone for any reason—I don't send mail to people who've obviously attracted the opprobrium of the entire Usenet community (with repeated posts of the same article, or whatever).
>In addition, consider this. The flam-
>ers go into the kill file. The file gets
>posted. The flamers see their names
>mentioned, and they begin to flame
>the kill file itself. Ad infinitum.

This is only a problem if you can't use said killfile. :)

Killfiles I've seen posted to other groups attract few flames . . . Even the most insipid of users can figure out that the people he or she is flam-

and been intrigued by the effect of the name.

Charter, Moderating a Group, FAQ; Off Newsgroup Contacts (e-mail Exchanges); Players and Lurkers

What are the (ideological) elements that make a news group tick?

For each newsgroup, the charter is supposed to set a standard, a rule of what is allowed and what is not, and according to which people can post their articles. Although the charter sets the rules, the gray area is large. Newsgroups vary in their agenda, some are information oriented (e.g., soc.culture.india.info), others are interested in a specific issue (e.g., comp.pc.laptop [fictive]), and yet there are others that are more general (e.g., soc.culture*). The more we move away from the narrowly focused newsgroups to broadly oriented ones, the more we face the fact that the interpretation of a charter becomes problematic. That is, deciding on what article does or doesn't fit the group becomes more difficult.

This is when deciding on whether a newsgroup should be moderated or not becomes crucial. Moderation refers to filtering out the articles before they actually appear on the bulletin board. It involves a reachable location and someone who has enough memory on their hardware and interest in interpreting the charter. The moderators are not generally popular people.

Historically, the USENET newsgroups that are more specifically ori-

ing can't read their flames if they generated that killfile!

I believe I also mentioned that people might be warned before they go into my killfile (via e-mail from me); if they want to flame me, that'd be the time to do it.

In any case, if
1) The charter is clear
2) People know how to use killfiles
3) People politely correct (via email) newbies on the purpose of the group
4) A FAQ is posted regularly
5) People are educated on the use of Followup-To: and Newsgroups: lines

the group will moderate itself in every way, just short of actually refusing to allow a given article to be posted. "Homer deserves to be thrown out of the contests and flogged."
—Heraclitus

————————

The following messages concern the charter itself and commentaries. The first one is the preliminary charter that was not posted and the second one is the charter that was posted (to compare), and there was only one comment. There are usually flame wars at this stage but it didn't happen for this newsgroup—partly a function of timing (not many people are at their terminals in August).

ented are advised to be moderated, as it is easier to decide what fits or what doesn't. Newsgroups with broader interest such as soc.culture* are advised to remain unmoderated. Most soc.religion* are moderated, strangely enough. This constantly causes flame wars on the one hand, and on the other hand there is always a fight over changing the moderators on the newsgroup. For example, there once was a movement to change the existing moderator of soc.religion.islam under the allegation that he had not been responsive to the fellow groupies. He responded at one point saying that "I am only responsive to Allah." Another instance that shows the problematic of virtual groups is the controversy over the creation of soc.culture.tibet. Soc.culture* groups are not advised to have moderators, but the creation of this group had become so controversial that the suggestion came through that this group should be moderated. The problem of Tibet, on the Net, as a category leaks to outside and its creation according to the Net rules was very much affected by the conflict over Tibet's political existence.

Another device to educate the participants is the FAQ (Frequently Asked Questions). This is usually a monthly posting which as its main task tries to answer what its title literally claims. It is, more importantly, used to create a *communitas* or maybe a common memory through which the groupies remind themselves of what is important or allowed in their group.

Suggested Chart for soc.culture.scientists:

_Name
soc.culture.scientists refers to contextualizing scientists in their milieu as they are always already situated in a social and cultural setting. Therefore the name reflects a decentering of scientists as "universal man" by situating them into the social setting, cultural background, and gender politics.

-What does qualify as a possible discussion?
(philosophical background and tenets)
The Enlightnement project in which the Western scientific discourse is rooted set up to rid itself of "tradition," that is any bias that would interfer with objectivity (such as religious bias). This tenet of the Western Enlightnment is taken for granted and replicated in most scientific discourse as objective vs. biased. When it comes to culture or gender politics the replication of this tenet manifest as culture/tradition and gender politics are biased and a "real" scientist should shy away from those categories. Therefore:
1-The news group, soc.culture.scientists, must not take objective vs. biased for granted when culture, tradition, and gender are discussed as part of science and scientific projects. This is to avoid labeling such as "you're religious, or this idea has nothing to do with science."

FAQ also has its limitation in that it is formatted as a document that contains information. This reduction to a database does not allow mediation over the content by the more experienced members of the group. Therefore the tradition is usually set by the individuals who are most active players.

There are often exchanges of e-mail among the players off the record of the bulletin board. These exchanges create more intimate knowledge of each other and some fragile consensus among some members which allows some orchestrated efforts to emphasize certain issues.

Soc.culture.scientists claims to be a home for non-Western scientists and women scientists. However, a survey shows that this ideological stand never materialized and those who post articles are by and large white male scientists. The number of female posters has drastically decreased since the conception of the newsgroup. I attribute this to the nonpromotional quality of this group. That is, all ideological elements thus far described have not been extensively used to promote the ideology of the group. Furthermore, this problem is a symptom of the larger concern that despite the large number of non-Western and women scientists, this virtual community cannot easily accommodate their participation and pushes them to the background.

-From what perspective do we discuss the issues?
Again, another tenet of the Western Enlightnment is to divide nature and culture, which resonates in division between natural sciences and human sciences. The academic divisions generally do not allow that an object of study be approached from different perspectives. Therefore:
2-The news group, soc.culture. scientists, must engage in an interdisciplinary study of social and cultural aspects of science and technology. Rather than imposing our own professional training, we should approach issues from different academic and intellectual backgrounds.

-What should be the focus of discussion?
The issues such as what is "real science" or "alternative science" should only lead to a flame war in a group such as soc.culture.scientists. The news group must not engage in defining what is science or who is a scientist, rather:
3-The news group, soc.culture. scientists, must engage in discussing the "real projects" or "school of thoughts" that respond to the Enlightnment and modernity (which might include religious challenges). Good examples that come to mind are collaborative projects of different scientists, education of scientists, and scientific projects.

-Knowledge and power are not separated. The political aspect of science can not be separated from the science and scientific projects. How-

Conclusion/Projections

The following is my e-mail inquiry and the responses that I have received concerning the newsgroupies' reaction to the group. I will submit my own conclusion and suggestions further below:

Warning: All Typos Are Original (not edited on purpose)

Hi
I am Mazyar Lotfalian who initiated the news group soc.culture.scientists. After a few months of on going activity on this news group, I am contacting you to get a feed back from you. I am writing a paper on this kind of community, known as virtual community, and am trying to get the opinion of many people who have participated at some level in creation of this news group. Your name came across as one of these people who might have posted, read, or had opinion about this news group.

Would you please take a minute and give me your reaction?

A couple of things came to my mind that might give you an impression of my thoughts:
-The charter of this group makes clear it that is interested in hearing voices of women scientists. Why is it then that more and more these voice have disappeared?

ever, this group is not a policy making group, the eccessive politiking might first, lead to flame war, secondly, overtake or overemphasize the political aspect.
4-The news group, soc.culture. scientists, must consider politic as inseparable from the science, but put the emphasis on cross-cultural.

Suggestion for the Charter for soc. culture.scientists:

Why "soc.culture.scientists"?
The soc.* hierarchy is home to many groups devoted to discussions of minority or regional issues (the soc. culture.* groups), as well as to groups interested in counterhegemonic (feminist) or other non-scientific, yet academic issues (e.g. soc.history).

Soc.culture.scientists is supposed to combine many of these currents in "soc" thought, providing a home for the serious discussion of how science has been affected by its own globalization.

The name of the group was chosen to reflect a decentering of the image of the scientist as a "universal man"—to acknowledge and accept as a valid concern scientists' social settings, cultural backgrounds, and genders.
Soc.culture.scientists explicitly encourages the scientists and engineers of different cultural background to participate in this newsgroup.

-The same thing about the non-Western scientists who have participated in voting for this group but their voices are virtually hidden?

-Some women poster are not posting as much anymore, what is the reason for that?

-Can you think of ways of correcting this or do you see an inherent problem in this kind of community?

Please send your email response to me:
mazyar@rice.edu

From:k.liddicott

Womens voices:
I disappeared because I don't have such frequent computer access anymore.

Also a few points I noted when I did have more frequent access (you're just lucky not to be waiting 4 weeks for a reply to this now)

a. there were a few very vocal women out there initially, who (though perhaps I was reading them wrongly) sounded as though they were verging on the hysterical, jumping down peoples throats etc at the slightest provocation. I can only speak for myself, but I don't like that kind of atmosphere. Give me something calm rational and interesting. there is also the fear that "if that's what women scientists are like I'd rather do without them". one author finished up in

What qualifies as a legitimate discussion?

—Discussion about the education of scientists and the effect of their cultural background on their scientific praxis.

—Discussions of scientific praxis in a cross-cultural perspective

—Discussions of the metanarratives from which certain ideas about objectivity and scientific rationality gain their authority

—Discussions of specific Big Science projects that demonstrate the globalizing processes of modernity (e.g. international research cooperatives)

—Discussions of social/technological developments that have tended to make scientific endeavors culturally heterogeneous

—Discussions about the actual projects, science cities, and collaboration of scientists (i.e., different countries).

—Posting news from around the world with inclusion of sources.

In general, anything which might be discussed at conferences or in academic programs devoted to science and technology studies, with the one major difference that this newsgroup automatically creates a culturally diverse context for the expression of personal viewpoints.

What does NOT qualify as a legitimate discussion?

This is tricky, because while discussions of the cultural contexts that have produced alternative scientific my kill file. however, more seriously there is an ingrained fear that all women will be tarred with the same brush, the vocal few giving everyone a bad name. It's silly of course, it needs the silent majority to speak out to rectify the image.

b. I participated in discussions tht interested me, and in some subjects didn't because I felt out of my depth. I'm a material scientist, and my knowledge of quantum mechanics and higher mathematics is cursary. a great many of the articles went into these subjects last time I got a chance to read it. I am interested in discussing these subjects, and I do have ideas. But my knowledge being limited I confess I was afraid of looking foolish. I didn't feel there was a sufficiently broad acceptance of people being igmorant in some areas and knowledgeable in others, to the extent that I could participate in a discussion about which I didn't know very much.

c. Not a great answer, but the stereotypical western male is not renowned for his listening skills. A great many things could have been discussed but appeared to be ignored after a first posting or two.

d. Perhaps men have more time to mess about on computers. I'm single, but if the proffesional women you are talking about have families then. . . . okay, the men have families too but do thy devote as much time to their families?

traditions such as (a lot of) X-Soviet Science and Vedic Science, etc., ought to be perfectly acceptable (insofar as they do not range into flamewars or simple-minded critiques of ideology), it is clear that this newsgroup should not be allowed to become a forum for the promulgation of highly eccentric, personal, "alternative" theories of science or the nature of the universe.

As a general rule, this is not the place for describing any scientific theory unless that description is being used as part of a larger description of the social context in which that theory was produced.

In short: We don't want to hear about why "time has inertia" or why certain crystals are good for my inner balance, but we wouldn't mind hearing about WHY "alternative" science enjoys some popularity today in many different places.

———————

Article: xxx of news.groups
Newsgroups: news.groups
Path: xxxxxx
From: DE
Subject: Re: A Draft Charter for soc.
culture.scientists
Message-ID:xxxxxxx
Organization: xxxxxxxx
X-Newsreader: TIN [version 1.1 PL8]
References: xxxxx
Date: Mon, 2 Aug 1993 21:10:56 GMT
Lines: 11

This would be a good place to discuss the strengths and weaknesses

e. As for correcting it . . . you can't force people to be more aware of everyone who is participating.

f. Finally, I was always curious about you. An anthropologist who appears to be studying the scientific community. It almost prevented me from signing up in the first place. Did I want to be studied? And it does make it difficult to take the group completely seriously. But I did think it was a great idea. What better way to study them than set up a group like this and watch. Perhaps I just have a susicious mind, but if anyone else had the same ideas . . . won't you have to account for that in your data?

I / __|I__
I/ ∧ I I-I I
N NI I I
I\ I _I_

_____

From:k.liddicott

An addition to my earlier comments; I've just caught up scanning the group, and ideas are fresh in my mind. The shear volume of information in daunting. And it was only the last 4 days worth. It was hard to follow the thread of the conversations with so many bits missing, and I skipped a lot. And because I can't follow the thread it's difficult to make any contribution at all.

of reductionism as a sole model for scuentists. Over the last fifteen years some prominent scholars have raised serious doubts about it. These include a past president of Yale and Houston Smith in his book 'Beyond the Post Modern Mind. The difference between the view of science in German speaking countries and English speaking countries is also something that could be discussed.

The proposal has a lot of potential.

DE

_____

The following messages came up after the CFV (Call for Vote) was posted. During this phase, the discussions on the charter are presumably wrapped up and everyone is ready to vote. The vote taking for this newsgroup was taken by an independent vote taker.

Original message was crossposted to:

] news.announce.newgroups,
] news.groups, sci.research.careers,
] soc.culture.french,
] soc.culture.indian,
] soc.culture.iranian,
] soc.culture.japan,
] soc.culture.pakistan,
] soc.religion.islam, soc.women
] soc.culture.arabic,
] soc.culture.asean,
] soc.culture.china,
] soc.culture.indonesia,
] soc.culture.jewish,
] soc.culture.korean,
] soc.culture.misc, soc.culture.soviet,
] soc.culture.turkish

There seems to be a wider range of topics being discussed now, which is nice. But, I just don't have the time to read them all properly.

The group doesn't seem very friendly though.

```
| / ___| |___
|/∧ | I-| |
N \| | | |
|\ | _|_
```

From:dyer
Hi.
First, I'm not really a scientist. I have a Bachelor's in Physics from Bryn Mawr College. I work as a computer scientist at Lawrence Livermore National Laboratory _with_ scientists.

I read the group for a couple of weeks. Why did I stop?

~ Each news group has its own personality. This one seemed to be interested in arguing for the sake of arguing. That can be fun and informative, to a point. But I find a steady diet of it to be unpleasant and a complete waste of my time.

~ There seemed to be little _communicating_ going on.

... and in it [independent vote-taker] writes:

>　　CALL FOR VOTES (1st of 2)

>Unmoderated group soc.culture.
>scientists
>
>Newsgroups line:
>soc.culture.scientists　Cultural is-
>sues about scientists & scientific
>projects.

.
.
.

>CHARTER

>Why "soc.culture.scientists"?
>_____
>The soc.* hierarchy is home to
>many groups devoted to discus-
>sions of minority or regional issues
>(the soc.culture.* groups), as well
>as to groups interested in counter-
>hegemonic (feminist) or other non-
>scientific, yet academic issues (e.g.
>soc.history).

>Soc.culture.scientists is supposed
>to combine many of these currents
>in "soc" thought, providing a home
>for the serious discussion of how
>science has been affected by its
>own globalization.

>The name of the group was chosen
>to reflect a decentering of the im-
>age of the scientist as a "universal
>man"—to acknowledge and accept
>as a valid concern scientists' social
>settings, cultural backgrounds, and
>genders. Soc.culture.scientists ex-
>plicitly encourages the scientists
>and engineers of different cultural
>background to participate in this
>newsgroup.

~ The favorite topic of conversation seemed to be about the existence (or lack thereof) of God. If I want to discuss religion, I'll go to alt.atheism or soc.religion. (Just for the record, I am a practicing Christian.)

Hope this helps . . .

"Time has little to do with infinity and jelly doughnuts." |

From: lefevre

Hi,
I as very interested in the creation of s.c.s, but I was really desapointed by the first debates there. I have to declare myself partly guilty because I did not post there.

I did not post for (IMHU) the same reason why the non-western scientist voice is hidden. (maybe I am an non western scientist myself as a French post-doc living in Germany:-). The reason is obviously my BAD american. I did not spend enough time in school doing foreign language, basically because I had to learn sciences, and it is not so easy itself. Now I have also to spend some time doing german.

I am very desapointed to see what s.c.s became. Mostly a place to argue about the meaning of the word relativ-

Is it just me, or does anybody else feel that there is a procedural problem here, in that this call for votes was only posted to one relatively insignificant sci.* group? It would seem to me that any proposal for the creation of a group whose purpose is to talk about scientists should be posted to the groups that scientists actually read. I gather that the RFD was not posted to (m)any sci.* groups either.

I am also curious why [independent vote-taker] felt that this proposal was more relevant to the readers of soc.religion.islam and soc.women than to the readers of any of the sci.* groups besides sci.research.careers.

Perhaps this whole proposal should be bounced back to the RFD stage, with the RFD crossposted to an *appropriate* selection of groups this time.

| Do not be alarmed.
| Be very, very frightened!

Article from #2

In article xxxx #1 writes:
> Is it just me, or does anybody
> else feel that there is a procedural
> problem here, in that this call for
> votes was only posted to one rela-
> tively insignificant sci.* group?

IMHO, this CFV *could* have legitimately been posted to all of sci.*, but since discussions of the sort for which this group is intended are rare in the sci.* hierarchy as a whole yet fairly common in the soc.* hierarchy, I'd

ism, or so. Even if I am able to understand most of the point, and sometime to have idea about them, the level of the language used, detered me to post. I know that somebody can flame because of poor usage of one word, or (worst) that I can not explain my thought because of not so precise meaning of words in american.

I know some russian and polish guy who thinks the same.

In others words, I felt sometimes a non-western scientist or to say a non native-US speaker scientist, and in a such philosophical group it's a fatal drawback.

Maybe I can lunch this thread on s.c.s, but not now due to 2 weeks beamtime coming tomorrow :-)
I don't think it will be a very successful thread.

As a matter of comparison, I don't feel the presure of language in group related to computer sciences like soc.culture.computer, or in sci.physics.particle, or .accelerator

Considering the women, it's a bit difficult to say. We don't have such a PC thinking in europe, (I believe the situation of minorities is better in Europe, so we don't urge it) and laws are trying to negates differences.

say the net has already sifted out which readers are most interested in this sort of thing.

The list of newsgroups to which this CFV was posted accurately reflects which readership populations tend to bring up cultural issues in their discussions of science. If you read very many soc.culture.* groups and sci.* groups, you've doubtless seen this in action: soc.culture.* folks very often discuss big science projects going on in their country; the status of science education in their country compared to others; their own education at home and abroad . . .
Similar topics occasionally arise in sci.research.careers (even through such discussion is clearly motivated by the third term in the group's name :), but not very often in other sci.* groups. (Just my impression . . . feel free to correct me if you know of some sci newsgroup where this otherwise itinerant topic has a regular home)

In fact, the only newsgroup I would add to the list is sci.anthropology—but for a reason very different from the one you're using to justify adding other sci groups!

> It would seem to me that any pro-
> posal for the creation of a group
> whose purpose is to talk about sci-
> entists should be posted to the
> groups that scientists actually read.

Maybe so . . . but your guess is only as good as mine, in this case. The groups listed above have demonstrated that they have readers who

I remember well the flame-war triggered by Patricia Schwartz. I never wrote my european way of thinking (mostly agree with patricia about the diagnostic but desagree about the way of saying it, and the way to cure abuses) just because a flame-war in such a subject with my poor american is almost a suicide :-) I archived some of the post about the subject, but I do not have time to browse them now to explain my feeling about.

Also women are not so many in sciences. I don't have time yet to give you my feeling about it. They are just hidden by the number in s.c.s as in real lab's life.

Also the number of post in too high. Too many post to read, and too many times the same arguments. I did try to read almost all thread for a long time, but I stopped in january.

I hoped to find in this group more scientists concerned with the impact of science in society, not philosopher arguing about some theories about how science SHOULD works.

Of course I have no cure :-0, but if it can help you in finding a diagnostic, I didn't lost my time.

Amities (~ friendship in French)

best wishes

---

might like to participate on soc. culture.scientists—or at least crosspost relevant info about their own countries, cultures, or experiences.

The sci hierarchy might be good for negative feedback, and I'm sure there are readers of sci newsgroups interested in cultural studies of science (even if they aren't talking about such things anywhere); however, the sci.* readership demonstrates primarily an interest in discussing scientific theories (of course! :)—which is taboo on the proposed group, except insofar as it is required to trace the sociocultural production of those theories.

>I am also curious why [mazyar@
>rice.edu] felt that this proposal was
>more relevant to the readers of
>soc.religion.islam and soc.women
>than to the readers of any of the
>sci.* groups besides sci.research.
>careers.

The relevance of the newsgroups to which this CFV was posted stems from the demonstrated tendency those groups have towards discussing issues which might be better served with a new newsgroup, soc.culture. scientists. I believe this was mentioned in the justification of the group's name posted during the RFD period and re-posted with the CFV.

I don't think the sci hierarchy has any parallel justification; rather, I'd say your observations are based on good old common sense. No problem with that except that it fails to reveal the counterintuitive truth that people on soc.women (see the recent "Women in Physics" and "Woman astronaut

From: k.liddicott

Hi,

Thanks for the reply. I would be really interested in hearing any of your conclusions.

One thing I forgot to mention that I was thinking about again last night re: my interactions here in the department with my peers. I don't know if it's relevant but I get on far better with the guys from a nonwestern culture, eg. Korea, Japan, China than the english guys here. Communication seems to be more open, that is perhaps that they actually appear to be listening. Furthermore general interaction and chatting with these guys is more comfortable. General chatting with the english guys is strained at best, they don't relax at all, and it makes scientific communication a lot more onerous. That's because if I do have something to contribute to the research group that would be of benefit to them, initiating the conversation is a big effort. It doesn't come about from general interaction. From my observation,and talking with one of them, the nonwestern guys also find the same problem with the english guys.

As for who is to blame, if blame can be attached I am not sure.

Anyway, your research all sounds very interesting.

tour" messages) and soc.religion. islam (see the recent "Number Theory in Islam" and the zealous but still interesting and relevant "THE IMPORTANCE OF ACQUIRING & SPREADING KNOWLEDGE" messages) discuss issues appropriate to soc.culture. scientists FAR more often than the readers of sci.physics, sci.lang, sci. math, and any other sci newsgroup I've ever read over the past seven years (a fair number).

> Perhaps this whole proposal should
> be bounced back to the RFD stage,
> with the RFD crossposted to an
> *appropriate* selection of groups
> this time.

I know the guy who proposed the group fairly well, and I'm sure he'll abide with the decision of the group-advice folks, if it comes to that.

__

+   "Homer deserves to be thrown
+   out of the contests and
+   flogged."
+   —Heraclitus

_____

Article from #1

#2 writes:

> In article xxxx #1 writes:
>>   Is it just me, or does anybody
>>else feel that there is a proce-
>>dural problem here, in that this
>>call for votes was only posted to
>>one relatively insignificant sci.*
>>group?

[Long answer deleted.]

Kathi

```
I / ___II___
I/ /\ I I-I I
N \I I I I
I \  I  _I_
```

From: patricia

>A couple of things came to my
>mind that might give you an im-
>pression of my thoughts:
>-The charter of this group makes
>clear it that is interested in hearing
>voices of women scientists. Why is
>it then that more and more these
>voice >have disappeared?

Women are interested in feminism
right now. Any mention of feminist
thinking in science was *not* tolerated in soc.culture.scientists with
open minds. Instead there was a very
defensive and reactionary response. I
understand that men feel like their
backs are against the wall regarding
social issues these days. But science is
still founded upon open-mindedness.
The defenders of the old regime
should remember that.

>-The same thing about the non-
>Western scientists who have par-
>ticipated in voting for this group but
>their voices are virtually hidden?

I think the white American men are
successful at dominating most the

Thanks for your explanation. The decision to only post the RFD & CFV on
the groups they were posted to makes
much more sense in light of what
you've said.

—

| Do not be alarmed . . .
| Be very, very frightened!
| —D. Adams

Article from#3

In article xxxx #2 writes:

>IMHO, this CFV *could* have legiti-
>mately been posted to all of sci.*,
>but since discussions of the sort
>for which this group is intended
>are rare in the sci.* hierarchy as
>a whole yet fairly common in the
>soc.* hierarchy, I'd say the net has
>already sifted out which readers
>are most interested in this sort of
>thing.

Crap. If it wasn't intended to keep
scientists in ignorance of this proposal, precisely what *was* intended?

>If you read very many soc.culture.*
>groups and sci.* groups, you've
>doubtless seen this in action:
>soc.culture.* folks very often dis-
>cuss big science projects going on
>in their country; the status of sci-
>ence education in their country
>compared to others; their own edu-
>cation at home and abroad . . .
>Similar topics occasionally arise in
>sci.research.careers (even though
>such discussion is clearly moti-
>vated by the third term in the
>group's name :), but not very often
>in other sci.* groups.

Net-space that is open to them, which is why all of the interesting conversations involving non-Western and non-male people happen in groups where Western men are not present in significant numbers.

>-Some women poster are not post-
>ing as much what is the reason
>for that?

Being called a stupid bitch might have alienated me, perhaps. Why spend the energy trying to contribute to the group when nobody to listen and everyone wants to hurl insults?

>-Can you think of ways of correct-
>ing this or do you see an inherent
>problem in this kind of community?

I hate to say this, I really do, but with my experience on the Net I think the inherent problem is with one group of human beings who were raised to believe the Earth belongs to them. You see them on the news. You hear them on the Net. The rest of us can f*ck off as far as they're concerned.

They colonized the dark people and brutalized the female peoples. Sorry to be so PC but I am fed up with "white male space". They just have not learned yet to actually listen to other types of people and grant credibility to other types of experience. Maybe the future generations will get better.

Completely false. I have no idea what this about or why, but the science groups very often talk about education, and on occasion about "big science" stuff such as the Human Genome project or the SSC

For some reason the this proposal seems to have been crafted to ignore or belittle actual scientists, and to produce a charter which will allow people to say "science isn't an allowable topic for discussion, please go away". Crap.

>The sci hierarchy might be good for
>negative feedback, and I'm sure
>there are readers of sci news-
>groups interested in cultural stud-
>ies of science (even if they aren't
>talking about such things any-
>where); however, the sci.* reader-
>ship demonstrates primarily an
>interest in discussing scientific
>theories (of course! :)—which is
>taboo on the proposed group, ex-
>cept insofar as it is required to
>trace the sociocultural production
>of those theories.

Great. A "science" group for pin-heads, where no science is allowed. I love it.

>> I am also curious why
>>[mazyar@rice.edu] felt that this
>>proposal was more relevant to
>>the readers of soc.religion.islam
>>and soc.women than to the
>>readers of any of the sci.* groups
>>besides sci.research.careers.

>The relevance of the newsgroups
>to which this CFV was posted stems
>from the demonstrated tendency
>those groups have towards dis-

So we take our marbles home and play in our own groups. I have much more open-minded and fascinating discussions about scientific philosophy on feminist and all-women networks than I can ever have out in that Western male-dominated public group.

Good luck with your group. But looking at this experience—the disappearance of women, etc, maybe you understand why some women's colleges will do anything to keep from admitting men. They dominate. It's their birthright.

And we're *tired* of having to put up with it, or outshout them.

———————

From: 6500lem

Dear Mazyar,

I would be glad to share my opinion of soc.culture.scientists with you. I think what has happenned here is extremely interesting.

The discussion in the group seems to have strayed very far from the original intent of the group, which (I believe) was to discuss cultural differences among scientists and how that might affect their work.

The current discussion is centered on debates and critiques of various aspects of the philosophy of science.

>cussing issues which might be bet-
>ter served with a new newsgroup,
>soc.culture.scientists.

Right. Sure. Uh huh.

———————

Article from #4

In article xxxx #3 writes:

>Crap. If it wasn't intended to keep
>scientists in ignorance of this
>proposal, precisely what *was*
>intended?

It seems to me that you are involved in a misconception: that scientists only read the sci.newsgroups. I would say that this is incorrect. Scientists also read the soc.newsgroups and in fact, a lot of other newsgroups as well. This might perhaps be due to the fact that they are human beings and therefore presumably have other interests than just science.

>From observing the charter of the
>newsgroup and the comments made
>by some of the people who pro-
>posed and support the newsgroup
>proposal, it seems to me that this
>newsgroup is not aimed at all
>scientists, but those that have ex-
>pressed other interests by reading
>some of the soc newsgroups as
>well.

———————

Article from #5

#1 writes:
>Original message was crossposted
>to:
>[big list]

The view of the people who comprise this community is that (as I see it) the very reason for this group to exist is irrelevant. That is, good science is good science, regardless of the cultural background of the practicing scientist.

I subscribe to this view as well.

With regard to the diminishing "voice" of people from under-represented groups, this again is a very interesting phenomenon. If you read soc.feminism you will see a similar effect almost 3/4 of the posters are male. It seems to be a natural tendency for the "empowered" group to take over. Whether that is due to superior ability or cultural training I don't care to speculate.

You do have the option to create soc.culture.scientists.moderated. Then you could keep the conversation focused on cultural differences.

I want to thank you for creating soc.culture.scientists. In my opinion, it is the most interesting newsgroup currently available.

If you care to ask me any other questions about this, I would be delighted to respond.

Laurence

From: haavard

Saa skriv Mazyar Lotfalian:

> I am also curious why [indepen-
>dent vote-taker] felt that this pro-
>posal was more relevant to the
>readers of soc.religion.islam and
>soc.women than to the readers of
>any of the sci.* groups besides
>sci.research.careers.

This was not his decision. The list of groups the RFD went to and which the proponent requested the CFV go to is the list he used. He's acting as the vote taker on this, not the group proponent, and it's the proponent's call on crossposting. It is a strange selection of groups, but it's not [independent vote-taker's] fault.

I'm trying to arrange my life so that I don't even have to be present.

Article from the independent vote-taker

In article xxxx #5 writes:
#1 writes:
>Original message was crossposted
>to:
>[big list]

> I am also curious why [indepen-
>dent vote-taker] felt that this pro-
>posal was |>more relevant to the
>readers of soc.religion.islam and
>soc.women than to the readers of
>any of the sci.* groups besides
>sci.research.careers. This was not
>[his] decision. The list of groups the
>RFD went to and which the propo-
>nent requested the CFV go to is the
>list he used. He's acting as the vote
>taker on this, not the group propo-
>nent, and it's the proponent's call on
>crossposting. It is a strange selec-

>A couple of things came to my
>mind that might give you an im-
>pression of my thoughts:
>-The charter of this group makes
>clear it that is interested in hearing
>voices of women scientists. Why is
>it then that more and more these
>voice have disappeared?
>-The same thing about the non-
>Western scientists who have par-
>ticipated in voting for this group but
>their voices are virtually hidden?
>-Some women poster are not post-
>ing as much what is the reason
>for that?
>-Can you think of ways of cor-
>recting this or do you see an in-
>herent problem in this kind of
>community?

The problems with s.c.s are, I think, typical of News in general: It is to a large extent a realm of *very* aggressive rethorics, and consequently of those who don't feel (too) uncomfortable about its use.

I'm no expert on gender differences, but I seem to remember that—on average—women feel more uncomfortable about such things than men.

Personal attacks run rampant, particularly—it seems to me—against those who question conventional wisdom.

———————————

(If you're such a complete and utter idiot that you didn't realize even before you were born that SCIENCE (TM) is TRUTH (TM), and since you are obviously out to destroy WESTERN CIVILIZATION (TM), why

>tion of groups, but it's not indepen-
>dent vote-taker's] fault.

What #5 said :-)

Yes—I'm just taking the votes on this proposal. Contact the proponent for an explanation on why the particular groups were chosen.

"You cannot pray to a personal computer no matter how user-friendly it is."
—W. Bingham Hunter

———————————

Article from #3

In article xxxx #4 writes:
>It seems to me that you are in-
>volved in a misconception: that
>scientists only read the sci. news-
>groups.

Utter rubbish. However, if you want to catch scientists, soc.religion.islam is not the right group to post to. Islamic scientists do not deserve special treatment. Why soc.religion.islam and not soc.religion.christian, or soc.motss, for that matter?

This whole thing stinks. Either the proposer is incredibly stupid, or is only normally stupid but is attempting something against the spirit of the newgroup creation rules.

don't you step in front of a bus?) The visciousness of the rethorics of some people (I won't mention names) strikes me as being far beyond what simple conviction of the correctness of one's own position and wrongness of that of the others would call for.

Another thing that I think scares some people (I know it has on occasion convinced me that engaging in debates wasn't worth it.) are the sheer time requirements. Turnover speed is *very* high, and if you feel you should keep up, you'll need to spend a fair amount of time at it. If you mull over your answer for a day or two, it will often no longer be as important as you feel it should be.

The only think I can think of that would have effect against at least some of the problems, is moderation.

—Hevard

What the world needs is not dogma but an attitude of scientific inquiry combined with a brief that the torture of millions is not desirable, whether inflicted by Stalin or by a Deity imagined in the likeness of the believer.
—Bertrand Russell

———————

From: Gordon

>-The charter of this group makes
>clear it that is interested in hearing
>voices of women scientists. Why is

If actual comments or votes by scientists were wanted, which frankly I doubt is the case, the RDF should have been posted to the basic science groups as well as certain other groups on which scientists are especially likely to be found. This would mean sci.physics, sci.astro, sci.bio, sci.chem, sci.med, sci.geo.geology and so forth for your basic "hard" sciences. Also sci.math, sci.nonlinear, sci.math.stat for your "mathematical sciences", and sci.psychology, sci.anthropology, sci.econ for the "human sciences".

You also want groups where scientists are especially likely to hang out. These would be sci.skeptic, talk.origins, sci.philosophy.tech, sci.research, sci.misc, sci.edu.

This wasn't what was done. I can only conclude that whoever proposed this is an imbecile. If they are attempting some kind of fraud, it won't work, since an unmoderated group is defined by the people who post to it, and any attempt to bring up a "charter" would be laughed at after an abortion of a "discussion" and "vote" such as this. On the other hand, if it was meant honestly, then it is still idiotic and insulting to have posted this to all kinds of irrelevant groups while ignoring the relevant ones.

Idiots either way, and turtles all the way down.

>This might perhaps be due to the
>fact that they are human beings
>and therefore presumably have
>other interests than just science.

>it >then that more and more these >voice have disappeared?

This is a common problem on the Net. It was recently taken up in alt.culture.theory. I know a number of women who might have a lot of interesting things to say but can't put up with thegeneral atmosphere of stupidity and hostility that prevails. As the Net is an anarchy, nothing can be done about this. There are moderated newsgroups, but typically they don't have thevitality of the unmoderated groups. There are also mailing lists; but I find the mailing lists have other problems.

>-The same thing about the non->Western scientists who have par->ticipated in voting for this group but >their voices are virtually hidden?

Same thing.

>-Some women poster are not post->ings as much what is the reason >for that?

Same thing.

>-Can you think of ways of correct->ing this or do you see an inherent >problem in this kind of community?

If more people outside the set of European-descended middle-class males would post articles, the nature of the Net would change, but the E-d. m-c. males can't do much about that. The question is whether they (the former group) value cyberspace enough to put up with its unpleasant qualities and use it anyway. In that sense, it's very much like a street.
Gordon

―――――――――――

Tell me about it. Do *you* work in a scientific field, by the way?

>From observing the charter of the >newsgroup and the comments made >by some of the people who pro->posed and support the newsgroup >proposal, it seems to me that this >newsgroup is not aimed at all scien->tists, but those that have expressed >other interests by reading some of >the soc newsgroups as well.

In other words, some complete nincompoop is hoping that real scientists will somehow never learn about the existence of this group?
Won't work.

―――――――――――

Article from #6

In article xxxx #1 writes:
>#2 writes:
>
>>In article #1 writes:
>>>
>>> Is it just me, or does any->>>body else feel that there is >>>a procedural problem here, in >>>that this call for votes was only >>>posted to one relatively insig->>>nificant sci.* group?
>
>[Long answer deleted.]
>
> Thanks for your explanation. The >decision to only post the RFD & CFV >on the groups they were posted to >makes much more sense in light of >what you've said.

No, it doesn't. If you want input from scientists and others interested in science, the RFD should have been posted to science newsgroups. Putting some kind of weird perceptions

From: gazissax

I posted to a discussion which was crossposted to sci.med. I have read sci.med for some years, off and on, because my mother teaches at a medical school, and so I have some interest. And I've been reading it regularly lately because I maintain a FAQ on a medical topic. As for soc.culture. scientists, it sounded somewhat interesting when I first heard it was created, but I've never gotten around to checking it out.

>Would you please take a minute
>and give me your reaction? A
>couple of things came to my mind
>that might give you an impression
>of my thoughts:
>-The charter of this group makes
>clear it that is interested in hearing
>voices of women scientists. Why is
>it then that more and more these
>voice have disappeared?
>-The same thing about the non-
>Western scientists who have par-
>ticipated in voting for this group but
>their voices are virtually hidden?
>-Some women poster are not post-
>ing as much what is the reason
>for that?
>-Can you think of ways of correct-
>ing this or do you see an inherent
>problem in this kind of community?

Hard to say, since I haven't been reading the group. I am a woman in a technical profession (technical support for computer software), and I've noticed that many newsgroups have a shortage of women posting.

about who reads what newsgroups into the crossposting selection still makes little sense, especially in light of some of the newsgroups chosen (soc.religion.islam comes to mind).

"I'm mentally OVERDRAWN!"

Article from #7

In xxxx #3 writes:

>If actual comments or votes by
>scientists were wanted, which
>frankly I doubt is the case, the RDF
>should have been posted to the
>basic science groups as well as
>certain other groups on which
>scientists are especially likely to
>be found. This would mean sci.
>physics, sci.astro, sci.bio, sci.
>chem, sci.med, sci.geo.geology
>and so forth for your basic "hard"
>sciences. Also sci.math, sci.
>nonlinear, sci.math.stat for your
>"mathematical sciences", and sci.
>psychology, sci.anthropology, sci.
>econ for the "human sciences".

>You also want groups where sci-
>entists are especially likely to
>hang out. These would be sci.skep-
>tic, talk.origins, sci.philosophy.tech,
>sci.research, sci.misc, sci.edu.

So what's preventing you from just crossposting the CFV to the groups that you consider appropriate?

One striking point about the news-group is the way people talk about it, using the face-to-face assumption of language to talk about a computer-mediated communication (CMC). This is done even by those who try to study this mode of interaction. It was this aspect of the technology that I tried to unpack—the enframing of the newsgroup.

The focus of most activists, the Net people (for example, moderators and advisors), is to suggest better ways of using the "tool" without being accountable for the way the it enframes. This approach creates discrepancies between what we think we are doing and what the effects are. Participants, in their commentaries above, suggest problems that are similar to the problems that exist with real life. But are these really the same problems or are they the same questions that we are facing anew, under different enframing?

I think it is the latter. As Heidegger said, "there is nothing technological about technology." We are asking the same questions under a new frame. The newsgroup is different from a community of people interacting face-to-face in at least three ways: the newsgroup is a community of "users" who interact in a mode that is hieroglyphic (a cross of picto-logo-phono language), the object of interaction is treated as confrontation, and it is rhizomatic in the sense that there is no beginning and no end.

Finally, I would like to suggest some points concerning the merits and potentials of this community. The

Article from #2

In article xxxx #7 writes:
> So what's preventing you from just
> crossposting the CFV to the groups
> that you consider appropriate?

First, it would start to look like a campaign.
Second, those groups weren't involved during the RFD period.

All you can do, at this point, is calmly answer accusations of irregularity and wait. Paranoid, conspiracy-minded, insulting rants (such as those posted by the infamous #3) are probably best left ignored. Posts which add no new charges (like the one from #6) are also best left ignored.

_

+   "Homer deserves to be thrown
+   out of the contests and
+   flogged."
                        —Heraclitus

—————————————

After thirty days, from the beginning of the CFV to the deadline, the newsgroup passed by almost two-thirds of the total vote. The newsgroup was created five days after the announcement of the tally.

The professional makeup of the voters: The following diagram is a survey of degrees sought or obtained in the given fields.

practice of newsgroups shows that those particular newsgroups that are formed around the information swapping do well. The same is not true for most other newsgroups. For example, soc.culture.scientists which caters to diverse groups of people and cultures, work against some demographic and real life problems, such as having access to the Net, enduring the intimidation of the white male flamers, and so on. The newsgroup soc.culture.scientists needs to change this "natural" flow by understanding the elements of interaction or this enframing, that is, the new language.

Art and Humanities	|*
Social Sciences	|*********
biological science	|****
engineering	|*******.
physics	|**********
mathmatics	|********
computer science	|**********
geology	|***
astronomy	|**
statistics	|*
animal sciences	|*
bio/chemistry	|********
cognitive sciences	|**
medicine	|*
info sciences	|*
material science	|*
marine biology	|*
sys. engineering	|*
astrophysics	|**
physiology	|*

References

Barthes, Roland. 1974. *S/Z.* Trans. Richard Miller. New York: Hill and Wang.

———. 1985. *The Grain of the Voice: Interviews 1962–1980.* Trans. Linda Coverdale. New York: Hill and Wang.

Deleuze, Gilles, and Felix Guattari. 1988. *A Thousand Plateaus: Capitalism and Schizophrenia.* Trans. Brian Massumi. London: Athlone Press.

Derrida, Jacques. 1974. *Of Grammatology.* Translated by Gayatri Chakravorty Spivak. Baltimore and London: Johns Hopkins University Press.

———. 1987. *The Post Card: From Socrates to Freud and Beyond.* Chicago: University of Chicago Press.

Goody, Jack. 1987. *The Interface Between the Written and the Oral.* Cambridge: Cambridge University Press.

Heim, Michael. 1987. *Electric Language: A Philosophical Study of Word Processing.* New Haven, Conn.: Yale University Press.

———. 1993. *The Metaphysics of Virtual Reality.* New York: Oxford University Press.

Stone, Allucquére Rosanne. 1991. *Cyberspace, Will the Real Body Please Stand Up? Boundary Stories about Virtual Cultures.* Ed. Michael Benedikt. Cambridge, Mass.: MIT Press.

Tyler, Stephen. 1987. *The Unspeakable.* Madison: University of Wisconsin Press.

———. 1993. *Descriptive and Theoretical Modes in the Alternative Linguistics. To Be Isn't to Be Represented.* Fifth Biennial Symposium of the Department of Linguistics, Rice University.

Ulmer, Gregory. 1985. *Applied Grammatology.* Baltimore: Johns Hopkins University Press.

———. 1989. *Teletheory: Grammatology in the Age of Video.* New York: Routledge.

II

THE ACTIVIST IMAGINARY

5

COMPUTING FOR TIBET: VIRTUAL POLITICS IN THE POST–COLD WAR ERA

Excerpt from Tibetan Bulletin November-December 1993
(Tibetan Bulletin, the official journal of the Tibetan government-in-exile, known as the Central Tibetan Administration (CTA), is published by the Department of Information and International Relations, Dharamsala, India. World Tibet Network News reprints each issue on-line.)

4.1 Dharamsala goes E-mailing

Bhuchung K. Tsering

After several years of feasibility study, the Central Tibetan Administration in Dharamsala is finally on e-mail. The idea of putting Dharamsala on the electronic mail map of the world was conceived in 1989 when a New York-based computer consultant, Ms. Indira Singh, suggested the setting up of TibetNet. Ms. Singh felt TibetNet would provide the Tibetans the technological ability to disseminate the Tibetan story worldwide. She made preliminary trials in collaboration with the Department of Information and International Relations (DIIR). The then DIIR Kalon Lodi G. Gyari shared Ms. Singh's feelings saying "TibetNet is the vehicle which will take Tibetans to the twenty-first century."

Despite the unreliable telephone system, an ad-hoc connection was made in early 1990. As a simple message, Hello from Dharamsala made its first journey from a laptop computer to the computer in the Office of Tibet New York, there was jubilation. Reporting on the event, this journal, in its March-April 1990 issue, said it was the first tottering steps the Tibetans, cooped as they are in their own little Shangri-la, are taking to catch up with what has bypassed them—telecommunications.

Since then much water has flowed down the Bhagsunath rivulet in Dharamsala. Some problems made the experiment remain as it was; just an experiment. But the Tibetans were given a taste of what was in store for us. Just as the shrewd business sense of a Tibetan does not let an opportunity pass by, this idea of a private electronic mail service became merely placed on the backburner, not totally forgotten.

Meanwhile, Dharamsala's Planning Council had set up the Tibetan Computer Resource Center to provide an organized computerised service to the Tibetan community. Simultaneously, in Canada, the Canada Tibet Committee had taken the initiative to enter Tibet into the e-mail world actively. The offices of Tibet in New York and London followed suits [sic]. They all had the experience of Tibet Information Network in London which had over the years become one of the few independent sources for objective news from Tibet. Dharamsala began to feel the pressure to set up a nodal point here . . .

Dharamsala is going e-mail. A small step for mankind, but a giant step for the Tibetans.

Much has been written in recent years about the explosion of computer-mediated communication (CMC) in the United States and elsewhere. Today, anyone with access to a computer, modem, and network account can be linked into the vast web of global electronic information flows known colloquially as cyberspace. The growth of new communication technologies has gone hand in hand with the proliferation of international and transnational movements and organizations, what Arjun Appadurai calls "complex postnational social formations" (1993:420),[1] and the emergence of a global civil society.[2] American discourse on computer networks, however, has been characteristically parochial, dominated by arguments over universal accessibility to the still-protean "information superhighway" and its potential commercialization.[3] Little attention has been paid to the relationship between CMC and these transnational social forms.[4] This piece offers a concrete example of how computer networks have been used by members of one such formation.

Since 1989, Tibetans and Tibet supporters around the world have used networked computers to communicate among themselves, mobilize grass-roots opinion, and inform the media about events in Tibet and the diaspora. This activity represents an increasingly common phenomenon in the post-cold war era whereby marginalized, diasporic, and dissident groups embrace new media technologies in order to assert their political presence in the international arena.[5] What makes electronic networks particularly significant for such activism is that they enable a form of intercultural solidarity that does not rest on face-to-face contact. Thus Tibetans and their supporters in New York, London, Geneva, Tokyo, Canberra, Toronto, New Delhi, and Dharamsala can all be connected and participate simultaneously in the Tibet struggle.

The interviews in this essay with Robbie Barnett, founder of Tibet Information Network, and Tseten Samdup, information and press officer, Office of Tibet, London, trace the emergence this "virtual community."[6] They are part of a larger study of the collaboration between westerners and Tibetans in the self-conscious production of "Tibetanness" in the diaspora and the Tibet Movement.[7]

The spread of new media forms and the tremendous growth of transnational and international movements and organizations has coincided with the breakdown of traditional cold war alliances and enmities. For interstitial groups such as the Tibetans, this confluence of events has meant the opportunity to create a new political space for themselves in the contemporary world order. By allying themselves with various nongovernmental organizations (NGOs) and taking advantage of sophisticated information technologies, for instance, Tibetans have been able to raise the Tibet issue in a number of important international fora with greater visibility than ever before.[8]

The Tibetan delegation's experience at the UN World Conference of Human Rights in Vienna (1993) is a case in point. Before the official UN conference opened, Chinese protests over a scheduled address by the Dalai Lama at the parallel NGO conference caused UN organizers to ban the exiled leader from speaking. The controversial decision attracted intense publicity, a large part of which was generated by online dispatches and faxes from Tibetans in Vienna to supporters, NGOs, governments, and members of the press around the world. By utilizing the on-site communications center set up by the Association for Progressive Communications (APC),[9] representatives of the Dalai Lama, including Tseten Samdup, interviewed below, learned firsthand the benefits of computer-mediated communication. Under mounting public pressure, conference officials eventually reversed their decision and allowed the Dalai Lama to address the NGO forum.

What are we to make of this form of disembodied communication and the virtual politics it facilitates? What sort of intercultural negotiations take place in the process of working across cultural difference and what are the limits of the solidarities engendered? The interviews in this piece attempt to answer these questions and to shed light on the increasingly mediated nature of political action in the late twentieth century. They touch on issues such as the ambiguities of an electronic forum for political discourse; the growing interdependence of decentralized communication technologies and the mass media; and the culturally complex character of transnational social/political movements which bring together "first world" and "third world" peoples. To fully understand the recent trajectory of the Tibet struggle, however, it is necessary briefly to examine the history of Tibetan/Western relations in the diaspora.

Tibetans and Westerners [10]

Tibetans have a history of deep involvement with non-Tibetan "friends" [11] dating back to 1959, when the Dalai Lama, fleeing Chinese occupiers, escaped Tibet, creating an exodus of Tibetans who followed their leader across the

Himalayas with only what they could carry on their backs. Nehru's government, international relief agencies, and sympathetic westerners hurried to aid
the tens of thousands of refugees who streamed into Bhutan, Sikkim, Nepal,
and India, all in desperate need of shelter, food, and medical care. Over the
next several years, scattered in settlements across the Indian subcontinent, Tibetans set about rebuilding their lives with help from the Indians and foreign
aid organizations.[12]

One of the Tibetans' top priorities in exile was to preserve their unique religious traditions, a decision which reflected the centrality of Buddhism in
Tibetan life. With the Dalai Lama's newly formed government in exile overwhelmed by refugee rehabilitation and educational responsibilities, the mon-
asteries in exile were forced to rely on a network of Western relief workers,
travelers, and other sympathetic individuals for donations. Over time, as high
lamas, or teachers, went abroad and established centers in the West to teach
Tibetan religion, meditation, and language, a network of Western practitioners
(what I call a transnational *sangha*) evolved which also supported the fledgling
Buddhist institutions in exile. This cultivation of outside "patrons," or *sbyin-
bdags,* is part of the cultural framework of *mchod-yon,* whereby spiritual guidance is exchanged for material and political support, and which characterized
interactions at all levels of society in old Tibet, from the perception of the
Tibetan state vis-à-vis the outside world to the relationship between an individual and his or her *lama.*[13]

Over the years, Tibetans have had no difficulty reinterpreting this social relation in exile because, unlike other refugee groups, they have encountered
many benefactors eager to offer support in exchange for contact with them.[14]
These potential *sbyin-bdags* often hold romantic fantasies about Tibet which
derive from a long history of Western representation of Tibet as Shangri-la and
the belief that all Tibetans, regardless of their spiritual training or accomplishments, embody spiritual values that have been lost in the West.[15] However
problematic, this first-world fantasy may account for the long-standing commitment many Western donors have made to helping Tibetans remain Tibetan
in exile, which in turn has enabled Tibetans not only to survive the trauma of
displacement but to keep their refugee status. Retaining this status, as opposed
to taking Indian or Nepali citizenship, is seen as an act of patriotism by members of the exile community, allowing them to fulfill the Dalai Lama's vision
that "the purpose of refugee life is to rescue the nation, the people, and the
cultural traditions of Tibet."[16] Western largesse, however, has been a double-
edged sword. While is has played a crucial role in helping Tibetans preserve
their cultural identity in diaspora, it has functioned as a conservative force in
exile society by privileging religious institutions over secular ones. In so doing,
it has hampered Tibetan efforts to overcome their stereotyped image and have
their political claims taken seriously by the world community.[17] At the same

time, Tibetans have made productive use of Western fantasies about Tibet as a sacred place and Tibetans as special beings in their efforts to generate support.[18]

It has only been recently, however, that Tibetans have put their unusual alliance with Westerners to work for the purpose of building an international movement. This change of focus was initiated by events which took place in September 1987, when major pro-independence demonstrations erupted in Lhasa, Tibet. China's violent response galvanized both the exile community and the latent network of Westerners who had always supported the refugees but who had never actively campaigned for Tibet. They joined together in publicizing the riots and in so doing attracted new recruits to the cause. Tibet support groups quickly sprang up in Switzerland, France, Germany, the Netherlands, England, Australia, and North America, many filled with young professionals who had no previous ties to the Tibet issue but who shared concerns about human rights, the environment, and other global issues. Since then, a definable Tibet Movement has emerged which, while still relying on Gandhian tactics such as demonstrations and boycotts, has also developed new strategies that are reflective of changing contemporary realities, namely, the deployment of traditional Tibetan "culture" in novel arenas and the use of computer-mediated technologies.

The Computer/Media/Information Nexus

Over the last several years I have been tracking the proliferation of Tibet-related computer conferences and newsletters, including CanTibNet (CTN)—now called World Tibet Network News (WTN), Tibet Information Network (TIN), Tibet News Digest (TND)—now part of (WTN), and talk.politics. tibet.[19] WTN, founded in 1991 by the Canada Tibet Committee, features daily news reports from wire services and from Tibet organizations such as the Tibet Information Network. It also posts press releases, "urgent action alerts," and other information from government and nongovernmental organizations such as the Central Tibetan Administration and its overseas offices and various Tibet support groups. WTN has also played an important role in the planning and launching of campaigns in support of Tibet, facilitating information exchange and coordination of activists dispersed around the globe. For example, WTN was involved with the campaign to free Gendun Rinchen, a tour guide arrested for reporting human rights violations in Tibet in 1993. It was also part of the effort to mobilize opposition to Beijing's Olympic bid, and to the renewal of Most Favored Nation trading status by U.S. President Clinton. Tibet-related postings have multiple (multimedia) lives: for instance, a story originating on TIN will be carried by WTN, broadcast on the BBC World Service and into Tibet by the Voice of America, and published by the *New York Times*. It will then be reproduced in Tibet organization newsletters and exile community publications. While this redundancy can at times create a circular effect, it is indicative of the increasingly complex global media environment in which political action takes place, an environment characterized by transnational information flows and technological innovation.

In my conversations with Barnett and Samdup, both pointed out the need to find fresh audiences for their material in order to avoid the common pitfall of preaching to the converted. As Barnett put it, "the value of Tibet news is that it is read by people who have nothing to do with it." Barnett and Samdup work hard to disseminate their material to the mass media, which they see as the most important outlet. Although Tibetans have many friends in the press, as one American media consultant recently put it, historically they have not been successful in getting the kind of hard political coverage they desired. There are numerous possible explanations for why this is so, including the mass media's tendency to filter out dissenting opinions in favor of the status quo; the Tibetans' refusal to "package" the Dalai Lama for media consumption; general Western ignorance about Tibet; or a stereotyped view of Tibet as somehow not of this world and of Tibet supporters as flaky or strange.[20] With the growth of computer-mediated communication such as fax and e-mail, however, news gathering methods have changed, opening the door a crack for marginalized groups like the Tibetans to inject alternative viewpoints into the public arena. In this piece, Samdup describes how he uses a fax/modem to "plant stories" in the media by faxing press releases and background information to Western wire services in Beijing. If China watchers in Beijing find the story to be newsworthy, they put it out on the wires where it can be picked up by radio, print, or electronic news organizations around the world, making Tibet "news" and Samdup its "source."

As one of a only a handful of Tibetan journalists trained in the West, Samdup is uniquely positioned to understand both Western news-gathering practices and Tibetan approaches to information. Born in exile, Samdup worked for the government in exile in the Department of Information and International Relations where his responsibilities included assisting Western television crews that traveled to the former British hill station of Dharamsala to film the Dalai Lama and record refugee life. He then won a Ford Foundation Fellowship to study at the Columbia Graduate School of Journalism in New York City. Upon graduating in 1991, Samdup moved to London to work for the Office of Tibet as information and press officer. In this role, Samdup mediates between two different cultural worlds, each with its own attitude toward information and what constitutes knowledge.

In old Tibet, a place where religion and government were traditionally intertwined and the head of state was considered to be an emanation of the Buddha Avalokitesvara, the most prized knowledge was spiritual in nature and the most respected individuals were *tulkus,* constantly reincarnating personages who had attained enlightenment but who voluntarily choose rebirth in order to assist other sentient beings. There was no civil society in the Western sense, because Tibet was not a democracy; there was no concept of the public's right to know or equal access to information. In the refugee community, information still has a different currency than it does in the West. Like many other non-Western societies that operate in what Eric Michaels (1985) calls an "economy of oral information," Tibetan hierarchies are based on differential access to information. As Samdup's comments illustrate, these hierarchies of power endure in exile and distinguish the ways Tibetans understand media. This deeply engrained orientation poses a problem for those reformers—including the Dalai Lama—who want to make Tibetan refugee society more open and democratic. Without the free flow of ideas and information, they argue, the public can not make educated decisions about the things they are supposed to decide upon, such as the government in exile's negotiating position vis-à-vis the Chinese. As a recent editorial in the *Tibetan Review* argues, "one of the peculiarities of our version of democracy seems to be that as far as the people are concerned, the less they know the better. When the people are kept in perpetual darkness, the government can do what it likes and call the system 'democracy'—or whatever happens to be the in thing at that time" (1994:3). As this internal critique suggests, even with the best of intentions, old habits die hard.

There are other differences between the way Tibetans and westerners approach information. Unsurprisingly, Tibetans view any story that comes out of Tibet as news. For instance, according to Tseten Samdup, the government in exile often fails to apply "Western notions of facticity" to stories coming out of Tibet; instead, he says, "it looks at any story that is happening in Tibet as important. If something is happening, that's news. But journalists would say, 'Okay, how many people were there, what time did it happen, why did it happen.'" Yet to confirm a story is difficult given China's strict control over information in Tibet. In addition, Dharamsala often has to rely on testimony from escapees, many from rural areas who are not media savvy and who sometimes "don't tell the entire story because they think, what good would it do?" or who "exaggerate their stories," perhaps knowing that the more harrowing their tale, the greater the chance they will have an audience with the Dalai Lama, who uses meetings with new arrivals to keep abreast of developments in Tibet.

Despite claims to objectivity and facticity, Western media has its own set of culturally embedded social practices that shape and are shaped by sources, journalists and audiences who coexist in a complex interrelationship.[21] Structurally, the imperatives of commercial mass media demand a continuous flow of information which is packaged in specific ways for mainstream consumption. At times, Barnett suggests, journalistic needs have been dangerous for some Tibetans: "the history of journalism in Tibet is the history of Tibetans being put at risk by freelance journalists for a story." Offering a thumbnail sociology of journalism, Barnett contrasts journalists who oversimplify, making "Tibetans look like victims," with the elite group of China watchers at the BBC World Service or the wire services, whose work reflects more of an interest in long-term processes in Tibet. Barnett sees his own work with Tibet Information Network as a corrective to the trend of representing Tibetans as victims; for him, Tibetans are active agents of their own history and TIN's purpose is to document this fact.

Witnessing for Tibet

Within the text I have interspersed postings from Tibet Information Network, World Tibet Network News, and other Tibet-related conferences in order to give readers a feel for the heterogeneous nature of computer-mediated communication and to alert them to what is at stake in the Tibet struggle. Despite the media attention Tibetans have managed to attract in recent years, it has not translated into political gains in the international arena. After more than three decades, the Dalai Lama's government in exile is still not officially recognized by any country, and Tibetans are persona non grata at the United Nations, never having been granted observer status. Meanwhile, the situation worsens for dissidents in Tibet: the number of political prisoners jumped significantly in recent years as the Chinese severely cracked down on all forms of resistance to their rule (Asia Watch 1994). Postings like the following one function as sober reminders of this reality:

> From: IN%"tin@gn.apc.org" "Robbie Barnett" 24-May-1993 10:28: 31:40
> To: IN%:tin-List@UTORGPU.bitnet"
> Subj: MAJOR UNREST IN LHASA, TIBET
>
> URGENT URGENT URGENT
> There has been a major outbreak of unrest in Lhasa today Monday 24th May involving 2-3,000 Tibetans stoning a police station and shops owned by Chinese migrants, according to foreigners contacted within the capital.
>
> Chinese are said to have been restrained at first but have since used large amounts of tear gas. There are vague and unconfirmed reports of gunfire. There is an unconfirmed report of one person killed . . .
>
> This is by far the most serious outbreak of unrest in Tibet for the last four years. Martial law, lifted only after 13 months, was declared on March 7th, 1989 after a series of very similar incidents. There have been over 150 known demonstrations in Tibet since the re-emergence of mass protests in the Himalayan region in September 1987. Al-

most all protests have been in support of the pro-independence movement . . .

In the period 1987-89 approximately 3,000 Tibetans were imprisoned for political activities and at least 200 killed by security forces during major demonstrations. Since 1990 there have been more protests, but involving only small numbers of Tibetans. However, political arrests from those small incidents doubled in 1992 from the previous year.

The first conversation in this piece is with Robbie Barnett, the founder of Tibet Information Network (TIN), an independent nonprofit organization that collects, analyzes, and distributes information about the current situation in Tibet. One of the Westerners radicalized by his experience in Tibet in 1987, Barnett began receiving information from Tibetans in Tibet through secret means upon his return to London. A Cambridge-educated journalist and actor, he felt a "moral responsibility" to disseminate this material to the outside world. Barnett's story of the birth of TIN reveals a fierce commitment to the standards of journalistic objectivity and intellectual independence. It also suggests the transformative effects of his experience in Tibet, a theme common to the personal narratives I collected from activists during the course of my fieldwork.

Barnett traces the evolution of TIN to Tibetan initiatives and events:

> I walked into a square, a lot of people got shot in front of me, I got very frightened and thought the best thing to do is to watch, to be a witness, which a lot of us Westerners did at the time. . . . other Westerners wanted to get involved, to deter shooting by standing in the middle. I'm one of the ones who wanted to organize witnesses and set up chains of people transferring film canisters. We tried to tell those taking photographs that you mustn't be left with a canister . . . in my case, it's a way of dealing with fear—to get bossy [*laughs*].

Barnett's witnessing took the form of reporting what he and others had seen, verifying rumors, and recording the names of Tibetan prisoners. The shift from what Barnett calls the "Western witness experience"—tourists sitting around recounting what they saw—to relying on Tibetans as a source of knowledge was an important moment in TIN's evolution. It entailed close collaboration with a few Tibetans, each of whom risked his or her life by passing information to foreigners. From the beginning, Barnett attempted to apply Western journalistic standards of "facticity" to the material being passed, some of which failed to distinguish between information and commentary and was written in a rhetorical polemical style according to Tibetan tradition:

> I was in a room in Lhasa and somebody brought in something that said, "Fifty babies had their hearts eaten out by Chinese for human sacrifice and then were thrown in the river." And I said, "This doesn't

wash." [*Laughs.*] Okay, so maybe it's true, but what are the numbers and when and how do you know and who saw it and how many? . . . I told them you can send as much comment as you like but it has to be kept separate from information. TIN is strongly committed to this idea of the fact.

Embedded in Barnett's belief that high quality of information is "the only thing we can offer the Tibetans" is a critique of the neo-orientalist tendency of those well-intentioned westerners who would see themselves as heroes, putting themselves between Chinese bullets and Tibetan bodies. Or, more likely, those who would see themselves as "saving Tibet." Barnett's narrative is thus complex and contradictory, moving between a strong commitment to his sources and an insistent detachment from Western-based supporters who make use of the information he publishes in their activism.

Barnett's work with TIN represents an ongoing extension of witnessing by Tibetans inside Tibet. He sees himself as a translator, facilitator, and communicator of information for a media that likes to listen to Western people "who patently know less about the situation than Tibetans," a phenomenon he labels as "deeply racist." At the same time, Barnett asserts that material coming from Dharamsala, which is translated into Indian English, can sometimes seem "florid" and "Victorian" to Western ears: "It never sounds believable, the semiotics of it are that it communicates fabrication. It is the English bequest to India, but it is a clerical language which is immobilizing." Although Barnett does not identify himself as an activist, his organization has nonetheless made a significant contribution to the struggle. TIN reports are currently distributed around the globe to more than a hundred paying subscribers who receive fax and e-mail versions. Another hundred receive TIN reports free, many of them via e-mail. TIN subscribers include members of the media, print, radio, and wire services in Asia, Europe, and North America, governments, human rights organizations, Tibet-related groups, and interested individuals. The organization survives on subscriptions and donations from foundations, individuals, and organizations such as the European Community.

INTERNET ADDRESS:
Tibet Information Network <tin@gn.apc.org>
DATE OF CREATION:
October 1987
COMMENTS:
The Tibet Information Network (TIN) is an independent non-profit making organisation which collects and analyses information about the situation in Tibet. It works to help protect fundamental human rights in Tibet by fostering the flow of information from Tibet about current conditions in that country.

The organisation began when a group of Western tourists witnessed the shooting by Chinese police of a number of Tibetan demonstrators in Lhasa in October, 1987. The authorities denied that police had opened fire, expelled journalists and tourists, shut down telephone lines and impounded foreigners' photographs of the incident.

As a result, a number of tourists came together to compile detailed accounts of what they had seen and to send these to the outside world. Later some of those who had witnessed similar incidents formed TIN in order to continue the collection of accurate and dispassionate information about the situation inside Tibet.

TIN, now based in London, UK, continues to conduct research into conditions in Tibet. TIN makes documents available on the APC computer network (including PeaceNet, GreenNet, GeoNet, Nicarao, Pegasus, Web and IGC) and has a special mail service for usenet/bitnet users. Relevant materials are distributed to subscribing organisations throughout the world including human rights organisations, international agencies, governments, parliamentarians, and the media.

The collection and distribution of the information is guided by several fundamental principles. TIN aims to provide accurate and objective information, and to be free from political bias or affiliation. It therefore maintains its independence from any other organisations as well as from governments. TIN supplies information and research materials to its subscribers irrespective of their opinions and takes no part in campaigning or lobbying activities. (Excerpt from TERG)

The following conversation with Robbie Barnett took place on 18 August 1993 in the TIN office in London.

McLAGAN: When you got on GreenNet and started your TIN conference, who did you envision you were addressing?

BARNETT: I don't really think like that. Because at that stage and even now, I'm still not sure who reads GreenNet.

McLAGAN: That's what I was going to ask you.

BARNETT: It's a passive, imaginative process, you're addressing an imaginary audience, you're not trying to reach anyone. Anyway, TIN is just creating a historical monument to the statements of these people in Tibet. I wanted to build a monument, like the monument in the middle of the square in Lhasa commemorating the eighth-century Tibetan conquest of western China. I come from a monumental tradition of historians who dig up those things. I'm just marking down in stone what these Tibetans say has happened for people who want to know.

McLAGAN: Some people would say, though, that you're using a most ephemeral medium, you're not using stone. I mean that's an interesting meta-phor you choose because it's about the least permanent medium.

BARNETT: Well, no, these conferences stay there. The conference is prob-ably still there from when I started it. I mean, all those postings on GreenNet, you could tap into now and read. But I didn't know about the life of these conferences. I didn't know what actual mental user activity there is; I never knew. I'm not sure anybody read them. But the network people liked them. They saw this as being somehow useful because all the things that were going on turned out to be human rights emergencies. So they felt this was a two-way process and as somehow vindicating their existence because here's this guy putting on stuff which is saying that people urgently need help. Whether any-body read it at that stage, I have no idea.

McLAGAN: But at the same time you were putting out hard copy versions.

BARNETT: Yeah, the printed reports were a priority. The conference mate-rial was just my personal desire to see something placed somewhere as a monument. So that people who were in that world could read it.

McLAGAN: You weren't thinking that this technology would be something you could use to connect to the Office of Tibet in New York or to different Tibet support groups in Europe?

BARNETT: No. Nobody seemed to have anything to do with GreenNet in the Tibet world at that time. That came much later. That's not really right. I specifically wasn't interested in connecting to the community of Tibet martyrs and fellow sufferers [*laughs*] and the emotional pathological there-but-for-the-grace-of-god-go-I people. I'm not interested in communicating. I mean that seemed to me to be the problem with Tibet was that it only communi-cated to the other fellow, empathetic martyrs. I remember the reason that I wanted stuff on GreenNet was because I wanted Tibet information to be read by someone who has nothing to do with the church of Tibet martyrs and would-be empathetic martyrs. I wouldn't have given a damn if the Tibet com-munity office somewhere had been on e-mail. I wasn't interested in that. I think the value of Tibet news is that it is read by people who have nothing to do with it. The lack of value of Tibet news is that it is only read by people who are already committed and predisposed to the issue. That's an inverse achievement, it is not a communication to have them reading it. That's why I put it online—it was outside the locked circuit of Tibet supporters.

McLAGAN: When we first met in 1990, you talked about some problems you were having with the TIN conference on GreenNet. Can you talk about that a bit?

BARNETT: Yes. Electronic communications has this tendency, once it is open ended, to appeal to the lowest common denominator. This is the unsa-vory side to the electronic world. It was very hard to get GreenNet, PeaceNet, and all the connected organizations to actually operate consistent with the policy that TIN was a moderated conference. There was an incident in 1990 when I deleted some material from the conference that someone had crashed into which was about forced abortion in Tibet and which I said was unsubstantiated and emotive. I put a notice in saying that I had deleted the material and one of network's sysops said, "How dare you do this, this is censorship." So I wrote a response, which he later accepted.

It's very interesting, this emotionality of the liberal conscience which one has to distinguish from the liberal intelligence. There is the idea that if everybody could say anything they like, somehow it's better. But we often end up with exaggerated, highly inflammatory anti-Chinese racist commentary. This is a huge problem within network culture. It is open to the most inflammatory material—to emotional fascism. TIN doesn't deal in that area at all. I'm not interested in it; I just use electronics as a way of putting out stuff that has our name on it.

McLAGAN: Do you read the other networks with postings and conferences on Tibet like CanTibNet or talk.politics.tibet?

BARNETT: CanTibNet is a big step up in the whole issue because it takes all our postings and sends them on to other people, which is great. We are keen on CanTibNet because they print uneditorialized text from Reuters and other wire services. They print some editorial material, too. They're intelligent guys and when they print something from Reuters it's from Reuters, and Dharamsala, Dharamsala. It is signposted, so that is healthy.

McLAGAN: Who subscribes to TIN? You've said you don't know who reads it online.

BARNETT: The key subscribers are the distributors of news, the wire services. It wasn't what we had in mind when we started, but the wire services, particularly the Beijing-based wire services, are important in terms of impact, because if they print something it goes to X million people. One or two governments also subscribe, which is of significance, as well as some newspapers.

McLAGAN: Like the *New York Times?* I've noticed they've been crediting TIN in their stories on Tibet more frequently in the last year.

BARNETT: Yes, but you see it has to do with the culture of China watchers. We're only perceived to be of significance by China watchers, by specialists in Chinese politics. It is only those people who see what we do as being of wider significance. This is the sociology of journalism. We don't bother with television journalism; it's a waste of time because they don't have any perception for the specialist interest. They respond to campaign groups, which shows how low they are actually. You know once they get on television it's because other campaign groups are hassling them, saying, "Look, we got video, we got pictures of people being shot."

The television journalists do not have a perception of real significance.

They only have a perception of incidents. That's very damaging to their ability to read into events and processes. I mean, their achievement in China has been so abysmally low, their achievement over Tiananmen, their misreading, their provocative action, their dangerous habit of putting people at risk is something I've written about. It is really a condemnation of their profession. But this also applies to freelance journalists. The history of journalism in Tibet is the history of Tibetans being put at risk by freelance journalists or being marginalized or being minimalized by the freelancer who had to pay for his trip and so exaggerates or distorts or even puts people at enormous risk, in some cases at the risk of their lives, for a story. But exaggeration or simplification is more common. Simply because it makes Tibetans look like victims. You've heard me say that before.

McLAGAN: Right.

BARNETT: But if you look at the journalists who are full time specialists, either because they are on radio, like the BBC World Service, which has an East Asia department, or because they are based in Beijing, their level of expertise, professionalism, intellectual resources, and the principles they bring to their work is entirely different. We communicate to those people. Those are the people that we admire, that we in a sense model ourselves on. In that we are Tibet watchers and they're China watchers and they have a long-standing commitment to being able to understand and interpret processes.

So this is a radical schism within the trade. We don't have a life really outside those China people, except in Hong Kong, because Hong Kong thinks that anything about Tibet is interesting now. They didn't when we first started talking to them, but they have changed in the last three years.

McLAGAN: Can we get a little more macro here and move beyond the mechanics. How do you think TIN has affected the Tibet Movement?

BARNETT: It has invited Dharamsala to adopt similar approaches and techniques. I wouldn't be able to say this authoritatively because I have no idea whether it's true, but I would guess that it has given Dharamsala ideas about how to present information in ways that are more Western-friendly. Updates, short items, focused targeted items on a factual basis. They might have been doing it anyway, actually, they were doing fantastic stuff in the sixties.

McLAGAN: But if you had to sum up for someone who didn't know anything about the movement, how would you say that you have affected things?

BARNETT: Well, in a sense, there wasn't anything else before, but we have created at least one area of information which appears to describe what's happening but doesn't have a political agenda. That's the optimum interpretation of what we've done. I would reject anything that was given to me by the exile government or a lobby group. I would look to see if there is any organization whose reputation, whose survival, and income depended on them being accurate, or relatively accurate. That's what we try to do. Because we don't have any other interest, we can't survive unless we produce accurate information, so it's in our own interest to get it right. Therefore, if we happen to find information that says something that Dharamsala is also saying, then there is a better chance of being believed. We make it into the media. Now Dharamsala has started to make it into media as well in the same way.

Two things are happening now which I don't entirely approve of, but they're very interesting. One is, in the last few weeks the wire services in Beijing have started to print Dharamsala releases, which they've never done before. Partly because there's one very, very smart Tibetan trained at Columbia, Tseten Samdup, who's started to copy his Dharamsala material to the same people we send stuff to—AP [Associated Press] and AFP [Agence France Presse] and so on.

McLAGAN: So he writes a press release in London and faxes it to Reuters in Beijing, and it comes out under the government in exile's name?

BARNETT: Yes. In the past this was always done by AFP and sometimes Reuters out of Delhi. But it was never highly rated, it just didn't have authority because it's not from a Beijing source. They are not experts, but now for the last month Tseten has been using our approach of going to Beijing, and they've printed a couple of his releases from Dharamsala. More importantly, we find him a really helpful person in that he supports entirely our principle of maintaining independence at all costs.

There's other very interesting news. There is material coming out of Tibet recently that is high in factual content. The latest appeal to come out of Tibet, which was a bit related to our own contacts and which ostensibly comes from a village in Tibet, appears to be very direct and purely factual. Although it came through our contacts—it may have been altered in the process, I don't know—but it has no rhetoric or emotional appeal. It just says we want support from the UN for the following situation and then describes the situation without exaggeration or flourish. That's culturally really extraordinary. That's exactly the kind of new culture we've invited and that has developed.

The link is that we were approached by the VOA [Voice of America], which has a daily broadcast in Tibetan, and they did a number of interviews with us about what TIN's ideas are regarding what constitutes valuable information. They then broadcast the interviews about facticity and the Western idea of what a valid statement is into Tibet.

They say that VOA has enormous impact, that it is the one thing Tibetans talk about all the time. VOA is quite strict itself in what it puts out. The increase in quality that I'm seeing is because VOA is probably broadcasting in that quality, not because I said it on the radio. It is because Tibetans are hearing everyday news broadcasts in a VOA form which is very careful. They report whether a story is confirmed or not, they use very restrained language and are very cautious and precise—it is quite impressive. So that is what is having the impact. The use of radio in Tibet is widespread. Actually, videos have a big impact as well.

McLAGAN: How do conferences and online journals or newsletters, such as CanTibNet or talk.politics.tibet, advance the Tibet Movement or serve the Tibetan community? Or is all this posting futile?

BARNETT: Well, I don't have any interest in the movement; I don't know what that means. I mean, I'm not interested in the Tibet Movement so I wouldn't answer the first part of your question. We haven't talked about e-mail; that's person to person. We get fantastic value out of being able to transfer large amounts of information directly to people with computers. Especially using confidential procedures.

McLAGAN: You are talking about communicating via e-mail with Amnesty or Asia Watch or with people who are outside.

BARNETT: Amnesty, Asia Watch, some of these environmental organizations, our specialists, people who are academics, people who work on the issue. It's incredibly useful for us to be able to send a detailed long stretch of something very fast. For example, the database analysis of prisoners is done by somebody who is changing addresses every week and phones into his e-mail box every day from wherever he is and picks up our prisoner list, which we e-mail to him and he then puts it into a database so the analysis of prisoners is done by some guy traveling around the world. And we talk to him everyday. And if we want to we can make it secure. In this respect e-mail is not futile at all.

We are creating a corpus of material that can be accessed by either conference or the CanTibNet archive. In a way, it's not very good because it doesn't do anything, it just sits there and waits for somebody to use it, but as it happens there are people who want to use it. So even though we are independent, it is an entirely dependent process because we don't carry anything through to anywhere. Although we call ourselves pragmatic action, we're not in that we don't have any end. The same with CTN in a way, although it does include some demands and requests for action.

McLAGAN: I would say that CanTibNet's orientation is activist and what you are saying is that your orientation is not activist, at least directly.

BARNETT: It isn't activist at all. It's just that the material is used by activists. We don't see ourselves as part of an activist movement, although we are aware that activists see us as part of their movement.

There is a complex subdivision. We say we are just providing resources, information, to people who want it. If the Chinese want it, that's fine. Information that says that China's wonderful, if it was news, we'd print it. As it is, we don't need to; China prints enough news saying it's wonderful. If we had news saying Dharamsala was committing atrocities, if it was news, we'd print that, too. No question. There is a sense of exposing atrocities as implicitly

activist, but I would say that journalists represent, by their existence, a prag-
matist activist statement that information should be allowed to flow.

The information that we print about human rights is incidental in the sense
that because it makes the most news at the moment, it gets printed. In two
years' time, it will just be news about social and economic conditions. Because hopefully they will have cleaned up the human rights problems in Tibet
and we won't be seen as activist in quite that way.

> From: IN%"tin@gn.apc.org" "Robbie Barnett" 19-May-1993 19:20:
> 12:24
> To: IN%"tin-list@UTORGPU@bitnet"
> Subj: Arrests, Torture Fears During Diplomats Visit
>
> TIN News Update / May 19, 1993
> Arrests and Fear of Torture in Lhasa During EC Visit
> Reports are coming in of a wave of arrests in the Tibetan capital,
> Lhasa, amidst growing fears that three key prisoners arrested last
> week are being tortured in prison. The arrests could torpedo last-
> minute attempts to get President Clinton to renew unconditionally
> China's special trade privileges with the US, due for renewal by
> June 3rd.
>
> Dozens of suspected dissidents are said to have been detained in
> Lhasa in the last few days, according to claims received today from
> unofficial sources in the city. The arrests appear to be an attempt
> to prevent Tibetans from disrupting a visit to Lhasa by a group of
> western diplomats representing the 12 countries of the European
> Community.
>
> Police are believed to have accused the group of planning to deliver a
> letter to the diplomats about human rights conditions in Tibet. Passing
> of information about human rights conditions to foreigners is re-
> garded in Chinese law as an act of espionage, which in certain circum-
> stances carry the death sentence. One of the three detainees arrested
> last Thursday, 46-year old Gendun Rinchen, from Eastern Tibet,
> speaks good English and is well-known to foreigners as one of the
> best tour guides in Lhasa.

The following interview with Tseten Samdup took place in the Office of
Tibet in the Kilburn section of London, on 23 December 1993.

McLAGAN: I wonder if you could tell me a little bit about your work. Has it
changed in the last few years, since you've been in London?

SAMDUP: Well, the Office of Tibet London is a de facto embassy, but without status and recognition. People expect us to have the same sort of services
as an embassy, except of course we can't issue visas. The nature of my work is

mainly to keep tabs on what the media are saying about Tibet, to try to plant stories, to keep the journalists happy. Whether a story is good or bad is not important. What is important is that they are getting information about developments inside Tibet as well as within the exile community. I do a lot of compiling and analyzing of information, and sending it on to organizations which in turn distribute it further.

There has been a big change in the flow of information with the introduction of new technologies. When you get more involved with this sort of work, you find that a simple fax machine is not enough. You need a fax/modem because that enables you to just sit there and type out something, for example, a press release, and use preprogrammed addresses to send it automatically at midnight, when the phone rates are cheap, rather than having to sit there and do it, one by one. That's the advantage of a fax/modem.

I have also been using e-mail, both Compuserve as well as GreenNet. I use GreenNet mainly to send out information and for networking, and Compuserve to download wire service stories on Tibet. I find England much more capitalistic than America in terms of communications.

McLagan: Really?

Samdup: Yes, there are so many more restrictions than in America. For instance, when I was at Columbia University, I could just go to the library and punch in Tibet, and I'd get all the newspaper and magazine stories from Lexis/Nexis. I can do that on Compuserve, but it's expensive. At Columbia, it was free. That is my frustration now. I know there is information out there but I find getting it is expensive. And because we don't have the funds, we have to depend upon people's generosity. With Lexis/Nexis you can get American and British newspapers, but here each time you want to search for a newspaper article on Compuserve, it's five pounds for a search. Plus ten pounds or something like that for each story you download. So it's forbiddingly expensive to do it.

McLagan: Please describe to me what your media strategy is.

Samdup: Our media strategy is very simple. To get as many positive stories on Tibet published as possible. Not in any sort of forum, but in mainstream newspapers or magazines that are important. We haven't been as successful with regional newspapers because of lack of resources.

McLagan: Your focus is on British media?

Samdup: Actually, this office is responsible for Tibetan affairs in the Nordic countries, the Republic of Ireland, Iceland, and the UK, but we have to limit our circles. As I said, with the British, we have done well, and I think it is partly to do with the media sympathy for Tibet. That is our advantage. If it wasn't there, we would really have a tough time getting our message across.

Also, it helps that I have a degree in journalism and that I know how a journalist functions, and how to judge whether a story that comes from Tibet, India, or Nepal is important or not. You can't put in every story because they will get annoyed and you will lose your credibility.

McLAGAN: Can you talk about that? How do you decide if something is important when it comes in?

SAMDUP: Well, for instance, when something comes across my desk which we have doubts about, we try to cross-check with different sources, or try to make sure that Dharamsala has more information. If there is no information, then I tell people that we can't confirm it. We try not to do that too often. I think because we represent His Holiness the Dalai Lama we are viewed as a credible source. On the other hand, because we are a government, people think that we are portraying our point of view and not the general consensus. Sometimes the media tend not to come to us, they try to go to independent organizations instead, which is frustrating, because sometimes we have information.

If something happens in Tibet, I should not be calling Tibet to ask what is going on. Being a government, you have certain unwritten laws that you are not supposed to break. So I call Hong Kong and Beijing, I talk to the journalists, mostly the wire service people.

McLAGAN: What do you mean you are not supposed to call?

SAMDUP: It's like an American diplomat might not call Cuba or Russia. There's no such thing as saying you can't do it, it's just that you censor yourself.

McLAGAN: So you wouldn't call Tibet to have a story confirmed?

SAMDUP: I've done it in the past when we have received reports of demonstrations. I have picked up the phone and called one of the Lhasa hotels or police station or bus station to say, "I have some relatives visiting Tibet, I haven't heard from them, have they been in the disturbance, I believe there was something today in so and so place, is it true?" Mostly people deny it, but when they do you know that they are doing it because the phones are monitored, and I have been able to sense the nervousness in the person's voice. So we do call. Sometimes when I try to call Lhasa to get a story, if I can't get an answer, I call Beijing to say, "Look I'm having problems getting Lhasa, do you know what's happening?" So that alerts them there's a story, check it out.

McLAGAN: One of the things Robbie said in his discussion with me was that you had started going to the Beijing wire services and were able to plant stories that way. Can you talk a little bit about this strategy?

SAMDUP: Basically, when you are a journalist, you are looking for scoops. You want exclusives that other people don't have. Sometimes I just show the Beijing reporters the tip of the iceberg, and if I sense that they are interested, I give them the entire story. I do it based on what they have written in the past.

I also have a list of people whom they can contact if they want to interview

someone. The moment they sense that you are not organized, that you don't
have the information at hand, they hesitate. Being a journalist, I have the advantage of knowing what things people are looking for. Not just supplying
stories but also giving them background information as to whether the story
was touched by somebody, if so, which angle it was covered, and so on. Most
journalists are pressed for time. How much homework you do helps a great
deal in planting the story as well as making the person feel easy, because if
he finds that there's a story but it's difficult to write, next time he hesitates.
I function as a backup, someone who's going to provide him information,
arrange for him to speak to different people. That's very important.

The advantage of being in London is that we have the BBC here. Besides
Americans, everyone listens to the BBC World Service. From that point of
view it is very important that we get our stories as much as possible on the
BBC. Of course, CNN is important, but people think that CNN is American
propaganda. Same for the Voice of America.

Anyway, one of my main tasks is to work with the BBC. They are very
interested in Tibetan developments. Whenever there's a story I make sure that
they can talk to someone higher up in India to confirm or to give the official
government line. Sometimes the journalists will talk to me, but because I'm
just an individual, with no status, they will take my background briefing but
they will not quote me by name, only as an official.

When I have a story, I send a press release. I call people, for instance,
David Watts at the *Times*. I say, "David, did you get the story?" He says
"Yes, except I don't think I'm going to do it this time." Then I call the *Financial Times:* "Alex, did you get the story? What do you think about it?" He
says, "Well, I'm sitting on it." It means it's not good. Then I try again, I push
and say, "Look, this is really important for these reasons."

One of the disadvantages of being in London is that there is no access to
Tibet. People can't just walk in or out of Tibet. So if there is something happening in Tibet, you can't provide the media with footage or sound bites. I'll
give you an example of what happened in May this year, when demonstrations broke out. I called the BBC television editor John Simpson—I've spoken to him before because he wanted to interview the Dalai Lama, so I had
his personal number. I called him up and said, "Look, this is happening in
Tibet, you've got to do a story on this, because this has not happened for three
or four years and the European ambassador is there." He said, "Look, you
guys never warned me about it." How could we have known? There's not any
warning, it happened spontaneously! Then he said, "There's no footage." I
said, "What do you mean there's no footage? Not everyone gets to go in!"
I told him, "You can use old footage, you can tell the story from that." Then
I said, "You know, you guys have access to Bosnia, and everyday you have
a story from there, but when something breaks in Tibet, why aren't you out

doing the story?" He said, "You have a point there." And they did a story. I'm not saying that it's because of me, but you've just got to push them, make them more aware. So from that point of view, perseverance helps.

I think the biggest advantage for us is when the Dalai Lama comes here, because all the top journalists call you. That's the time when you can say, "Can you give me your private number?" Then you are able to keep the number and use it in the future. I take advantage of that when His Holiness is coming to town.

McLAGAN: And then they meet him?

SAMDUP: Not all of them get to meet him, but if they want to interview him they have to give me a number where I can contact them, and usually they have high hopes that they are going to get the interview so they give me a number, which is more or less a classified or private number.

McLAGAN: So you find that you have much greater access when His Holiness is coming to town?

SAMDUP: Oh yes, definitely. Much greater. When His Holiness comes to town, we are really important [*laughs*]. Otherwise we are not important. We are important, I suppose, from the story point of view, because the Dalai Lama is a story. He creates stories.

McLAGAN: Tell me why he is a story.

SAMDUP: I guess he's a story because he's this mysterious man. He's always laughing. So much has happened to his country yet he talks about compassion, love, and doesn't talk about violence. Most leaders, whose countries have suffered, talk about violence, so I think they want to know what's so special about this person. They might know the Dalai Lama but they might not know about Tibet. He's more important; he's more of a known entity than Tibet itself.

McLAGAN: So that's what makes him news?

SAMDUP: Yes, I think that is what makes him news. Being head of a refugee community that's doing well, also Chinese oppression in Tibet, all the Tibetan people have stuck together as a community under a leadership which causes people to ask what makes him so unique.

From: IN%"ctn-editors@utcc.utoronto.ca"
To: IN%"ctn-list@utcc.utoronto.ca"
Subj: CTN 93/06/10 20:10 GMT
--------------------------CanTibNet Newsletter --------------------------
Published by: The Canada-Tibet Committee
Editorial Board: Brian Given (bgiven@ccs.carleton.ca)
Nima Dorjee (amnesty@acs.ucalgary.ca)
Conrad Richter (richter@gpu.utcs.utoronto.ca)
Submissions to: ctn-editors@gpu.utcs.utoronto.ca
or fax to: +1-416-640-6641

We encourage discussion on articles. Send us your comments, announcements, news or items for discussion.

Anthony Whitworth, WCHR Project
Association for Progressive Communications

FOR IMMEDIATE RELEASE—10 June 1993

Dalai Lama's Address to NGO's Forum in Vienna Cancelled

His Holiness the Dalai Lama's planned address to the Non-Governmental Organization Forum at the United Nations World Conference on Human Rights in Vienna has been cancelled due to Chinese pressure.

Mr. Manfred Novak, the Director of the Vienna Ludwig Boltzmann Institute of Human Rights and senior member of the Joint NGO Planning Committee informed the Tibetan delegation this afternoon that due to strong pressure His Holiness' participation in the NGO forum has been cancelled.

In addition, the planned seminar, Tibet: 43 Years of Human Rights Violations, on June 22, part of the NGO parallel activities, has also been cancelled.

Tashi Wangdi, the leader of the Tibetan Government-in-exile's delegation, said he regrets that under pressure His Holiness' address to over 3000 Non-Governmental Organizations will not proceed.

His Holiness the Dalai Lama, the 1989 Nobel Peace Laureate, was invited to Vienna by the Austrian Foreign Minister Dr. Alois Mock to participate in parallel events in connection with the World conference. His Holiness is due to arrive in Vienna on Sunday, June 13.

Contact Tseten Samdup in Vienna
Telephone No. 4028666 ext. 809
The Tibet Bureau
rue de l'Ancien Port 13/3
1201 Geneva, Switzerland
Tel: 022 738-79-40
Fax: 022 738-79-40

McLAGAN: The Dalai Lama was certainly news last summer. I know you were in Vienna at the World Conference on Human Rights, and I wondered if you could tell me what role you played in shaping the story that came out about the controversy?

SAMDUP: My main role was to work with the media. What happened was this: China tried to block the Dalai Lama from speaking. Neither the journalists nor the NGOs knew why the Chinese were doing it, why China was being so bad. So that became a story. Why won't they let a person who won the Nobel Peace Prize speak? Why is this person so powerful that China doesn't want him to speak? So China became the bad guy. They became even more so when they did not allow the NGOs to sit in on the drafting committee of the declaration.[22]

It is like what His Holiness says, "Your enemy is your best teacher. Your enemy lets you do things for yourself." If His Holiness is traveling and China just keeps quiet, he might not get that much attention. But because China makes so much *noise,* because it tells the British Foreign Office that it must not receive the Dalai Lama, it's a story! To give you the latest example, there was a documentary film about Mao Tse-tung that was broadcast here on Monday. Before that, the Chinese tried to tell the British they couldn't air it. The Chinese don't have the faintest idea of what a free press is, what they can or cannot do. When they behave like that, people wonder, why is China so vicious? If they think they can tell us here what we should or shouldn't do, imagine what they do to their own people.

McLAGAN: How did the decision to bar His Holiness get reversed?

SAMDUP: I think it got reversed in various ways. There was strong, strong pressure from the press.

McLAGAN: Press, meaning print journalists or everyone?

SAMDUP: Everyone. CNN had a story almost every day saying, "The Dalai Lama has come here, invited as a guest of the Austrian government, to a conference on human rights, why isn't this man allowed to speak?" Also, the NGOs were frustrated because they were there to make sure that everyone had human rights and here a world leader was being denied his rights. Third, the Austrian government invited His Holiness, and their guest was more or less being told that he couldn't come to a conference that had been organized in the Austrian capital. So there were various factors.

McLAGAN: Did you put out stories from Vienna?

SAMDUP: Oh yes. My main story was about what was happening, what we thought about it. But it was a very tricky situation for us. We couldn't really put out too many stories. We had to talk to people more or less in confidence. We didn't try too hard to project the Dalai Lama because that's not what we consider important. We wanted to talk about the Tibetan issue, not the Dalai Lama. The Tibetan issue is the major issue, the Dalai Lama is one individual, he's our leader, but he is not the story. The story is the suffering of the Tibetan people in Tibet. The Dalai Lama, being the leader of the Tibetans, he's the spokesperson of these people, so therefore he has to get the opportunity to speak. That was our point. We wanted to be careful as to how it was portrayed. We wanted the journalists to know that there was real concern among the honorary delegates that they be able to hear what the Dalai Lama had to say. But we didn't want it to appear that we Tibetans were imposing our view on the organizers that the Dalai Lama should speak.

McLAGAN: What was your communications strategy?

SAMDUP: We haunted the e-mail center set up by the Association for Progressive Communications every day. Actually, I will read you something [from the IGC newsletter] which you will be quite surprised at. It says, "APC at Vienna UN Human Rights Conference. The first day APC opened for public use, the Tibetan delegation pounded out messages, appeals, press releases, and endless e-mail messages to their office in London in an effort to get the Dalai Lama to be allowed to come to the conference. Their effort paid off. The Tibetan leader visited the Austrian center a couple of days later. A large number of the Tibetans here experienced how e-mail can help them in their work, the London office communicated daily with the Tibetan delegation in Vienna."

McLAGAN: So they actually made your use of their network a story?

SAMDUP: They made it into a story to demonstrate how people were using their online center, how so many people used it, including these Tibetans, who were using their computer and e-mail services to send messages and press releases, and so on. As I said, that's how we become stories.

McLAGAN: It sounds as though the APC communications setup was effective.

SAMDUP: Oh yes, very effective. Frankly, it would have been more effective if I had known more about e-mail. But at that time I had just been online a couple of months. In Vienna I made sure that all the stories I was putting out on human rights came out in the APC United Nations Human Rights Conference because that is a permanent record, it houses all the official documents, press releases, etc., and people have access to it.

McLAGAN: That is how I got interested in the Vienna Conference, when I saw on PeaceNet that APC had set up an online center for people to use to communicate with other conference participants and with the rest of the world. Then when His Holiness was barred, I became interested in how this technology was being used to mobilize public support.

SAMDUP: The day we were told that we were not being allowed in, I don't remember the exact date, but it was a Sunday. We did a press release, went to post office to fax it, but it was closed. I was stuck. Then I ran into one of the organizers of the APC center who said he knew about the Tibetans. "Don't worry," he said, "I will help you send out all your e-mail, you can send faxes to Dharamsala and your other offices." So we went to the center, and there were a whole lot of nice people there who knew about Tibet and were sympathetic to us, and they let us use the facilities.

McLAGAN: Do you read the Tibet conferences on the computer?

SAMDUP: In the last two years the conferences on Tibet have developed from nothing to something really big. My worry now is that it is getting out of proportion.

McLAGAN: Really? In what sense?

SAMDUP: In the sense that every story on Tibet is getting put online. I find that rather scary. Now that I'm the European editor of the *CanTibNet Newsletter,* each day there are six or seven stories, and it's a little overwhelming, especially since I have other responsibilities.

If we had access to Lexis/Nexis, then we'd have a wider range to choose from and could be more selective as to what we publish. At the moment, we are limited by what people give us; we are at the mercy of our sources. Suppose that *CanTibNet Newsletter* gets access to Lexis/Nexis and they start using it, I think most of the subscribers would just say, "Okay, we don't want it anymore, it's too much, we can't handle it." So from nothing you go to something and then when you reach that something, people are worried that it is too much.

McLAGAN: So basically you are feeding Nima and Conrad [coeditors of the former CanTibNet] in Canada with information that comes to you.

SAMDUP: I'm just a broker, I take it and pass it along [*laughs*]. So that's what I'm getting scared of, it gets too overwhelming. I think we should break up CTN into different conferences. Political, cultural, economic.

McLAGAN: So you don't feel that computers are the answer to everything in terms of publicizing the Tibet issue?

SAMDUP: Everyone says that the computer will solve everything. The computer will not solve the problem of spreading information. It's just a vehicle in the sense that technology enables you to do something at a faster speed; at no time does it lessen your workload. I would challenge anybody who says otherwise. It gives you more work.

McLAGAN: To get back to the issue of computer networks and conferences, what purposes do you think they serve?

SAMDUP: These networks save the person who is doing a story a lot of time if he can send it online. He doesn't have to send a fax, he doesn't have to seal envelopes, he can e-mail his story directly to everyone on the mailing list.

In terms of the various conferences that one can go into, like the Asia human rights forum on GreenNet, I think those are the areas that we should look into. We need to contact different networks and ask them what forums they have and then target the appropriate ones. We need to not only reach more people but reach different areas. That's very important, but we haven't been able to do that yet.

McLAGAN: One of the things that people in America always assert is that computer-mediated communication like fax and computers facilitate democracy. I wondered if you've heard that.

SAMDUP: Well, in America anything promotes democracy. What's the first act in the Constitution?

McLAGAN: The First Amendment?

SAMDUP: Yes, the First Amendment. You Americans go for anything First Amendment. When I was doing my Columbia journalism course, we had an American lawyer as well as a *New York Times* columnist, Anthony Lewis, teach us about the First Amendment, and it came to a point when I was telling somebody, "I think the First Amendment will do the job for you, it defends you against the government, against everything."

But the issue of democratic use of computers has practical aspects as well. In America, you can make one phone call and speak for three hours for ten pence. In this country you can't. I was talking to the *CanTibNet Newsletter* people and I said, "Fine, you have a lot of stories, but you've got to realize that people have to spend money to read them."

McLAGAN: So in that sense information is costly.

SAMDUP: Outside of North America, information is costly. For instance, if Dharamsala wants to send something, they have to dial New Delhi, they can't just dial locally, there's no local host. It gets very expensive.[23]

McLAGAN: What do you think about the discourse on cyberspace?

SAMDUP: I think it is totally overblown. Does everyone in the third world have access to a computer, do they own a phone? If you don't have them, how can you say that these technologies help democracy? If people have to boil water, but they don't have fuel, how can they boil water? If there is no water, how can you wash your hands? You can wash your hands with some dirty water, but that doesn't do the trick. I think it is democracy for the privileged. I would call it democracy for the haves, not for the have-nots.

McLAGAN: One of the ways in which people claim that these networks are democratic is that supposedly they enable people to shift positions from being consumers of information to being producers of information.

SAMDUP: That's true, but it varies from person to person, frankly speaking. Previously I was a consumer, now I'm sending out information, so my position has changed. It is part of my work. Someone like you would only send out information regarding you.

One thing I've noticed is that you become much more greedy, not in terms of economic materialism, but you become obsessed with the technology, with upgrading. Now that I have a fax/modem, I want a scanner.

McLAGAN: Yes. It's very addictive. I wanted to talk to you a little bit about your idea of what constitutes information. When you put your stories out, are you putting them out with an end in mind?

SAMDUP: Well, I put out information according to our own agenda. What we want people to know about, what our organization is doing. A lot of the information that CanTibNet puts out is what other people are saying about Tibet, but here at the Office of Tibet London, it is what the government in exile wants to say about Tibet.

McLAGAN: And how is that different from what Robbie does?

SAMDUP: Robbie is not accountable to us. He is independent and writes what he thinks is important. He is credible, but I wouldn't say he is more credible than us. See, our agendas are different. Our agenda is to create more of an interest in Tibet.

McLAGAN: What is his agenda?

SAMDUP: His agenda is to monitor developments in Tibet. Those two things are different.

McLAGAN: How would you say the media typically represents Tibet over here?

SAMDUP: Very sympathetically.

McLAGAN: Is it a sophisticated representation?

SAMDUP: What do you mean by that?

McLAGAN: Well, is it stereotyped? Is it dumb, stupid, uninformed?

SAMDUP: Yes, sometimes it can be really dumb, and I get frustrated. Why don't they just call on the phone and ask us, "Is this story true or not?" Or, "Can you comment on this?" But as a journalist I know the limitations people face. There's a five o'clock deadline, you have no time to make a phone call, so you write something, and sometimes you make a mistake.

McLAGAN: For instance, during the Year of Tibet I collected press clippings, and it seemed like a lot of the coverage was fairly inane and problematic in terms of making Tibetans seem like cuddly panda bears. In other words, not serious about their struggle.

SAMDUP: It is an attitude everyone has. You want to make it sensational. A Tibetan, does he know how to eat? Can he work a computer? Does he know what's inside a computer? They try to give an image that this guy is from another world, who doesn't know what's happening. That has its advantages and disadvantages, because people say, "Oh, this is interesting," then they learn about Tibet. But you have to go beyond the impression that creates. The first step is that people know about Tibet. The second step relates to what their knowledge of Tibet is. Do they think Tibetans are primitive or barbaric, do they think Tibetans are advanced? Do they think Tibetans are sympathetic, compassionate? What do they think of Tibet? First reach them and then work on what they think about Tibet. Sometimes when journalists write, my boss gets mad but I just don't take much notice of it because I'm a journalist and I tend to identify with the problem.

For instance, if someone calls up and asks, "What shoes does the Dalai Lama wear?" or, "Are the glasses he wears made by so and so company?" I think to myself, is it important? Is it relevant? It is not important but people want to add flavor to their story. But when you add too much flavor, you lose the real central theme that we would like people to talk about.

McLAGAN: Which is?

SAMDUP: Which is the suffering of Tibetans, the loss of their country, the fact that they are refugees. Again, when you say refugees, people talk about you as though you are pathetic, that you need attention. It has a lot to do with people's understanding of the situation, of what a refugee is and what a refugee goes through. If that understanding is not good, then the story suffers.

I take myself as an example. When I was at Columbia I specialized in international and diplomatic reporting. I had no problems with it, though some of my American classmates did because their knowledge of international affairs was not as good as mine. But I had problems in terms of local reporting. I didn't know much about the drug or housing problems in New York and didn't want to do things like court reporting.

McLAGAN: Do you think this job is something you will stay with?

SAMDUP: I will stay with this so long as I feel the environment is good and that I'm useful. If someone asks me do you think you will go back to India, can you do the job effectively there, I would say no. Because in this office, there are two people. If you get something from Dharamsala, the boss gives it to you and you do it. If there's something happening in Tibet, I can pick up the phone and talk to the foreign minister and say, "This is happening, they are going to call me for more information, what should I say?" I'm able to talk to the people who are responsible for making policy. If I was in Dharamsala, I might not be very close to His Holiness—I'm not talking about a close working relationship, but in terms of close physical contact. When he comes here, I am close to him. Of course, I would go back to India if the government asked me to.

McLAGAN: One of the things I talked with Robbie about was his commitment to Western standards of facticity. He said that he felt that at times Dharamsala did not show this commitment. Do you have any thoughts on that?

SAMDUP: I agree with him, but at the same time, Robbie has to understand that when you are dealing with an organization or a government that is in Asia, it is not in the West. So the person is not in Hampstead. The person is how many kilometers away? How people look at journalism there is different.

McLAGAN: How do they look at journalism?

SAMDUP: They look at any story that is happening in Tibet as important. If something is happening, that's news.

Also, being a government, they wonder if this has come from so-and-so source. Can we release it because it might compromise somebody? But Robbie has to make a decision for himself, he doesn't have to consult the Department of Security or the Kashag. He can just say, "Okay, I think I can do it." As the size of an organization grows, the flow of information and communication deteriorates. When you are small it is more effective.

McLAGAN: But is there a difference between the Tibetan notion and the Western notion of what constitutes information? Do they have different attitudes toward information?

SAMDUP: I think there is a difference in terms of the possessiveness of information. People in the East tend to keep things to themselves. The problem is that the Tibetan people who have escaped from Tibet sometimes don't tell the entire story, because they think, what good would it do? They may report that something has happened, but they don't often give the specific details of how, when, or where it happened. Or various people have come out who exaggerate their stories. So for us the biggest problem is providing accurate information, being observant.

Plus, if we get some information from Tibet and don't use it properly, if we blow covers, we are in trouble. Not only do we put someone at risk but we lose an important source of information. That is one of the reasons why there are a lot of restrictions—we are accountable to the people in Tibet.

The use of computer-mediated communication to address political issues represents a new practice in the post-cold war era, one that is being negotiated piece by piece. In the meantime, we need to develop a discourse that allows us to critically discuss the complexities of this new form of social action. As the interviews with Barnett and Samdup suggest, despite utopian first world (and ethnocentric) pronouncements on computer activism and "virtual communities," which are rooted in a McLuhanesque belief in an electronic democracy, there is still a disjunction between the promise of intercultural solidarity and the reality of cultural, political, and economic differences. Mediators of knowledge like Barnett and Samdup may be able to (temporarily) transcend the limitations of time and space in their computing for Tibet, but it remains to be seen how effective this "virtual" mode of engagement will be in the future. The existing structures of power in Tibet and elsewhere continue to pose a formidable challenge to even the most innovative of activists, and the circulation of information, so often taken for granted in the West, often comes at a high personal price, as this last posting suggests:

> From: IN%"tin@gn.apc.org" 26-JUN-1994 02:37:33.92
> To: IN%"tin-list@UTORGPU.bitnet"
> Subj: 250+ Political Prisoners in Lhasa
>
> TIN News Update / 22 June, 1994 v2/ total no of pages: 3
>
> There are now over 250 political prisoners in Tibet's main prison, more than double the number four years ago, according to detailed reports received from unofficial sources in Lhasa. The number of

women political prisoners in the prison has tripled in the last three years . . . One man, a former school teacher, is serving a 28 year sentence for shouting or writing pro-independence slogans . . . The majority of the 255 prisoners have been convicted of "spreading counter-revolutionary propaganda", a term used by the Chinese to describe shouting a political slogan or distributing a pamphlet. Most of the sentences of 15 years or more have gone to people who formed "counter-revolutionary organisations", meaning that they were in groups that supported independence . . .

Meanwhile unofficial reports continue to emerge from Tibet of the transfer in early April of just over 300 prisoners to remote labour camps in Qinghai, 1200 km north east of Lhasa. It is not clear how many if any of these prisoners were being held for political offences. Although it is common in China itself for prisoners to be sent to re-mote prisons, this is the first time since the current wave of unrest began 7 years ago that prisoners from the Tibet Autonomous Region have been shifted to another province. The development, a major change in security policy, will enormously hamper monitoring efforts as well as attempts by local Tibetans to ensure that prisoners are sup-plied with adequate food and clothing.
- end -

Notes

This paper is based on research conducted in London in 1993 with the generous support of the Wenner-Gren Foundation for Anthropological Research. The writing of this study was made possible by a National Endowment for the Humanities Dissertation Award (FD-21450-93) and a Dean's Dissertation Fellowship from New York University. I am grateful to Robbie Barnett and Tseten Samdup for fitting me into their busy sched-ules. I would also like to thank Brian Larkin, Faye Ginsburg, Chris Pound, Robyn Bren-tano, Lisa Keary, and Patti Sunderland for their helpful comments on this piece.

The following is a list of e-mail addresses for some Tibet organizations and offices around the world:
    --International Committee of Lawyers for Tibet, USA
    <iclt@igc.apc.org>
    --Canada Tibet Committee <richter@utcc.utoronto.ca>
    --International Campaign for Tibet <ict@igc.apc.org>
    --Office of Tibet, New York <otny@igc.apc.org>
    --Office of Tibet, London <tibetlondon@gn.apc.org>
    --Alaska Tibet Committee <dpaljor@igc.apc.org>
    --Tibet Computing Resource Center, Dharamsala
    <tcrc@cta.unv.ernet.in>

1. According to Appadurai, "postnational social formations" are organizations, movements, ideologies, and networks which are not contained or defined solely in re-lation to the nation-state. They are "more diverse, more fluid, more ad hoc, more pro-

visional, less coherent, less organized, and simply less implicated in the comparative advantages of the nation-state" (1993:420). They include organizations and movements that monitor activities of the nation-state, such as Amnesty International, as well as those that "work to contain the excesses of the nation-state," such as UN-related organizations, nongovernmental organizations (NGOs), and biopolitical movements like the Greens. They also include such things as transnational philanthropic movements, international terrorist organizations, and refugee camps, bureaucracies, and support organizations that float in between the "certainties and stabilities of the nation-state" and which are part of "the permanent framework of the emergent, postnational order" (1993:419).

2. Scholars argue that a new kind of global community has emerged in the last decade, one that is increasingly a force in international relations and whose development has been fostered by the explosive growth of NGOs. This community, what Hamelink (1991) calls "global civil society," has gained even more influence with the reorganization of political alliances during the post-cold war period. See also Boulding (1988).

3. In saying this, I do not mean to belittle the political significance of the issue of universal access to digitalized computer networks in this country.

4. Edwards (1994) is an interesting exception. In his account of the use of computer conferences by diasporic Afghans, Edwards argues that Afghans around the world engage in a form of "simulated politics" through heated debates on the USENET newsgroup <soc.culture.afghan>.

5. In the last decade the spread of new media technologies, such as portable video cameras, VCRs, networked computers, cable television, fax, satellite communications, and cassettes, has created the potential for decentralized communication and collective self-expression for many groups around the world (see Ginsburg 1991, 1993; Turner 1990, 1991). Recently, these new media forms, especially computer networks and faxes, have played an important role the political crises in Thailand (see Hamilton 1993), Russia, and China (see Calhoun 1989).

6. "Virtual communities" are defined as groups of people linked together by their participation in computer networks. See Rheingold (1993) for an explanation of one of the most well-known electronic communities, the WELL (Whole Earth 'Lectronic Link).

7. Doctoral research was conducted 1990–93 in the following locations: New York City, Washington, D.C., San Francisco, London, Dharamsala, India, and in multiple sites in Switzerland, including Zurich, Geneva, Horgen, Flawil, Rikon, and Trogen.

8. For instance, the Tibetan delegation, led by the Dalai Lama, made a big splash at the United Nations Conference on Environment and Development (UNCED), otherwise known as the Earth Summit, in Rio de Janeiro, Brazil, in June 1992. While the Tibetans were shut out of the official proceedings, they attended the simultaneous NGO conferences and events, where they drew attention to environmental devastation in Tibet. The Tibetans' high profile was a result of Chinese attempts to pressure the Brazilian government into denying the Dalai Lama a visa. This generated a barrage of local media coverage, calling on the government to resist such arm-twisting, and ensuring the Dalai Lama large and sympathetic audiences wherever he went.

Tibet has also been on the agenda at the annual meeting of the UN Commission on Human Rights in Geneva since 1991, when a Tibet resolution was sponsored for the first time in twenty-four years. Although China has managed to persuade enough member nations of the commission to vote for "no action" four years running, the number of countries refusing to criticize China's human rights record has diminished with each passing year.

Finally, Tibetan women has already begun preparations for the UN Fourth World Conference on Women which will be held in Beijing in September 1995. While Tibet organizations may run into problems receiving NGO accreditation in order to attend the parallel NGO forum, they plan to work with other NGOs to ensure that Tibetan women's issues and concerns are raised at the meeting. Much of the preliminary networking being done by the Tibetan Women's Association, based in Dharamsala, and Western NGOs and Tibet support organizations has taken place via e-mail.

9. The Association for Progressive Communication (APC) is a prime example of the new forms of political association and mobilization which have emerged in recent years. Based in San Francisco, the APC is an international partnership of computer networks that provides low-cost and advanced communications services to activists, educators, community leaders, and policymakers in more than ninety-five countries through a distributed network of host computers. Since its establishment in 1990, the APC has overseen the global operations of PeaceNet, GreenNet, and many other "partner networks" which have sprung up in countries around the world, including Nicaragua, Sweden, Brazil, Canada, Australia, Costa Rica, Uruguay, Russia, Germany, Czechoslovakia, Kenya, and Bolivia. For more information on the history of the APC, see Howard Frederick's "Computer Networks and the Emergence of Global Civil Society: The Case of the Association for Progressive Communications," distributed on-line via the GASSHO newsletter 1, no. 3 (1994).

As of this writing (summer 1994), there are a number of other electronic networks and organizations dedicated to serving the human rights community, including Digital Freedom Net, a Gopher site in New Jersey which houses a library of material by censored writers around the world (the Internet address is <gopher.iia.org>, and Human Rights Network (HRNet), a multilingual information service which solicits and publishes updates on human rights issues around the world. APC networks also offer human rights conferences <igc.apc.org>. See "On the Internet, Dissidents' Shots Heard 'Round the World," *New York Times,* 5 June 1994.

10. In the context of this piece, *Western* is an analytic, political, and geographical category referring to members of industrialized societies in the Western Hemisphere. It is in keeping with the Tibetan term *inji,* which originally referred to the English, the first non-Asian foreigners Tibetans had extensive contact with, but which today is used by Tibetans to refer to any person from the West, regardless of nationality. It usually connotes whiteness.

11. My use of the term *friends* is not an attempt to be ironic; it is the word used by Tibetans when speaking to and about their supporters in public. I draw attention to it simply because the word encodes a particularly Tibetan conception of social relations between individuals and political entities, that of patron-client, or *mchod-yon,* which is explained in the text.

12. The total number of individuals who fled in 1959 is unknown; estimates range anywhere between 60,000 and 80,000. Today there are roughly 100,000 Tibetans living outside Tibet, the majority of whom are concentrated in settlements in India and Nepal.

The largest concentration of Tibetans found outside of Asia is in Switzerland, which is home to approximately 2,000 refugees and their families. The second largest concentration of Tibetans in the West is located in the United States, which has a population of roughly 1,500 Tibetans.

13. Klieger argues that the conflict between Tibetans and Chinese can be seen as a "differential misunderstanding of the traditional pattern of the patron/client framework that defined the relationship between the two polities in the past. . . . According to native Tibetan interpretations, in both modern refugee praxis as well as in native records back to at least the 17th century, no hint of client subordination can be seen. In native practice, the Tibetan state, as the estate of the Dalai Lama, should be considered at least equal to those agents which support it materially. A patron, however powerful, has no rights of interference in the affairs of his or her sacred client. The empire, by entering into a *mchod-yon* relationship with the Tibetan hierarch, and consequently Tibet, according to native interpretation, obtained no rights of sovereignty" (1992:19).

There is no stigma attached to being a recipient of patronage; in fact, quite the opposite is true, as Klieger noted while conducting fieldwork in Dharamsala: "The acquisition of foreign patrons is a device for obtaining prestige in the lay refugee community" (1992:104). Indeed, from a Buddhist perspective, it is honorable to be in a position to receive, as the client is providing the patron a vehicle by which the latter may accumulate spiritual merit. See also DeVoe (1983) and Nowak (1984).

14. Though the focus is on Western supporters in this piece, India's long-standing support of Tibetans must be acknowledged. First and foremost, the Indian government gave refuge to the Dalai Lama and his government and thousands of destitute Tibetans. It also provided land in a number of places, including Himachal Pradesh where the Dalai Lama settled, and Karnataka, in the south, where several large settlements were established. The Indians helped the refugees create a Tibetan school system and supplied other resources in the early years of resettlement. Indians have always felt a spiritual connection to Tibet, which preserved a form of Buddhism that originated in India but has long died out.

15. See Bishop (1989) and Lopez (1994).

16. Quoted in DeVoe (1985:1230).

17. In a recent article in *Tibetan Review,* United Kingdom-based scholar Tsering Shakya articulates a view of Western involvement with Tibet that is held by many of the Tibetan intellegentsia: "The West has always reduced Tibet to its image of Tibet, and imposed its yearning of spirituality and solace from the material world onto Tibet. In the same process, the West has sought to define the Tibetan political struggle. Tibetans are seen merely as victims who are unable to speak for themselves. . . . After decades of being reduced to the status of mere recipients of charity and sympathy, the process of reduction of Tibetans to an endangered species of the human family is nearly complete.

18. The Dalai Lama himself frequently describes old Tibet as a uniquely spiritual place and Tibetans as peace-loving, nonviolent, spiritual people. By proposing, as a first step toward resolving the future status of Tibet, that the plateau be established as a zone of peace, or *ahimsa,* the Dalai Lama is evoking a traditional Buddhist eschatology which associates Tibet with Shambala, thought to be both a physical area in eastern Turkestan (just north of Tibet) and a metaphysical "pure land," filled with enlightened

beings. In so doing, the Dalai Lama is imagining a future for Tibet in keeping with the Kalachakra tantra's prophecy of a golden age of peace and one that offers the possibility of spiritual fulfillment in a secularized world (see Brentano 1993).

What does it cost Tibetans to represent themselves in this way? Tibetan complicity in perpetuating a stereotypical image of Tibetans as victims and/or special spiritual beings cannot be gone into here, but it is worth pointing out that at the heart of the Tibet Movement is a contradiction. The contradiction is between the need to portray themselves a certain way (for example, as refugees, victims of human rights abuses, people whose unique religious culture is endangered) in order to garner support and reproduce themselves in exile, and the need to put themselves forward in the international arena as empowered political actors with an agenda of their own. By accepting Western discourses and representations, Tibetans facilitate their struggle in certain arenas and inhibit its progress in other fronts.

19. The address for World Tibet Network News is <wtn-editors@utcc.utoronto. ca>. Tibet Information Network's address is <tin@gn.apc.org>. Tibet News Digest has been merged with CanTibNet to form World Tibet Network News (see above). The TIBET-L discussion list address is <Listserv@iubvm.ucs.indiana.edu>. <Talk. politics.tibet> is a USENET newsgroup.

The Tibet Electronic Resource Guide (TERG) is a directory of computer network addresses of research facilities, archives, online databases, and resources of interest to the scholars and students of Tibet and Tibetan studies. To access tibet-electr-rsrc-guid-terg.txt, use the following Gopher: <coombs.anu.edu.au@/coombspapers/ otherarchives/asian-studies-archives/tibetan-archives/network-inf-sources; type 0, port 70>. For more information, contact <tmciolek@coombs.anu.edu.au>.

20. In some cases, the current trendiness of the Tibet issue in artistic/celebrity circles has led to a tendency by the Western media to treat Tibet as more of an entertainment issue than a political one, focusing on personalities as opposed to conditions in Tibet.

21. There is nothing new in arguing that television, and the media generally, can not be regarded as a mere observer and reporter of events and that they have become an integral part of the reality they report. In a familiar argument, Bennett (1982) has suggested that the media are "definers of social reality," a view which challenges one of the central tenets of Western journalism: that reporters must be objective, neutral and impartial. For a discussion of each side of the debate, see essays by Schudson, Gurevitch, and Lichtenberg in Curran and Gurevitch 1991.

22. Samdup is referring to the Vienna Declaration and Programme of Action, the final document adopted by participants at the World Conference on Human Rights.

23. The situation has changed somewhat since the interview in December 1993. The Canada Tibet Committee is currently funding the costs of operating a computer network connection from Delhi to Dharamsala and the costs of a local network that connects Tibetan government and cultural institution offices to the international computer network.

References

Appadurai, Arjun. 1993. "Patriotism and its Futures." *Public Culture* 5, no. 3: 411–29.

Bennett, Tony. 1982. "Media, 'Reality,' Signification." In *Culture, Society, and the Media,* ed. Michael Gurevitch et al. London: Methuen.

Bishop, Peter. 1989. *The Myth of Shangri-La: Tibet, Travel Writing and the Western Creation of a Sacred Landscape.* Berkeley: University of California Press.

Boulding, Elise. 1988. *Building a Global Civic Culture: Education for an Interdependent Planet.* Boulder, Colo.: Westview.

Brentano, Robyn. 1993. "The Wheel of Time: Symbolic Transformation in the Cross-Cultural Transmission of a Tibetan Buddhist Ritual." Master's thesis, New York University.

Calhoun, Craig. 1989. "Tiananmen, Television, and the Public Sphere: Internationalization of Culture and the Beijing Spring of 1989." *Public Culture* 2, no. 1:54–71.

DeVoe, Dorsh Marie. 1983. "Survival of a Refugee Culture." Ph.D. diss., University of California, Berkeley.

———. 1985. "Psycho-social Dimensions of Cultural Conservation Among Tibetan Refugees in India." *Proceedings of the International Conference on China Border Area Studies.* Taipei, Taiwan.

———. 1987. "Keeping Refugee Status: A Tibetan Perspective." In *People in Upheaval,* ed. Scott Morgan and Elizabeth Colson. Staten Island, N.Y.: Center for Migration Studies.

Edwards, David. 1994. "Afghanistan, Ethnography and the New World Order." *Cultural Anthropology* 9, no. 3:345–60.

Frederick, Howard. 1992. *Global Communication and International Relations.* Pacific Grove, Calif.: Brooks-Cole.

Ginsburg, Faye. 1991. "Indigenous Media: Faustian Contract or Global Village?" *Cultural Anthropology* 6, no. 1:92–112.

———. 1993. "Aboriginal Media and the Australian Imaginary." *Public Culture* 5, no. 3:557–78.

Gurevitch, Michael. 1991. "The Globalization of Electronic Journalism." In *Mass Media and Society,* ed. James Curran and Michael Gurevitch. London: Edward Arnold.

Hamelink, Cees J. 1991. "Global Communication: Plea for Civil Action." In *Informatics in Food and Nutrition,* ed. B.V. Hofsten. Stockholm: Royal Academy of Sciences.

Hamilton, Annette. 1993. "Video Crackdown, or the Sacrificial Pirate: Censorship and Cultural Consequences in Thailand." *Public Culture* 5, no. 3:515–31.

Klieger, P. Christiaan Klieger. 1992. *Tibetan Nationalism: The Role of Patronage in the Accomplishment of a National Identity.* Berkeley, Calif.: Folklore Institute.

Lichtenberg, Judith. 1991. "In Defense of Objectivity." In *Mass Media and Society,* ed. James Curran and Michael Gurevitch. London: Edward Arnold.

Lopez, Donald S. 1994. "New Age Orientalism: The Case of Tibet." *Tibetan Review* 29, no. 5:16–20.

Michaels, Eric. 1985. "Constraints on Knowledge in an Economy of Oral Information." *Current Anthropology* 26, no. 4:505–10.

Nowak, Margaret. 1984. *Tibetan Refugees: Youth and the New Generation of Meaning.* New Brunswick, N.J.: Rutgers University Press.

Rheingold, Howard. 1993. *The Virtual Community: Homesteading on the Electronic Frontier.* Reading, Mass.: Addison-Wesley.

Shakya, Tsering. 1992. "Of Real and Imaginary Tibet." *Tibetan Review* 27, no. 1:
    13–16.

Turner, Terry. 1990. "Visual Media, Cultural Politics, and Anthropological Practice:
    Some Implications of Recent Uses of Film and Video among the Kayapo of Brazil."
    Commission on Visual Anthropology Review (Spring): 8–13.

———. 1991. "The Social Dynamics of Video Media in an Indigenous Society: The
    Cultural Meaning and the Personal Politics of Video-making in Kayapo Communi-
    ties." *Visual Anthropology Review* 7, no. 2:68–76.

KNOWING EACH OTHER THROUGH AIDS VIDEO: A DIALOGUE BETWEEN AIDS ACTIVIST VIDEOMAKERS

Alex, Juanita, and the Women's AIDS Video Enterprise

Alex's Introduction

Since 1985 there have been thousands upon thousands of videotapes about AIDS produced outside of broadcast television by and for communities as diverse as black gay men into sadism and masochism, Hispanic teens who are homeless, or Jewish parents of persons with AIDS (PWAs). In unprecedented volume, individuals, communities, and organizations have used inexpensive video technology to speak about and to AIDS, a brutal biological phenomenon with massive personal and political impact. People affected by AIDS videotape marches and protests, oral and anal sex with dental dams, funerals, women feeding sick babies—the shapes and sounds of living in a world with AIDS. I watch, make, and write about such work to understand why there is so much of it, how or if it is different from other media, how it affects its viewers and makers, and what, if anything, it accomplishes in the face of AIDS.

In my work I attempt to make sense of and enact a cultural practice rooted in both a distrust and a celebration of representation and the deepest ambivalence about the uses, meaning, and power of the media. I learn many things from and about AIDS activist video. For instance, unlike commercial television or Hollywood film, it is inexpensive to make and distribute and requires little technical know-how or professional credentials. In contrast to traditional ethnographic film, the "disempowered others" of our society have access to the form, technical apparatus, and authorship of representational work about their condition. Yet unlike so much of the camcorder production currently being promoted on broadcast television—featuring slapstick, catastrophe, amateur gaffes—activist producers use the medium to articulate carefully constructed ideological positions made to convince others of who they are and what they believe, if not at least to communicate these things.

Activist video production challenges current theories and practices of media as it enacts not another field of dominance begging for resistance or negotiation but instead a site for intimate and local identification and consolidation. Yet, of course, making a low-budget, alternative, or activist AIDS video does not grant you hegemonic control, nor does it abate bodily pain or bring back the dead. Or does it? I saw my friend Jim kissing a cute East Village clone a few nights ago in the Castro Theater. Jim has been dead for a year and a half. His image, a part of the crowd at an ACT UP "kiss-in" in Gregg Bordowitz's video *Fast Trip, Long Drop,* propelled me back to him.

The gains of activist video are small—one viewer recognizing, at last, what dental dams are for; one viewer bringing back the dead. But after seeing so many of these videotapes, I am certain that these isolated effects begin to explain the motivation for this unprecedented media movement which is perhaps the first political and social cause to be told and made and seen and fought, to such a large extent, through video. And there are other reasons. The AIDS community is vast, diverse, dispersed: to reach others you must speak carefully, taking account of difference, taking stock in your own position, taking responsibility for the real effects of words. This is where video's power of scripting, using talented and knowledgeable interviewees, editing, and VCR exhibition are so important for the movement. Video allows words to be spoken with care and precision and on places many speakers could never go. The AIDS crisis is without origin, center, logic: to speak of it, or within it, or to it, you inevitably converse from a position where identity is both certain and uncertain, as are community, politics, and meaning. Thus AIDS activists use video which is a medium itself based upon many of the contradictions found underlying AIDS. Video is both impermanent (images which can be edited, digitized, or lost due to magnets or time) and frozen (a face in a crowd can be recorded and live as an image more finally than his own mortality). Video is both entirely objective (the camera's mimetic hold on reality) and subjective (our abilities to mold that reality to our liking). Video is both precise and technical, like biology, and creative and political, like poetry.

The overwhelming needs to counter the (mis)information about AIDS represented on broadcast television, to represent the underrepresented experiences to the crisis, to communicate with others who feel equally unheard, coincide with the formation of a new condition of media practice, the low-end, low-tech video production enabled by new technologies like the camcorder, VCR, inexpensive editing, and cable. Thus the new possibility of media production for those individuals and communities who could never afford or master it, occurred just as there was a social crisis of massive proportions and multiple dimensions that begged to be represented in a manner available to the most and the least economically and culturally privileged. The politics of AIDS—the diverse demands for a better quality of life for the people affected by this epidemic—are well matched by the potentials and politics of video.

This is what alternative AIDS TV is about: the use of video production to form a local response to AIDS, to articulate a rebuttal to or revision of the mainstream media's definitions and representations of AIDS, and to a form community around a new manner of political identity forced into existence by the fact of AIDS. The process of producing alternative AIDS media is a political act that allows people who need to scream with pain or anger, who want to say, "I'm here, I count," who have internalized sorrow and despair, who have vital information to share about drug protocols, coping strategies, or government inaction, to make their opinions public and to join with others in this act of resistance. The process of viewing alternative AIDS television—lying on a couch at home watching a VCR, sitting at church, or joined with friends and neighbors at a local screening—is always an invitation to join a politicized community of diverse people who are unified, temporarily and for strategic purposes, to speak back to AIDS, to speak back to a government and society that has mishandled this crisis, and to speak out to each other. Thus AIDS video exists for the same reason most political, cultural production does—just faster, or newer, or more desperate—because in the face of horror people are motivated to do whatever they can in whatever forum that they can get their hands on.

Yet although I am certain that it is important to theorize how AIDS video—in its quantity, trendiness, impact—has altered the media landscape, in this piece I attempt to do something different, or at least to approach this concern from a different vantage. Rather than from the outside in, here I intend to look at AIDS video from the inside out: what it feels like to make it, to put your hands on a camera, to work with others, to be vulnerable and powerful all at once. In this dialogue I will use one of my own video projects—the Women's AIDS Video Enterprise (WAVE)—as a jumping-off point. But instead of describing the project as whole and how it fits into the larger activist video scene, I wish to home in on what I am certain is another critical impetus behind a great deal of the production and viewing of AIDS activist work, namely, its power to allow people who are different from each other to "know each other," as well as to know themselves (at least as they wish to be known on videotape).

At the end of this introduction I will outline the Women's AIDS Video Enterprise as background for a much more difficult enterprise, an attempt to engage in a mutual and respectful dialogue with a fellow member of this project—my friend and colleague Juanita Mohammed—who is also, at least superficially, something like my polar opposite. Like so much ethnography (and most of the work in this book), we are separated by the typical markers of difference, with the imbalance of power seemingly on my side of the binaries of race, class, education, and profession. But I hope that this dialogue with Juanita evidences how our participation in an activist AIDS video project differs from (while sometimes resembling) the typical interactions between filmmaker and subject in both ethnographic and mainstream media—processes which serve to preserve, unexamined, power imbalance and prevailing assumptions about difference. We hope to show how many of the distinct features of camcorder video allow for such interactions.

We are interested in using this forum to understand the obstacles and bridges incurred by cross-cultural, activist, and educational video production. To this purpose we have attempted to devise a form for writing that both acknowledges the power disparities that frame every act of interpersonal communication while working to ameliorate and question them. This was also the motivation behind the WAVE project, and, as is evidenced in the discussion of that project below, we both succeeded and failed. The structure for our dialogue is simple, if at first a little off-putting. We each conceived of five questions to pose to ourself and our friend about the meaning, importance, and theory of activist AIDS video. After writing our answers to these questions in isolation, we shared them with the other conversant, who edited and critiqued them. Finally, we met and discussed our answers, the piece as a whole, and the process. (These after-the-fact conversations are identified by the use of italics.) Although the only instances of "real" dialogue (two friends and colleagues talking together in person) in the piece, it is important to understand how initially writing our individual responses in private liberated us to have these later, difficult, in-person conversations about the WAVE project, about video, about ourselves and each other.

I met Juanita in the winter of 1990, when we joined up with four other women from Brooklyn and one woman from Queens in an innovative "video support group" of my design. WAVE was organized to empower women from the communities disproportionately affected by AIDS (urban, lower-income women of color) to produce their own educational video through the structure of a long-term AIDS support group. I hoped that this structure would serve to disperse the imbalances of power typical of educational video projects where an outsider enters a community with a project and process already in mind. At this stage in my AIDS activist video career I had already made one too many videos "about" poor, HIV-positive women of color. Yet the support group would still allow me to continue to make use of the knowledge and power (money, skills, equipment, education) that I had. Coupling video education with an AIDS support group seemed an obvious choice for other reasons as well. Integrating video production into a typical AIDS support group gave the group a focus, an output, and a method of communication. Integrating a support group into the production of community-specific AIDS educational material acknowledged the complexity of making public the very private experiences of AIDS, especially for women.

During twenty-two three-hour sessions, Aida, Sharon, Carmen, Marcia, Glenda, Juanita, and I met to discuss AIDS, the media, the politics of representation, and video production. We shared the goals of video education, AIDS support, and video production, but had little else in common. In our group were six women of color and one white woman; working women, housewives, and the unemployed; women with a great deal of education and some with very little; women who had a variety of relations to HIV, through infected spouses, relatives, or friends, or through political or religious commitments to the crisis. The seven of us held in common only two readily apparent traits: our gender and our commitment to making a contribution toward abating the affects of the AIDS crisis.

From these similarities, and across all our other differences, we formed a temporary community and collectively produced three videos: *We Care: A Video for Care Providers of People Affected by AIDS; WAVE: Self Portraits;* and *A WAVE Taster. We Care* is widely distributed. We sent out nearly one thousand copies of the tape free of charge to community AIDS service organizations across the country. The tape has been shown in major art museums, AIDS conferences, churches, and in group members' living rooms. The effects of the group continue for the participants: in economic terms, as the tape continues to make money; in activist terms, as we continue to take the tape to people and organizations that can use it; in emotional terms, because over four years later we are still friends. Juanita has gone on to achieve a career in AIDS educational media. She is currently working full time for the Gay Men's Health Crisis (GMHC) "Living with AIDS" cable program. Glenda has worked on several other videos at her job at the Brooklyn AIDS Task Force (BATF). Sharon is currently organizing a tape on anger. I focus upon the success of this group, and our video project, because it points to the most powerful and unique aspect of alternative AIDS media: the strategic and conscious claiming of identity and recognition of community across differences for the accomplishment of shared and progressive ends in the face of an epidemic.

Juanita's Introduction

When I signed up for the WAVE project, little did I realize that the producer Alex Juhasz would be instrumental in transforming my life. She awakened my self from a deep sleep. My self had been locked away because of economics, family, peer disapproval, and self-abasement. For too long no one had reaffirmed my talent; no one trusted me enough to show me how to use it. Until that time I had let go of my dream to be a director. Instead, I had devoted myself to working with PWA. You can not imagine the flame that flickered when Alex let me take home her expensive video camera. To be able to use it without guidance gave me the determination and courage to put forth my ideas. I was truly afraid to use the camera. I knew my hands would shake. Thus in the first segment that I shot I purposefully tried to make it look like an artistic endeavor by shooting body parts here and there. As we looked at videos by other video-makers, I always fantasized about making the same type of videos and working with the people who make them. To me, that's just what it would remain—a fantasy. It's amazing that I am now a peer with those very same people.

In the beginning the WAVE project was, in my eyes, Alex Juhasz's vision. I saw her as the director—that when she asked for ideas she was really doing research to help her do her own project. Although she said we would use the camera, I always thought it was in the context of using it under her direction. But my opinion changed as we began to work on the video. I think the time I took the camera home to shoot my self-portrait was so successful because Alex had trusted me to take it home. I probably worried more about the safety of the camera than the project.

Trust was what the WAVE project was built on. Alex trusted us to stay committed and focused. We trusted her to listen and understand us. We trusted each other to be nonjudgmental and caring. When one of us did not show up, the others were concerned. When we were together, we were like a family, full of bickering, favoritism, stupidity. When I think back, I always wonder why we didn't tape our group sessions. We all claim we just didn't think about it. But these were the scenes which should have been on tape. These would be scenes which showed us bonding, crying, sharing, taking, and giving.

When I first met Alex, she was the "white girl." As I got to work with her she became my mentor. Only after she gained my trust did she become my friend. It is my mentor with whom I am corresponding in this dialogue. But it is my friend with whom I have chosen to discuss two of the most important facets of my life. AIDS and video production are on the same scale for me. For this reason, being able to discuss them with someone I trust, respect, and envy teaches me more than any school ever could.

The Questions

Alex's Questions

1) Describe yourself in relation to AIDS.
2) Describe Alex/Juanita in relation to AIDS.
3) What have you learned about yourself through AIDS video production?
4) What have you learned about [the other conversant] through AIDS video production?
5) What is the relationship between AIDS, community, and video?

Juanita's Questions

1) What preconceived prejudices, stereotypes, or biases do you start out with when doing a video dealing with a community of people either infected or affected by AIDS?

2) What are the personal issues you have to deal with when you enter into a group dealing with AIDS where you are the "other"?

3) Is it necessary to detach when dealing with an AIDS group? How do you manage to detach from the real emotions, or do you?

4) Coming from an academic, middle-class background, how do you adapt that to dealing with people who come from poor, working-class backgrounds and have very little education?

5) Why do you think it's important to allow communities to tell their HIV/ AIDS stories through video?

Answers to Alex's Questions

Describe yourself in relation to AIDS.

Juanita: I thought this would be an easy question, but it was the hardest to answer. I figured that I'd be self-effacing. But I didn't mind saying the things I was good at, the positive things, that I was talented.

Alex: This is also a hard question for me, but more for the issue of infection versus being affected. For myself, I know profoundly how I am affected by AIDS, but in a public statement like an article, I find I am very defensive.

Juanita: I have the same defensiveness. But I feel it through jealousy. When I'm with a group of people who are all HIV-positive, they seem to be so happy and friendly. I'm the sole outsider. It's illogical, but they seem so close and you can never be in it.

JUANITA: When I think about it, it seems easy to describe myself in relation to AIDS. The immediate answer would be, I am a person who is concerned about people with AIDS. However, once I am forced to look into it, I have to admit that it is much more complex. I see myself as an information gatherer and dispenser. My biggest function is to act as a conduit dispensing and acquiring information. This information comes from those I see as the "real" people who are affected and infected. This is information which is generally ignored or not allowed to be valued by the general public; it is information on humanity that they need to know. An important role in this concept is that I do not add my agenda, nor do I hide the fact that I am also a part of this issue. When I tape a family, I am allowing the viewer to see themselves. I am putting a face on a disease. Through my private and public talks with people I interview, I come to see them not as tokens, political tools, or numbers, but as people. I guess this is the public description of my work and myself.

The second part which I would describe as my private self is much more complex because it has more roles. There is the part who, like everyone else, is afraid of AIDS, who still does not practice what I preach (safer sex), someone who still wants to find a fall guy. On the other extreme, there is the outreach educator who puts on an optimistic face and goes out to preach the safer sex word every day in any little way, be it by wearing buttons, giving out pamphlets, correcting statements, handing out condoms, or volunteering. The me who is a buddy is the hardest to describe, as she is the one who is the most unsure of herself, the self who has to deal directly with a person who is positive on a day-to-day basis, never knowing what will develop, good or bad.

ALEX: I am a woman who believes herself to be HIV-negative. (I was last tested in 1990, but have not practiced safer sex with either my male or female lover since that test). I have been involved with AIDS activism, education, video production, and scholarship since 1987. Since then I have produced videos, written several scholarly articles and my dissertation (now a book) on the representation of AIDS, watched my best friend die painfully of HIV-related illnesses, known of many other friends and colleagues who have died or are currently dealing with HIV infection, and have organized within my small college community around issues concerning HIV and college students.

When I think of myself in relation to AIDS, I see that it is probably the largest political, intellectual, personal, biological, sexual, social, and metaphysical force that has structured and given meaning and focus to my adult life, even as I am not infected by HIV.

Like Juanita, I struggle with what it means to have dedicated myself to a cause which affects but does not infect me. This was particularly difficult in the early years of my activism, when as a straight, white, highly educated woman engaging in a crisis thought to be affecting only gay men and low-income people of color. Although my activism was precisely to make others see what already seemed clear to me—that AIDS was an issue for everyone who was sexually active or used intravenous drugs—there was still an undertone at places like ACT UP, GMHC, or BATF that I was colonizing others' issues and pain. Today I continue to struggle with my distance and difference from the majority of people infected by HIV, and I struggle with what motivates me.

And then I know. I remember. AIDS became my issue in 1987 because I recognized that it was a crisis building upon what directly affects and angers me: sexism, racism, sexual conservatism, and a healthcare system rooted in capitalism. AIDS was my issue in 1987 because I understood that all sexual people (white and black, straight and gay, educated and less educated) were at risk for HIV. AIDS continues to be my issue because it has scarred by vision of mortality, humanity, dignity, and sexuality.

I continue to feel uncomfortable about struggling for an issue which does not directly affect (infect) me until I remind myself how limited is this vision of AIDS—a global catastrophe that personally affects many of our lives, that politically and economically affects all of our lives, and that exposes the hypocrisy, greed, and indifference under which it is suggested we continue to live these lives.

Describe Alex/Juanita in relation to AIDS.

Juanita: I had a terrible time with this one. It's hard to describe other people. I'm worried I'm going to insult them. Also, people never know a person as well as they think they do.

Alex: What I said is true to my concept of you, but I don't know if others will get a good picture of you.

Juanita: Your answers amazed me. I never believed that any one could describe me like I could myself. You got into the real me, the one I don't want people to know. You saw that I was shy, and most people think I'm confident or even aggressive.

JUANITA: I would describe Alex as a person who has made a commitment in relation to getting the message out about AIDS. While she is observing others, I am often observing the way they react to her. I have seen that she is not a person who is out to make a lot of money. The fact that she has chosen to work on half-inch video, with a low budget, untrained crew, and in dangerous locations more than anything reinforces my view. Alex is a person who believes in people helping others by helping themselves. She is not only out to put a face on this epidemic, but to also allow the people infected and affected to show their view. If I had to define her, I would say that Alex Juhasz is not someone who remains an outsider. She takes time to go in and get to know her subject while letting them get to know her.

During the WAVE project Alex was able to divide her time and emotions equally between those who wanted technical knowledge and those who wanted practical knowledge. Instead of telling us what to do, she was willing to show us. Much of her success comes from the fact that technical quality is not her number one concern. The visuals do not have to be perfect, lighting can be a little off, audio can be too low or too high. Many of Alex's peers would consider this irrelevant because they would not understand that her main concern is to the story being told and the person who is telling it. Isn't it more effective when you provide lunch, transportation, and information to subjects than purchasing an expensive piece of equipment? This is the type of thinking that helps community AIDS videomakers realize that they do not have to go to college or technical schools to show their views through video. Many of these people do not have time to think about camera angles, lighting setup, or theories for the simple reason that they are dealing with life and death issues.

ALEX: I am not actually sure what brought Juanita to AIDS. However, I do know that when I approached BATF about the WAVE project they told me about this wonderful woman who had been doing volunteer work at the agency; they thought she would be a perfect member for the group I described. In the context of the WAVE project I learned that Juanita was an extraordinarily productive, creative community activist; a mother of two young children; married to a Bangladeshi; a funny, shy, beautiful black woman; a little-tutored artistic genius; a part-time college student; a full-time housing inspector; a woman concerned with a great many issues that affect poor people of color; a person who has always wanted to tell stories with film.

Knowing Juanita as I do now, I would guess that her initial motivation to do volunteer AIDS work was much like mine: a personal and political commitment to combating the sexism, racism, homophobia, and economic oppression that she confronts daily from the mainstream culture and often from within her own community. She has told me that she faces more oppression, disapproval, and blockage from her own community than from outside it. I would guess that AIDS gave her a focus for all of those concerns and a site upon which to enact the enormous amount of energy, passion, and desire, which fills and sometimes paralyzes her, to work with and know others. It has provided a field of action that allows her to work within her community as well as to move into others.

Four years later, because of her work for GMHC and her activism outside of the agency, I believe that Juanita Mohammed has come into a new professional and creative power because of and through AIDS. She has made countless AIDS videos, done even more AIDS educational forums in her neighborhood and throughout New York City, has made (and lost) many friends, and has come into her own as an AIDS activist video maker.

What have you learned about yourself through AIDS video production?

Juanita: I hadn't realized I'd learned anything. When I answered the question I was amazed at all I had learned. I see the changes I made personally. This was one of your analyzing questions and it got on my nerves.
Alex: What do you mean by "analyzing"?
Juanita: Asking me a question that I'm going to have to think hard about, that's going to open me up, make me think about who I was, where I am, and where I'm going.
Alex: I go through different moods about this work. On paper, for this answer, I'm very positive. But in fact I'm often more cynical about AIDS video production. Maybe not about what it's like to do the work, but about what it takes to get energized and committed to do it because it's so much work, funding it, remaining optimistic and enthusiastic. With all the hard parts, it's easy to forget how much you get from it.

JUANITA: Through AIDS video production I have learned many things about myself, the most important being that I have a talent and skill that I can use to help others. In producing AIDS video I have been able to see myself more clearly. It has helped me in overcoming my reluctance to meet people different from myself. I realize that even though I do not always agree with different people, I am still able to be open to their ideas and beliefs.

While I have an excellent vocabulary, it was not until I got involved in AIDS video production that I felt the freedom to use it. Dealing with diverse populations has reinforced my belief that no matter what race, class, sexual orientation, or gender, the human family continues to strive to survive. The gay and straight family still worry about insurance coverage, the Catholic family can be as dysfunctional as the Muslim and Baptist family. The poor, single mother can be just as confused as the multigenerational family.

AIDS video production has also allowed me to see that I can be mechanical. That although my hands shake there are tools like the tripod and stabilizer. Tools like this have enabled me to teach children, handicapped people, and illiterate individuals to use the camera to get their ideas across. In terms of conveying ideas or information, the video camera has proven to be an excellent time-saving visual tool.

Because when I make AIDS video I have to ask personal questions and make decisions that effect the lives of others, I have come to learn what I will and will not accept, deny, or exploit. For example, even though an HIV-positive person might want to self-disclose on camera, if I feel they are not able to accept the fallout from this disclosure I will allow them to say what they choose but I will not use the tape for broadcast. Yet at the same time, even if I strongly disapprove of a person's ideas, I will still broadcast them. This has helped me see myself as a responsible educator. Once, when videotaping, I asked a question which caused the interviewee to cry. From a voyeuristic position, I thought it was great, but felt uncomfortable showing a person in a vulnerable state. So I shot it again when she was more composed. On showing it to Alex and the other women in WAVE, we all decided that the segment without the crying got the point across, while the segment with the crying took the focus off the point.

I have come to the conclusion that Juanita can be flexible. The idea of making choices was something I shunned before: I did not want to take the responsibility. Today I am willing to make choices and live with the consequences. If not for AIDS video production, I would still be working at a job I hate, still hanging out with people who were narrow minded, still thinking of myself first. I would still be a phony, denying my bisexuality to the world, denying my humanity to myself. AIDS video production has given me the freedom to be my real self.

ALEX: Through AIDS video production I learn many different things which help me. First, I learn that I am not alone in my grief, anger, pain, or even daily experiences with AIDS. Making (and screening) video is a collective act where I can be engaged with others who are living with and thinking through this crisis. Interviews are the most obvious example of this: a camera between two people allows them to converse in ways and about issues that are usually unavailable to them in the real world. But also the immense amount of work that goes into making a video is itself an incredibly social act, full of negotiations and attempts at expression, arguments and reconciliations. Screening your work is perhaps the most difficult aspect of the communication made necessary by video production. I always feel very vulnerable showing a video: during a screening it feels so big and concrete. But the tape between me and others often provides a springboard for conversations which would be less comfortable without the video there, especially if I am trying to engage in conversation with people who seem "different" from myself. A video provides a common point of reference: "you know that scene where the woman shows her house . . . ?"

Through AIDS video I am also given an opportunity to discuss, challenge, and expand my own AIDS knowledge: how I understand the politics and implications, as well as the daily experiences, of this crisis. Seeing and speaking with others about something I'm concerned enough about to make or watch a video allows me to learn that my ideas and experiences are valid but also limited—only one vision of AIDS, only one interpretation, but also something that might matter to someone else.

I learn that I can make a contribution, something that is valuable to others, even though I spend most of my days feeling overwhelmed by the magnitude of suffering, indifference, and death which is AIDS. Sometimes I believe that this work is entirely selfish—busywork that at least allows you to feel like you're doing something. But this is one way that video is so exceptional. If you are willing to do the hard work of distribution after the already hard work of making a tape, you get to see your entirely selfish busywork affect other people, whether the work is good or bad, liked or disliked. It's such a public form. From an initial inspiration to feel useful you are forced to actually imagine and then image what could be of real use to other people.

Of course, this work is also frustrating—people don't show up for meetings, don't get their work done on time, a project always takes more of a personal, emotional, and time commitment than I initially expect. So I learn that I am sometimes intolerant, but also resolute. I learn that I am committed, as are many others.

What have you learned about [the other conversant] through AIDS video production?

Juanita: I learned that you are not as secure as I first thought. I always had the idea that if you started a project, you knew what would happen. If you wanted to do B, B would happen before C. I always think the other person knows more than me.

Alex: I don't know why you have this overestimated view of who I am and what I do.

Juanita: I know that it is wrong consciously, but it's the unconscious level that is more difficult to change.

JUANITA: Through AIDS video production I have learned many things about Alex. The first would be her commitment to the use of half-inch video as a vehicle for involving everyone in the taping process. While her peers have gone for the political, educational video look, she has left her focus on the views of the people involved. Her videos reflect the hands-on work of the nonprofessional people she works with. I have seen her pain or happiness when a friend with HIV got sicker or healthier. Alex is the type of person who analyzes everything. She does not allow people to make blanket statements; she looks into these statements and makes them look into their statements as well. I believe that Alex has become much more self-assured from working with the WAVE group. She no longer has to ask constantly for affirmation. In getting to know her, I have seen Alex as an individual who dresses and says what she pleases; a romantic who is in love with everyone being in love. While she constantly changes hairstyles, her beliefs and commitments remain steady.

Watching Alex in the editing room is amazing. She turns from this liberal producer who makes sure that everyone is in total agreement into this mother lion fiercely guarding her cub. Throughout the project she was always worried if people did not attend meetings. Throughout editing, I think she was relieved when we all weren't there. During editing, she came into her total, true self. She was comfortable showing her expertise, arguing with others, overriding people's opinions, being corrective and political. I think I like this side of Alex best.

ALEX: Through AIDS video I have learned that Juanita is very vulnerable and very strong. That she is incredibly nervous and entirely self-assured. That she longs for more and more and more in her life—more people, new experiences, many projects—even as she takes comfort in the life she has, and often chooses to stay home rather than go to the events I invite her to. I have learned that Juanita is held back by the world into which she was born—by her race and class and gender, by getting married early and having two kids, by not getting her college degree in film when she began it at eighteen—and that she is entirely capable of breaking through these confines. Video is a powerful tool that allows someone like Juanita—who is not always confident in person, who may worry that she might not say something right, or that she is the only person of color or woman in the room—to take control of a situation, both through the authority of the equipment and the power of editing, where an argument can be rehearsed, fine-tuned, consolidated. I have learned that school smarts are only one way to know, and that creativity is not something that can be learned in school, through books, or even through the access to high culture that money and education allows. I know that Juanita looks up to me, what I've accomplished, and wonder if she knows that I also look up to her.

What is the relationship between AIDS, community, and video?

Juanita: This is my favorite question. Video production is a connection between the three. You can't have one without the other.

Alex: This question is important to me—it's the focus of my academic work, but also the inspiration for it, why I think that video production is so powerful for myself and others. I'm almost like a missionary, trying to bring people in to try it. People are so rarely afforded the opportunity to think hard about what they believe, to work through how best to communicate this to others, and then to see this actually put out into the world in a form which carries authority.

Juanita: Originally, when I wanted to go into film, I saw myself as the director, a god. Now I don't feel right if I make a video without input from everyone involved. This makes for good teamwork, better videos, and real relationships.

JUANITA: I believe the relationship between AIDS, community, and video is the human side of people being infected and affected by AIDS. By "human side" I mean the knowledge that the AIDS crisis is affecting real people. AIDS, the community, and video come together to help educate, support, and hook up people who need each other—people who otherwise might have never come together. When a community of people made up of different and similar backgrounds view a video about AIDS, they are allowed the opportunity to see that others are going through the same things. Seeing two gay men's dedication to their HIV-positive baby in my video *Two Men and a Baby* makes one realize the love gay couples can project. A video like *Invisible Women* (Ellen Spiro and Marina Alvarez) shows women their connection with each other: the issues they share such as children, dreams, education, fears, and strengths. Gregg Bordowitz's video *Fast Trip, Long Drop* ties the individual to the community, which in turn ties the community to the individual. When communities feel that AIDS only affects them or overlooks them, video is an excellent tool to reinforce the motto that AIDS affects everyone.

During the WAVE project the women in WAVE became the string which connected the community and AIDS through working on video. For example, one of the participants who never dealt with politicians called a local politician to interview him on how the community was working on an issue. As a result of the meeting, the politician learned about agencies dealing with issues of AIDS and the woman was able to start a support group in the area. Another example was when we shared *We Care* and other alternative videos with a church group and this prompted that church to have an annual AIDS Day and to publicly open its door to PWAs and their families. When I asked the preacher why, she said because the people in the congregation thought the videos were about people like them.

ALEX: I believe that activist AIDS video—its making and viewing—provides a format which allows people to form transient but useful communities around issues that matter to them. By making AIDS into video, we make sense—not conclusively or irrevocably, but partially and transitionally—of ourselves and our lives in the face of AIDS. The medium allows us a place to ruminate and then express. And while this is true of many other modes of expression, video differs from them in significant ways. Like activism, video attempts to interpret and interrupt the status quo of both intimate experience and large institutions; yet it is also permanent. Like academic work, AIDS video focuses upon analysis, making sense of experience, history, and culture; but AIDS video is accessible to many and is most successful when used in familiar and creative ways. Like other forms of art, video allows us to speak our individual pain; but unlike most other forms, video can be a collective act. Many of us who are profoundly affected by AIDS use video—it's making and watching—to communicate. Which is not to say that we don't communicate constantly about AIDS in other forms: on the telephone, over dinner, through writing. But communication through video allows for other levels of power: a larger audience, a mimetic hold on history, an accessible and familiar form.

When I make an AIDS video with others—those like me and those who are not—around the issues upon which we can agree, we are making an intervention that will contribute to change. These images serve to confirm a larger, politicized community—larger than any single AIDS identity—engaged in an ongoing struggle. Thus alternative AIDS video is about how identities are turned into communities because of AIDS and through video. The production and reception of alternative AIDS TV is a form of direct, immediate, product-oriented activism which brings together committed individuals who insist upon being industrious.

Answers to Juanita's Questions

What preconceived prejudices, stereotypes, or biases do you start out with when doing a video dealing with a community of people either infected or affected by AIDS?

Alex: This was the hardest question for me. It was embarrassing to express to myself, and especially to others, my prejudices. I probably wasn't exactly honest. I had to let my political understandings of these issues color my answers.

*Juanita: I hated this question, too. When I answered, I thought I could be to-
tally honest. But I realized I can't say this about this group or that group.
So I was more politically honest. But I learned how prejudiced, biased, and
stereotyping I really am. Even if I am a person's friend, I'm thinking about
them as a member of some group.*

*Alex: Yes, I know. You have to struggle so hard with all that you've learned
before from the outside. Those messages of prejudice are always there, getting in the way of having open interactions. All of the difficulty this society
has in dealing with difference ends up being played out on an individual
level, even if you try not to, even if you know better. The worst of it is that
even when you try to unlearn these prejudices, they seem to haunt the under-
currents of a relationship, they become that which isn't said. It takes courage and work to say them and in this way perhaps to begin to make them
go away.*

ALEX: Of course, my answer to this question depends upon the community
with which I am producing video, because I carry different biases for different
communities. If I was describing my preconceptions about the women in
WAVE versus what I thought I knew about the Swarthmore College students
with whom I produced *Safer and Sexier: A College Student's Guide to Safer
Sex,* I would have two different but related answers.

In the first case, working with the women in WAVE who were for the most
part less educated than me, and who were all women of color who lived outside of Manhattan, I was certain that some of my lifestyle choices would not
be accepted by the other group members: living as a single woman, living in
the East Village. It is interesting to consider why I cared about this acceptance. Did I want them to like me, respect me, understand me, follow me? I
remember trying to keep my political beliefs and commitments quiet: I didn't
want people to know I was a feminist, or that I had gay friends, or even that I
was an AIDS activist. I was embarrassed about what I perceived to be my economic and educational privilege, and tried to hide it by not talking like an
intellectual, or not referring to the ways and places in which I live my life
(trips I had taken, where I went to college). Yet, of course, as Juanita reminds
me, we were all quick to make assumptions about each other, give each other
titles: Sharon the strong one, Carmen and Aida the religious housewives,
Marcia the cold social worker, Glenda the comedian, Juanita the weird one,
Alex the white girl.

Of course, being white did not help in this awkward camouflaging process
where we all tried to hide the weird parts from each other. Initially it seemed
that in this context my whiteness was my greatest liability—I couldn't erase it
or cover it up—and everyone could see that I did not fit in. The misconcep-
tions allowed by privileging my difference (whiteness) were rooted in my
simple-minded conflation of race, education, class, and politics: as if a less

educated person couldn't be politically liberal or radical, as if a Christian women couldn't challenge her religion's dogma, as if a working-class black woman couldn't be highly educated. It took time and conversation to begin to understand the very inaccurate way that our skin colors gauge the full meanings of our differences. For of course it was not only my whiteness that was "different" here. The six women of color in our group—from a variety of ethnicities, religious upbringings, classes, educational backgrounds, and political outlooks—were as different from each other as they were from me.

Making video together allowed for, made necessary, the kinds of conversations that forced us to see beyond the visible differences that tend to disallow communication across difference in our society (I'm thinking here not only of skin color but also the markers of class, neighborhood, and ethnicity that are worn on the body: clothes, jewelry, hairstyle, weight). When you're working closely with people on a difficult project like a video about issues that matter to each member of the group, it's almost impossible to not speak with the words that make you most comfortable, or about your particular life experiences, or about your beliefs and values. And as you begin to reveal those politely protected spaces to people (my parents are professors, I eat bagels, I am not planning to get married or have kids for a long time, if ever), others begin to do the same. When people who are different from each other start talking together, they begin to see how their stereotypes are inaccurate, they see the ways that their most obvious or visible differences mask both similarities and differences. What I learned seems obvious but hard to know in a society that teaches us to place a premium upon what distinguishes us from others: I learned that race, class, gender, education, life experiences, political beliefs, and social values don't line up neatly, don't necessarily imply any one thing about the others.

On the other hand, when I worked with my college students (a group who shared only an elite liberal arts college educational background in common), the prejudices which structured this interaction were similar, if only coming from the opposite direction. I assumed that we were all *similar,* that we could take political beliefs, class, race, lifestyle, or values for granted because of our shared educational position. When we talked with each other in the process of making a video around an issue to which we are all committed, we learned how different we are. In this case, the group was constituted of men and women, a cheerleader, a frat boy, a safer-sex educator, a premedical student, a videomaker. The students were white, African American, Asian American, Jewish, Catholic, straight, bisexual, asexual, conservative, liberal, sexually naive, and sexually active. We all said we were HIV-negative and we all shared a commitment to making a safer-sex video, but our interpretations of safer sex, not to mention sex, varied: we disagreed on the viability of showing real sex on screen, about the importance of celibacy as a method of safer sex, about how to represent women's bodies. It became clear that our shared educational privilege served to mask the other traits which distinguish us. The only way to work together on the video was to talk together to learn about what we could agree upon.

Whereas I believe that race falsely marked what I perceived to be irreconcilable differences for the participants in the WAVE project, education (and thus, class) signified what I misperceived to be a common base for the individuals involved in the *Safer and Sexier* project.

JUANITA: I have to admit that when I am shooting a video with community groups, I find that a lot of my own personal prejudices, stereotypes, or biases come up. This generally happens when I am dealing with people whom I consider different from myself. When I am with people from less educated backgrounds, I try to not talk with words that I assume they will not know, or I try to talk their language, but at many times I just sound phony. I am more careful of what I wear; if I am with a church group, my pants will not be as tight, no low-neck blouses or jeans. If I am to be with a homosexual group, I try to dress trendy. Many times this even extends to where I choose to take people from different communities to lunch. I have found many times that people from lower income groups are more relaxed eating at fast food places rather than restaurants.

Although I have been around many people affected or infected by AIDS, I still feel that I have to be cheery and go out of my way to show that I am not afraid of them by drinking and eating their food or touching them. I tend to expect people to not know or want to know as much as I do about AIDS. When I am dealing with people from different races, classes, and genders, I tend to feel wary, that they will not accept me. To ward off these feelings interfering with the video and to get the chance to experience the real people, I have to make an effort to accept them. I do this through listening to and communicating with the real people rather than their races, classes, or genders.

What are the personal issues you have to deal with when you enter into a group dealing with AIDS where you are the "other"?

Alex: It was interesting to me how both our answers expressed how hard it is to do work with people who feel different from you: we both spoke of being very vulnerable, uncertain, and lacking self-confidence. But then, especially if you're in charge, you have to be able to put a good face on it anyway.
Juanita: I always feel like I am the other. When I enter a group, I am the other. But I also know that sometime during the process I can become friends with everyone in the group because I can find something in common with each of them. Yet when its over, I am the other again.

ALEX: If I am making video with a group of people who are HIV-positive, I deal with my sadness: I wish they weren't infected. I deal with my lack of confidence about how to be with people who are infected: I don't know what is the right thing to say. Should I mention their illness, should I act like they are or are not sick, like they will or will not die? I deal with my own stubborn belief in my mortality, as if their infection confirms my own health. I deal with my own fear of death, my own hypochondria, as if their infection is proof of my own.

If this is a group where I am "other" due to race, class, or sexual preference, I deal with my own uncertainty about how others see me. What do people of color really think about white people? What do poor people really think of more privileged people? What do young people think of older people? What do married women think of single women? Do they like my clothes, my hair, do they understand how I talk? I worry that I have to like everyone and if I don't it's a sign of my internalized racism or sexism or classism. I worry what they say about me when I'm not around. Maybe I'm too bossy, too closed, too much in command. I worry about what my responsibilities are to others. What do I owe people with whom I make educational video? What do they think I owe them? I carry a great deal of guilt, always thinking people want more of me than I can provide.

JUANITA: When I have to deal with any group in which I am the "other," personal issues pop up. The fact that I am shy and insecure makes me anxious, which stresses me both emotionally and physically. I am very liable to have an anxiety attack when meeting a group. The main cause not being because I dislike the people, but because I do not want to offend. I take great pains with dress and how I am going to introduce myself. Many times I have to overcome learned prejudice and stereotypes. The only way I can do this is to open my eyes, ears, mind, and heart to people. When I find myself uncomfortable with a different race, class, or culture, I make it a priority to extend myself. For example, I will go to their homes and eat their food, or I will take them to my home. I get to know them and let them get to know me. I do not talk down or up to them, nor do I make judgments. I have even overcome automatically expecting people from my own race, culture, and gender to behave and have the same beliefs that I do.

Another personal issue for me is being the responsible person. I have never liked assuming this role. Responsibility carries with it the expectation that one is in the know; I am rarely in the know. I do not know what goes on in people's lives when I am not around. I do not know what affects them and what does not.

It is especially hard for me to take responsibility in producing a video about AIDS because even after four years as an AIDS activist and two years as an AIDS video activist, I still feel like a novice. This goes back to my insecurities based on the fact that I am the "other" even with people I work with. As I see it, they do not come from the ghetto and I live there; they have more political savvy and are not tied down with children; they know how to speak and have no insecurities. I know logically that they all have problems just like I do, but still it's hard to see from my eyes. I see them as free and a part of each other. I see me as a part, but also on the outside.

Is it necessary to detach when dealing with an AIDS group? How do you manage to detach from the real emotions, or do you?

Alex: This was a hard question for me because since my friend Jim died I have been doing a lot of work to not think about this part of AIDS work. It's easier to think about AIDS as a political issue. This question asked me to reveal more about the other, more emotional stuff.

Juanita: That's often why people have a camera in front of their eyes.

ALEX: Yes, I guess it is necessary to detach when dealing with the emotions and experiences raised when confronting AIDS. But the funny thing is that as much as I try to protect myself from being hurt or vulnerable in an AIDS video group, there are always words, or images, or experiences which make their way in. I imagine, finally, that this is why I do this work: not because I want to be safe but because I want to be confronted or shocked or upset. I want to feel deep emotions, even if they hurt. This is because the only way to live day to day in a life surrounded by AIDS is to be numb. In my day-to-day life and in AIDS video groups, I detach from difficult emotions or thoughts by thinking that I've already heard or seen something before, I've already worked through or resolved a particular crisis (what someone with Kaposi's sarcoma all over his body looks like, what to say to a wife with two children who has recently lost her husband, how to talk to someone who is too young to die). In my day-to-day or within a group, I deal with each upset as practically as I can, and then I can tell myself I've resolved that, it's out of the way. In AIDS video groups we all enter with these hard shells defending us—all the issues we've confronted and gotten past. The power of working on a video with people who are affected by and committed to AIDS is that you know, often without saying, that they've seen similar horrors with their eyes, that they've confronted similar traumas, and that they too have lived through it, probably also by hardening up and closing down. We all enter a group pretending that we would never want to share what really happens in our lives. It is startling how rarely we can keep up this pretense. Producing video is about making a commitment to externalizing, making visible these fears and images, to yourself and to others. But this is not a simple purging, or a release for release's sake, like saying it will make it go away. Rather, making and watching video allows both a context to release and expose vulnerability and also a forum with which to productively transform these emotions into knowledge, communication, images, or sounds from which we and others can learn.

JUANITA: I believe a certain amount of detachment is necessary when dealing with a group around the issue of AIDS. In my case, I know it is hard for me to detach my emotions. I feel for the person who is not only facing an incurable disease but also a society which seems incurable in their prejudice. I cannot just forget a person or their family when the taping is over. I have to keep in correspondence with them in some form. For this reason I am the buddy to many HIV-positive people. When someone with AIDS dies, I cannot cut my attachment to the family because I know they will still be affected by AIDS.

On the other hand, I have trained myself that there are times when I must detach. I realize that I need to detach so that I may view and hear what my subjects say without letting my emotions cloud my judgment. Many times I will set aside the questions and just ask the subject to say what she wants. Another way I detach during taping is to focus on the technical aspects like lighting and audio rather than analyzing the person's speech. Nevertheless, I do believe that it is important to not become completely detached, as it can lead to losing the image of the real person.

Coming from an academic, middle-class background, how do you adapt that to dealing with people who come from poor, working-class backgrounds and have very little education?

Alex: *This was a difficult question about something I worry about a lot. It made me feel defensive.*

Juanita: *During the time I was writing it, there were things happening at work that made me upset. Someone asked me why, if I didn't know something technical, I just didn't take a class about it. I didn't have the money. So the question to you was an attack for something you didn't do. However, initially, I thought it was written for both of us. I've always thought that I came from a middle-class background. Then I realized that I was one of "them," those poor people I asked about. I never saw you as a privileged person. It wasn't in my mind. I saw you as you. A weird person who dresses in weird clothes.*

Alex: *Why didn't you see me as privileged? When did you decide that I was?*

Juanita: *You were free. You're not a mother stuck in your house with those children. You were going on a trip or something. But even so, I think we have the same commitments. It's just that I can be more jealous or envious. You want to be that person.*

Alex: *What do I have that you think you want?*

Juanita: *Freedom.*

Alex: *Freedom to do what?*

Juanita: *Go where you want. Not have to be the other.*

Alex: *That's probably true. I do have those freedoms. So I can say as much as*

I want about our similarities, and how video can bring us together, but the
bottom line is that I always have certain privileges. I can always leave.
Juanita: *You said that you couldn't hide being white in the WAVE group when*
we were all black. We all should have had that feeling of difference—that
we were all different from each other.

ALEX: My answer relates a lot to Juanita's question 1, about biases. Because of course, even after I've done many videos with communities who are "different" from myself, and have learned how my biases, stereotypes, and the ineffective interpersonal strategies they promote get in the way of good work, it's still very difficult to do anything but treat people like the visible traits they present to you when you initially begin a video project together. So beyond the mistakes I inevitably make where I assume I can figure all of a person out because of one noticeable component of their personality (education, race), I deal with my difference by asking myself difficult questions. What compels me to work with people who are less privileged than me? Why don't I work with my peers? Who *are* my peers? Am I motivated by liberal guilt? Am I motivated by a voyeuristic curiosity about others? Am I slumming?

I created the WAVE project (and others like it) out of a belief that although these questions are vital, their often scary answers should not invoke paralysis. Instead, I attempt to work from the belief that people who are different from each other can work together, get to know each other, strive to understand what they share in common; the belief that the access I have to funding, equipment, and knowledge is better shared than hoarded. So instead I supplement the first set of questions with another. How can I account for my power and privilege while also accounting for others' power and privilege which may take forms which are less obvious to me? How can a group of people see beyond their obvious differences to begin to acknowledge their similarities? Why would they want to? Why would people who are less privileged than me want to work with me? The answers to these questions support a new model of video production based upon an attempt to destabilize overt power imbalances while maintaining a sense of self-awareness about how and where power does exist.

I created a model for video production that attempted to learn from ethnographic films' failings, from cross-cultural film work that did not account for the power of using a camera, asking the questions or answering them, or getting to leave when the project is over. Thus I envisioned and then implemented a long-term, support group-based, collective form of production where everyone in a group would shoot, script, and edit, where everyone would be emotionally vulnerable, where everyone shared a political commitment to the video project. WAVE worked because we became coworkers and friends. Not best friends. Nor film and video equals (I was the teacher, I had the grant money, I was the project director). Not people who pretended that we weren't separated in important ways, but people who worked hard at getting to know each other so that we could respect each other, learn from each other, and produce something we could all be proud of. We so rarely struggle with how and why we can communicate with people who are raised and live differently from us. A video project can be a perfect forum to reach for this kind of revealing, if challenging, interaction because there is the potential of something tangible, respectable, and important at the end of the process—a video.

JUANITA: I believe this question should be, How do you adapt yourself to people who have backgrounds different from you? In fact, when I think about it now, I believe this question was written as an attack on you as being a "privileged person" versus myself as a "put-upon person."

There are many situations where I find that I have to adapt when involved in AIDS video production. I find that I need to adapt myself to the moods of the subject. My attitude can become aggressive or passive to match the situation. Sometimes I can even be myself when I feel in tune with the subject. I find that I adapt by putting on many different hats. The Juanita who goes after funds has to be one hundred percent confident and dress presentably. As opposed to when I go out to shoot on location with butterflies in my stomach.

When interviewing an HIV-positive person who wants to talk about AZT, I can become very political, yet interviewing an HIV-positive person who has kids can turn me maternal. I have had to adapt myself to thinking that it is not my right to argue with a woman who takes AZT, not my right to argue with the HIV-positive senior who is into radical therapy. I have had to adapt myself to the realization that I am dealing with real people and real issues, not just abstract ideas. When I am on a deadline but my subjects cannot make it due to personal reasons, I do not throw a fit but instead offer a helping hand.

Why do you think it's important to allow communities to tell their HIV/AIDS stories through video?

Alex: That's an easy question. I've thought about it so much. I didn't want to answer it. It's what all my work has been about.

Juanita: Right, you can't do this work without the community involved in it because no man's an island. Everything affects everything. It made me think of something Sharon said: "Alex ran the group, all the ideas were really hers." It was easy, really, to forget our different races and backgrounds, but it is much harder to forget the hierarchy of control.

ALEX: First off, it is important for communities to tell their stories through video because the mainstream media provides us with such a limited vision of what AIDS is, what it means, who it affects, how and why. Those of us involved with AIDS, and those who are not yet, need to understand the many experiences of AIDS and need to pass each other information.

People affected by AIDS are the best AIDS educators. They speak with the words and images that their communities understand and feel comfortable with. Video is central to this task because it provides people who have little opportunity to imagine that their ideas count with a medium that organizes their thoughts into a recognizable, legitimate, and public form.

Finally, video provides a permanent archive of what we've done, what we've known, who was here, and how AIDS has taken so much away.

JUANITA: I think that it is important to allow communities to tell about their experiences dealing with HIV/AIDS because no one can understand or tell the real story better than those who see it happening every day. An outsider can only tell so much. There is much that I do not see when I produce a video on cultures different from my own. There is also a lot they do not tell me about. Take for example when I was videotaping one family. I showed them as carefree although they were dealing with the disease. It was only later when I was trusted in the community that neighbors let me know that this family was dealing with more than one person who was HIV-positive.

When AIDS videomakers come into a community, they have their own agenda which often does not correspond with that of the community. You have to grasp the concept that you can not tell the story without the community's involvement.

Conclusions to the Conversation

Juanita: One of the things I learned from writing this with you was more about the ways we see each other. The ways we figure that the other person saw us. I came to see you more as a person than a filmmaker. You can have insecurities. When I realized that you could have insecurities, it was okay for me to have them and then it was also okay to put forth my own ideas and advice. I had so many stereotypes about you. The biggest thing that broke them was that video you made with your college students with all the sex in it. I always thought you were a goody-goody.

Alex: I don't understand why you think that about me. It makes me uncomfortable. I think that you think too highly of me. It's a big burden.

Juanita: Well, here's something I didn't say during WAVE. Even though you were very committed to the project and the people, you took some things for granted. You didn't get releases, and some people turned out to not want to be in a video that was shown all over the country. Then you put Aida's picture on the flyer, and her boyfriend saw it, and it caused a big fight.

Alex: I felt vulnerable. It seemed to me that in many ways you all had the power. Like, for instance, what does "the white girl" mean?

Juanita: It's playful, teasing. It's self-effacing. We used it to bring us all together. It was a way for all of us, who didn't have so much in common, to talk and share. It kept you on the outside.

Alex: Did you stop thinking that that's who I am?

Juanita: Sure. After working with you you became "the dizzy girl with the

*weird clothes." We were more sure of each other and ourselves. We didn't
need one person to get us all together.*

Alex: Did you worry that this article, like WAVE, was ultimately my project?

*Juanita: In the beginning I didn't want to do it. I thought you'd end up wanting
to do it with a real video person. Then I was afraid to write my questions
without seeing yours first. But I pushed myself and wrote mine before I saw
yours. When I saw that yours weren't gigantic, I felt very good about mine.
Two people who are supposed to be such opposites say pretty similar things.
For instance, I also try to camouflage parts of myself to get along with
others.*

*Alex: I was most interested to see that difference affects us in similar ways.
What distinguishes us is simply that it is in different contexts where we feel
different.*

REPRESENTING "BHOPAL"

In the ten years since the Bhopal disaster, political activists have worked both to rehabilitate victims and to establish the legal and organizational structures necessary for the prevention of similar disasters in the future. At times these agendas have seemed contradictory. Health and economic rehabilitation of victims requires reliance on government resources and a legal strategy which advocates an intensification of the state's role in community affairs. Preventive measures involve attempts to reinforce community infrastructures and to shape government policy in ways which limit dependence on foreign resources. Thus a primary challenge for activists is the articulation of ideological positions which work through tensions which are largely ignored in established models for progressive social change. An important forum for this work is the practice of political writing wherein strategic representations must be made but without a clear sense of an overarching logic. The writing itself represents both tentative conclusions and practical attempts to recognize limited understanding without absconding from the responsibility to react.

The following excerpts attempt to tell a story about representing "Bhopal," both through language and through social practice. The excerpts are from press releases, pamphlets, legal documents, and other means of correspondence produced by Bhopal Group for Information and Action (BGIA), a group of middle-class activists who work as interlocutors between gas victims and the official rehabilitation apparatus, which often operates within and through the authority of the English language. Gas victims are primarily Hindi speaking, as well as poor and, often, illiterate. Since 1986, BGIA has attempted to rework this resource deficit through representations which attempt to actively cut across the social and rhetorical boundaries which sustain it.

The excerpts were written between 1989 and 1991, during the time I worked with BGIA as part of an ethnographic fieldwork project. My primary task within the group was writing. However, none of the writing was done alone. Whatever the signature on various excerpts, all were collaboratively constructed, both within BGIA and across our alliances with other groups, par-

'CHILDREN OF BHOPAL'. A PAINTING BY KISHORE UMREKAR.

ticularly the mass organization of women victims with whom we had daily interaction.

The excerpts themselves do not reveal the extent to which understanding of our representation of "Bhopal" was continually mediated. Neither the social nor rhetorical negotiations which shaped the production of the documents are evident. Thus an important part of the story must be read beyond the text, through recognition that the language used here is used strategically, undermining the easy assumption that activists believe what they say, adhering to simple notions of language and truth. Though such simplicity was often yearned for, it rarely allowed the repose often associated with a leftist party line, sure of itself and at home in the world.

Particularly within the grassroots environmental movement in India, within which Bhopal activists position themselves, language is understood as vehemently operative in the production of the world, and of possibilities for resistance. There is overt acknowledgment that language, world, and consciousness relate in mediated ways, which both opens up possibilities for change and creates the most rigid of barriers. Such understanding of the language games within all representation marks a mode of politics that differentiates contemporary Indian leftism from older modes. It also cites an understanding of the dramatic change within which political work must now occur, and a tentative attempt to remain committed to "Indian alternatives" despite awareness that the phrase, and the politics associated with it, has been exhausted of critical force.

In themselves these excerpts demonstrate numerous processes of mediation. Most overtly, the diversity of rhetorical modes shows a recognition not only of the diverse audiences but also of the diverse possibilities of language. Through this recognition it is also possible to get a sense of the diverse alliances imagined as necessary in responding to "Bhopal." The correspondence seeks to connect with other grassroots organizations, with the courts, and with the mainstream media. Diverse styles are relied on to mediate the various expectations of both content and form, showing the way activists perceive the difference between audiences as marked as much by accepted modes of narration, as by different social positioning.

The excerpts also tell of some of the projects imagined as necessary or possible within the overall response to the disaster. These projects demonstrate commitment not only to the literal rehabilitation of victims, but also to a reworking of conventional conceptualizations of "Bhopal." Therein, writing itself is acknowledged as a political project, undertaking one aspect of the broad agenda to realign dominant social relations, and the moves of language which legitimate hierarchy and exclusion. Some of the excerpts included here are not about Bhopal itself. I have included them to demonstrate a practice of political work that attempts not only to advocate, but to engage with a new configuration of social issues.

FILE: Anniversary announcement to grassroots network
DATE: November 1990

Dear Friends,

The sixth anniversary of the Bhopal gas disaster is drawing near. In the past few months, communal and casteist forces have caused widespread damage

and dissension all over the country. The media and, through it, the attention of the general public, has remained dominated by issues such as Bofors, Mandal Commission and the Ram Janambhoomi-Babari Masjid controversy. While these are important issues, they are but manifestations of the deeper malaise that pervades all aspects of life in India. The media, as it happens to be, has engrossed itself with such manifestations and the deeper political/developmental/environmental issues have been relegated to secondary positions of concern. Narmada dams, Kaiga Nuclear Reactor, Balliapal Missile Range, increasing automation, rising foreign investment, work hazards, amniocentesis, displacement of tribal people and the impoverishment of peasants are hardly copy in these times. Neither is Bhopal.

Unbeknownst to the media, the most critical medical, rehabilitation and legal issues on Bhopal remain to be addressed in a meaningful manner. Death, disease and despair continue to stalk the shanties; the suffering continues in Bhopal. So does the struggle. The "valiant victims" continue their battle on the streets for rehabilitation and for punishment of the guilty officials of Union Carbide responsible for the genocide in Bhopal. It has been difficult for the courageous women of the Bhopal Gas Peedit Mahila Udyog Sangathan (Bhopal Gas Affected Women Workers Organization), the largest organization of gas victims; many of them continue to suffer from gas related diseases.

They have been harassed, beaten and arrested by the police; the organization has run into huge debts and the press is more often inclined to ignore them. And yet they continue to struggle. Sometimes they win.

Your support in this struggle is essential. The solidarity expressed by individuals and organizations from different parts of the country and the world has significantly strengthened the resolve of the victims to continue with the struggle. Bhopal needs also to be remembered and acted upon so that we are more aware of the "silent Bhopals" happening around us, more equipped to pre-empty Bhopals likely to happen in the future. Through this letter, we seek your support of the demands of the gas victims, as follows:

1. Union Carbide Corporation should be held liable for the death and destruction caused in Bhopal and it should pay compensation that is adequate to take care of the medical care and rehabilitation needs of the gas affected people.

2. Officials of Union Carbide responsible for making the decisions that led to the disaster should be criminally prosecuted.

3. The illegal, unconstitutional and immoral settlement reached between the Government of India and Union Carbide in February 1989 should be overturned.

4. Union Carbide should pay interim relief to the Bhopal victims as ordered by two Indian courts.

5. Union Carbide's assets in India should be handed over to the workers and there should be a ban on its future business operations in India. Particularly, the now closed pesticide plant in Bhopal should be completely dismantled and Union Carbide should pay for environmental clean-up of the grounds.

6. The Government of India must set up a National Commission on Bhopal which meaningfully addresses the issues of medical care, injury assessment, economic and social rehabilitation of the gas victims with the urgency they deserve.

With these rallying points, the Bhopal victims will be observing the sixth anniversary of the gas disaster on 3rd December 1990. On this day, the sorrow and anger of the people of Bhopal would collectively be demonstrated—rallies will be organized, marches will take place, effigies of Carbide officials will be burnt and oaths will be taken. Through this letter, we invite you to come to Bhopal on that day and participate in the observance of the sixth anniversary.

For those who cannot come to Bhopal, may we suggest the following solidarity actions:

1. Organize public demonstrations, meetings, exhibitions, burning of effigies, die-ins, etc. before Union Carbide plants and offices of other public places.

2. Organize press conferences around the issues of Bhopal and demands of the gas victims.

3. Organize letter campaigns supporting the demands with letters being sent to the Prime Minister of India (Prime Minister, North Block, New Delhi) and the Chairman of Union Carbide Corporation (Robert Kennedy, Union Carbide Corporation, 39 Old Ridgebury Road, Danbury, Connecticut 06017-0001).

If you send us reports of your protest actions or wish to send messages of solidarity, we would be happy to include them in the news sheet that we publish and distribute to gas affected people.

Remember Bhopal! In solidarity,

Dr. Rajeev Lochan Sharma, Satinath Sarangi

Bhopal Group for Information and Action

FILE: Pamphlet for distribution at anniversary rally
DATE: December 1990

Voices of Bhopal

On the night of 2nd–3rd December, 1984, 40 tons of toxic gas was released from a Union Carbide pesticides plant in Bhopal, India. In the immediate aftermath, 3000 died and over 400,000 others were exposed and have continued to die and suffer. Misery in Bhopal increases daily as victims begin to suffer the long term effects of toxic exposure and the consequences of damage to their immune systems, which makes them prone to debilitating infections. Meanwhile, the struggle for justice continues. Victims continue to speak out about the need for proper rehabilitation programs and for punishment of Union Carbide.

Interview with Bano Bi, age 35, resident of Chhawni Mangalwara

The night the gas leaked, I was sewing clothes sitting next to the door. It was around midnight. The children's father had just returned from a poetry concert. He came in and asked me, "What are you burning that makes me choke?" And then it became quite unbearable. The children sleeping inside began to cough. I spread a mat outside and made the children sit on it. Outside, we started coughing even more violently and became breathless. Then our landlord and my husband went out to see what was happening. They found out that some gas had leaked. Outside there were people shouting "Run, run, run for your lives."

We left our door open and began to run. We reached the Bharat Talkies crossing where my husband jumped into a truck full of people going to Raisen and I jumped into one going towards Obaidullahganj. It was early morning when we reached Obaidullahganj. The calls for the morning prayers were on. As we got down, there were people asking us to get medicines put on our eyes and to get injections. Some people came and said they had made tea for us and we could have tea and need not pay any money.

Meanwhile, some doctors came there. They said the people who are seriously ill had to be taken to the hospital. Two doctors came to me and said that I had to be taken to the hospital. I told my children to come with me to the hospital and bade them to stay at the hospital gate till I came out of the hospital. I was kept inside for a long time and the children were getting worried. Then Bhairon Singh, a Hindu who used to work with my husband, spotted the children. He, too, had run away with his family and had come to the hospital for treatment. The children told him that I was in the hospital since morning and described to the him the kind of clothes I was wearing.

Bhairon Singh went in to the hospital and found me among the piles of the dead. He then put me on a bench and ran around to get me oxygen. The doctors would put the oxygen mask on me for two minutes and then pass it on to someone else who was in as much agony as I was. The oxygen made me feel a little better. The children were crying for their father so Bhairon told them that he was admitted to a hospital in Raisen. When I was being brought back to Bhopal on a truck, we heard people saying that the gas tank had burst again. So we came back and went beyond Obaidullahganj to Budhni, where I was in the hospital for three days.

I did not even have a five paisa coin on me. Bhairon Singh spent his money on our food. He even hired a taxi to take me back to Bhopal to my brother's place. My husband had come back by then. He was in terrible condition. His body would get stiff and he had difficulty breathing. At times, we would give up hope of his survival. My brother took him to a hospital. I said that I would stay at the hospital to look after my husband. I still had a bandage over my eyes. When the doctors at the hospital saw me, they said, "Why don't you get admitted yourself, you are in such a bad state?" I told them that I was all right. I was so absorbed with the suffering of my children and my husband that I wasn't aware of my own condition. But the doctors got me admitted and since there were no empty beds, I shared the same bed with my husband in the hospital. We were in that hospital for one and a half months.

After coming home from the hospital, my husband was in such a state that he would rarely stay at home for more than two days. He used to be in the Jawahar Lal Nehru Hospital most of the time. Apart from all the medicines that he used to take at the hospital, he got medicines like Deriphylline and Decadron from the store. He remained in that condition after the gas disaster. I used to take him to the hospital and when I went for the Sangathan meetings, the children took him to the hospital. He was later admitted to the MIC ward and he never came back. He died in the MIC ward.

My husband used to carry sacks of grain at the warehouse. He used to load and unload railway wagons. After the gas, he could not do any work. Sometimes, his friends used to take him with them and he used to just sit there. His friends gave him 5-10 rupee notes and we survived on that.

We were in a helpless situation. I had no job and the children were too young to work. We survived on help from our neighbors and other people in the community. My husband had severe breathing problems and he used to get into bouts of coughing. When he became weak, he had fever all the time. He was always treated for gas related problems. He was never treated for tuberculosis. And yet, in the post-mortem report, they mentioned that he died due to tuberculosis. He was medically examined for compensation but they never told us in which category he was put. And now they tell me that his death was not due to gas exposure, that I cannot get the relief of Rs 10,000 ($400) which is given to relatives of the dead.

I have pain in my chest and I get breathless when I walk. The doctors told me that I need to be operated on for ulcers in my stomach. They told me it would cost Rs 10,000 ($400). I do not have so much money. All the jewelry that I had has been sold. I have not paid the landlord for the last six years and he harasses me. How can I go for the operation? Also, I am afraid that if I die during the operation, there would be no one to look after my children.

I believe that even if we have to starve, we must get the guilty officials of Union Carbide punished. They have killed someone's brother, someone's husband, someone's mother, someone's sister; how many tears can Union Carbide wipe? We will get Union Carbide punished. Till my last breath, I will not leave them.

Interview with Natthibai, age 55, resident of Rajendra Nagar

My husband's name was Dukhishyam. He got a lot of gas in him. On the night the gas leaked, both of us ran towards the forest. He remained sick afterwards. He used to get breathless, cough and his eyes would get very big. He could not see properly after the gas. Twice he was admitted to the hospital. The second time he was admitted, he never came back. He died in the MIC ward. I gave an application for Rs 10,000 ($400) in interim relief, but they haven't done anything about it yet. Last year, he died in Kunwar (autumn). They haven't yet told me whether I will get Rs 10,000 or not. I gave them all the medical prescriptions of my husband with my application.

I stay sick. I have come back from the hospital on 13th of this month [November 1990]. I was there for one and a half months. I never got breathless before the gas; I used to work as a laborer. Now I get badly breathless and my chest pains. I was in the hospital during the Festival of Lights. This gas has destroyed us completely.

Interview with Ajeeza Bi, age 30, resident of Kazi Camp

Ever since the gas, my head aches 24 hours a day. I have pain in my stomach and sometimes feel giddy. My daughter, Nasreen, cannot see properly, cannot thread a needle and she is only eleven. My other daughter, Sofia, also stays sick and she is eight. I have three children from before the gas disaster and after the gas I have aborted thrice. All three times it happened in the hospital. Once I was six months pregnant; the second time I was seven months pregnant and the third time I carried the baby for eight months. They were all born dead. All with black skin like the color of coal and all shrunken in size. The doctors never told me why such things are happening to me.

Interview with Mohini, age 32, resident of Mahamayee Ka Baug

Our organization, the Bhopal Gas Peedit Mahila Udyog Sangathan, started from a sewing center. After the gas disaster, in September '85, a rehabilitation center run by an organization was started with government help. About 600 women used to be given sewing jobs from this center. There were 30 of us employed who were employed for cutting cloth at the center and this cut cloth was given to the women for sewing at their homes. In December 1986, this center was closed down. All of a sudden the women who were dependent on the sewing job became jobless. The 30 of us decided that something must be done to get the center reopened. So we, along with 600 other women, marched to the Chief Minister's residence. We went on several demonstrations and had to face the police on many occasions. In April '87, 225 of us were arrested and put in jail. It was a long and hard struggle. Most of us were quite sick due to the gas. During one demonstration, a woman named Hamida Bi fell unconscious with chest pain and died 4 days later. We finally managed to get the center reopened and now 2300 women are getting sewing jobs.

After we got the center reopened our organization grew in number and we took up the issues of medical treatment and economic rehabilitation of the gas victims. We also campaigned against Union Carbide, organized rallies demanding punishment of the guilty officials of the company and adequate compensation for all gas victims. We opposed the unholy settlement between Union Carbide and Rajiv Gandhi's government. On five separate occasions, more than 3000 women from the Sangathan have gone to Delhi and voiced our opposition to the settlement.

We have also filed a petition in the Supreme Court challenging the validity of the settlement and now it is being heard. Earlier in August 1988, we had filed a petition seeking interim relief from the Government. On 13th March 1990, the Supreme Court ordered the Government to pay Rs 200 ($8) per person per month to all the residents of the 36 gas-affected wards of Bhopal for three years. This amount is being disbursed but there are a lot of problems in the manner in which this is being done. We know that the struggle against Union Carbide will be a long one and we are determined to carry on with our struggle till justice is done.

FILE: Letter to editor, Free Press
DATE: December 1990

Dear Sir,

I read your editorial "Legitimating Fascism" and want to commend you for taking such a forthright position against communalism. As you point out, gathering "historical evidence" to support Advani's claim about a Hindu temple having existed on the site of Babri Masjid is a devious political maneuver that seeks to take advantage of the legitimacy of "facts." It is disturbing but not surprising to see scholars put to such use. Scholarly claim are grounded on the assumption that only the academic elite has access to the truth and that such truth is objective-neutral and universal, not tied to vested interests. Yet, history is replete with conflicting records, the production of which is clearly connected to narrow political aims. The "facts" of history thus must always be seen as political, particularly when legitimated by scholarly claims to neutrality.

By claiming that the facts they present are neutral, the elite is able to co-opt others into believing that their cause is a common cause, thus creating a mass base to support issues which only serve elitist agendas. The BJP's maneuvers to establish Adyodha as the birthplace of Ram through "proof" of prior existence of a temple there is an instance of such co-opting. Garnering evidence for their claims about the birthplace of Ram is a way to suggest that the interests of all Hindus are unified, hiding the Brahmanic, upper class motivations which communalist tensions have served.

Hence, it is of utmost importance that we expose the political interests which motivate the production of facts and thus expose Advani as a fascist leader who has used religion to mobilize a mass base for the BJP's pursuit of governmental power. As you suggest, Advani's offering of archeological proof to support his claims about Adyodha is a con game that must be exposed.

Sincerely, Suresh Joseph

FILE: Position paper for presentation at Bhopal convention
DATE: April 1991

Rebuilding as Subversion-Independent Initiatives towards Rehabilitation of the Gas Affected People of Bhopal

Rehabilitation is a neglected area for revolutionary thought and practice. Mass disasters (destruction in Iraq, Chernobyl, Armenian earthquake or Bhopal) have given rise to situations that call for innovative political intervention in the aftermath of such disasters. Yet there is scanty evidence of such intervention, if at all. We believe that through intervention in such situations simultaneous with one's fulfillment of the essential task of rehabilitation, it is possible to act and think in ways that can encourage mutual cooperation and expose the illegitimacy of the State. The following agenda for long term voluntary action on Bhopal has been drawn up with such ideas in mind.

1. Growing without Pesticides

If there was any need for it, the industrial genocide in Bhopal demonstrated that pesticides are hazardous. The aim of "Growing without Pesticides" will be to demonstrate further that they are unnecessary.

The idea is to purchase agricultural land near Bhopal with the gas victims (members of the Bhopal Gas Peedit Mahila Udyog Sangathan) contributing to the common pool from the compensation/settlement amount they receive from Union Carbide. And then participate in pesticide free (natural or organic) farming to grow vegetables. Cucumbers can then be sold as political statements against Union Carbide.

2. Production and Distribution of Nutritional Supplements

We know of gas affected people who buy so called "health additives" (produced mostly by multinational companies) in the hope of putting some life into their toxin ravaged bodies. Voluntary and even government sponsored studies have highlighted the need for nutritional supplements for the gas victims. The aim of this project will be to fulfill this need (to an extent possible) and encourage cooperative efforts in the community.

The idea is to promote the formation of a cooperative (either in a community or in the organization of the victims) that would produce low cost nutritional supplements that incorporate traditional recipes. A number of groups have demonstrated the possibilities of production of such supplements from locally available materials through low technology methods. Efforts need to be made to ensure that such a project is self-sustaining in terms of resources. . . .

4. Vocational Rehabilitation

As in other such situations, an overwhelmingly large section of the population affected by the disaster consists of people who had been, prior to the disaster, earning a living through hard physical labor. A substantial majority of such people have been, due to gas exposure, incapacitated to continue with such work and most carry on with their traditional jobs like pushing hand carts, carrying loads, rolling bidis, construction labor only because their economic condition forces them to. The government's efforts towards providing jobs in accord with the health condition of the gas affected have been scandalously inadequate and singularly lacking in innovative ideas.

It will need a few volunteers with some experience in such matters to initiate income generating activities (garment stitching, health food production, running fair price coops have been suggested) among the gas victims. Widespread support, especially in the marketing of products, would be required for such an activity and it can be initiated only after such support has been assessed.

Given the spectrum of misery and the reasons for hope presented by the Bhopal situation, the list of possible independent initiatives can grow. However, to facilitate participation of groups/individuals (based in Bhopal and other parts of the country) in putting the ideas into practice, we suggest the formation of a network to begin with, which can be called "Friends of Bhopal's Valiant Victims." We hope that the need for rehabilitation activity in Bhopal will be appreciated by members of such a network and that such activity will be carried out with a spirit of subversion.

Satinath Sarangi
Bhopal Group for Information and Action

FILE: Press release
DATE: April 1991

Re: Proceedings of the National Convention on Bhopal Gas Leak Disaster and Its Aftermath, Delhi 8-9 April 1991

The Bhopal convention was convened to revitalize awareness and support for issues which have emerged in the aftermath of the 1984 gas disaster. Participants included journalists, trade unionists, representatives of political parties and activists from a range of people's struggles.

The meeting was divided into three sessions addressing the February '89 out-of-court settlement between Union Carbide and the Government of India, rehabilitation programs for gas victims and legislation regarding hazardous industry. Final discussions formulated resolutions to be presented to the public and an action plan specifying required initiatives by convention participants.

The most urgent demand articulated by the Convention was that the settlement be overturned and Union Carbide made subject to the continuing jurisdiction of the courts. This requires a reversal of the "full and final" clause of the settlement which bars further legal action against Carbide. It was emphasized that introduction of a legal category of "continuing liability" is the only way to ensure sufficient funding is available to care for victims of toxic exposure, particularly when the long term effects of exposure remain undetermined.

FILE: Press release
DATE: April 1991

Re: Union Carbide Boycott

To commemorate Earth Day 1991 (April 22), Bhopal gas victims ask for a renewed focus on the boycott against EverReady batteries. EverReady batteries are produced by Union Carbide; consumer rejection of EverReady batteries through a boycott is a means to protest Union Carbide's abuse of people and environment.

"Bhopal" has become a symbol of the problems of industrial society. Revitalization of the EverReady Boycott will both demonstrate solidarity with the struggle for justice in Bhopal and be a statement of public concern about the way global society is "developing." Industrialization means that safety of people and environment is determined by corporate quest for profit. Bhopal is only one example of the suffering caused by corporate greed and of the importance of regaining local control. Revitalization of the EverReady Boycott will be a statement of non-cooperation with corporate enterprise which continues colonialist patterns of outside control and local exploitation.

Revitalization of the EverReady Boycott on Earth Day is of particular importance due to recent corporate attempts to takeover the environmental movement. Through expensive advertising campaigns, corporations have tried to convince the public that they are concerned about the safety of people and environment. Yet, the record of corporate abuse is endless. Witness the destruction in Bhopal, at Exxon's Alaskan oil spill, in Italy's Sevesco. Bhopal gas victims believe this hypocrisy must be exposed and the environmental movement preserved as a forum for debate on the critical issues of sustainable and just development. Earth Day focus on the EverReady Boycott will highlight this concern for the integrity of environmentalism and remind of the urgent need for noncooperation with transnational corporate exploiters.

Perhaps the clearest lesson of Bhopal has been the need for extra-legal struggle. It is clear to many observers that the relief received by gas victims has not been the result of an efficiently operating legal system but due to sustained protest by gas victims. Victims themselves often argue that unless they had organized and marched to protest deplorable conditions, compensation and health care would be even less available than it is today. Further, attention to victims dissent against the February '89 settlement has only come through vigilant agitation. Clearly, continued and extended public pressure is essential to the on-going struggle. Mass participation in the EverReady Boycott is a way we can directly contribute to this goal.

FILE: Civil liberties report, slum clearances
DATE: June 1991

Encroachment on Civil Rights: Report of an investigation into the "anti-encroachment drive" in the gas-affected slums of Bhopal

People's Union for Civil Liberties, Madhya Pradesh

A large part of the population in cities lives in slums. In the eyes of the law, most slum are considered illegal settlements, but for the people who live in these slums there are no options. An estimated 40 million city dwellers live in slums, which is 20% of the urban population. Almost half of the population of Bhopal, like in many other cities, resides in slums. A majority of these slums happen to be affected by the world's worst industrial disaster—the toxic gas leak from Union Carbide's factory in December 1984.

Since last one year, the State administration has been carrying out an "anti-encroachment drive" as a part of its "city beautification plan." This drive has led to a situation of terror in the slums.

During this drive, there has been large scale demolition of slums situated along the Upper lake of the city. A large number of people have been evicted from their settlements. The Peoples Union for Civil Liberties has carried out an investigation on this matter. This is the report of the investigation team which included Mr. Om Prakash Rawal (Eminent social-thinker), Mr. Lajja

Shankar Hardenia (Journalist, Economic Times), Dr. Arun Kumar Singh (Geologist), Ms. Tultul Biswas (Student, Barakatullah University) and Dr. Rajiv Lochan Sharma (Doctor).

The city of Bhopal, besides being the capital of Madhya Pradesh, is popularly known as the cultural capital of India. The city, situated in the plateau of Malwa in Central India, can be divided into three distinct areas. The old city, which was established during the reign of the Nawabs, where most people are dependent on wage labor and petty trade for their livelihood. The new city, where government offices and staff quarters were built after Bhopal was made the Capital of the state, is to the south of the Old City. Most of the residents of this part of the city are government officers and other employees. The industrial township of Bharat Heavy Electricals Limited (BHEL) is the third distinct segment of the city of Bhopal.

The total population of Bhopal is about 10 lakhs (1,000,000), out of which approximately 6 lakh people reside in the old city. About half the population of the old city is settled in slums. According to the records of the government, close to 50,000 people in Bhopal live in 160 "illegal" slums, most of which are in the old city. The city has many large and small lakes, the upper Lake and the lower being the two largest. Shakir Nagar, Fatehgarh, Sajda Nagar, Sidhi Ghat are some of the densely populated slums along the upper lake. About 15,000 people had been living in these slums in small dwellings made of wooden planks, stones or mud. The land along the lake is owned by different individuals and institutions. Some of the land belongs to the Madhya Pradesh Wakf Board, some owned by people who hold entitlements (pattas) given to them by the government. Some of the residents do not have pattas.

Most of the men in these slums are either autorickshaw/tempo/minibus drivers, hand-cart pushers or daily wage laborers. Women work as wage laborers, housemaids or beetle-nut cutters. People also roll beedis at home to make a living.

A survey conducted by the Indian Council of Medical Research (ICMR) after the 1984 gas disaster indicated that 55% of the population in the old city is Hindu and 43% is Muslim. Though the two communities are close in size, it is the Muslim community that has suffered due to the demolitions. Our investigation team found that among 800 families evicted, only four were Hindus. Mr. Babu Lal Gaur, the State Minister for local self government told the investigation team that 30% of the population in demolished slums are Hindus. However, the Superintendent of Police informed the team that 99% of the affected people were Muslims. Most of the residents of these slums were known to have traditionally voted for the Congress Party. According to Fazalludin, a retired army man and resident of Sidhi Ghat, during the recent elections, a majority of the names of the residents had disappeared from the voters list. According to the local English newspaper, the people in these slums who were Muslims and supporters of the Congress Party were shifted out from one assembly constituency known to have Hindu fundamentalist inclinations. Both the minister for local self-government and the superintendent of police held that such charges were without any basis.

The demolition of houses

As one goes across the slums along the Upper Lake, the first one is at Retghat and is called Lal Imli wali Masjid ki Basti. The demolition of the houses started here on the 26th of May. Early that morning the city authorities accompanied by about 200 policemen, 10 with arms, descended on the settlement and demolished 75 houses in one day. Some of the houses that were demolished in this slum were more than hundred years old including Nazar Mahal which was a building of archaeological importance. Most of the residents here had ownership rights over their pieces of land. Aftab Ahmad, who lived in this slum, reported that he had his land registration papers but his house was demolished after issuing three notifications to him in twenty days. He was not paid any compensation for his house. The minister for local self-government, however, informed the investigation team that all people having ownership rights have been compensated for their houses and that they have been provided with plots of land to build their houses. According to Aftab Ahmad there are many like him who have not been given any compensation. The demolition continued till 30th May. Every morning the employees of the municipal corporation came with their bulldozers and a large posse of armed policemen and demolished 100 to 150 houses. The policemen and their guns were too intimidating for the people and they watch on silently as their houses were turned to rubble. A few who tried to oppose this destruction were assaulted by the police, abused and threatened. The investigation team was told by Liyakat, Mansoor, Shahban and Munni Bai that the demolition of the houses was carried out in this manner till 30th May.

Terror and protest

Meanwhile, terrorised by the thought of their houses being demolished, two women—Musarrat (30) and Pan Bai (36)—from Ammu Khalifa Ki Bagiya, committed suicide by drinking kerosene oil. The other residents of the settlements protested against the destruction of their houses and threatened to commit mass self-immolation. They also submitted a list of demands to the authorities in which they asked for stoppage of demolition during the rains and payment of compensation for their houses. This slum was built on land belonging to the Wakf Board and there was an order from the High Court staying demolition of houses built on this land. The municipal administrator refused to accept the order and the demolition of the slum was stopped only after three people threatened to immolate themselves en masse.

The next slum to be demolished was Fatehgarh. In the morning of 31st May when the demolition squad reached Fathgarh, about 50 women stopped them in the way holding kerosene cans threatening to immolate themselves. Ms. Shahbana who was leading the group said that she had dowsed herself with kerosene and that had scared the officials from going ahead and they went back. After this hundreds of women sat on a dharna (sit-in) in the slum. The dharna continued for three days and demolition of the houses was discontinued by the officials. According to the superintendent of police most of the people participating in the dharna were outsiders but Ms. Munni Bai, Nafeesa Bi and Rabia who were arrested while on dharna informed the investigation team that all the women who sat on dharna belonged to that locality.

On 3rd June at five in the morning Fathgarh was encircled by policemen, armed men from Special Armed Force (SAF) and Central Reserve Police Force (CRPF) and mounted police. All access to the slum was blocked. Three of the women sitting on dharna, Ms. Munni Bai, Nafisa Bi and Rabia Bi said their slum was surrounded by hundreds of policemen. After the encirclement a policeman came to the women on dharna and told them that some police-women wanted to talk to them and asked them to come to the main street. All the women sitting on dharna went off to the main street where they were arrested by the police and told that their houses would not be demolished and no one would be harassed. Sixty women were arrested in this dramatic manner causing a major setback in the growing opposition to the demolition. It is possible that some of the local leaders connived with the police and the city administration and allowed such arrests to happen and were later rewarded with land plots in the city itself.

After the arrest when all opposition was silenced demolition of the houses was carried out under heavy armed police presence. Masood, a resident of Shakir Nagar reported that there were two to three policemen at every house. The whole slum was surrounded by hundreds of policemen and no one was allowed to go across the police cordon.

In this manner 130 houses of Fatehgarh were destroyed on 3rd June and the demolition drive was restarted. Houses were demolished by bulldozers and in the presence of a massive police force. By 6th June the whole of Fategarh was razed to the ground and several houses were demolished in Sazda Nagar on 6th and 7th June.

FILE: Affidavit to U.S. courts
DATE: August 1991

Before, the undersigned authority appeared Kim Laughlin, known to be, and after first being sworn, dead upon her oath, state, swear and affirm as follows.

My name is Kim Laughlin; I am over the age of twenty-one years; of sound mind, and make this statement on my own free will and state that it is based on personal knowledge.

I am a doctoral candidate at Rice University in the Department of Anthropology. My educational background has prepared me to assess the role of science and technology in society. The subject of my Ph.D. research is the long term social and economic impact of the Bhopal gas disaster of 1984. I resided in Bhopal from September 1990 through June 1991. During this time I worked directly with the leaders and members of Bhopal Gas Peedit Mahila Udyog Sangathan (Bhopal Gas Affected Working Women's Union, BGPMUS), the largest victims' organization in Bhopal. I have also worked with leaders of Bhopal Group for Information and Action (BGIA), an organization of educated volunteers who serve as English language representatives of BGPMUS. I also have had numerous discussions with Indian legal experts, political leaders, health professionals, and bureaucrats who have been involved in the Bhopal case. I also have done archival research to analyze documents and other materials generated in the six years since the disaster. The following statements are derived from my research efforts and material:

Regarding the Motion to Dismiss Based on Adequate Alternative Forum and the Motion for Summary Judgment Based on the Alleged Effect of the Settlement Negotiated in the Indian Proceedings

Since 1985, it has become clear that India cannot provide an alternative adequate forum. The February '89 settlement pre-empted a trial on the merits of the case and came about through numerous failures of due process:

1. On March 29, 1985, the Indian Parliament enacted the Bhopal Gas Leak Disaster (Processing of Claims) Act, granting Union of India (UOI) the exclusive right to represent the victims in India or elsewhere. Thereafter, UOI has represented the Bhopal victims in the capacity of parens patriae. The Bhopal Act itself is a breach of due process because it involves conflicts of interest: while representing the victims, UOI also owns a substantial portion (22%) of UCIL stock and controls the courts, since judges are appointed and there are no juries. Thus, in the Indian proceedings, UOI has been plaintiff, defendant and the court.

The overlapping responsibilities of UOI has precluded the possibility of an impartial tribunal. This structural problem is magnified by the current political-economic environment in India. Since the early eighties, the orientation of Indian development has changed. In the decades following Indian independence in 1947, there was an overt attempt to maintain self-sufficiency through minimalized dependence on foreign investment and technology trans-

fer. This agenda did not provide adequate growth to keep up with the demands of a growing welfare state and increasing national indebtedness.
Hence, policy changes in the eighties redirected the economy toward greater
utilization of outside resources.

The current dependence of the Indian economy on foreign investment has
undermined the capacity of the Indian State to fairly evaluate the distribution
of risks and benefits which accrue through industrial development. Because it
is obliged to attract foreign investment, the Indian government is forced to let
market considerations override all other concerns. Thus, it is impossible for
the Indian government to fairly adjudicate the claims of those victimized by
corporations fulfilling investment demands. It is publicly recognized in India
that a harsh decision against Carbide would be a deterrent to economic goals.
The problem of Third World governments being caught in a double-bind
wherein they promote their economies at the cost of safety for their citizens
is well recognized in the social science literature.

2. There has been a failure of representation on the part of UOI as parens
patriae of the gas victims. This failure is indicated by the paucity of research
carried out before arriving at a settlement amount. At the time of the settlement, fewer than 50,000 victims had been assessed for personal injury. The
results of this initial assessment were not made public until April 1989, two
months after the settlement was finalized.

The great majority of victims contest the adequacy of the settlement because it is insufficient to cover compensation and rehabilitation costs. Approximately 600,000 persons have filed for damages based on physical proximity to the plant. Medical monitoring of the health status of these claimants
alone would cost in excess of $6,000,000. Conservative estimates for full
compensation range between one and two billion dollars. Please see Appendix 2 for details. Further, according to the terms of the settlement, the Indian
government has first access to reimburse itself for litigation costs, interim relief payments and general economic loss. Government reimbursement alone
could easily consume much of the settlement, leaving little for the present and
future claims of victims.

Within India, it is not possible to correct the settlement's inadequacies
because of UOI's involvement in denial of the magnitude of the disaster.
Medical categorization data produced by the Madhya Pradesh State Government and released in 1991 indicates that out of a gas affected population of
over half a million people, only forty individuals are permanently disabled.
The release of this data generated disbelief and outrage within the medical
community. Doctors affiliated with the organization Socially Active Medicos
(SAM) have denounced the data as corruption of scientific means for political
ends. They critique the testing protocol for being insufficiently thorough and
for blatantly ignoring long term and multisystemic ailments. Please see Ap-

BHOPAL: THE SUFFERING CONTINUES. SO DOES THE STRUGGLE

pendix 3 for elaboration on problems with medical categorization data now available in India.

Attempts to produce alternative medical documentation through the voluntary sector has led to confiscations and arrests. Officially produced data is not available to interested health professionals. Hence, the research basis for representation of gas victims in India is unavailable.

3. Victims were given no notice of the settlement prior to it being finalized and publicly announced. Such notice was clearly possible through public news releases or through mailings to victims included on a computerized list used for registering claims. Notice also could have been given through any of

the victims organizations in Bhopal. The Supreme Court of India itself recognized this failure of due process during its review of the Bhopal Act. While the Supreme Court upheld the validity of the Bhopal Act, it conceded that victims were not given notice.

4. The 1989 settlement order did not contain a distribution plan. Such a plan still has not been publicized. Thus, it is not known how much will be allocated to each individual, particularly since the Government has first option to reimburse itself for expenses. Further, the settlement order did not give attention to future claims.

5. Victims have never been given the opportunity to opt out of the February '89 settlement or of the litigation all together. However, sustained protest by victims has clearly indicated opposition. In a major demonstration protesting the settlement in August 1989, police brutally attacked demonstration participants. This attack is publicly recognized in India as a show of the government's refusal to attend to victims' demands. See Appendix 4 for documentation on victim protest against the settlement.

FILE: Letter to ICMR, response to women's groups
DATE: November 1991

To: Indian Council of Medical Research
From: Bhopal Group for Information and Action

We write out of concern over recent moves to introduce hormonal implant contraceptives into the Family Planning Program. Our concerns are as follows.

1. Research done in Bangladesh has indicated serious side effects during use of hormonal implants, including acute muscle ache and menstrual irregularity. No research has been done to predict possible long term effects. Research has connected other hormonal interventions to both cervical and breast cancer.

2. The "convenience" of the hormonal implants over oral contraceptives is offset by the loss of user control. Rather than becoming more independent in her birth control decisions, a woman using hormonal implants becomes increasingly dependent on her doctor. Research in Bangladesh documented severe injury to women who attempted to remove the subdermal implants themselves when unable to get cooperation from their doctor.

3. Introduction of hormonal implants without regard for women's health issues demonstrates that the Family Planning Program continues to prioritize population control over the well-being of Indian women. Orienting the Program toward the creation of family structures adaptable to a consumer society implicitly accepts further marketization and ignores the injustice which accompanies. Contraceptives should be available to women so that they have

more options regarding their sexuality and reproduction, not to further economic aims that serve the elite.

4. In the West, hormonal implants have not been accepted as a safe means of birth control. Introduction of hormonal implants in the Third World must therefore be seen as a ploy of pharmaceutical corporations who need to dump their hazardous waste.

5. Inviting women's groups to help in implementing the implant program suggests an attempt to legitimize the program through the involvement of these groups without actually being open to their critique. Failure to actively seek the critique of the voluntary sector on this issue demonstrates the tendency to use health care as a means of state control. The hormonal implant program also gives false legitimacy to the health establishment by suggesting that innovate technologies have been developed to serve women's needs. Because hormonal implants are so dangerous, the program must, instead, be seen as an effort to hide the shocking lack of priority given to women's health issues, including the development of safe contraceptives.

Thank you for your attention.
Bhopal Group for Information and Action

FILE: Letter to Left network, including international listings
DATE: November 1991

Program for a Medical Care Cooperative Among the Gas Victims of Bhopal

In January 1992, Bhopal Group for Information and Action (BGIA) will initiate a cooperative health care clinic to serve the gas affected community of Bhopal. The functions of the clinic will include both treatment and monitoring, guided by information gathered during a trial, mobile clinic run from March 1991 through the present. This proposal is a request for support and funds from sympathetic individuals and organizations.

Program Objectives

The specific objectives of the Cooperative are as follows:

1. To establish and popularize therapies based on rational drugs. This will include efforts to halt irrational drug use and to minimalize overall drug dependencies.

2. To involve victims in the diagnosis and treatment of other gas victims and thus evolve a system of participatory disease care.

3. To generate and disseminate information related to the health conditions of the gas victims.

4. To monitor the health status of the gas victims and to involve them in their own monitoring.

5. To perform a "watch-dog" function in relation to private and government medical care of gas victims.

6. To generate and disseminate information so to present a critique of the prevalent system of medicine.

Work Organization and Scheduling

The Cooperative will be a group of volunteer doctors and para-medical workers along with victim activists who have the inclination and potential to become health workers. All members of the Cooperative will have equal rights and access to decision-making and responsibilities will be shared likewise. The Cooperative will be a group which sees health in general and the issue of health of the Bhopal victims in particular as a political issue; activities of the Cooperative, all relationships within the Cooperative and all relationships between the Cooperative and its patients will be guided by this central understanding.

Budget Requirements

The funds for the clinic will be generated through contributions from individuals and organizations concerned with the health condition of the gas victims and in solidarity with the struggle for justice in Bhopal. The Cooperative will not accept funds from corporations, governments and funding agencies. It will be dependent on trade unions, mass organizations solidarity groups and sympathetic individuals for financial and other forms of support. To ensure continued and unhindered functioning for at least two years, commitments for regular financial contributions for this period would be appreciated.

FILE: Police report, Kesla incident
DATE: December 1991

First Information Report (copy)

Police Station: Kesla   *Crime no.:* 48/91
Name: Budhram *Father's name:* Bhajna *Caste:* Korku

I live in Rajamarihar and I am engaged in agriculture. Today morning my brother Sejram went out between 6 and 7:00 A M. Around 10 to 12 Sardarji (Sikhs) started beating him. When I went to protect Sejram, I was also beaten. I received injuries on the wrist and thumb. Sejram received injuries on his back, thigh, etc. These people beat other villagers also. Umrao s/o Kanak Singh, my mother Suddo Bai, sustained injuries on the head, left shoulder and left hip. People were beaten here and there. My mother was sitting near the fire and her ten rupee note was burnt. Baran s/o Teji, Antram, Rameshwar, my wife Sukhwati, received injuries on her left fingers. Phoolwati's matka (water pot) was broken. Sukhdev and Lalsaheb were also injured. Sejram s/o Bhajna, Atarsingh s/o Babloo and Atarsingh's wife also received injuries. The Party was accompanied by Excise Sub Inspector Jain. The attackers had gone to seize liquor. Sejram and Atarsingh are serious. These attackers surrounded and beat villagers. I report for proper action. The report was read to me. It is written correctly. SD/-

FILE: Letter to Legal Aid Committee, Supreme Court, Delhi
DATE: January 1992

Sir,

We are residents of village Rajamarihar, block Kesla, Dist. Hoshangabad, Madhya Pradesh. We are all tribals. We were displaced by the establishment of a proof range around 20 years back. This literally destroyed us. We do not have any proper employment opportunities. By tradition, we brew our own liquor for our own consumption. We are harassed by the local Excise Department and the goondas of the liquor contractor on this ground.

In a recent incident on December 25, 1991, Excise Sub Inspector Mr. K. C. Jain, accompanied by 15-20 hired goondas of the liquor contractor, attacked our village at around 6:00 A.M. The first villagers to be attacked were the ones returning after nature call. After this, the "raid" party entered people's houses and attacked them. They even beat up children, women and the old. The attackers were armed with lathis and swords. Around 20 people were injured, out of which 4-5 seriously. In addition, the goonda party also threatened to rape women. They also took away a lota and a shovel. They ransacked the houses and damaged things.

The whole incident was reported to the Kesla police station the same day. Nine of the injured persons were medically examined. The local MLA, Dr. Sitasharon Sharma, also arrived from Itarsi and demanded strict action. Yet, the police let the criminals go away. Two days after the incident, on December 27th, villagers held a demonstration at Kesla Police Station, after which 8 goondas were arrested.

1. However, they were charged with very ordinary crimes (such as IPC 147, 148, 149, 323, 452), which were extremely insufficient, looking at the seriousness of the crime and injuries therein. When questioned on this issue, the police officials said that new charges would be instituted after medical reports were received. However, even 15 days after the incident, medical reports have not been received from the hospital, according to Kesla P.S. In the meanwhile, the goondas were released on bail just after two days.

2. Excise Sub Inspector K. C. Jain, under whose leadership the attack was planned and executed, has neither been arrested nor suspended nor transferred. In other words, no action has been taken against him as yet. Jain is known to have committed such atrocities before and always uses private goondas.

3. Although swords were also used by the goonda party during the attack, police have only shown confiscation of lathis.

It is quite clear that police are trying to shield and protect the criminals. We are afraid that this will act as a morale booster for criminals and the incident might recur. In the whole of the tribal area where we live, excise, police, forest and other government officials harass people and commit atrocities day in and day out. Yet, no action is taken against them nor any preventive measure adopted. Therefore, we seek help in this incident to secure justice and ensure non-recurrence of such incidents in the future.

Residents of Village Rajamanihar,
Block/Police Station Kesla,
Dist Hoshangabad, (MP)

FILE: Letter to publisher regarding Chouhan's book
DATE: April 1992

Dear Director,

I write to you to inquire about your interest in publishing a book documenting my experiences as a worker in the Union Carbide plant in Bhopal. The book, Inside the Killer Carbide Plant: A Bhopal Worker's Story, traces the history of negligence in the plant in the years leading to the disaster and thereby argues against Carbide's claim that the cause was an isolated incidence of worker misconduct. This argument has gained increasing relevance with the recent re-initiation of criminal proceedings against Carbide officials. The book offers careful documentation of a series of managerial decisions that precipitated the leak and then made it impossible to respond responsibly once disaster had occurred. The book also includes brief interviews with 29 other former Carbide workers who collaborate my testimony.

Since the disaster, I have served as an informant for both journalists and official investigators from the India Central Bureau of Investigation. Using my access to eyewitnesses in combination with my own experiences, I have tried to wage a vigilant campaign to expose Carbide and to raise awareness of the problems caused by corporate domination. This book is the culmination of this effort.

I have also participated in numerous meetings addressing industrial hazards, including two held in the United States which focused on human rights aspects of corporate control. These conferences increased my awareness of the continued relevance of the Bhopal story. I hope you can help me in ensuring that it is properly told.

                                                        Sincerely, T. R. Chouhan

Note

The illustrations in this chapter are from postcards produced for sale and to commemorate various anniversaries of the Bhopal disaster. They are reproduced courtesy of the Bhopal Group for Information and Action.

URBAN MEDIASCAPES
ON THE VERGE

Horizons of Interactivity:
Making the News at Time Warner

Time Warner is in the news. As the world leader in entertainment revenues and one of the largest American publishers of books and journals, Time Warner is a vital force in the social, cultural, and economic processes which shape contemporary configurations of power and the ways we perceive them. The products distributed by Time Warner are both instance and explanation of emergent social processes which promise to dramatically change the ways we live. As part of this process, Time Warner is a leader in the game to build and acquire access to the information superhighway, which now has become a powerful metaphor as well as potential artifact of the Clinton administration.

A Time Warner pilot project in Orlando is anticipated to be one of the most ambitious moves being made to hook American televisions online. Billed as "the world's first digital, interactive, multimedia communications system," the project promises a wide array of options to subscribers. Relying on new technologies that

Subj: What would you want?
Date: 93-11-20 15:58EST
From: Walt Isaacson
Posted on: American Online
This past week, we at Time Inc. announced a proposed new interactive TV service called News on Demand.

It will provide televised news and information to your TV sets via a broadband, switched network, such as the Full Service Network that Time-Warner (our parent company) is launching next Spring in Orlando.

I have been asked to help invent this product along with Paul Sagan, who was the news chief at Channel One, Time-Warner's local all-news station in New York.

Our news service could—at least in theory—put any news and info programs or segments that you might want to watch onto a big server and to watch and call them up whenever you want them.

You could watch, for example, a traditional evening newscast whenever it was convenient for you. Or could watch special in-depth reports compress data and deliver it on call, viewers will be able to stroll an electronic mall, choose from hundreds of movies, and customize the news, including, perhaps, both esoteric foreign coverage and coverage of neighborhood events such as PTA meetings or little league baseball games. One day, subscribers may even be able to use the system as a picture telephone or for videoconferencing, paving the way for the "virtual corporation."

The interactive project is both made possible and inhibited by the merger of Time and Warner Communications in 1985. Time purchased Warner for $14.1 billion, acquiring, in the process, both the resources of one of the largest film and record companies and major debt. By limiting possible investment, Time Warner's debt could be a major deterrent to competitive advantage with other players who have accrued similar resources through stock swaps or other mechanisms which minimize liability. The sale of approximately 25 percent of Time Warner to US West, a regional telephone company, has been one means to offset the imbalance. The deal, closed in May 1993, offered Time Warner the chance to acquire switching and billing telephone technologies, as well as cash. Following closure, Time Warner's debt was reduced from $16 billion to $14 billion, and commitments established for a $5 billion investment to update the cable system.

Deals such as those between Time Warner and US West give both shape on big issues, such as Health care, Gun Control and NAFTA. It could also have entertainment reviews, weather, sports scores, sports highlights, business news, local news and community news.

Perhaps we should even encourage people to post their own news of their localities—such as by taping a PTA meeting or a Little League game and having us put it on the server. Maybe there will be a viewer feedback capability, where you can post your own video op-ed opinions.

We're now trying to figure it all out. What should the user interface screen be like? How should you navigate (there will be no keyboard, just a TV remote control)? How many categories of offerings should there be? What type of news and info programs or segments would you like to have access to at your convenience, on demand? Would you prefer to watch a rebroadcast or a name-brand evening news show, such as the CBS or NBC evening news? Or would you rather have a summary of headlines? Do you think we should offer the network news shows as well as the ones we make ourselves? Which are your favorites, and which would you like the chance to see at your convenience? How important would it be for you to be able to go deeper and hear more about certain stories? To see unedited video from major hearings, press conferences and events? To post your own news? To get local or community news? Movie reviews?

There are hundreds of questions

and substance to new media developments. The project is dependent both
on new technologies and new organizational structures. Entertainment/in-
formation companies such as Time
Warner would hold huge libraries of
information in archived digital form,
similar to juke boxes. On request, stored information would be loaded into
video servers, which do not yet exist on a commercial scale but are being developed by computer and software companies. Information would be piped
from the video servers over optical fibers, which would have to be installed in
home and, perhaps, paid for by residents. Ensuring that the right information
gets to the right place in a reasonable amount of time involves complicated
switching equipment that has been developed but never installed for an application as large as interactive television. When digits arrive over the fiber and
into the home, conversion is necessary but the required converter boxes have
not yet materialized, partly because a grand alliance put together by Bill Gates
to speed development is being contested by his competitors. Least developed
of all are the user interface technologies which would guide viewers through
options with on-screen software that would finally realize the interactive aspect
of the project.

we have to address. And we would
like to hear any questions or opinions
you have.

—Walter Isaacson, Editor of New
Media for Time Inc. (formerly Assistant Managing Editor of Time)

Advanced interactive networks are still on the drawing board. Basic questions involving what products and services will be offered, the format of the
services, and the amount of money customers will be willing to pay remained
unanswered. The politics of it all remain even more ambiguous, even if vigor-
ously debated. Nonetheless, talk about interactive media has become a vehicle
for late twentieth-century utopianism. According to some, interactive media
promises to replace the passive, homogenized consumer of mass media with
critical individuals in control of their own destiny, uncompromised by false
advertising, which has been replaced by information. The vision is Faustian
but without a blueprint. The hero will not be a technocrat but a pioneer exhib-
iting the daring creativity of the symbolic analyst. The promise of interactive
media may be shaped by high-modernist faith in technology, but it is grounded
in daily practice which cannot be performed by rationalized workers who are
efficient but only able to perform one discrete function as part of an unimagined whole. In sum, interactive media is a test not only of technology but also
of a general capacity for change that must do without a secure sense of management, expertise, and political implication.

Some say that interactive TV is not ready for prime time. Most often, it is
the technology which is said to be half-baked. While it is true that the technologies upon which interactive television are dependent remain underdevel-

oped, they are only one aspect of an endeavor which requires inventiveness on all fronts. Hardware and software are not the only missing links; the organizational, legal, and financial structures necessary to sustain the project are also in preliminary stages. However, this is not to say that the project is even less ready for trial than the technology critics suggest, at least in the eyes of those involved. Perhaps the most interesting and innovative aspect of the project as a whole is the overt recognition of working without a blueprint, creating necessary modes of operation in process. At times it appears that the crisis of perspective is not so much seen as a problem but as a workable mode of operation with deep historical roots in the media industry's never-ending attempt to innovate fast enough to keep pace with contemporary conditions. Nonetheless, the mandate for profitability prevails; components of the interactive project which don't promise quick returns are dependent on those which can take over existing businesses, diverting the source of a product rather an attempting to create a new market niche.

It is within this context that Time Warner is in the news, both because of what it does and because of what it promises. Amidst the fanfare of the promise, Paul Sagan is at center stage. As managing editor of the News on Demand program at Time, Inc., he is part of the only interactive media project which is developing a news component. Throughout this interview Sagan has retained the identity of a journalist, distancing himself from conventional corporate motivations. Yet he is clearly aware of the complicated organizational overlay in which he is embedded. The metaphors available to describe and strategize this positioning are both old and new, suggesting that while visions of the future carry a sense of departure, they also carry the faith in eventual arrival that has sustained twentieth-century commitments to progress. Nonetheless, the social field in which established cultural forms are now played out is clearly undergoing dramatic change. For now, we watch, and perhaps respond to the e-mail circulated by Walter Isaacson.

LAUGHLIN: This may be a good time to specify. Who are you, at this point?

SAGAN: This is a company that seems to accumulate titles. I am senior vice president of Time Warner Cable Programming, Incorporated, which is the programming arm of Time Warner Cable. As such, I am most responsible for long term supervision of New York 1 News, the twenty-four-hour news channel in New York, where I am also the senior vice president. I serve as an officer in various other entities because it allows me to transact business in various roles inside separate companies, under a wholly owned company. Also, in my corporate role on the cable side, I help them look at other news channels and other programming, ventures in other places. On the Time, Inc. side, where I spend 80 percent of my time now, I am managing editor of News on Demand, Incorporated, which is the incorporated name of this—the video digital news project that we are trying to establish using Orlando as a proto-type. I know that doesn't answer your question, but . . .

LAUGHLIN: No, but that itself helps identify you. Clearly it's a complex structure. Do you have to have a two-fold strategy—one to strategize the world, one to strategize things inside the corporation?

SAGAN: There are certainly lots of office politics. There are recurrent and parallel competing interests. For example, outside of my universe, Warner Brothers Studios and HBO both produce first-run feature films. They are both out there bidding for rights; sometimes they compete with each other. Our cable systems want to be full-service networks but they want to expand, not cannibalize their business. Technically, News on Demand, Inc. is a business that we will sell to them, because we want to sell it to other cable systems, because our cable systems don't reach the majority of the country. So we will probably make some decisions to make it broadly sellable and competitive that may or may not be exactly what the cable systems want—and, down the road, our cable systems will ask whether we are the best service at the best price. If not, we need to maximize subscriber revenue and we may not buy you; we are going to buy the other news service. There are some competi-tions, and I think its a very healthy thing.

MONBERG: Tell us about the work at New York 1. I'm told that it has re-quired an integration of newly available technologies, along with new styles of expertise.

SAGAN: I don't want to overstate this, but yes—at New York 1 we rewrote the rules. While we did hire journalists, we hired people who never would have been considered for TV in the traditional broadcast world. We hired people who were print people, people who really lived in the neighborhood, people with expertise and specialized competencies. Because the equipment was much less expensive and easier to use, we could train them and use people who never would have been given a television opportunity. So we didn't step outside the professional realm, we used people who were in the business, but never could have been on (broadcast) television. On television they can reach far more homes. So it is a step that indicates that technology expands the roles we play.

LAUGHLIN: What if I came to you at New York 1 with a liberal arts educa-tion and no knowledge of the technology?

SAGAN: Most of the staff had no technical knowledge. What we wanted were bright, well-educated people and, because it's a New York City-only ser-vice, we wanted people to have worked here, or grown up here, or have gone to school—because we put a premium on New York City-based information.

LAUGHLIN: How has this effected the distinction between television and print journalists?

SAGAN: I think that the boundaries are starting to break down. Eventually they become completely artificial. Boundaries that now segregate newspaper reporter, television reporter, print reporter—some of them cross over even now. In the future, I think that multimedia reporters will deliver various pieces of information in various ways. A reporter's basic job does not change, regardless of the medium. So they will go out and find stories and a lot of them will be required to come up with a video version and a text version, which they will deliver, maybe, to a magazine, a newspaper, online, maybe a video version to a TV network or digital service. More and more, the technology is coming down in cost and complexity; more and more, reporters will do all of the things instead of having separate technicians performing technical functions.

MONBERG: How did the older distinctions operate in the past?

SAGAN: At the risk of overgeneralizing, I think there has been a feeling of jealousy—print reporters have a feeling that something is more pure about what they are doing; TV people are overpaid airheads. On the other hand, TV people are a little arrogant in thinking that television has this great power because it reaches more people. I think these attitudes probably carry forward, breaking down slowly as skills merge and individuals handle a wider array of tasks. As these distinctions break down, those who do well will be those with combined expertise.

LAUGHLIN: How do people learn to do all these things at once? It seems hard enough to become competent within tight specializations. How can formal education prepare people for this?

SAGAN: I think there is a great deal of concern about whether the formal education for journalism still makes sense. Even in the old school, there's a real question about how much you can really learn in the classroom about being a reporter that you couldn't learn in your first two or three days on the job. Some have been very vocal that there should not be journalism schools—just shut them down. Just educate people and teach them to write before they send them to us. I think this argument is a little far-fetched, but it's not that far off, either. I think that the best journalism programs are not going to teach you things like a trade school, particularly in the area of television. They will turn out educated people who have some background in journalism because there are some things that are hard to learn in the crossfire of the job—the history of the business, the history of mass communication, ethics, and journalism law, which is expensive if you don't know it. These things are worth teaching, but a course load of more than ten to twenty percent probably does not make sense.

Even without changes in preparation, all things being equal, a journalism degree from one of the best schools—and there are three or four or five of them—may help break a tie. But I would still prefer someone from a major university with a good general education—which overspecialization works against.

As we move toward television, the traditional schools are going to have an even bigger problem, which is that even a modicum of success in preparing people requires a capital investment difficult to make. Students may train on equipment that's completely out-of-date; there's almost no value in that. As the equipment changes more and more quickly over the next five years, it's going to be harder and harder for schools to keep up. The real skill I need from people is the ability to write—in any of these forms you can't succeed if you can't express your ideas clearly and concisely.

LAUGHLIN: What about the training you got, that lead you into this? Do you think your generation was trained in ways that fed into current trajectories of media work?

SAGAN: I don't think so, but let me back up. My college training was at Medill School of Journalism at Northwestern University. That's where my degree is from. But most of my course work was in liberal arts and political science—just a basic, liberal arts education. Most of my training is practical; my family was in the newspaper business and all of my professional experience has been as a journalist—at newspapers, magazines, and electronic, both and broadcasting and cable.

LAUGHLIN: At the time you received formal training, was there a paradigm in place that, perhaps, defines you as a generation? One thing seems apparent: incredibly young people are now in very powerful positions.

SAGAN: I think it is our having been brought up on television. This is the first adult television generation—those of us who grew up with Bozo the Clown, all of the cliches are true.

We are now running, but did not found, many parts of media—entertainment, news, information. The economics prize youth; certainly, what advertisers want to buy—this is where their emphasis is. This is a high-energy business that tends to burn people out. It turns over a lot of generally young people. And, probably, those who are in it, who are more interested in the futuristic stuff, tend to be young people, who are a little more open or a little more accepting of technology. Although that's not always true. John Malone, Jerry Levin—all those people are not thirty years old; they are fifty or sixty years old.

LAUGHLIN: Is there a sense that there is an old school that is still powerful?

SAGAN: I don't think there is a generational division. I think there are people with more traditional business plans, and those who are willing to bet more that the changes in multimedia will happen more quickly. But I don't think that it is age or tradition. I think it tends to match the economic outlook of the companies, where they come from, where they think they can go. Telephone companies are entering their first really competitive period. I think they are scared by it, and are trying to figure out how they can take what they do, which is a switched network and transactional business, charging for a minute of phone call, into something for today's market.

MONBERG: Traditional, large scale corporations often have a recognizable internal focus. Here, particularly within the attempts to develop interactive media, it seems there is also an eye looking outside the corporation, recognizing that today's market can't be taken for granted, that it must be understood as the effect and context of dramatic social change?

SAGAN: Unlike some industries, I think that media has always been very competitive. I think people are very used to keeping their eyes on outside competitors. Whether it's the studios or music or news, it's a very competitive business. I think that the pace has accelerated with people like the phone companies coming to the table, but I don't think it is the question of steel or automotive, where they just didn't compete. I don't know if they conspired as the old cartels or robber barons certainly did, but there was certainly the appearance of that "Hey, don't rock the boat, we're all doing great" mentality. Suddenly, the Japanese and the Germans were creaming them.

LAUGHLIN: Today's market, as well as these new technologies, seems to complexify the difference, or tension, between the local and the global, sparking questions about what's relevant for whom, who's interests are served, and so on.

SAGAN: The challenges are too numerous to list, and I don't think I know half of them yet. Every answer results in two new questions. There are a lot of technological things that have to be solved and there are a lot of consumer questions. How will people use the technology? Will they respond favorably? Which information? This will involve the most vicious rating system ever because people will be selecting individual items or stories or movies—unlike the overnight TV ratings, which are questionable statistical samples, or even a newspaper or magazine circulation—where maybe you know how many people bought it but you don't know how many people read it, and you certainly don't know story by story. We're going to know second by second exactly which things were watched and which were not, which things were started and not finished. The ratings on digital will really be scary—the cruelest form of public opinion.

LAUGHLIN: What if you had very low ratings on news from a certain part of the world; news that you would need for comprehensive coverage but couldn't get the ratings? Would you pay its price?

SAGAN: I have a very positive view of that question. A lot of people are very worried about this, that since it can't pay its price, esoteric news will get lost. I think what will actually happen is that we will be able to track who really uses such news, and those will be real premium users. I would suspect that there will be a very upscale audience for world news, for example. People involved in international trade and business, highly educated, motivated people, people advertisers would pay a huge premium for access to if they knew they were getting to that group efficiently. I think that these niche markets will serve themselves because you can actually identify for advertisers people who care about Indians in your area of India—well, here, there are all twelve of them right here. Instead of wasting your advertising on a million people who would never buy a ticket, give me a commission to get those twelve names. So I think that the interest group is actually better served.

There are lots of things that we have to figure out how to add value to, and it may turn out that there are things we create that we can't, or that the business winds up being a distribution business, much like these online services which are charging you for usage time—basically, a phone bill going through their database. That may wind up being a very good business. I don't know that that's exactly a News on Demand business, although we may develop it and be able to get revenue from it as part of what we do.

I do think that this is going to be an area where a business somewhere will develop—whether the phone company, a cable company, a common carrier, or somebody else. One could ask, How can anyone ever create money out of delivering the mail? The post office does that. Don't tell that to UPS or Federal Express or Airborne or DHL. Because they all do a better job of it, more efficient than the post office. So maybe there is the Federal Express of digital communication, in that there is some form of technology that somebody is selling. I don't know the answer to that, but I think that there are real alternatives there.

LAUGHLIN: Mainstream media coverage of interactive media projects suggests that if you are not in it, you are out of the game. Does this translate into resources for you?

SAGAN: Within the corporation we certainly feel fully supported. Interestingly enough, you don't hear as much about News on Demand as you do about all of the other applications. The movies, the shopping, the games— they are getting the bulk of the attention. I don't question that. If you ask what is the real business here at News on Demand,—I'm not sure.

Shopping is something of a business with QVC and such but it is still easily criticized for being low scale, etc.—spread across the gamut of retailing in the analog world and games somewhere in between. But with movies, the home video rental business is already a multibillion dollar business; you are not inventing a business, you are trying to move a business—from the Blockbuster store into the home. Taking that whole pie of movie rental and increasing the video pay-per-view on the cable system—at the expense of the video store, probably. So I see movies as an easier first target. It is an existing business; we just want to compete for it aggressively. That is why people want to jump on that first—because you are not saying let's make it up, you are saying let's just get it, let's make it more convenient and at a lower price.

You don't hear as much about news. We are the only ones to announce a division to go after this. Because I think a lot of these companies are not journalistic at their heart; certainly the phone companies are not, and even a lot of the studios basically are not. The number of companies in the news business is much smaller and those who are in the position of Time Warner are even fewer. So I think, I hope, that we are really in the forefront in this area. Journalism is at the heart of what Time Warner is all about.

LAUGHLIN: So the movie aspect of the project seeks to displace an existing commercial enterprise. The news aspect is different; there is nothing to displace so you are obliged to create?

SAGAN: In the short run you can see why going into the movie business makes sense because there is a business to go after. Which means that there is not only a market, but a time-space for it. None of us have an application that gives you a twenty-fifth hour of the day. Whoever figures that out will really make money. We will all make money with that. So, ultimately, if we create a compelling visual menu, if you will, for News on Demand and people make use of it, they are going to be taking from somewhere, presumably from other news activities, that may be analog television viewing, magazine or newspaper reading, radio listening, or chatting over the back fence. The only thing I am sure of is that you can't add time to the day. Some of these tools will be more efficient but they still don't add another minute.

LAUGHLIN: This experimental approach, figuring out what you are doing as you go, is it a style that people within the media business are comfortable with?

SAGAN: No. Generally, I think that it is not done. Generally, I think that people are much more conservative. They either just don't do it or wait until they are pretty sure that it'll be a good business, although often they are still wrong. For News On Demand, a working approach is the only solution, or it can't be done. There is a lot of wisdom in it; I think the payoff will be great. But it is still based on the premise that we really think there is a successful business readily available in movies. Movies are going to be profitable, and also allow us to do other things that we will want to do. It's not as simple as investing money to create a network for news. The network is being created for entertainment reasons and will also allow us to do news.

MONBERG: To generate revenue for a service like News on Demand, could you offer some kind of authoring service, that you could offer as a product?

SAGAN: Or you could do a story about a theater performance, and then charge for tickets. You could do a story about a doctor, and then make an appointment for the doctor. Now you are starting to cross editorial lines, and there is a church-state issue. Are you selling a product or are you providing pure information? It may turn out that news makes its money on pure, unbiased information. People will pay a premium because they want it unbiased.

A shopping component or area may be developed, linking you to a product, sort of like a rudimentary yellow pages. Can I find a hardware store and figure out how to get there? Or, can I go to a virtual hardware store in a virtual mall, see the shovel and have it delivered. Hit the buy button. Really, it would be a much more sophisticated version of the French Minitel, where all it does is give you the address and phone number.

MONBERG: Traditional notions of objectivity, believability, credibility—how do you see these evolving?

SAGAN: It's very complicated. You could argue this point a couple of ways. On the one hand, you could argue that what the digital arena does is handle the job of the editor. What the editor of *Time* does is decide what you get to see, like the editor of the evening news. In a digital realm, where everything is on a database and everybody can make a separate decision, then the challenge is not necessarily pure reporting—because you could have more people gathering information and putting it on the server, reporting still being a challenge, but the editing process is reduced.

The flip side of the argument is, "Oh my God, none of us have enough time in our day and now you're going to give me even more choices." There may, then, be an even bigger premium on good editors, editors who are either brand names or are specialized by subject matter. They could command a premium in the digital realm because they will be—you know, there is this term *smart agent*—your person who is going to find your customized stuff.

Probably, there is truth on both fronts. Traditional editing, the sort of broadcast and newspapers that sort through massive amounts of stuff, perhaps gathered by multiple news organization, will go on, but shifting where we are heading in the process.

LAUGHLIN: Within the curriculum debates that are running through the universities, there is an argument that students may be acquiring analytic skills but not synthetic capabilities—the capacity to link fragmented knowledge into something to work with. What's relevant here? Are certain intellectual skills necessary to make use of the systems we are talking about?

SAGAN: Right. You can get on the Internet now and there are ten lifetimes of information in a minute. The difficulty is the ability to sort it, understand it. Another point is that of serendipity. Certainly, a lot of news is serendipity—unless you are reading a very focused trade journal of some sort. If you watch newscasts you could say, "I only want weather, sports, and what's happening in Bosnia, but I don't care about South America," or whatever. But if you tailor the news too much, then you miss the serendipity that people get when they are watching a general news show—"Gee, I didn't know about bone marrow transfers or something down the block." A lot of news is about something that you don't know about. If you don't know about it, how are you going to ask to find it unless someone is there? Well, they could have a random story generator—you could put into our preference list that I want these things and those things and then I want every fourth random story from all of these broad topics. A bizarre sort of artificial intelligence editing function—

we're not quite sure about that. But I think that we would all become pretty boring if we got only what we said we wanted before we knew what had happened.

MONBERG: Especially if we're getting lots and lots of what we want.

SAGAN: Lots and lots of what we wanted, even sorted. We'll probably drown in what we think we want. So there is a real risk of sorts in this idea of virtual communities—that is, "I don't care about my neighbors across the street because I never leave my home; between my toaster, my TV, my VCR, I have everything I ever wanted." A world so complete you don't know you miss out on good things.

LAUGHLIN: Some critics seem concerned that interactive media could create new forms of social stratification, that communities will be codified around the selections people make in accessing new information and advertising sources. Is this a real threat?

SAGAN: I'm an optimist, so I don't think so. I think that the new services will expand people's ability to obtain information, unconstrained by their regular schedule. My sense is that people will love to surf through this the way they do through the Net, or that less sophisticated users do through on-line services. I think it will expand their ability to find out about other areas of the world, in the same way you may wander through a video store and rent a video about a part of the world that you may never have thought of seeing. I think that people are by nature inquisitive, so there is a tendency to ever expand. A lot of it will come down to how it is priced.

LAUGHLIN: Who will create the surf? Who will surf?

SAGAN: I think that the ones who are doing it now will have a leg up but that the technology will have the capability of dramatically lowering the cost of producing news—so that you can take a pocket camcorder and anybody, for that $800 investment, can go shoot a video, do a story. So if you start linking various network servers, you could have people doing their kid's play and mounting it on a server so that the other parents see it, or somebody covering every schoolboard meeting and mounting it on a server. When you get in the position where storage costs drop and bandwidth is virtually free, now all of a sudden it really expands roles—the question of who is the reporter and who is the editor—maybe there are no gatekeepers and everybody is a journalist, and we will be reporting, all of us will be sending messages and no one will be there to consume them. But I think it will radically expand the definition of who is a journalist.

MONBERG: The National Information Advisory Council has just announced that their vision lies in trying to create an environment that will reward the risk necessary to create the infrastructure while preventing corporate abuses of monopoly power, etc. Is this a realistic goal? Are the concerns appropriate?

SAGAN: That's interesting. I met with the vice president this week when he was here and the conversation was an off-the-record conversation so I will leave the specifics out, but what I realized is that not much has changed—the answers I heard were very much the same with taxes added on. Tarification is the key word. Tarification means that instead of the user getting charged—well, the user ultimately does get charged—money will come via the provider. It raises the costs. I think that the position of the government is very sound. Competition is the right way to do it. I think that a lot of regulation does not make sense—the government has had a great deal of difficulty dealing with things like financing regulations for the networks. The changes have come too late. The whole cable regulation, regardless of which way you thought it should go, nobody would argue that they should have said that rates would go down and they seem to have gone up and that they should put out a five-hundred-page rule book explaining it. I think that nobody would argue on either side that that's what was supposed to happen. So I'm not sure that government can be better—certainly no better—than the market. Whether they can really, truly create a model that simply encourages companies to compete and then get out of the way—it's really tough. I hope that's what they can do, but it's a lot easier to say than do.

MONBERG: Are there any specific government regulations that prohibit you from doing some of things you want to do?

SAGAN: There aren't any because none exist. But a good question would be about universal service and guaranteed access. It's one thing to say that low-cost telephones for dialing 911 will be available; it's different than saying that people can get MTV for free. What do we mean when we say that people can get a level of universal service for information? We don't even have subsidized newspaper and magazine subscriptions. We don't subsidize going to the movies. So we haven't had a constitutional right to those things in the analog world, and yet, at the same time, it is very important that everyone gets information. But, again, it is very easy to say it, much more difficult to define. What is it that we are defining? What is it that people have rights to?

And I think that there is another interesting critique—and that it is not meant as a critique of the administration but, I think, of our whole society. It is lot easier to sit here and say that we are going to guarantee access for poor people to something that might exist in five or ten years. Well then, why don't we even provide them libraries now? It is kind of absurd to sit here talking about access to technologies that are not proven and do not even exist when we are not providing people with medical care or education or other resources that we now have. There are inequities now. But, nor would it be right to say, "Gee, why worry about the future? Let it be screwed up, too." This, also, is not a good response.

LAUGHLIN: This legislation that doesn't yet exist. Do you hope to actively take part in the creation of it?

SAGAN: That's really a corporate issue, and my guess is that the company does pay people to do that, but I'm not one of them. I'm a journalist. As a journalist, I want to be removed from that.

LAUGHLIN: It's interesting—at this point, before having a clear sense of what the product is going to be, even within those spheres working to produce it, it seems that the people best informed for influencing legislation are precisely those with vested interests.

MONBERG: On the one hand, you seem to face an extraordinary urgency to be competitive. On the other hand, a lot of the technologies required for the interactive project are cutting edge, or bleeding edge. It creates extraordinary risk—the technologies haven't been combined into robust products yet. How do you manage this process?

SAGAN: That is one of the $64,000 questions. And, keeping your metaphor alive, I'd like to say that we try to stay on the cutting edge, but behind the blade. A friend of mine has a great expression: pioneers get the arrows and settlers get the land. I wouldn't mind getting a couple of arrows in the back, particularly as long as I get my 40 acres and a mule when it's all over. That's one thing that we are right in the middle of in News on Demand, as a distinct operation within Time Warner, as a part of Time, Inc.—that is, how much can you invest, and it is a lot of money, in, for example, the Orlando project, where you know with a 4,000-home model we will never make any money. Even if it is successful beyond our wildest dreams, we'll lose lots and lots of money.

How can we invest in order to test our theories? One of the critiques of videotext, which has been a miserable failure several times in the last fifteen years, is not that the ideas are not good but that the product is either too much and too complicated for the unsophisticated user or not nearly good enough for the person who wants to make use of it. Now we finally see the online services, and even on the Internet, where the products are now robust enough for the sophisticated user, who's interested in making great use of some of these things. In some ways they are text services, but then videotext will be taken off the TV and put onto the computer, making them sophisticated enough, yet simple.

My demands may be fairly sophisticated from a business point of view, but not from a computer point of view. I do not want to write code to get information out of a sea. How can we finally cross that bridge? One of the challenges for News on Demand, or any of the interactive electronic multimedia services, is to determine how to invest a reasonable amount to create a model—that's very difficult to do. Especially since the definition of what constitutes an interactive service remains unspecified.

MONBERG: The Orlando project hinges on the convergence of a number of new technologies—advanced switching equipment, high capacity video servers, new set boxes. Are any of these a particularly crucial link?

SAGAN: I think the answer is yes. I am not an engineer, but I know that it works like a chain—the crucial one is the one that doesn't work. They all have to work for this thing to work. So they are all critical and they are all developmental. Some systems and some vendors may not work, but if they don't they will be replaced by other people with different solutions. Even the ones that do work will be improved upon. We are already speccing on gear that won't make it through its depreciation cycle, which is a year or two. Some of the compression stuff will be obsolete before it arrives. Things are changing so rapidly that any breakthrough is like drawing a line in the sand. I think the reason that these projects are even remotely possible now is the convergence of the things you listed—the broadband server and the switching capability, cable boxes in homes. The question is how to merge all these things at once.

If this wasn't the question of the day, a technical question, it would be akin to producing a daily newspaper and not worrying about how I am going to distribute it every morning. There is no point in designing a product that requires more server capacity than will fit on a disk, or applications that are more complicated than the system can actually execute, or a VCR type capability that exceeds the capability of the control boxes of the system. It is almost uncomfortably critical. A lot of what we do will be based on learning what we can do, in process. We learn and immediately say that we have to accomplish something else, which means we have do a lot more of it—quicker, faster, bigger, better. The technology is limited; its potential is infinite.

LAUGHLIN: How informed do you, personally, have to be about the technical aspects of things?

SAGAN: I do not have to be a programmer; I do not have to write code; I am not an engineer. But I think you have to have more than a passing understanding of some of these things or you get lost—even so, we still make mistakes. For example, I am pretty literate on the Macintosh; I can operate programs. I used to know how to write FORTRAN; I can't read UNIX code.

LAUGHLIN: What kinds of skills are required to make the collaborations work? A motley crew has to come together to make this project happen, depending on alliances across expertise that may not have been exercised before. You call yourself a journalist. Don't you also have to be a coalition builder?

SAGAN: I'm really a journalist with a specialization in operations. The people who are actually building the network are engineers from the cable company. They spec things out, then a video engineer on our staff interfaces with them and then tells us what the capabilities are.

These engineers often approach things from a network capability rather than a user or producer point of view. They spec it on a blackboard; they don't necessarily consider when people will buy, what they want to watch. Nor do they consider the programming point of view, telling me when I will need to upgrade and how much it will cost.

LAUGHLIN: How often do these interfaces from different perspectives happen?

SAGAN: Our engineers are at a developers conference right now, with some of the code writers and applications producers. Many different kinds of engineering expertise, and styles of working, around a table. It is very much a collaborative process.

LAUGHLIN: Do the engineers you work with seem prepared for this type of collaboration? Has their formal education prepared them for such teamwork?

SAGAN: I think the question is itself a cliché—we are talking about things better learned in kindergarten. I don't think I can teach somebody these things. You either grow up learning to share the blocks, or whatever, or not. Clearly, loners will not do. The media has always been this way—producing a newspaper or movie requires a lot of collaboration; writing a book, perhaps less so.

LAUGHLIN: Do the collaborations undermine the significance of status?

SAGAN: All the same ugly trappings.

LAUGHLIN: Is the structure any less hierarchical because the collaborations are so necessary? Wouldn't it be a contradiction to insist on a top-down approach?

SAGAN: I can't overgeneralize; it's different everywhere. But I do know that you still need some rigidity to survive.

MONBERG: As far back as the 1970s, Warner set up QUBE. Was that a useful learning experience or lesson?

SAGAN: I'm not an expert on QUBE—that predates my professional life in a lot of ways. It certainly predates my exposure to Warner or Time Warner. But I think what is interesting is that what was seen as a failure was not nearly as unsuccessful as some of the text services. QUBE only finally shut down in the last twelve months. But, out of that, grew MTV, Nickelodeon. Some of the people who were there—Bob Pittman, for example, started MTV, and is now at Six Flags. So they learned a lot of things that became very much a part of our lives. MTV is a dynamic force around the world and has changed the way a lot of visual communication is done in all forms of media.

And some of the people who were there, maybe the best and the brightest, or just lucky and in the right place, learned a great deal. The problems were with the technology, not the programming—it was a very convoluted box, not even using infrared; it had wires so that you were tethered to your TV. It wasn't really interactive in the sense that the audience could respond—you could answer questions, but it wasn't digital control. It didn't let you pick programming—and that is what the next generation of switch technology is about. It really will let you pick exactly what you want to watch, when you want to watch it. It is a very different thing than what QUBE was about.

MONBERG: QUBE did offer a wider variety of services and products.

SAGAN: I think so, but within confines. They did shopping, they did auctions. Again, very crude technology, a very crude number of channels.

So things were learned—just because things were not rolled out does not make them failures. A lot of the tests, particularly Orlando and Omaha, may work out in a similar way. Now maybe there's too much hype, talk of the great future—so that if that model is not found everywhere in the future then there's a tendency to say that it's a failure. Well, that's not quite right. But I think that the punishment may equal the crime of too much hype. The critics were too harsh about QUBE, but they deserved it, to some extent. But I don't think they really were failures. Some may say that this is true of videotext as well. But I think, hope that there may have been less expensive ways of learning those lessons.

LAUGHLIN: Earlier you mentioned the French Minitel system. Doesn't it allow access to a database, and interaction between users?

SAGAN: Basically there is a computer terminal in every home—text, used for searching for phone numbers, like a yellow pages, sort of.

LAUGHLIN: I read a research article which argued that the success of the French project, as compared to similar projects in Britain and Germany, was due to the person-to-person interaction it allowed.

SAGAN: Yes, I believe that's right, and that certainly parallels what's happened to Prodigy. They may lose a billion dollars on a product with lots of users because they miscalculated the e-mail component, and that's exactly the same thing—what people are using the technology for is to communicate with each other. In a way, that's really what we use radio for, and television, too. But you're right, it is one way. But it is a window on the world that lets us go to places we couldn't go. Where there's even an inkling of two-way communication, like with the telephone, people sort of jump on that.

Asynchronous forms of communication seem to be what is driving a lot of the online products, whether it's e-mail or bulletin boards. I think that it will be behind one of the major applications of this new, interactive media. Which is interesting because that's not merely time-shifting existing programming that is controlled by media companies.

One of the big businesses may be what really is a form of two-way communication. But I don't think it is as simple as the picture phone—it's not going to be, "Gee, now I can call my mom and see her." It will be, "Gee, Mom, did you see this? This is really interesting." To make up an example, "This doctor I just saw on TV here in Orlando has a new treatment for migraines. I'll send you the story and why don't you call your doctor and ask him what he does now." I'm making this up as an example, but I think it is going to be taking some of what exists but adding the two-way.

You use the network as a way to send things to someone else, not as a database—this is important to recognize. At News on Demand we think that it's important. I can't tell you too much about it at this point, but we think that it is important, and we're going to try to build it in. But technically, that's several magnitudes more complicated than simply allowing database access.

LAUGHLIN: Are there concerns about intellectual property rights?

SAGAN: Huge concerns. Time Warner is the largest copyright holder in the world and there are always conflicting opinions about what it is you can copyright. Certainly, still photographers are scared to death of this, and I think overly so. The music people are very afraid of it. There was a whole debate over CDs and DAT, digital audio tape. Once you have one digital copy out there, you are in the distribution business. It may be illegal, but that's a real concern. Then again, it was the same way with movies, and the VCR has become a huge revenue stream for studios, and not their downfall. So that is a concern; that is an area where the government is going to step in to define intellectual property. The flip side—the patent office gave a patent to Compton's for interactive media. And the way that Compton's is interpreted implies that they would be entitled to something from anyone who does any kind of multimedia, any format, at any time, forever. And the government has decided to review its own patent because that clearly wouldn't be right, either. That would be like saying that one guy owns the idea of breathing and everyone owns him money every time they breathe in or out.

Trying to write contracts for News on Demand—for products, inside and outside. It's tough. There is no boilerplate to even express what we are talking about developing. In some cases, we don't know what the valuable property is going to be five years from now.

LAUGHLIN: The classic argument is that if there is no promise of financial return, you won't have creativity. If, in these new ways of production, we have less capacity to protect in classic ways, do you think we will see a corollary decline in creative activity?

SAGAN: I don't want to sound like I have all the answers. I don't. I think that it won't come to that. I think that because of the fear that that's what would happen—that huge corporate interests would prevent starving artists from expressing themselves—people will insist that there are means of prevention. That's what this company's business is—copyrights.

MONBERG: You mentioned how difficult it is to come up with appropriate contract language. What are some of the specific difficulties you have?

SAGAN: When you take something that is in analog now, when you take a news story and digitize it, what kind of product is it? Because once someone has, say, got it in their home, they could reedit it then, over a switched network, ship it to grandma. But you really aren't supposed to reproduce an article for your business, say, as seen in the *New York Times*—you are not supposed to do that; people do it all the time, but it is against the law. What happens digitally? What happens when, say, I've collected lots of stories on some subject and then I start creating a digested video product? Well, somebody else shot those pictures and licensed them to a news organization for some use and the news organization made money on it. Do I have the right to take it and reedit it? What rights are being protected? Or do I not have that right? Can I manipulate it for my own use and cut it up into pieces? Do I not have the right to use the whole thing?

LAUGHLIN: You seem to be suggesting that we need to figure out where the creative activity is.

SAGAN: What is the creative activity and what is fair use and what is public domain? If I paid to watch a film, why don't I have the right to show it to someone else? If I bought stock information, why don't I have the right to resell the stock price now that I know it?

LAUGHLIN: It may be that we should see a difference between the educational realm and outside. One thing I see in the university is that the requirement to get copyright permission for photocopying has seriously limited our ability to use print media. I think it is a shame. If you find an article in the *New Yorker* that seems good for teaching, it usually seems too much of a hassle.

SAGAN: Someone worked hard writing that article and they are in the business of paying the bills by selling the textbook. So the question is, how far should we go? It's very difficult to answer. I think that you are right that in the educational realm there may be exceptions, but don't forget, you are going to make your living on your creative ideas. You don't want somebody just copying them away.

LAUGHLIN: I guess I am in the business of copyrights also?

SAGAN: Maybe more tenuously because your audience is small. You could almost argue that while piracy takes some business from film, we are still making back our investment. Yes, they are concerned about bootleg copies of the Batman label, but no one went hungry over that. In academia your potential market is a whole lot smaller.

MONBERG: Another tension—in academia there is a tradition of open inquiry and sharing knowledge to encourage critique from as many directions as possible.

SAGAN: All of these things are in conflict.

LAUGHLIN: Practically speaking, the problem is not so much the idea of the copyright but getting the permission. No one seems to know whose job it is.

SAGAN: It's chaos and it's a hot potato. No one wants to be the first to say yes.

LAUGHLIN: Do you have legal people on staff whose job it is not just to create contract language but to go beyond that and anticipate the next ten years?

SAGAN: The same people are trying, but it is very hard.

MONBERG: There is a lot of talk about a public space on the digital information highways. What kind of responsibility do you see yourself having?

SAGAN: I feel very strongly about the public. That is one of the reasons I am in journalism—to create an informed public. But I don't think that it is any different in digital, except maybe that some of the risks are different. Even without digital, the Soviets used to erase people.

In digital, what is real and what is not is going to be really hard to control. So I think that, if anything, we need to build some firewalls and some standards. But I don't think they are fundamentally different than in the situation now. In broadcasting, at this stage, you can't take bribes, etc. But I think that there is a responsibility for people to uphold those standards from analog and carry them over into digital. The public needs to know the difference between a review from a critic and a trailer that a studio might buy and produce. A commercial is clearly a commercial if it is just thirty seconds. Infomercials very much blur the line. With video on demand you have the ability to create through editing what looks like a review or a feature story but is nothing but a shill for a movie. And when you give people the ability to buy a ticket at the end, it really blurs the church-state separation. And I think that is a very big risk.

LAUGHLIN: Why do you use this church-state metaphor?

SAGAN: Because I'm at Time, Inc. It is a Henry Luceism. At this company and at the *New York Times* and at most of the good news organizations, there is this integrity, which is that the church is editorial and they make their own editorial decisions and that the state is the business side and they can sell ads but they don't have a say in the content. There is that wall; that is where the metaphor comes from. And I carry it forward. This being a Time, Inc. business, it seems appropriate.

LAUGHLIN: Is this integrity sustainable in a world where competition clearly creates enormous pressure?

SAGAN: I think that there are some steps forward and some steps backward. I think that the talk shows and the tabloid shows have blurred the lines, and I think that, in some cases, the networks have given into the pressure to play by the same rules and have blurred the distinction.

MONBERG: One of the ways in which the line is blurring, even in the case of print products, where it is not obvious to people, is through the targeting of editorial content according to database consumer information. *Sports Illustrated* is at the forefront of this.

SAGAN: You know more about that than I do, about *Sports Illustrated*. But I do know that lots of organizations are trying to take their database information about their subscribers or consumers, assess them, do market research, then figure out what that means in terms of program provision. Which is not necessarily the worst thing in the world. If you don't have readers, you don't have a business. And, to some extent, editors are just using a more scientific tool. That's not necessarily bad, not de facto evil.

LAUGHLIN: When people compare the new media to older forms, the talk is highly utopian. They claim that mass media is media for a crowd, asking its audience to submit to the authority of a standardized message laden with emotional images that call for memorization, indoctrination, purchase of the commodity. New media is said to be more individualistic, a source of information rather than advertising, a means to interaction and intimacy.

According to this view, the promise of new media is extraordinary. Media will no longer be feared as a form of persuasive authority; both individuality and communal solidarity will be preserved, even fostered—built through processes with built-in momentum.

SAGAN: This really is a utopian view; it wouldn't be bad if it turned out. I do think it is consistent with what I see so far.

LAUGHLIN: Does your role ask you to unilaterally support the interactive media project, or do you also have a role in asking the hard questions, saying, "Hey, wait a minute; the purpose of journalism may not be being served here?"

SAGAN: It's complicated. However, I think that the public is and should be the check—you can't get away with information that is not credible for very long. People will figure it out and go somewhere else. I think there are checks and balances within the economic model; the consumer puts those checks in place for us.

LAUGHLIN: You put a lot of faith in the reader-consumer, even while admitting that older media forms prepped its audience to be submissive?

SAGAN: I do put a lot of faith in the public being gatekeeper. I think the public is a lot smarter than people give them credit for. Further, I am very leery of journalists or government agents, or anyone, walking around with a veil on, hiding the fact that their judgment is often no more reliable than anyone else's. Public official, journalist, doctor—all operating in terrains where they can play the holier-than-thou role.

Also, people are much more sophisticated in their assessment of media than they were just a few years ago. Even if this is revolutionary technology, perhaps *because* it is, people are much more aware.

MONBERG: It is often said that technologies have revolutionized societies. The railroad transformed the world of small villages by linking them to mass markets; highways helped create suburbia. How will information highways transform the social order?

SAGAN: Dangerous to predict, but also to underestimate. Western Union was offered Alexander Graham Bell's telephone patent and they said no, certain that everyone would want a hard copy. They had a good run for a while. But then they died.

What would I like to see? People with greater information, greater access to information that enriches their lives, enables them to live better. It is very utopian to hope that people can get all the information they know they need—but that is the direction we should go. I don't want to be discouraged because the track record of many of these changes is not all positive. There is a lot of chance for good.

LAUGHLIN: Assessment seems difficult because of the speed of it all, the ways both everything and nothing seems to have changed.

SAGAN: It may be a rare time when we are anticipating, paying attention but moving so quickly that we really can't study what we are part of. Or maybe it happens a lot more slowly than we imagine—which also means that we can't study it very well.

Meanwhile, it's all being made up as we go—which is exciting.

REWRITING NEW YORK CITY

You're standing there in the station, everything is gray and gloomy, and all of a sudden one of those graffiti trains slides in and brightens the place like a big bouquet from Latin America . . . The city is like a newspaper anyway, so it's natural to see writing all over the place.[1]
Claes Oldenburg, 1973

New York City is always already written on in a million ways: written in alphabets, in images, in the vocabularies of architecture and street, in fashions passing by, in noise and sound and tune, in rubble, in human life, in motion, in established institutions. In this forest of signs, public space itself is a medium of communication, but there is no DJ, no production manager, no editor organizing all the messages being broadcast through the glance of everyday life. Instead, the messages are organized through the denizens' attention, sometimes focused and intent, sometimes wandering. We might notice, preoccupied: litter, the *Daily News* and the *New York Times,* street addresses, new advertising advertising old advertising, dilapidated buildings, people in rags and suits, billboards and neon, ART SALE!, the sidewalk detours around the de/construction of another skyscraper, groups of people, a change in the price of roses and crack, intention and confusion and conflict, peddlers selling books new and used, traffic on empty streets, food and eating and no food, flyers being handed to you now in the garbage cans now blowing down the street, a dozen languages on the subways and that's not enough. The city's public space—its public sphere[2]—is encoded, overcoded, and coded over: a palimpsest order of change and monumentality, constantly rewritten, never blank, in dialogue with people and place. Every city in the United States is like this, but not on the scale or the density of New York City.

As the authorized city codes attempt to order and subdue the others, the continual activity of rebuilding, maintaining, renegotiating, using, repairing—literally, the continual remaking (rewriting)—of New York City means that

CAVS, 1988

any singular ordering is constantly disrupted, rewritten, a matter of struggle, localized, partial. Only in official fantasies does the city embody a singular logic: in the engineer's blueprints, in the planning commission's charts, in the bureaucratic plans for efficiency, in the laws, in the imagination of individuals. Outside of these fantasies, New York City has no stable zero state. Outside of these bureaucratic fantasies there is only the constant reencoding and clashing of multiple social orders overlaying each other: the codes of architectural aesthetics and city planning, the codes of advertising, property and ownership, the codes of class and race, the gendering of urban space. All these codes are written on the crowded empty streets, the white-washed walls covered with theater and movie posters, the swept sidewalks cluttered. These codes are as so many languages that give shape to the city itself. The city is the multiplicity of codes that order, disorder, and reorder New York.

Writing **New York City** [3]

A new language appeared in New York's public sphere in the early 1970s. Young people had been writing their names on the walls in their local neighborhood areas for some time in New York City,[4] but in the late 1960s a few innovative practitioners began to expand outside these neighborhood boundaries, and saw the entirety of New York City as a venue for their names. They

Poem, 1992

wrote their names everywhere: on public walls, on buildings, on subway stations, on the insides and outside of subway trains, anywhere their *writing* might
be seen. The notoriety gained by this expansion quickly attracted others, and
within a few years a new set of practices had been defined. Calling themselves
writers, the members of this emerging culture generally wrote their names in a
stylized manner, not unlike a signature. But the names they wrote were not
those on their authorized certificates of birth. *Writers* invented and borrowed
names, or created a namelike pattern of letters, initials, and symbols. These
invented names were invested with a much more dramatic sense of public self
for having been created by their users—each name was uniquely designed and
open to scrutiny by other *writers*. If more than one *writer* claimed the same
name, they added numbers at the end to distinguish between each other.[5]

Establishing an economy of prestige and status among peers is nothing new
in human history, nor is it confined to youth cultures, of course. *Writing* developed in the city that contains the majority of the world's major advertising
agencies, many of the nation's major fine-arts institutions, publishing houses,
and music, television, and movie studios, and is rivaled only by Hollywood in
its celebrity-producing capacity (Mollenkopf 1991). New York is a city of the
name and the renown attached to status; *writers* created a New York alternative
to the economy of prestige that functioned on Madison Avenue. A *writer* could
establish a reputation among other *writers*—fame—through a couple of different methods. A *writer* could saturate the public sphere, *writing* his or her

Illy, by Twoill, 1992

name everywhere; a *writer* could *write* in what appeared to be impossible places, like the bridgework of the subways and highways, or in places that required considerable daring, like the fender of an occupied police car; a *writer* could create an exceptional style, inventing new letters, adding cartoon characters or colors, or becoming very skilled in his or her technique. But the fame gained in *writing* was a unique blend of identity and anonymity. A *writer* could be quite well known among other *writers* for his or her style or for "getting up" (saturation), but be otherwise unrecognizable in public since the *writer*'s birth name or any other identifying marks were not written. The common mode of greeting among *writers* who did not know each other was not "Who are you?" but "What do you *write?*"

AUSTIN: So why do you think everything got so concentrated on the name? You guys could paint anything.

IZ THE WIZ: Okay: Mr. Mobil; Mr. Amoco; Mr. Exxon. They're rich. They can put their name on any sign, any place. Build a gas station and there's their *name.*

TWOILL: Macy's. Alexander's.

IZ THE WIZ: Mr. Gimbel's.

TWOILL: Sears.

Iz the Wiz, 1993

Iz THE WIZ: Okay, now you're on a poor economic level and what do you have? Years ago, and even today, a boxer makes a name for himself in the boxing ring. So when this art form starts developing, why would it be any different? It's all in the name. When you're poor, that's all you got.

As the culture of *writing* developed, *writers* borrowed what was around them, taking lettering styles and figurative characters from advertising, the commercial mass media, and comic books. Soon after the new *writing* began in the early 1970s, *writers* also appropriated the New York City subway system, and gradually transformed it (rewrote it, so to speak) into the primary institutional arena where *writing* developed. The subway trains offered a number of advantages. First, the trains were stored in yards at locations throughout the city, allowing access for *writers* in different boroughs. *Writers* entered the yards late at night after the trains were taken out of service and swept, and became quite skilled at avoiding detection and capture by police and workmen patrolling the yards. Second, each yard contained a large number of trains and could therefore serve several functions simultaneously, allowing *writers* at all levels of development to share a common space and develop a common set of practices. The yards were at once a production studio for the advanced *writers,* a school for novices, and a common gallery for examining and critiquing com-

Uzi, 1992

pleted works. Third, the trains circulated throughout the city, which allowed *writers* from distant areas to see each others' works and to display the work to the entire city. In short, the trains were a much more efficient mass communication network than the city walls. *Writers* in the Bronx could "broadcast" their work all across the city, all the way out to Coney Island, as the trains circulated. As the trains and yards became the primary institutions for gaining fame, the number of young women, who had always been in the minority of *writers,* decreased. By the late 1970s, a female *writer* was an exception.

Graffiti

Writing appeared at the end point of the 1960s, during a historical period when the common understandings of "urban problems" were being reconsidered and debated. New York City was an important example in the national debates surrounding the "urban crisis," which included the income gap between the poor and the prosperous, riots, brutal state repression, the priorities of administering and financing municipal and social services, the racial segregation of urban and suburban space, and a host of "problems" associated with urban youth: drugs, unemployment, radical political agendas, crime, the influence of countercultures on teenagers, the failing public schools, gangs. Although the New York

City mayor in 1970, John Lindsay, was nationally known as a liberal attempting to integrate minorities into the urban political system, he was nonetheless concerned about the business image of his city, particularly the number of Fortune 500 companies that were leaving New York.[6] Despite New York City's reputation as a liberal city, *writers* were never welcomed or even tolerated by city officials, and have been uniformly condemned by successive city administrations as vandals. *Writing* developed in dialogue with these views of urban youth, the city, and the administration's representation of their work.

Writing challenged the accepted practices of commercial and public property by *writing* (un*author*ized) names on it. One of the primary markings (codings, languages) of ownership is the ability to control the appearance of a property, even if that property is publicly owned or if its outside surfaces are an unavoidable part of the public space, like the outside of the buildings that meet the sidewalk almost everywhere in New York. Since the language of property ownership is among the foundational languages of the modern state and the economy of prestige that supports the contemporary elite, the state recognized the new *writing* as a threat to the order it was charged with maintaining. As a result, the city-state has refused to recognize *writing* as anything other than "graffiti vandalism" for the last twenty-five years. These guardians of the public order and their allies frequently wrote themselves to be virtuous Roman citizens, and the *writers* as invading Vandals and Visigoths.

The writing about New York City (in print, in photographs, in everyday conversations, in televisual representations, in other media), is an important part of the city's constant remaking. Understanding the new *writing* to be a "problem" for the city-state, various public agencies set about addressing it and informing the public of its plans and intentions. Part of that process involved shaping the public understanding of what the new *writing* was and what it represented.

From the *New York Times,* 1972:

> City Council President Sanford D. Garelik . . . proposed yesterday that New Yorkers band together . . . to wage a massive war on graffiti. "Graffiti," Mr. Garelik said, "pollutes the eye and mind and may be one of the worst forms of pollution we have to combat." [7]

> The Mayor said it was "the Lindsay theory" that the rash of graffiti madness was "related to mental health problems." He described the scrawlers as "insecure cowards" who sought recognition from their peers.[8]

From a 1992 interview with Phase 2 and David Schmidlapp, editors of *IGTimes,* a *writers'* magazine:

PHASE 2: I think it's kind of weak to connect [graffiti] from the stone age to now, when the whole attitude, the whole placement of *writing,* the whole reason for it is totally fucking different. What *writing* consists of and why it consists of that is totally different too. And now there are so many aspects to it. But some people don't even see the disconnection between what we're doing now and what was done 2000 years ago. They don't even see the disconnection of it.

SCHMIDLAPP: Especially in a name. You know, a 15 year old kid in '73, when he heard the word "graffiti" probably looked up the word in the dictionary. "Oh, is this what I'm doing?"

PHASE 2: Exactly, exactly. I never even heard of the word "graffiti." It had no significance to me what so ever. And that's exactly what I did. Because we said we were "*writers.*" I think we read it in an article. It probably said "graffiti writers." I don't think it said "artists." I think we sat around and had a debate about whether we should call ourselves artists. We are artists, we're not just *writers,* you know. I remember looking "graffiti" up in the dictionary, and it was appropriate. But basically, you still didn't call what you did "graffiti." Even if someone said that what you did was graffiti on the trains, you had names for your stuff. More so than "I'm doing graffiti. I do graffiti. What kind of graffiti do you do?" It wasn't even like that. It was "style," "piece" and stuff like that. And the dictionary said: "Writing on the walls." What else were you going to think? What else are you going to say? If you never thought about what you were doing in the first place, and somebody says what it's called is writing on the walls, and here's another word for it, of course it makes sense. In the *IGTimes,* we've denounced the term "graffiti" in every way, shape and form.

SCHMIDLAPP: Another way that certain "allies" or so-called "friendly critics" start excusing it, and I think they *excuse* it, is that they'll describe it as a "raw ghetto expressionism."

PHASE 2: Whatever that is.

SCHMIDLAPP: Whatever that is.

The commercial mass media had covered the appearance of the new *writing* before the city administration began rattling swords, and it was their misrecognition of the new *writing* as "graffiti" that established the term. The *New York Times* was perhaps the first of the print media to notice, and was certainly the most involved with the conflict. Initially adopting an attitude of benevolence and mild bemusement, the *Times* quickly mobilized the editorial pages and joined the mayor and the Metropolitan Transit Authority (MTA), who administered the subway system, in the "war."

> The handwriting is on the wall . . . and the ceiling, floor, seat, door, window. It is day-glo bright and multicolored, sometimes obscene,[9] always offensive . . . This painting binge . . . tends to reflect the utter disregard by many people, and not only the young, for the rights and

NIC 1, 1992

property of others. It is a form of immature ego-tripping . . . The graffiti are no longer amusing: they have become a public menace.[10]

The *writers* were much more excited about the appearance and circulation of stories about themselves and their *writing* in the media than the threats encoded in the military metaphors, even if the media coverage was coincidental. On rare occasion, *writers* were interviewed or covered in a story, but "getting up" in the *Times,* on television, in magazines, or in a film usually meant that someone's *writing* appeared in the background of a photograph or a location shot. This was nonetheless an enviable mark of prestige, although it meant little if the *writer* had not already established his fame among other *writers* (Castleman 1982).

The initial attempts in the war failed miserably, and since the war was fought in and over public space, the administration's defeat was clear to everyone. Having challenged *writers* openly, the city administration had turned this conflict into something like a sport, but it was a sport in which the city administration was a minor league player. For instance, in the fall of 1973, the MTA spent $10 million to repaint every train in the subway fleet—almost seven thousand cars. Within three months, the *writers* had completely rewritten the trains again. In fact, the transit authority's efforts had assisted the development of the art form by offering fourteen thousand new "blank" canvases, and the new, mural-like "masterpiece" thereafter emerged as the dominant aesthetic form for *writers*. Although the MTA continued to strategize and pursue the war, it avoided notifying the media of its efforts for several years.

"Graffiti 2": The Elite Discover that New York City Is Out of Control

During the 1970s, *writing* had been pursued and represented as a form of juvenile delinquency and a moral outrage. The city's strategic representations had focused on the *writers* themselves: their lack of respect for property, their supposed pathologies, and the denial that their work was art. To remedy the situation, the city had created new laws, new punishments, and attempted to catch *writers* in the act, but these had all failed. During the 1980s, the authorities adopted new tactics and a new representational strategy.

New York City recovered from its mid-1970s financial crisis with remarkable swiftness and not a little suffering from its citizenry, and its economy boomed during the next decade. Hoping to wipe away the tarnish of the financial crisis, New York City set about rewriting its image to match its commanding position as a major node in the global, postindustrial economy. The subways were one of the main infrastructural elements in need of attention, having suffered the same fate as the city itself. Maintenance had been neglected during the 1960s and 1970s in an effort to keep fares low and to make up for a lack of operating capital. The system suffered a series of panics about subway crime, ridership continually dropped, and the system fell into decay. Accidents and delays in service became commonplace. The MTA began a new effort to rebuild the system in the early 1980s, which included the purchase of a large number of new subway cars and a plan to prevent *writers* from appropriating the system.

The earlier focus on the moral outrage of business owners, landlords, and public officials had created only minimal popular support, and was tinged with an uneasy race and class tension. What was needed was a more sympathetic *victim* for the *writers'* crimes. Not to deny the power of visual appearance in late capitalism, *writing* presented something of a rhetorical problem in this regard since it doesn't actually destroy or harm anything *but* appearance; *writing* is an un*author*ized use of the public sphere. Following the neoconservative trends of the period, *writing*'s new "victim" was represented as the city's hardworking, "decent" citizens, and what *writing* supposedly destroyed was the decent citizenry's psychological sense of safety and social order that the city-state was supposed to protect. The most elaborate statement of this new representation of *writing* came from the esteemed sociologist Nathan Glazer:

> The subway rider . . . now has to *suffer the knowledge* that his subway car has recently seen the passage through it of the graffiti "artists" (as

they call themselves and have come to be called by those, including the police, who know them best). He is *assaulted continuously,* not only by the evidence that every subway car has been *vandalized,* but by the *inescapable knowledge* that the environment he must endure for an hour or more a day is *uncontrolled and uncontrollable,* and that *anyone can invade* it to do whatever damage and mischief the mind suggests. I have not interviewed the subway riders; but I am one myself, and while I do not find myself making the connection between the graffiti-makers and the criminals who occasionally rob, rape, assault, and murder passengers, the sense that all are part of one *world of uncontrollable predators* seems *inescapable* [emphasis added].[11]

The risk in this rhetorical turn was actually quite substantial since it hinged on an admission that the hegemonic social order had never been anything other than a matter of appearances (a matter of writing) all along. But by the time the new rhetoric was deployed, the few cultural critics who had been willing to take up the *writer*'s side of the issue in the major commercial media in the 1970s were preoccupied with other, more life-and-death struggles with the neoconservative revolutionaries.

The city administration, the MTA, and their allies repeated this new representation of the threat of *writing* like a mantra. It was accompanied by a much more aggressive legal pursuit of *writers,* which has included civil suits against parents, and by a $24 million construction project to build special fences around each of the nineteen train yards, remaking them into something akin to medium security prisons. The new fences consist of two concentric chainlink fences, ten to twelve feet high and about four feet apart. Each of the fences is topped with coils of ribbon wire and two to six coils of ribbon wire are also placed in the space between the two fences, which makes cutting through the fences extremely dangerous if not impossible. After a fence was completed, the MTA began a "clean train" program in that yard, which meant removing the *writing* from one train at a time, and not allowing it to circulate through the system if *writing* appeared on it thereafter. This was supplemented with the purchase of large numbers of new trains with surfaces that make removing paint much easier. The first clean train program began in 1984; the last painted train in service was cleaned five years later.

But despite the valiant war on graffiti that has now lasted a mere quarter of a century, *writing* has not faded away. During the years of the clean train program, *writing* transformed itself in several ways. One of the ways *writers* have transformed their culture is to find new methods of circulating *writing;* that is, new media have been appropriated. Part of the "zine revolution,"[12] *writers* began publishing small-run, self-produced magazines containing photos, interviews, and matters of concern to the culture.

A second transformation of *writing* culture was also made possible by the print medium. In 1984, sculptor Henry Chalfant and photographer Martha

SAR, 1993

Cooper published their photographs of New York *writing* in *Subway Art* (Chalfant and Cooper 1984). Although the *writing* culture had already spread outside of New York City to some extent, *Subway Art* offered a much more concentrated and elaborated presentation of the artwork. The book was distributed in the United States, Europe, and the Anglophone countries, and new, local *writing* cultures subsequently developed in several major cities, including Paris, Copenhagen, Berlin, Munich, Amsterdam, Stockholm, Dortmund, Sydney, and several others. There is now a *writing* culture in almost every major city in the United States, and in many of the major cities of Europe and Australia. By 1987, *writing* was an international art movement.

The interviews that appear here were recorded with the editors of three of New York's *writer*'s magazines. Phase 2, Vulcan, and David Schmidlapp are the editors of the *International Get Hip Times* (more commonly known as the *IGTimes* or simply *IGT*), the first *writer*'s publication. The first segment is a transcript of a lecture/slide show they gave in the American Studies Program at the University of Minnesota in February 1991. It serves as a basic introduction to *writing* culture from the perspective of those who developed the culture in the early 1970s. The questions and comments that are attributed to Graduate Student below are from various members of the audience of that lecture.

Phase 2, 1991, © Aerosol Archives

PHASE 2: We're going to speak on the art, its roots, how it started in general as an art form, and how the art evolved. And why, when we hear the word *graffiti,* those of us who are elder statesmen do not relate to that in a sense, because the art has evolved.

GRADUATE STUDENT: About elder statesmen, what do you mean? Since when?

PHASE 2: Since the early seventies, '71 or '72. The difference being that most of us who have been able to experience the art from day one have a different sense of what it's all about, as opposed to guys who just started *writing* in the last two or three years, because there is a history behind it. The art started about 1969. I wasn't there at that point, but the early seventies is when everything that you're seeing now started, the foundation of it. Those of us, like Vulcan and myself, have a keener sense of understanding that, because it's more important to us. Our lives, everything surrounding us, the Black Power movement and so on, those were the things that concerned us. That's how we go about living—to understand that which we are and that which we're doing. I think that it's not as much an issue now with kids, even though you have a certain amount of so-called Afrocentricity. In general, I think people in America are not being told that they should understand themselves culturally *outside* of American society and inside their own family roots, that is, to know self. That's how we approach the whole art. It's not just writing on walls.

SCHMIDLAPP: Scratching one's name in public might have ancient roots, but the development, the technique, and the placement of this art, which is the foundation of what we call aerosol dynamics[13] comes in the late sixties and early seventies, when in large numbers, inner-city youth from upper Manhattan and the Bronx started placing their signatures, the names they called themselves, in public places. And those public places tended to be environments that the public was neglecting, like the subways.

If anything, the artists used the subways, because that was a way to be known and to know others, so from the very beginning it was a very creative and communicative activity. It was a way to participate. Also, remember that the subways went everywhere—it was a nineteenth-century kind of design to bring the city together. The way I see it, the city was falling apart during the early seventies and the youth of the city took it upon themselves, in their own way—which was not understood by the adults or the guardians of the city— to bring it together. Unlike gang graffiti, which is territorial, this was the subway, which was supposed to bring the city together.

VULCAN (referring to two slides of artwork, *Topcat,* 1972, and Hash, 1991): You can see the evolution of the artwork as it has come along. This one (Hash) is about twenty feet long, and this (Topcat) is just a signature, a couple of feet long. Even though probably no one in this room can read that one (Hash) but me and Phase, and although it's not a political statement per se, like to overthrow a government or anything like that, it *is* political in its undertones, where it says, "I can do this and you can't stop me. This is who I am. And it doesn't matter how much money I have or where I come from, I can do this and you can't stop me." When people compare it to straight-up political activism, it might not always be consciously or overtly political, but there's always something in the subconscious of it that is connected with the way you were brought up and how you relate to the person that you are. Until recently, people who paint on trains and paint on walls like this didn't get any notoriety. You don't get to see the people behind the painting, so you don't really have a voice except what you leave there.

PHASE 2: Basically *writing* started to become a tradition. It was a system. You had a name and the numbers. Like 1 or 2—that was who first wrote that name,[14] or if the number was higher, it was probably your street number. Like "Mike 171," he probably lived on 171st Street. You had certain rules about not going over each other's names. If you went over someone's name, it was disrespect. It was *not* total reckless abandon.

GRADUATE STUDENT: Is there still a sense of respecting the work [on the public walls]? Will people *write* over your work?

VULCAN: Right now there's really not. I think things are changing right now. But I'm used to a really high code of ethics where other artists don't *write* over your shit unless they have a reason. They'll *write* over you if you did something to them or you did something to their friend. But now there's a lot of kids who don't have a sense of self or self-worth in their own work, so they don't respect anybody else's either. But almost everybody who has a reputation for being good respects each other's work, even if you hate them.

PHASE 2: Most signatures are identifiable more by the shape than by the legibility. And that was one thing you could identify with yourself. Super Kool 223 (1972), rather than just *writing* small signatures on the trains, came up with what we know as a masterpiece.

VULCAN: But at that time, the art form was evolving really fast. It went from small signatures to these big things on the sides of the trains that no one really had a name for. Even though that work looks really crude now, I remember when I was a kid just running down the platform. I mean, I couldn't understand; I didn't know how you did it or where you did it. How do you get the train to stay there for a couple of hours?

PHASE 2: As opposed to now, when younger guys can look in books and get ideas about how to paint, back then there was no such thing. The only thing you had was what you saw in comics and whatever you saw in the newspapers. So the way I come off talking about symbolism as a science is that I think it was being approached as a science even without anyone consciously knowing it, because what we were doing is just totally distorting language as we knew it. My reason for doing it was just being bored with the same old thing, A-B-C-D-E-F-G. Here's a Phase 2 here [gestures to a slide of his early work]—these letters are not the way I was taught to write. That was one of the things that pushed me to keep on *writing* because I realized I could *write* my name any way I wanted to write it and it would still be my name.

GRADUATE STUDENT: Phase, when you were first starting out, what did you look at? You mentioned there wasn't the same kind of books that are available now. What did you look at that got you making the bigger letters and things like that?

PHASE 2: First off, I always had a problem with writing the way it was, so I think that drove me to do something different. But you look at things around you. When the movement started, it was basically bombing trains[15]—to get your name on the trains as much as you could. It was something else for you to do, besides going to school, doing your homework, playing ball. That's how I approached it. Like, "Wow, I'd like to check this out." And in some respects there was a negative attitude that I had toward what I was being given by society, and how I was being treated—I knew something was totally not right. So I could see myself going against a law that says that you're not supposed to write on trains. Nobody looked at it like that, but in some senses you didn't care. Who are you really hurting? Guys like Super Kool inspired me to say, "Wow, let me try out this in my own way." What happened is that if you take one hundred *writers,* about ten of them will take what they see and try to do something else with it.

VULCAN: I think most *writers* have been inspired by the alphabet, of

Vulcan, 1994, © Aerosol Archives

course, and they've seen letters in advertising or whatever that they can relate to. That's what most people have done. Within the art form of *writing,* it's the wilder you can twist this letter and destroy it and put it back together in another way, and the wilder you can get within your definition of what style is. If you can do it and make it look nice, it can be totally unreadable to someone who is not into your style. But that's the point—you don't want it readable. To be readable is to be lame. To get it wild so nobody can read it but they still know who you are, that is the mission, and that's mostly what I'm known for. Some people do straight letters [16] that everybody can read, some people do stuff that most people can read, and then there's people who just totally don't give a fuck who can read it. That's where I'm coming from. I can read it, I know what it says. That's the epitome of it for me. The letters are twisted so you can see something, you might be able to relate because of the colors or some other aesthetic quality of it, but as far as reading it like you read English, I don't care if you can't see a word or my name in there. But it does revolve around the letter.

Now there are kids painting all over the world. They have different concepts of what their reality is. A lot of kids just draw. Their concept of art is characters [17] or something that you can see a face in. That went on in New York, too, but it was always secondary to the name. So as the art form opens up to the rest of the world, I guess they'll have to define what it is for them, too. But in New York, the name was always primary.

GRADUATE STUDENT: Phase, why did you pick up the letter? Out of all the things you could have picked up, you picked up language, which most people don't think of as visual to begin with. They usually think of it as something you hear.

PHASE 2: I look at language as something that was created. It wasn't already here, like a rock. Once I saw that you could manipulate it and change it, I got involved just to say that I can do this or I will do this. And I know that I can create a language, because you can go all around the world and even English has been manipulated and changed around. I can speak patois or I can speak it in an accent in a way that you'll think I'm from England. A lot of times we look at people who speak English in a different manner as being ignorant, sometimes because they can't read. But *I* can read this [gestures toward a slide of a piece that is illegible to the grad-school audience], *you* can't, so who's the one with knowledge and whose the one that's ignorant? I know what this says and you don't, *and* I can read what *you* write also.

It's like a fascination for me. And also I create things that don't have anything to do with English, either. You're not going to take the time to recreate English, because you already have this language. I'm not satisfied with that language. That's what keeps me going. When I look at Old English, I think it's more complicated than what we're writing now. This [standard English] doesn't do anything for me.

What is language, what is communication? Is communication something where I have to make a statement that you can read or is communication just putting something on the wall that you can absorb something from, that is not necessarily a message—even if you just feel a good vibe from it? Do you have to understand something to appreciate it? That's my culture and I *write*. I think once you start to *write for* people and paint for people, you lose a sense of self.

GRADUATE STUDENT: I was wondering if you could say something about how you got started. I mean, did you just go out and start painting trains?

VULCAN: Actually, the art form was just beginning when I started and the pieces, the big stuff, hadn't really started yet. You knew these were kids doing it. They were probably a little older than me—I was about eleven then. But I couldn't understand how you could do this. Do you run along with the train in the station? How do you do this and not get caught? That fascinated me at first. And then I saw the first piece, the Super Kool 223. I remember being on my way to school and seeing this thing come into the station and it looked like the biggest thing. I couldn't understand. When I think about it now, the piece was probably only four or five feet long and it was totally drippy and sloppy by today's standards, but in the scope of all the thousands of pieces I've seen and all the artwork I've seen hung in museums as "great art," that first piece was probably the most influential thing that I ever saw. Because it was something that I could not understand.

SCHMIDLAPP: The interesting thing from the very beginning is that the artists took photographs, because they knew it wouldn't last. They became their own archivists.[18]

VULCAN: One of the most significant things about Phase 2 back then was that once people started doing their names big on the sides of the trains, they usually derived it from the ways they signed their names, in their signatures. They learned how to do it big and then did it just like that over and over again. You could have guys who did a hundred pieces and they all looked the same. Phase was the first one to come out and every time you go to the trains, you do something different. That was the concept: I can *write* my name, and I can *write* it differently every time.

GRADUATE STUDENT: Do you sit down with pencil and paper beforehand?

PHASE 2: No, I did this [gestures toward a slide of his work] out of my head.

GRADUATE STUDENT: So, when you go to the wall, that's what came up?

PHASE 2: Well, not really. It's like blueprinted in a sense, where I have a certain approach. To me, it's no longer my name any more, it's just symbols and I'm building them. Getting your name around and having everybody know your name, that's not the game anymore [for me]. It's just playing around with language, no matter what the language is. I think I'm inspired by all the different languages of the world and the way they were written, the characters, because of the fact that I see a beauty to them without knowing what it says. It doesn't have to say something to me, it just has to "work" in a sense, to come across to me, and that's how I paint. So when I paint, I don't care if you can't read it, because it's not significant to me. It's just a structure, it's something to build on—letters to me are just something to build on.

VULCAN: But if you're asking if, in general, *writers* use outlines for what they do, the answer is yes. For the most part, they sketch it out first, depending on how complicated it is. It would be the exception not to use an outline for something really complicated.

GRADUATE STUDENT: Would people be able to tell that you did these, even though it's not apparent what it says?

VULCAN: Yeah, people know my styles.

SCHMIDLAPP: Both Phase and Vulcan are known as innovators of style.

VULCAN: But that's what you want. You want to be set apart from the others.

The characters are more or less ornamentation. That would be the one thing that most people could relate to—you know, little cute cartoon characters—but as far as a hardcore *writer,* that would be the last thing you would really be concerned about. But you put it there to give those people who can't relate to the rest of it something to catch their eye, something for those people who think drawing is art. You give *them* something to think about, too.

There's a lot of *writers* that don't relate to the totally unreadable style. Because if you pull it off well, the amount of recognition that you get is not as much as if you pull it off and did it readable, because other people could read it. There's a lot of people that can't relate to doing shit you just can't understand. But for me, that's the hardest thing and it's the thing that I like the most.

GRADUATE STUDENT: So is it just your name that you are trying to vary? Because you were saying that you would use more realistic characters to make it more approachable for other people, but in some of the same works you were using your name in ways that can't be read by people from the outside.

VULCAN: Yeah, my name or *a* name—just letters. People *chose* their own

names around letters that they like, and that they like to draw.[19] They like the
shape of the letters, and they like what they think they can do with those letters. I didn't really choose my name like that. I would never choose a name
with a V because it's pretty hard to come up with stuff for. I like to make it
totally unreadable but within a style that I've established. Just because you
can't read it doesn't mean it's good. It has to fit into some kind of philosophy
of what your style is. And that can only be established by doing piece after
piece.

GRADUATE STUDENT: Why do you *write* "Vulcan"?

VULCAN: Actually, I got the name from another person that wrote it when I
was in grammar school. I thought it was kind of cool. And I was always pretty
good in school, so it kind of fit.[20] I didn't think it was a particularly nice-
looking name or anything. When I picked the name I wasn't doing pieces because they didn't exist yet. I was just *writing* it in a signature form.

GRADUATE STUDENT: Are there still neighborhood differences [in styles]?
Styles based on where guys are from?

PHASE 2: Guys will say that.

VULCAN: I don't think you can say that much anymore about New York.
But there were only *writers* in New York City back then, and some in Philadelphia. You could tell the difference. But now it's on a worldwide scope. I
can look at pictures and tell if the *writer* is from London or from San Francisco, or if he's inspired by Los Angeles or Australia.

GRADUATE STUDENT: When did the art establishment become interested?

PHASE 2: I think they were interested as early as 1972, as soon as they saw
that they could sell it. I think the Europeans were more serious about it. They
respected it more as an art form.

SCHMIDLAPP: There was a big hype in the late seventies and early eighties,
and that's when a lot of people who never wrote on trains but had art skills
cashed in. It was kind of a downtown, lower Manhattan thing: real estate
boom, a lot of money, cocaine, dealers looking for inner-city art. You have to
see it in that context. Certain people made a name for themselves then, but
when you look at it now, five or ten years later, their art has bottomed out.
Keith Haring, by his own right, did something; but he profited by [his association with *writing*]. He was inspired by *writing*.

PHASE 2: But there's no way in the world that you'd ever call him a *writer*.
You pick up books and you get mislead because you see someone like Keith
Haring or maybe Jean-Michel Basquiat and Kenny Scharf, and these are the
guys who kind of coexisted around us. But they were put out there in the front
as though these guys were inspired by what we did and then took it to a level
that we couldn't take it to. Which is total nonsense, because you can't connect
on the level of content what we were doing and what Keith Haring or Jean-
Michel Basquiat were doing.

VULCAN: Most of the people who were in galleries who made a worldwide

name, or their galleries made worldwide names for them, and labeled them graffiti artists are not people that wrote on trains or wrote on walls from a hardcore perspective. I don't know any *writers* that wanted to draw like Keith Haring. The only thing they would want is to have the money, to sell paintings, and not to have to work. I spent ten years developing my style and this [Haring's work] is what people all over the world think I do now, these little stick figures. I don't have any problem with him per se, but I do have a problem with him not disassociating himself with being the leader of this art form.

GRADUATE STUDENT: Can you talk about the state of *writing* right now?

VULCAN: The contemporary art scene in the United States is kind of a joke. When you pick up art magazines, the people that are hot are only hot for a couple of years. A career that lasts twenty or thirty years, like a career should last, doesn't exist in the art world. You're either a superstar or you're a nobody. It's a sign of what the United States is, this consumer thing. We have to build an enigma around everyone who does art. People like Andy Warhol,

Layouts for *IGT,* no. 13. © *IGTimes*

who has to be this larger-than-life character. The art world in the United States caters to that—you want to see eccentricities in people. That's one thing about a lot of the people that do this art form, that are good at it—they don't bow to that pressure. They're going to be who they want to be. They're not going to walk into a gallery with a tuxedo on or stuff like that. They don't give a fuck about that. The person from Park Avenue that buys your art probably never rode on a subway anyway. You only care about that kid that stands out there when it's ten degrees below zero looking for pieces to take pictures of, who thinks your work is the greatest thing since the wheel. That's a bigger compliment than someone who spends $50,000 on your painting. Although you could probably use that $50,000.

PHASE 2: Here's the layout for our new *IGT.* Our newspaper is not just about aerosol art. Like Vulcan said earlier, we tend to point out that just the act of *writing* your name on the wall is political, whether other people see it that way or not. With that in mind, it's not only about writing on the wall. Nicaragua to the South Bronx, or whatever we think that other people need to hear. The things that you're not going to read in the *Daily News* or hear about on television.

Like other aspects of *writing, IGT,* the first *writers* magazine, was originally something else. Currently in it's fourteenth issue, the magazine has become a work of art in itself. This interview with David Schmidlapp and Phase 2 was done in the summer of 1991 in David's apartment.

AUSTIN: Tell me how *IGT* got started.

SCHMIDLAPP: About '81 or '82 we started reading about the death of graffiti. The art world had put their grasp around it. You'd read from these so called graffiti representatives that the art on the subways was dead and now it was time for these artists to corner the market. I think that anyone who was living in New York could see that the trains were just as painted as ever. There must have been a whole army behind this little front.

I came into it very ignorantly, not even knowing a *writer* and for some reason I wanted to put out a publication.

AUSTIN: So what gave you the idea of doing a publication?

SCHMIDLAPP: I don't know. This goes back into my own art. I'd been involved with the printed page. I had a good opportunity to do some photo layouts—I did these photo stories for this cultural rag called the *Soho Weekly News.* It started when Soho became an entity. Artists had lived down there probably all through the twentieth century, but by the 1970s, it started becoming a pinpoint of the art world. The gallery scene blossomed. I was working in a restaurant and I was doing photography. I did photo stories. The printed page was my venue. I guess I would define myself as a journalist who did fictional stories. I was the only person who conceived, executed, designed, photographed, and wrote my own stories in that paper. So I was involved with an idea of publishing and printing. That was from 1976 to 1980, and there were some things that happened. You have to put it in perspective.

There was a point at this paper [*Soho Weekly News*], after maybe three or four years of doing these pages, when things changed. I had developed a little reputation. But there was a backlash—gentrification, money, attitude. All of sudden the galleries started to become boutiques. And then the boutiques became chain stores. All this economic development happened in the late seventies and early eighties. And my artwork had a social edge—I was accused of being too political. There were a lot of weird stories; I found myself just being blackballed. So there was a period from about 1980 to 1982, before I started *IGT,* when I didn't have an outlet. I think that's when I started my slide shows. I was started using nightclubs as my venues, working with punk bands.

It was also the time that the aerosol world came downtown again. It had been downtown in the early seventies. There was the first generation of *writers* working with Twyla Tharp,[21] and UGA,[22] and the exhibitions at the Razor Gallery. But then there was a gap in the mid seventies. Subway art was developing like crazy, but it didn't come back downtown with shows and all until '79. And being on the outside anyway, I just observed it. I was doing slogans on the sides of buildings, so I had this little thing going on myself that came from a political slant—a social commentary on the streets. See, I'm a child of the sixties and related to the streets like that. And I just got more and more interested in this art form. What was this about? And from what you read about and from going to the shows, you knew there was something else behind it all. I think I just put two and two together and said I want to put out a publication. I wanted to do a forum on this. A couple of other people were involved, helping out and getting printers and so forth.

And immediately it became a *writer*'s paper. I had interviews in the first issue with Revolt, Quik, Sak, and Rise. The *writers* wanted to read about what was being said. I first thought the audience who would be into the paper would be people like myself—the culture downtown. There were a lot of admirers and supporters of that art.

And then you're dealing with the city, and an indigenous culture and an indigenous art form. I thought it was just disgusting how one set of people related to it, a so-called art establishment. Something was right here in their midst, and they couldn't understand it unless they were selling it or dancing in front of it. This paper wasn't only a critique of society as a whole. It was a critique also of this hip art world.

It's funny, some times you feel like you immediately become establishment yourself, and in some weird way you do. When you put out a publication, you become an authority. Why not an authority of change? It was anonymous for a long time. That was part of the charm and excitement, too. Why don't I put something out and see how people respond to it? And leave it open to who ever wants to get involved.

AUSTIN: You didn't put your name on it?

SCHMIDLAPP: No. Even to this day. Well, sometimes I do. I don't know if that makes any sense.

But that's the thing about this art. It has a lot to do with respect and it's easy for someone to just grab it and take off and then ignore where it's coming from. This art form had a lot of openings. It has a very natural edge to it. Maybe you have to talk about it as a postmodern vision. It's not from academia, it's not even a mutation. It was something natural to do. You have spray cans and you have inner-city youth and they put their signatures on what's around them and made an art.

And utilizing the subway, I think it was amazing. The subways were in decline. You have this nineteenth-century design, this environment that is put upon us, through history, through tradition, through capital, through money, all the social forces, politics. The design was pull the city together in an economic way, to bring the workers in cheaply. Then I see in the seventies how this thing just kind of—there were a lot of offshoots from the inner city, post sixties era: black consciousness, minority rights, and the intermixing of cultures. Kids took it upon themselves to say this is a vision of unity. The subways became a vision of pulling something together as it was falling apart— the infrastructure, the city politics, the who's-going-to-pay-what. It seems something so simple. They grabbed onto a technological tool that was sitting around, the spray can, that had—I remember in the sixties, you picked up the spray can because it was something that made it easy to paint on the wall. It became a revolutionary tool. It took inner-city kids to develop it into an art form, and into the culture that it is today.

AUSTIN: Tell me what happened after the first issue.

SCHMIDLAPP: One thing lead to the next. I thought, what have I got myself involved with? People started calling me up, and saying, "Oh, do you know this, do you know that?" I knew immediately there was a history behind it all. I opened myself up to it. So that second issue had some early *writers* who were with UGA. That's when I met Phase, Coco, Richie AMRL, Wicked Gary; Stan and T.B. were in there, some other people.

AUSTIN: So the second issue had more people working on it? I remember you saying that the first one had only you and one other person working on it.

SCHMIDLAPP: I guess I wanted to involve myself more with the photographs. I didn't have many aerosol pieces in here. The photography had kind of a cryptic nature. The Michael Stewart thing.[23] I guess it was just putting the issue together. With the second one, I was introduced to more *writers*. More and more *writers* got involved by the third and fourth issue.

AUSTIN: When you say "got involved," what did they do? Do you mean you did more interviews? Or that they got more involved in making the text? Taking photographs?

SCHMIDLAPP: Yeah. As I'll take credit for putting it together, I can't take credit for people's involvement, whether it's photographs, text, stories. I started going with ideas and layouts. The first issues were single issues. There were people who gave ideas and artwork. [*Phase comes back in and there is some talk about the bargains he's found at the store.*]

PHASE 2: So what you been lying about, man?

SCHMIDLAPP: I've been lying about . . . everything I've said is a lie [*laughs*].

PHASE 2: You started the whole movement, right?

SCHMIDLAPP: I started the whole movement . . . [*laughs*].

I went through how I came into it basically ignorant, and I saw something happening. Part of it was where I was coming from. I talked about my cultural background being about photography, being involved with the printed page and layouts. *Writing* was peaking at that time in the art magazines and media hype, in this framework of the "art world." And being a scenester down here, I knew what was going on, and that there was something beyond the bullshit. And not knowing anybody, getting to know people. It was a way of getting to know this whole new world, an indigenous art form that was in the midst of this cultural capital.

It's *from* somewhere. I think the fact that *writers* called themselves *writers* said something about culture. Period. At that time, it said a lot. Sometimes it's looked at as this failure of the liberal dream. I mean their little idea was to have inner-city kids express themselves and do—blah, blah, blah.

PHASE 2: In some kinds of ways. I think they blew the whole identity shit out of proportion.

SCHMIDLAPP: It failed. Yeah, totally.

PHASE 2: You know, "You have a lack of identity, so you paint the trains to be known." All the books say that basically. That isn't why I was *writing*. Actually, I didn't want anyone to know who I was. It was more fun to me to do it with everyone wondering who you were as opposed to everyone knowing who you were.

The paper probably focuses more on the art now than it did before. Now everyone expects that.

AUSTIN: In earlier issues, there were a couple of pretty political things that are about what's going on in Nicaragua.

SCHMIDLAPP: Yeah, we've strayed away from that.

AUSTIN: When you were doing that, what were you thinking about?

SCHMIDLAPP: Well, it's like I said, the publication did not start out as a publication for *writers.*

PHASE 2: That's for sure.

SCHMIDLAPP: Where I was coming from, there is politics and then there is politics. I wanted to open it up this paper and see what this art was about. Let artists speak for themselves. Let's see what's up.

PHASE 2: Mind you, before *anyone* else. Before anyone even *bothered* to focus on anything that had to do with it, outside the stupid art galleries.

AUSTIN: Phase, how did you get involved with David? How did you find out about *IGT* and why did you get involved?

PHASE 2: I think he would remember better than I do. How did we get together with the paper? I just remember doing this one interview. But actually it wasn't until five issues later that I got involved with the paper. Do you remember who set that up?

SCHMIDLAPP: A reader set it up. I called her up and told her I wanted to speak with some old *writers.* I said some original *writers,* and she said, "Oh yeah, no problem." But like I said, I didn't know what was going on.

PHASE 2: When did you start working with AMRL? Was that the third issue?

SCHMIDLAPP: Yeah, the third issue AMRL got involved. He did the hall of fame story.[24] T.B. worked on a couple of issues. Revolt, Sharpe, James Top—there were others. All kinds of *writers* were sending in photos.

PHASE 2: When I first started getting involved with the paper, there were a lot of different ideas. It's funny. In some ways, [some of the *writers* working on *IGT*] were involved in all this shit more than I was, right or wrong. They were involved in the gallery scene. All I was doing was flyers. I was more into what we call hip-hop, which is not spray painting. I had just started getting involved with this gallery. But these guys had been around for a while. They were involved with it, but they weren't fixtures in the arts. No one knew them that well. It's strange that I ended up being the one more into it and more dedicated to it. These guys are supposed to be militant, and came up during all this crazy shit, during the Black Panthers, during the Watts riots. And yet, they didn't have anything to say about Eleanor Bumpers, unless I'm wrong.[25]

SCHMIDLAPP: No, but nobody did.

PHASE 2: They didn't have anything to say about Michael Stewart, or anything to say about the state of the state, or the mayor. Which was the kind of thing that all the youth that were into, certain scenes were into. Speaking out against what they thought was wrong. I started talking with Dave, saying that to me, none of these guys were doing their job. Because they weren't really getting involved. They were just floating around.

SCHMIDLAPP: There was a new focus with the paper by number 8, and that was when Phase got his hands on it. I think the seeds were planted a little before that.

PHASE 2: Yeah, you hit on some shit in number 7. But the difference between you and them is that you were always hitting on shit.

SCHMIDLAPP: Phase and I work well together. We are people who are our own hardest critics. We have a touch when it comes to editing photos and words. I don't like to use the word *we*. But here I speak. Even our differences have added to a better publication. You have to think of the *IGT* as a publication with a mind of its own. It has its reputation. The *IGTimes* promotes the real shit, and believe me, there's many barriers and shortcomings to this.

Putting out the *IGTimes* has never been easy. See, I have a million other things I do and many more millions I want to do. I have tried to give it up. Aerosol isn't my art. It's Phase who has recently been pushing up on the *IGT*. Still, I will say I have had and will continue to have the privilege to render my underground skills to this inner-city worldwide culture.

Today there is another new generation, and they're putting out all of these aerosol zines throughout the world, building this infrastructure of the movement. They were just babies [when *writing* began in New York City].

PHASE 2: Yeah, even eight years ago, they didn't even exist. These guys weren't even *writing*.

SCHMIDLAPP: Even four years ago, three years ago, it didn't exist. Aerosol has become international. It has crossed boundaries and you were having very

ID, 1990

legitimate inner-city phenomenon happening everywhere. Even if it's happening in the suburbs, it still has impact. Kids are picking up the spray can, looking at photos, trying their hand. The *IGT* peeped and pushed this. The *IGTimes* not only reflects the times, it initiates the times. The very first volume of the *International Get Hip Times* had that idea—this is a worldwide culture for youth. And then it happened. This rag gets around. We receive thousands of letters from you name where and that's just each year. This is publishing, in effect.

There is substantial continuity between the *writing* culture of the 1970s and the contemporary *writing* culture. But changes in the way public authorities approached *writing* as an urban problem in the early 1980s radically changed the way that *writing* is now produced. Phase 2, Vulcan, and David Schmidlapp discussed the ways the art world has reshaped one set of meanings for *writing* through the promotion of a group of artists through the gallery system. Although the galleries had a powerful impact on *writing,* the MTA's clean train program eventually foreclosed on the shared culture that had developed in the yards. No longer able to occupy this central institutional site, *writers* moved to other venues: to the streets and the "halls of fame." Ironically, most of the antigraffiti personnel that I spoke with during fieldwork in the period from 1990 to 1993 admitted that the MTA's clean train program had resulted in more *writing* in the public spaces of New York City than ever before, particularly on businesses and public buildings.

The move to a static institutional base, one that does not circulate, created
two major new developments. First, it fragmented the culture, so that new *writers* entered the culture on a more narrow local basis, often without much contact with *writers* from other boroughs, and sometimes without contact with the
more skilled *writers* creating pieces. Many new *writers* never develop their
skills beyond street bombing, since this practice frequently brings more recognition than a well-executed piece in an obscure location, like a hall of fame.[26]

But the fragmentation has been counteracted by a second development. As
the subways were fenced off and their function as a broadcast medium was lost,
writers and their allies took up print media, film, and video in their place. *Style
Wars,* a documentary, was produced in the early 1980s by Henry Chalfant
about *writing* on the subways. Chalfant approached the subject respectfully, as
a new aesthetic practice.

By the late 1980s, xeroxed publications containing photographs and interviews with well-known *writers* were appearing in growing numbers. A few of
these publications are now publishing on printed stock, allowing color photographs to be circulated. In 1989, *Videograf,* a video magazine for and by *writers,* appeared on the market, opening another avenue of circulation. As the
clean train program fragmented New York *writing* culture, it was simultaneously reconstructed through these new media and dispersed to other cities in
the United States, Europe, and Australia. These media now constitute one of
the major modes of circulating and reproducing *writing* culture as an international art movement.

What follows are two interviews with Air, who currently produces two xerox
zines: *Move* and *Styles for Miles.* Several generations younger than Phase 2,
Air became a *writer* during the 1980s.[27] The diversity of the *writing* culture
even within New York City does not allow a "typical" *writer* to be cast. Nonetheless, the differences between the ways *writing* was organized and understood by those, like Phase 2, who first developed *writing* culture, and those,
like Air, who inherited it during the MTA's clean train program in the late
1980s, are reflected in their views. The first interview was conducted in Washington Square Park in 1991.

AUSTIN: When did you start your magazine?
AIR: Last year.
AUSTIN: What influenced you? What made you want to do it?
AIR: *Styles for Miles* came out first. A lot of kids don't have the knowledge
of where the halls of fame are. A lot of kids are struggling for style and they
don't know how to go about it. They are just biting off the same old styles that
have been in their neighborhood for so long.[28] Nobody is creating anything
new because they don't see it. That's one thing about New York. If you walk
around the city, you're not going to see any fresh pieces. You're not going to

see them on the trains. You're not going to see them on the streets. They're in abandoned buildings and under bridges. Graffiti has really crawled under the covers. It's kind of a shame that nobody's putting their art out in the public's eye, because all people see is shit. I mean, street bombing is cool but, if you want to have an argument *for* graffiti, then the public has to see some of the work.[29] You can't just have photo exhibits.

Anyway, the reason for *Styles for Miles* was so that some of these kids could bite and get some style from it. So they'd have more exposure. Before 1990, I didn't even know there were graffiti magazines out. It's because it just wasn't talked about, I guess, I don't know. I didn't know where any halls of fame were. It was just because I made a conscious effort that I was able to find them.

AUSTIN: When you saw the first couple of magazines, did that give you the idea to put one out, or did you already have the idea?

AIR: Yeah, I already had the idea, but I didn't think anyone would buy it. When I was freestyling, we had a zine.[30] But what really made me come out with it was I saw another magazine and I thought I could do better. That's why I came out.

AUSTIN: But you'd seen other kinds of zines before?

AIR: Yeah. I knew the alternative press was a reality.

AUSTIN: How do you see the difference between *Styles for Miles* and *Move?* Why did you make two of them?

AIR: Well, one is outlines. That in itself is something totally different than the artwork that is put on the wall. And, I don't know why, it seems like kids have a hard time biting off photos. It seems to me that if you present it in its original form, on paper, kids can get better ideas. It's easier to approach. And then for the pure art of it, photos are like a canvas. It's saved forever. So that's why I came out with the photo one. I didn't want one taking away from the other.

AUSTIN: How do you produce them? Do you do it by yourself? How do you get your photos?

AIR: Ninety percent of the photos in my magazine, I take myself. I take a lot of pictures. I also know a lot of kids overseas, so they send me photos. I know kids in Chicago and California. It's really amazing where you'll find graffiti. All sorts of places. Pennsylvania, Georgia, Washington state, Washington, D.C. Everywhere.

AUSTIN: How did you make all these contacts?

AIR: Through other people that I meet. For instance, there was this guy, Fume, who came to New York and a friend of mine couldn't hang out with him because he was going to college. So I hung out with him, took him to do a train, and we kept in contact. He came back the next year with another of his friends. And we stayed in contact. It just snowballed. And then I went out to Chicago and I met some kids there. We did a couple of yards. They hooked me up with addresses, I hooked them up with addresses. You know.

AUSTIN: Do you put them out by yourself?

AIR: Yeah, it's my little brainchild. I like having control over the quality.

AUSTIN: How do you distribute it?

AIR: Through friends. Through stores. There's Soho Zat. There's the Golden Apple. There's comic shops in New York. Friends play a big part in it though, kids who are active in *writing*. They know a lot of young kids who are just starting out, and just a lot of *writers* in general. That's how it gets out there. And then pen pals.

AUSTIN: Are you national or are you mostly focused on New York?

AIR: No, I'm focused on all aspects. I'm not prejudiced toward California or Germany. You know, at a certain point in time, maybe kids were biting off New York styles, but I really don't see that happening anymore. Once people get it in their head, and it becomes a normal thing for them, they start to evolve and their own style comes out. Germany has its own style. England has its own style. California has its characters. It's all different now. And everyone is going at their own pace. Oh, and Australia, too. They got some cool shit out there.

AUSTIN: How much do you see the graffiti community being politically aware of what it's doing?

AIR: Indirectly, everyone is aware. You grow up in a society that is geared against its youth and you grow up in an impoverished neighborhood or you just don't have access to like—not everybody can be an actor, not everybody can be famous. Then you see somebody that's living large off fame, and you know you could do it better. You want to be famous. And society is not willing to give that to everyone. Fuck that. I want fame. To that extent, *writers* are politically aware, even if they don't understand why they're doing it. You want fame, you can't have it, but you're going to take it. Or you want to advertise yourself. That's rebellion. That's going against the state, whether you know it or not. But not too many are deeply political. If they were, you'd see messages up everywhere.

AUSTIN: I was over at Soho Zat, and I thought, Oh, this is where it's happening. This is where everyone is seeing each other's work now that the trains are gone.

AIR: That's the main drive behind it anyway. If it weren't for photos and zines and *VideoGraf,* if it weren't for those media, nobody would be doing trains right now.[31] Because the *writer*'s prerogative is to be seen. This is the reason why I didn't go to the layups back in the days, because nobody would see it.[32] You're not going to get fame from it. If you tell someone that you did a train, so what, who saw? My tag on the corner is getting me more fame than your train. But with zines and videos and photos, that changes it totally. Suddenly, you're seeing everyone's work. Suddenly, trains are the new shit. Throughout time, you're not really a *writer* unless you *write* on trains.[33]

AUSTIN: Are you thinking about staying with publishing for a while?

AIR: Yeah, publishing has always been a big interest for me. I mean, you can't read about graffiti in the *New York Times* and get the whole story. It's society's view of things and society isn't always right—that's been proven throughout time. You can't always believe what you hear. If you don't *write,* you can't really tell people what it's about. Only a graffiti *writer* is going to be able to tell you how it is done, who does it, and who's on top. That's the only viewpoint I trust anyway.

In graffiti, you don't really meet a lot of people who are up on current events or whatever. If you let anything dominate your life too much, it's going to get ahead of you. That's what a lot of graffiti artists do. They don't take any outside interests except graffiti. Their politics are, you know, graffiti wars, whose getting up now, whose a dick because of what, what's happening with the MTA, why is the MTA fucked up—they're very selective with their politics.

AUSTIN: They're involved in community politics?

AIR: Yeah. Only a few will take the big picture into account. Like *why* are they trying to stop graffiti? Is it because graffiti is the only medium of expression that can't be controlled? The only thing that they can't censor unless they arrest you? Unless they break you? Unless they wage war against you? That's why they're doing it, because they don't want anyone to have freedom of speech. This is supposed to be a free country, but it's not.

To me, my zine is a way of getting people to be creative. Letting people know that this is the reason that people are trying to stop graffiti. This is your art form. It's not just what we always thought it was—it's something different to other people. It's one thing to us, but it's different to society. It's a threat to society.

It's acceptable when it's used in advertising. When it's selling something, that's okay. If it's on the side of a train, and you didn't pay for that space, well it's, "We got to catch these motherfuckers. God forbid people should think they can get free advertising." There's a whole bunch of money makers out there.

AUSTIN: What do you see the future of graffiti being?

AIR: I hope for graffiti's sake that it comes more out in the open. I think halls of fame are really cool to practice in and do really complicated productions that you couldn't do anywhere else, but that's like hiding and shit. The whole reason why graffiti came out in the first place is to go against the state, to fucking rebel. All the kids are doing now is sitting in legal halls of fame and *writing* their names on walls, with nothing to say. Which is okay, I mean everyone wants their little fame. After a while that's not enough, though, you want to say something. I hope it comes out in the open more.

The second interview took place during the next summer (1992) in a small park near Soho. We began by looking at a recent issue of a German *writers* magazine that had photographs of work from all over the world. I asked Air to explain some things about the aesthetics of *writing*.

AIR: [*Points to a photo in a magazine*] I don't know, man, I mean, there's not too much heart in that, is there?

AUSTIN: Okay, but when you're thinking about that, how do you see it? Show me something that does have heart.

AIR: Graffiti artists are just like any other artists. I mean, it's got to be the best, that's the whole point of graffiti. Your letters have to have the most style. California is a prime example. They concentrate more on colors and blends and characters, and their letters kind of lack. So the blends are helping out the letters and the characters are supporting the piece. California's story is basically the world's story, except for New York. New York concentrates on letters. In New York, and very few other places, the letters are the hipest part of the piece. The colors complement the letters, the characters complement the piece, but nothing is *supporting* the piece, nothing is helping the piece. The letters are the high point. That's the raucous part, that's got the most heart. This [*gestures toward another photo*], that's like, unimaginative. A lot of *writers* that don't have style hide their shit with a lot of arrows. You create a lot of action and it takes your concentration away from how weak the letters are.

AUSTIN: Why do you think New York has concentrated so much on letters?

AIR: Because that's the way it evolves.

AUSTIN: Because that's how it started?

AIR: Yeah, it was the tag. That was the base part. *Writing* started out as tagging. Then people started putting on more styles to their letters. Back in the days, you'd see a fill-in and it was just two widths of a spray nozzle with an outline—it was weak, right? Then they started saying, Yo, doing a fill-in is just like tagging, you've got to juice up your fill-in. So they started making it thicker in some areas, copied from commercial art and comic book letters and stuff, and they juiced it up. Since then there's always been an emphasis on letters. It's always been the most important thing. [*Turns back to the photographs in the magazine.*]

I like Mode 2's characters a lot. It's like I said, graffiti artists are just like any other artists. If your character is ugly, it's wack. In graffiti, it's the best and nothing less. Your proportions have to be correct. It has to be realistic. If you're going for something that is cartoonlike, it has to be the freshest cartoon style. That's where originality comes in. I mean, look, he has flesh tones and everything.

AUSTIN: Where's Mode 2 from?

AIR: He's from France. Germany has nice simple styles.[34] They do a lot of sharp edge stuff. That's what I like. But that's just simple style.

AUSTIN: Did you take art lessons?

AIR: No.

AUSTIN: So you learned how to do this by doing it and talking with other *writers* about it.

AIR: Basically, yeah. As you progress, you just figure out better things to do. So when you were young in your career, you might have kinged the tunnels with tags.[35] Now that you've got some style, you've been out a few years and know the ropes a little bit more. You know how to get away a little easier. You might want to do a top to bottom on everything.[36] You might want to rock a really fresh piece that people will bug out on. It just keeps going, it just keeps piling on. I mean, look at this wall [*gestures toward a concrete wall on one end of the playground where we are sitting*]. It's got tags on it right now. But if they didn't keep buffing it, after a while there would be fill-ins, after that a few pieces.[37] It just keeps progressing more and more, you just keep doing better and better stuff.

AUSTIN: So where you do it is not that important?

AIR: Yeah. Your mind will always be coming up with new ideas. It's just that trucks, trains, highways, stations, streets, halls of fame, all those things—that's your media, that's where you apply it. The caliber of the *writer* is judged by how much you can get away with and how well you can do it. It's like with trains. A lot of people are doing simple styles now because this is the hall of fame generation. In the hall of fame, you've got all the time in the world to do your shit. So a lot of kids get used to going slow and spending all day, wasting time, and taking three hours to do their simple style. So when they go to a train, it will take them an hour to pull off a simple style where a guy back in the days could have pulled off a fresh top to bottom. As you get better, you can pull off more in that hour.

AUSTIN: In *VideoGraf* there has been a lot of emphasis on these guys that are doing clean trains, and other, sort of, outlaw stuff. In some ways, *writing* has always been outlaw. But now it seems like part of the aesthetic is the ability to get in there, do it and get out without being caught. In the older train yards there was always the possibility that you'd get caught, but it wasn't as great. Not like now, when you have to plan things out to the nth degree. Those clean train bombings are really exciting to watch on film. But what is the push to do that?

AIR: I'll put it this way. I was in Boston and we went to this museum where these kids had done this piece [legally, by invitation]. Now, even though they had done this piece, they couldn't get in to take photographs of it unless there was a supervisor there. Now is that what you want to happen to graf [graffiti]? Do you want it to be controlled? Graf isn't something to be controlled, that's why it came about. Kids were unhappy with the way they were treated in society. Kids didn't want to be a part of society. To get fame in society, you've got to make the most money, you've got to do all these things. I don't mind making money and shit, but in order to make money in society and in business, you've got to kiss ass. That's not what I'm out there for—that's not how anyone should have to play it. These executives, they live a nightmare because they are always worried about their job, worried about how their boss looks at them, worried about their next pay check. So the graffiti artists are saying, "Fuck it, man, I'm getting my own fame. I'm getting fame from my peers. I'm getting fame from putting my name *out there*."

You have to stare a billboards all day, like [*gestures toward a nearby billboard*] Discount Liquors and Wines. But no one would even know what my name was down the street, so I'm going to do a throw-up right there. Graf *should* be outlawed, or else it's going to lose its flavor.

AUSTIN: Some *writers* in the late seventies and early eighties were trying to talk to the MTA, saying, Okay, just let the masters have the trains and they'll control it. They'll make sure the toys don't.[38]

AIR: I don't know if that would have worked. Graffiti, being that it's chaotic—it's anarchy, really. But even in anarchy there are rules. But there's not anything that one individual, ten individuals, twenty individuals, can do to control a thousand others. There's always going to be someone out there who's a dick. That's just the nature of people.

And there's another thing. Okay, so say now trains are legal. What rules are we going to set up? You can't curse on the trains? You can't draw naked girls on the trains? You can't put any message you want on the trains? So what's the point? Graffiti has got to stay chaotic. Graffiti has got to stay outlawed to be interesting. There's got to be rebellion there. There has got to be no rules in order for people to be able to create. You see all these problems that the National Endowment for the Arts is going through, right? Just imagine that graffiti gets put under all that. What's going to happen to graffiti? It's going to die. It's going to die.

I came to the conclusion that everyone is going to be offended sooner or later. Someone who lives in Minneapolis, who hasn't grown up in New York, who doesn't deal with the day-in, day-out of living in New York, who doesn't know how it was being a youth in New York, who doesn't know anything about the history of graffiti, graffiti is always going to be dangerous to them.

They're always going to find something that they don't understand, something that is foreign to them, they're always going to be afraid of it. Especially something that, let's face it, that has minorities and no rules: the earmarks of everything that most of America is afraid of, that most of America is threatened by. It embodies everything—it embodies political unrest. It's a true mirror of society. Wherever you go, graffiti will be different, because it's a mirror for that society. Boston is different. Chicago is different. New York is different. Everywhere.

AUSTIN: Today, a new *writer* gets more socialized into the scene through magazines, or that's a major way now. It used to be more through black books [sketch books] and through the other *writers*.

AIR: It's totally possible for someone to take a trip to Soho Zat right now, spend fifty bucks on all the magazines, practice for two or three months, get an all right style, and start *writing*. For two years I was a tagger. I had to work on my throw-up for a year. If I had known about graffiti media back then, I wouldn't have been original, but I would have had a fresher style right away. Back then, it took me two years.

In 1975, how else were you going to get involved with graffiti unless you came to New York? If you were in Minneapolis, how were you going to hear about graffiti? You were going to see it when you went to New York, or if someone went to New York, they took pictures. You didn't see too much graffiti in Europe, and if you did, it was weak as hell because they only had a few pictures that didn't really represent the New York style. When *Subway Art*[39] came out, *Boom!* Worldwide, every train, every wall. That shows you the effect that graffiti media can have on the world. Then there were a couple of magazines. That was basically following *Subway Art* and *Spray Can Art*[40]— those kids that wanted to stay in touch with it, and wanted to keep getting an idea of new styles and stuff. Now there are a lot of magazines, so there is a broader spectrum. Now not only do you see New York styles, but you have New York *writers* being influenced by European styles, by Australian styles, by other states. It's a world society now, everyone is getting influenced by everyone.

Writing has a significant history: an art history, an intellectual history, a dialogic history with the commercial mass media, popular culture, and the city authorities. From the perspective of the academy, these are fractured and metamorphic histories: advertising and "fame" are appropriated and transformed into an expression of "heart"; names are altered and redesigned, and placed in circulation in another system of prestige and renown; the alphabet is abstracted until its visual elements can be linked only loosely to language; the New York subway was transmuted into a mass communication system and an art gallery;

Rated, 1992

writing became an international art movement, even if the academy and the galleries failed to notice. For twenty-five years, *writers* have rewritten New York City.

Contacts:

Flashbacks. Into its seventh issue, this is a slick-paper zine, with clear black-and-white photos and four to six pages in full color. Great layouts. Strong connections to *writers* who have been in the scene for some time; also strong connection to European *writers.* Interviews. A lot of attention to trains. Ads for products, American and European zines. This zine keeps getting better. Quarterly. *Flashbacks,* P.O. Box 7372, FDR Station, New York, NY 10150. Back issues available. Subscriptions: $20 cash or money orders payable to J. Edwards.

Move and *SFM* (*Styles for Miles*). Two high-quality xerox zines put out by the same *writer. Move* covers the contemporary New York City scene, with some national and international coverage. Lots of photos, plus articles of interest. Planning to come out in color in *Move* no. 7. Probably the best writing on the contemporary scene, certainly the streetwisest. *SFM* is an "outline" zine—drawings and sketches for works to be executed later. It has, among other things, a kind of "education" mission, showing new *writers* how designs are made, and so on. Also covers sticker scene. Both zines have interviews and ads for products, including distribution networks. Lists contacts for a lot other zines not listed here. Back issues available. Price: *SFM* $3, *Move* $4. Cash or money order payable to *Move Magazine, Move/SFM,* 51 MacDougal St., #106, New York, NY 10012.

IGTimes. "The Original, Whole School, International Magazine of Aerosol Culture." In publication since 1984, this was the first *writer*'s zine to appear. Slick paper, large format, with two to four pages in color. The recent photo collages are really magnificent. By far the most political-minded zine, the editors see *writing* as the art of a historical, worldwide youth culture movement. Interviews and articles of interest. A few ads. Back issues available, great subscription deals. $5 per issue. Subscriptions: $20. Cash or money orders payable to *IGTimes.* Box 299, Prince St. Station, New York, NY 10012.

GSEL (Graphic Scenes and Explicit Language). High-quality xerox zine put out by a poet, so the writing is first-rate. Occasionally takes up political subjects. Lots of photos. A few ads. Hasn't been active in a while, but promises to come back soon. Back issues available. For information send a self-addressed stamped envelope to: *GSEL,* P.O. Box 2328, Astoria Station, New York, NY 11102.

Grafnews. Connected with the United Five crew in Brooklyn and Queens, but by no means limited to that crew or that area. Some national coverage. Published as a high-quality xerox zine, it consists mostly of photos and drawings, with a few interviews and reprinted articles of interest. Nice layouts. A few ads for other zines. *Grafnews* has probably put out more issues than any other *writer*'s zine. Bimonthly. Contact: Vargas, 10 Rinaldi Blvd., Apt. 11M, Poughkeepsie, NY 12601. Subscriptions: $25, check or money order payable to Ruben Vargas.

VideoGraf. The first video magazine of the *writer*'s scene, *VideoGraf* has put out seven issues since 1989, with every issue getting better. Last four issues make MTV look tame indeed. Interviews, in-action painting, train bombing, and hundreds of stills, plus some original music. New York City, national, and international coverage. Some history lessons. A few ads. Thirty to forty-five minutes in length. For information, send a self-addressed stamped envelope to: *VideoGraf* Productions, P.O. Box 1933, New York, NY 10274.

Forbidden Art. A new video magazine, now working on the third issue. In-action piecing, train bombing, and interviews. Lots of attention to the bombing scene. New York City focus, with some stuff from Miami and other cities. Music. One hour long. $20 cash. *Forbidden Art,* Nassau Ave. 106B, Box 244, Brooklyn, NY 11222.

The Great Train Robbery. A large-scale, ongoing documentary project about the history of *writing,* with emphasis on New York City. Still in production, it promises to be a blast when it comes out. For information, send a self-addressed stamped envelope to: *The Great Train Robbery,* P.O. Box 1531, Old Chelsea Station, New York, NY 10113.

Notes

1. Claes Oldenburg, quoted in "The Graffiti 'Hit' Parade," *New York,* 26 Mar. 1973, 64.

2. My ideas about the communicative and political properties of the shared public space of cities are based on the spacial metaphors embedded in Habermas's notion of the public sphere (Habermas 1962; 1989) and the elaboration of his ideas in Negt and Kluge (1972; 1993). Ryan (1992) has explored these ideas with regard to the political activities of women in the nineteenth-century United States. Debord (1967) offers another passage to these ideas.

3. The italicized word *writing* is meant to distinguish the culture of writing from the word's more common usages. See Phase 2's comments on the term *graffiti* below.

4. Kohl (1972) observed what appears to be the precursors of the contemporary movement in New York City in 1967, although that name-writing practice may be older. Stewart (1989) traces New York City *writing* to Philadelphia origins. See also the interviews with *writers* from the early part of the movement in Phase 2 (1994).

5. Aside from interviews I conducted with *writers* themselves, the historical information on the *writing* culture in this section was gathered from Stewart (1989), Castleman (1982), and Chalfant and Cooper (1984). Stewart's (1987) and Miller's (1993) interpretations of aspects of the movement have also influenced my thinking about *writing.*

6. Bellush and David (1971) offer a very thorough analysis of Lindsay's administration in the context of the race and class conflicts of this period. Fox (1985) and Beauregard (1993) locate New York City's importance in the larger "urban crisis" of the late 1960s and early 1970s.

7. "Garelik Calls for War on Graffiti," *New York Times,* 21 May 1972, 66. Although Garelik's plan, which called for a public action akin to Earth Day, was never implemented, the military metaphor behind his call to action has been sustained in the statements by city officials and by the commercial mass media throughout the history of the "graffiti problem."

8. Edward Ranzal, "Ronan Backs Lindsay Antigraffiti Plan, Including Cleanup Duty," *New York Times,* 29 Aug. 1972, 66.

9. References to obscenity in *writing* are markers that the author has, in fact, not observed *writing* on the subways to any great extent, not surprising for a *Times* editor, perhaps. *Writers* saw no value in this practice, and did not consider anyone who wrote anything other than their name to be part of the culture.

10. "Scratch the Graffiti," unsigned editorial, *New York Times,* 16 Sept. 1972, 28.

11. Nathan Glazer, "On Subway Graffiti in New York," *The Public Interest,* no. 54 (Winter 1979): 4.

12. *Writer*'s zines are part of a much wider publication phenomenon. See Gunderloy and Janice (1992).

13. This is a different term for what I am calling *writing* culture.

14. Since *writers* enter the culture independently at disparate locations, usually beginning their involvement on a local scale, several *writers* may be writing the same name at the same time. The smaller numbers (1 through 5, usually) are a way of differentiating between these different names as they become aware of each other.

15. *Bombing* is a term for covering a surface with *writing*.

16. A blocked, sans-serif style of lettering.

17. *Writers* usually use the term *characters* to refer to any type of figurative representation in a piece, not be confused with the characters of the alphabet.

18. *IGT* has also created the Aerosol Archives, a repository for photographs of work by *writers.* The archives contain the photo collections of several early *writers,* and is probably the most complete collection of this art in existence. Its competitor would be the photo collection maintained by the Transit Authority Police Department, which is not accessible to the public.

19. Almost every *writer* has changed their *writing* name at least once. This is probably more true for those *writers* who became part of the culture after the late 1970s. It is also not unusual for a *writer* to *write* more than one name; I've met several accomplished *writers* who have as many as three names they are *writing* at the same time.

20. Vulcans entered the popular consciousness through Leonard Nimoy's character Mr. Spock on the popular science fiction TV program *Star Trek.* Vulcans were a race of hyperlogical beings.

21. Twyla Tharp placed six *writers* on stage to paint a large backdrop *during* each of the performances of *Deuce Coup* at Lincoln Center in 1973. Eighteen *writers* participated in the performances in all. See Stewart (1989): 332.

22. UGA, United Graffiti Artists, was a group of the best *writers* in the early 1970s, organized by Hugo Martinez, a sociology undergraduate at the time. Martinez wanted to direct the *writers'* talent toward canvases and galleries, and UGA members had to promise to *write* only on legal spaces. UGA is significant as the first organized recognition of *writing* as an art form. The group held several exhibitions of their work, and several *writers* sold canvases. The group lasted until the mid-1970s. See Castleman (1982): 117–26.

23. Michael Stewart was an African-American male in his twenties who died in September 1983 while in the custody of the Transit Police, having been arrested for allegedly *writing* in a subway station. The officers were acquitted, despite the testimony of numerous witnesses that say they saw the police beating Stewart just prior to the time of his death and strong evidence that the chief medical examiner had falsified the autopsy. The incident, in various incarnations, remained in court until August 1990.

24. The hall of fame that Schmidlapp is referring to here is a Harlem school yard where *writers* were given permission to paint the walls as part of a summer youth program during the 1980s. Since that time, several new halls of fame have been founded, either tucked away in spaces that are not accessible to the casual observer (under bridges or in or around old warehouses) or in other schoolyards. These became the primary institutions for the contemporary *writing* culture as the subway yards were fenced off. See the interview with Air below.

25. Eleanor Bumpers, an African-American woman, was shot by police in 1983 as they entered her apartment after battering down her door to serve an eviction notice. She was unarmed.

26. Street bombing is the practice of *writing* on the walls of buildings, including the roll-away gates that cover the storefronts of most New York City shops at night, usually with tags, throw-ups, or fill-ins. Tags are smaller, signature-like *writing,* often done with a wide-tipped marker or spray paint. Fill-ins and throw-ups are much larger than tags usually, but much less complex and smaller in size than most (master)pieces. They usually consist of three letters or less taken from the *writer*'s piecing name and are painted in a single color with a dark outline, or may be simply the outline of the letters alone. These forms are preferred by bombers because they can be painted quickly; a skilled bomber can do a respectable two-color fill-in in less than a minute.

27. A generation in *writing* culture is approximately three years.

28. Biting is the practice of borrowing aspects of someone else's style. For instance, a *writer* will innovate on the shape of a popular letter, and other *writers* will bite that shape. Probably all *writers* have done this at some time during their career. However, some *writers* are able to transform their borrowings into a unique style that no longer bears the traces of the originator's style.

29. Street bombing is the probably the most common form of *writing* practiced currently. The subways were the central institution of the culture while they were accessible. However, after the MTA successfully removed and prevented the circulation of *writing,* the culture began to turn its attention to other public spaces, including the streets. Street bombing places a high value on quickness and stealth rather than intricacy and traditional visual aesthetics; it is frequently contrasted with piecing as the "bad" or less desirable aspect of *writing* culture. It is important to note the city's part in bringing this form to dominance.

30. Freestyling is a kind of acrobatic bike-riding style that became popular during the 1980s.

31. *VideoGraf* is a video magazine created in 1989 by two former *writers.* It contains interviews, still shots, and footage of *writers* creating works, along with some original music. Since the third issue, *VideoGraf* has presented footage of *writers* gaining entrance to New York subway yards and bombing and piecing on clean trains. Although the artwork was never allowed to circulate through the train system, it nonetheless circulated through *VideoGraf,* rekindling an interest in the trains. For instance, in the first eight months of 1992, there were over 225 trains with "major hits" (throw-ups and/or pieces), according to Transit Police Detective Jerry Dassaro (author's interview with Detective Jerry Dassaro, 21 Aug. 1992; see also Stephanie Strom, "Subway Graffiti Back and Bothersome," *New York Times,* 11 Feb. 1991, B1).

32. A layup is a train yard. Air came of age during the MTA's clean train program.

33. Specifically New York subway trains. Each year, a number of *writers* from other U.S. cities and from other parts of the world come to New York to *write* on the subway trains and certify that they are "true" *writers.* For instance, in the summer of 1992 I met *writers* from California, the Netherlands, Australia, and Germany who were scouting out connections with New York *writers* to bomb clean trains.

34. *Simple style* refers to a legible printing style with clearly defined edges, but not necessarily a block-printing style ("straight letters").

35. *King* marks a writer as the most prolific among his peers, and is usually related to a specific location. Here, Air is referring to the subway tunnels, but a *writer* could be a king of any bounded location, from a building to a subway line to the entire city. The king of a line usually was able to exercise some control over who *wrote* on that line. See Castleman (1982), Chalfant and Cooper (1984), Stewart (1989), and Miller (1993) for elaborations on this term.

36. *Top to bottom* refers to a large-sized work. The term originally referred to a work that covered the side of a subway car from top to bottom, but not necessarily the entire length of a car.

37. *Buffing* means removing the *writing*. The buff was the *writers'* terms for the MTA's attempts at a chemical wash to remove *writing* from the subway trains. See Castleman (1982), 152–57.

38. Castleman (1982): 176–77. See also Bruce Chadwick, "The Great Graffiti Talk Conference," *New York Daily News,* 4 Feb. 1982, magazine section, 1. A master is a respected *writer* whose style is well established and widely acknowledged, and whose commitment to the culture is unquestioned. A toy is an inexperienced or unskilled *writer,* whose commitment to *writing* is uncertain or doubted.

39. *Subway Art* (Chalfant and Cooper 1984) documented the New York *writing* scene at that time and provided a view to the way the culture was organized. The book is reputed to have been a best seller in Europe and in Australia. In any case, its impact was significant, and is generally credited with being the major transmission line from New York to other cities outside of the US east coast. Any *writer* whose work appeared in *Subway Art* acquired a world wide reputation.

40. *Spray Can Art* (Chalfant and Prigoff 1987) documented the worldwide *writing* movement in much the same way that *Subway Art* had documented the New York City movement earlier.

References

Beauregard, Robert. 1993. *Voices of Decline: The Postwar Fate of U.S. Cities.* Cambridge, Mass.: Blackwell.

Bellush, Jewel, and Steven David, eds. 1971. *Race and Politics in New York City.* New York: Praeger Press.

Castleman, Craig. 1982. *Getting Up: Subway Graffiti in New York.* Cambridge, Mass.: MIT Press.

Chadwick, Bruce. 1982. "The Great Graffiti Talk Conference." *New York Daily News,* 4 Feb., magazine section, 1.

Chalfant, Henry, and Martha Cooper. 1984. *Subway Art.* New York: Holt, Rinehart, and Winston.

Chalfant, Henry, and James Prigoff. 1987. *Spray Can Art.* New York: Thames and Hudson.

Debord, Guy. 1967. *Society of the Spectacle.* Detroit: Black and Red.

Fox, Kenneth. 1985. *Metropolitan America: Urban Life and Urban Policy in the United States, 1940–1980.* New Brunswick, N.J.: Rutgers University Press.

"Garelik Calls for War on Graffiti." 1972. *New York Times,* 21 May, 66.

Glazer, Nathan. 1979. "On Subway Graffiti in New York." *The Public Interest,* no. 54:4.

Gunderloy, Mike, and Cari Goldberg Janice. 1992. *The World of Zines.* New York: Penguin Books.

Habermas, Jurgen. 1962; trans. 1989. *The Structural Transformation of the Public Sphere.* Cambridge, Mass.: MIT Press.

Kohl, Herbert. 1972. *Golden Boy as Anthony Cool.* New York: Dial Press.

Miller, Ivor. 1993. "Guerrilla Artists of New York City." *Race and Class* 35, no. 1.

Mollenkopf, John H. 1991. "The Postindustrial Transformation of the Political Order in New York City." In *Power, Culture, and Place: Essays on New York City.* Ed. John H. Mollenkopf. New York: Russell Sage Foundation.

Negt, Oskar, and Alexander Kluge. 1972 [1993]. *Public Sphere and Experience: Towards an Analysis of the Bourgeois and Proletarian Public Sphere.* Trans. Minneapolis: University of Minnesota Press.

Oldenburg, Claes. 1973. Quoted in "The Graffiti 'Hit' Parade." *New York,* 26 Mar.

Phase 2, orchestrator. 1994. "Aerosol Armageddon." *Vibe* 2 (Oct.): 80–84.

Ranzal, Edward. 1972. "Ronan Backs Lindsay Antigraffiti Plan, Including Cleanup Duty." *New York Times,* 29 Aug., 66.

Ryan, Mary. 1992. "Gender and Public Access: Women's Politics in Nineteenth-Century America." In *Habermas and the Public Sphere.* Ed. Craig Calhoun. Cambridge, Mass.: MIT Press.

"Scratch the Graffiti." 1972. Unsigned editorial. *New York Times,* 16 Sept., 28.

Stewart, Susan. 1987. "Ceci Tuera Cela: Graffiti as Crime and Art." In *Life After Postmodernism.* Ed. John Fekete. New York: St. Martin's Press.

Stewart, Jack. 1989. "Subway Graffiti: An Aesthetic Study of Graffiti on the Subway System of New York City, 1970–1978." Ph.D. diss., New York University.

Strom, Stephanie. 1991. "Subway Graffiti Back and Bothersome." *New York Times,* 11 Feb., B1.

SHADES OF TWILIGHT: ANNA DEAVERE SMITH
AND *TWILIGHT: LOS ANGELES 1992*

22 March 1994

I am sitting in the darkness in the Newman Theater, the largest of the performance spaces in the Joseph Papp Public Theater, in New York. It's the last preview of Anna Deavere Smith's acclaimed one-woman show, *Twilight: Los Angeles 1992,* a play based on the Los Angeles "riots," "uprisings," "rebellions," "civil unrest."[1] I was one of four dramaturgs for the piece during its world premier at the Mark Taper Forum in Los Angeles in June 1993, and I've made a special trip to New York for the official opening tomorrow night and for my interview with Anna.[2] In a few weeks I'll return when *Twilight* opens on Broadway. Anticipation mounts. It's an older, largely white crowd, not what I would have expected at the Public, especially for this piece. (Later, we find out it was the press opening; these people are the critics!) We have good seats, dead center, near the front but not too near. I know this play virtually by heart in its L.A. version, and I strain with excitement and curiosity, dying to see the changes that Anna, director George Wolfe (artistic director at the Public, director of *Angels in America*) and dramaturgs Tony Kushner (author of *Angels in America*) and Kimberly Flynn have made.

The house lights dim, and the title is projected at the top of the stage: "Twilight: Los Angeles 1992." "Prologues," flashes the next title. A video projects the horrifying images of the Rodney King beating, and as the images fade, the loudspeakers "boom!" A pool of white light stage right suddenly illuminates Anna. A tall, light-skinned African-American woman, she wears the white shirt and black trousers that will be her basic costume—now with a tie. In deep tones she begins speaking in Korean. Yes, this is familiar. Identified in the supertitles is Chung Lee, head of the Korean American Victims Association, in a vignette entitled "Riot." As he speaks solemnly, then passionately, we see the translation flashing above us. His store is burning down. The "riot" has begun. The segment lasts a few minutes. The split second Anna finishes, almost in midsentence, we hear another boom! Blackout. White spotlight. Now she's

Anna Deavere Smith as the juror Maria. Photo by William Gibson/Martha Swope Associates.

farther toward audience right, removing her tie as she talks. As she does so, she becomes Chicano-Salvadoreno writer and commentator Rubén Martínez. In his characteristic quick, incisive delivery, he tells us about police harassment of Latinos: you can be stopped for just not "walking right," the title of his segment. Again, virtually in midsentence, boom! Blackout. Lights up. Anna, even farther to audience right, has become a confident, defiant, sometimes jocular Keith Watson, one of the "L.A. Four" tried for the beating of white truck driver Reginald Denny. Watson revels in how they "rocked" L.A. Blackout, then jaunty music. Now Anna is stage left in an upright, controlled posture. The slide flashes the supertitle "Dorinne Kondo, Scholar/Anthropologist, 'Sunset Boulevard.'" I gasp and almost hide my head on the shoulder of my theater companion, anthropologist Kamala Visweswaran. I can hardly look, especially since people are laughing. I sound spacy, all light energy, spouting distant academic observations about "the social geography of Los Angeles," a stark contrast to Watson as the homeboy "down" with the community. A few seconds later I sound more sensible as I talk about driving along Sunset Boulevard, beginning with its Asian and Latino businesses in the east to the trendy restaurants of West Hollywood to the broad avenues of the "compound" of Beverly Hills. Driving down Sunset becomes a demonstration of the city's race and class segregation. Personal mortification aside, I am a bridge to the next section, beginning with Beverly Hills real estate agent Elaine Young, ex-wife of actor Gig Young. Her "Safe and Sound in Beverly Hills" enacts the notion of Beverly Hills as white fortress. And so the show continues, briskly, poignantly, humorously. One after another, Anna Deavere Smith "becomes" some of the two hundred or so people she interviewed for *Twilight,* switching age, gender, race, every few minutes, with a change in speech rhythms or a few gestures, perhaps donning or removing a shawl, a sweater, a tie. Mostly, these characters are residents of Los Angeles. Some—like Reginald Denny, ex–police chief Daryl Gates, police officer Ted Briseno, an anonymous juror from the Simi Valley trial—are directly involved in incidents involving the uprisings. Some— like Black Panther Party leader Elaine Brown, legal scholar Lani Guinier, Senator Bill Bradley, opera star Jessye Norman, scholar Homi Bhabha—engage themes that resonate with the unrest of April 1992. Mostly, these people are not "famous." A Panamanian woman, Elvira Evers, cheerfully and engagingly relates a tale in which her baby, still in the womb, caught a bullet in the elbow, thus saving Evers from death. An anonymous talent agent describes in hilarious detail the sight of "aging—or aged—yuppies, Armani suits, fleeing from the office" after the "riots" had broken out. "All they needed was Godzilla chasing them—aaaaggh!" In two hours, we meet people who sketch out for us a history of the uprisings and of an American past of race and class oppression, creating a vast collage of sometimes utopian, mostly sobering views on L.A.'s—and the nation's—continuing "state of emergency."

By the time the evening ends, I am deeply moved, overwhelmed at the transformations wrought in *Twilight.* Brisk pacing and an expansion from an uninterrupted ninety minutes with twenty-six characters to a full-length, two-act play with forty-one, allows Smith the opportunity to display more vividly her quick-change artistry. Simultaneously it gives the play an epic embrace, encompassing the events of April 1992 and L.A.'s many contradictions, possibilities, and colors. Paradoxically, this New York version of *Twilight* actually does justice to the daunting yet exhilarating complexity of Los Angeles and to the critical state of race relations as we face the new millennium.

A Quest for "America"

Twilight: Los Angeles 1992 forms part of a series of performances begun in 1979, called *On the Road: A Search for American Character.* With it, Anna Deavere Smith has invented a new genre. The difficulty people have in classifying what she does indexes the ways her art subverts and escapes conventional categories. Journalism, documentary theater, shamanism, one-woman show, play, ethnography—her work is all and none of these. Like an ethnographer or a journalist, she gathers perspectives on a place, a gathering (an academic conference, for example), an incident, by interviewing people. Unlike ethnographers and journalists, she constructs her art through performing these people and their words onstage. These are not impersonations, Smith says—that is, a form of mimicry and caricature—but impressions based on the person's speech rhythms, body language, and, often, the context in which they were interviewed. (For example, the people she interviews by telephone are sometimes, though not always, depicted with a phone in their hands.) It is an extraordinary sight and a testament to Smith's virtuosity to see an African-American woman "become" a Korean-American merchant, a fearful white mother, Motown executive Suzanne DePasse, a (female) Salvadoran political leader in exile, a Chicano artist.

The effect of these multiple enactments via a particular gendered, raced body is complex. The Rashomonlike multiplicity can be well suited to depicting volatile events and bristling tensions, as in *Twilight* and its immediate predecessor, the highly acclaimed *Fires in the Mirror,*[3] that focused on the Crown Heights riots in Brooklyn and the conflict between blacks and Jews. In its best moments Smith's technique presents an array of points of view, but also suggests the historical and political forces that construct those "individual" perspectives. This, for example, is my reading of the stage version of *Fires in the Mirror.* Various people speak from complex subject positions, usually seeming both persuasive and problematic in different ways. As a spectator, the play made me understand "both" or multiple sides in the conflicts, but also gestured toward the historical intractability of these cleavages and the ways individual responses are overdetermined by forces of power and history.[4] The danger of this multiplicity, both for Smith and for her dramaturgs, is that it might be too easily read as a form of liberal pluralism in which "everyone has a right to his point of view," and the artist is simply "presenting all sides." Yet the claim that Smith's work is reducible to a flabby form of liberal pluralism misses the degree to which there is a point of view expressed through the questions asked in the interviews, the selection and arrangement of material, the performance, and the production itself—lighting, sets, music, costumes, placement on the stage. Having worked with Smith, I know that she sets out to frustrate (white) audience desire for closure, for a central unifying voice, and for a liberal humanist reading of "we're all human beings" that always ignores historically specific power relations.

Twilight's combination of technical virtuosity, the addressing of critically urgent themes in ways that are political but not "heavy-handed," and the epic scale of the undertaking, paved the way for a celebratory critical reception. *Newsweek's* Jack Kroll (1993) deemed *Twilight* [the Taper production] "an

American masterpiece." *New Yorker* critic John Lahr wrote, "In its judicious daring, 'Twilight' [the Taper production] announces that a multicultural America is here and functioning and is capable of noisy but brilliant collaboration. . . . 'Twilight' goes some way toward claiming for the stage its crucial role as a leader in defining and acting out that ongoing experiment called the United States" (1994). David Richards (1994) at the *New York Times* hailed the version I saw at the Public, ending with this: "For its restless intelligence and passionate understanding, it will be welcome. For its appreciation of the singular voice in the howling throng, it should be treasured."

The Process

Sonorous words, impressive claims. But the process of reaching this point was as epic as the scope of the piece itself. For an academic unaccustomed to the behind-the-scenes of the theater, and indeed for theater people unaccustomed to an "ethnographic" process, the play's development is an amazing saga, which I tell from my dramaturgical perspective—a partial account that inevitably omits or minimizes parts of the production of which I had little or no knowledge.

In 1992 Gordon Davidson, artistic director of the Mark Taper Forum, impressed by Smith's performance in *Fires in the Mirror,* commissioned her to develop a similar piece based on the riots. Immediately, Smith became the focus of controversy, as a coalition of Los Angeles–based artists, mostly artists of color, protested the Taper's selection of "an outsider" to portray their city's trauma, though Smith herself had lived and taught in Los Angeles for a number of years.[5] Furthermore, Los Angeles presented daunting challenges. Even relating a history of events would be a troubling task. In the Crown Heights case, two acts of violence sparked the conflict: the original killing of the young West Indian boy, Gavin Cato, by an out-of-control automobile driven by a Hasidic Jew, and the (apparently retaliatory) killing, by black youths, of Yankel Rosenbaum, a yeshiva student from Australia. Where to begin in Los Angeles, the site of multiple acts of violence, many never reported in the media? Where to begin in a city where race is as far from the black-white binary as it can be at this moment in the mainland United States? Crown Heights, with its two sides, two incidents, and its black-white tropes of race, could form an elegant piece of point-counterpoint in a satisfying narrative arc. In Los Angeles, any neat and tidy narrative was bound to do violence to the complexity of events and to the sprawling multiplicity of the city.

Fall 1992

To address this challenge required intensive "fieldwork:" contacting people, doing interviews, mobilizing networks. Whereas Smith was able to do her interviews for the Crown Heights piece in four days, the more than two hundred interviews for *Twilight* began in the fall of 1992, extended through the actual performance in the summer of 1993, up through the present performance in 1994. Initially, the Taper provided Anna with a rented car and an assistant to drive and to accompany her on interviews. My first contact with the project was a call from Anna's car phone. Steve Park, the Korean-American actor who appeared as the merchant in Spike Lee's *Do the Right Thing,* was taking her around L.A. and suggested she contact me for suggestions on Asian Americans she might interview. I had already known Anna for a couple of years through the American Studies Association, where we both served on the national program committee. (In fact, she had already interviewed and "performed" me and several other participants in a conference at Stanford in a piece called "Identities, Mirrors, Distortions.") Later in the fall, the Taper organized "focus groups" for each group of color in order to further the interview process. In October, I participated in the Asian-American gathering, where a number of us talked about our experiences of the riots/uprisings as Anna asked questions and recorded our discussions. During the winter I was asked to come on board as a dramaturg, along with *Los Angeles Times* reporter Héctor Tobar, who is of Guatemalan descent. Later, Anna asked African-American poet and scholar Elizabeth Alexander and Taper resident director Oskar Eustis to join the dramaturgical team. Emily Mann, artistic director of the McCarter Theater in Princeton, known for her work in docudrama, directed.

February 1993

Initial shaping of the piece began with a two-week workshop. We gather in rehearsal room B at the Taper Annex, a boxy, institutional-looking building (and an eloquent statement about funding for the arts). Anna sits in the center of the room, Walkman in hand, headphones in place. A bank of video equipment sits in front of her and to her left. A cameraman stands poised, ready to record. At a table facing her sit director Emily Mann, Héctor Tobar, and myself; at a table in back of us are Taper staff in charge of scripts, Anna's assistant Kishisa Jefferson, and an occasional visitor, such as Lynell George, writer for *Los Angeles Weekly.* Anna turns on the Walkman and begins to repeat sections she thinks are potentially usable for the show, reproducing inflection and, sometimes, body language. When she is through—either with the single piece, or with a group of interview segments—she stops and asks for comment. Everything—theatricality, content, the politics of representation—is up for discussion. Given the nature of Smith's work, the conventional role of dramaturg—doing research, working with text, acting as a "third eye" between playwright and director—was stretched in unconventional ways. Both Héctor and I had already suggested names of people Anna might interview, and both of us conducted interviews (Héctor more than I), though these were not part of the New York production. I tell Lynell George that the dramaturgs are "in-house critics": alert for potential misrepresentations, for what might be missing, for unintended consequences. As the workshop proceeds, I gradually seem to be assuming the role of the hypercritical academic, for whom the politics of representation are always problematic.

Though fascinating, it is a difficult process. At this point, the Asian Americans Anna has interviewed are mostly Korean Americans, of whom most are male shop owners—neither representative of the larger collective identity "Asian American" nor of Korean Americans. Whoever is organizing interviews at the Taper seems not to be following the suggestions I give them. Korean-American friends express concern, noting how mainstream institutions exploit communities and artists of color. At one point, I talk to Anna about my misgivings about my ability to represent the so-called Asian-American community—as though such a diverse population could be exhaustively represented. I am especially aware of being a Japanese American, descendant of the colonizers of Korea, in a drama that so centrally highlights Korean Americans. I articulate my worries about being "a minion of the dominant culture," a phrase that disturbs Anna. She listens carefully and promises to keep me from such a fate. The workshop ends. March is mostly a hiatus while Anna is in London performing *Fires in the Mirror*. I continue to fax names of potential interviewees to the Taper. Héctor, I think, is conducting some interviews for Anna. I advocate for a Korean American to do interviews in the Korean-American community, and a UCLA student, Nancy Yoo, is hired both to find more Korean-American interviewees and to accompany Anna on her interviews.

April 1993

By the time rehearsals begin with the full production team, Oskar and Elizabeth are onboard. We are now in the larger room A, with set designer Robert Brill, production stage manager Ed DeShae, composer Lucia Hwong, sound designer Jon Gottlieb, lighting designer Allan Lee Hughes, among many others. Together we make an impressive multiculti tableau. We dramaturgs react to Anna's performances of her interviews, giving our ideas on what works, what needs cutting, how sequences might work. The designers ponder and experiment with the sounds, music, props, sets, lighting, costumes, for particular characters. Anna and Emily must deal with all this and more.

May–June 1993

The rehearsals sometimes go smoothly; sometimes they are fraught. Upset with the presentation of Asian Americans, at one point I tell Anna that if I were an Asian American viewing the production as it stood, I would walk out—a statement that provoked, shall we say, a heated discussion. To Anna's credit, we are able to work things out. Mostly, rehearsal is not quite this dramatic, but it is clear that the stakes are high. When the production goes into rehearsal in the theater itself, the process becomes more fraught as opening approaches. When we go into preview, the list and sequencing of characters changes nightly (causing no end of trouble for the tech crew, who have to rearrange sound and lighting cues and negotiate the sets with each change). At one point, the preview performance comprises two acts and a good three hours, as Anna—sometimes on book (reading from the script)—valiantly tries to accommodate a broad sweep of events and characters that suggest the history of L.A. as a third world, diasporic city of migrants, refugees, and dream chasers (mostly at the suggestion of the dramaturgs). This clearly became too much, both for Anna and the audience, and Anna—in what was no doubt a difficult series of decisions—makes substantial cuts and revisions. The official opening is postponed; the play must be substantially revised, there are lines to memorize, interviews yet to conduct. (Indeed, two of the most important figures in the L.A. production, truck driver Reginald Denny and "Maria," a juror in the federal trial, were interviewed and added after the play had entered previews.) As opening approached—no other postponements were possible—our dramaturgical arguments centered on a handful of characters. For Héctor and me, the black-white binary was still far too much in evidence. I lobbied until the end for the inclusion of Dan Kuramoto, leader of the jazz fusion group Hiroshima, who to me embodies Los Angeles. His speech patterns are African-American, his identifications with people of color—African American, Asian American, and Chicano; in fact, growing up in Chicano East Los Angeles, he had always wanted to be a *cholo*. (He is part of the New York production.) He would be, I thought, a welcome presence, since all the Asian Americans included so far were still Korean-American store owners or members of their families. Many of us wanted the inclusion of Chicano artist Rudy Salas, whose often humorous rantings about police brutality provided a necessary history of racism and police harassment of Latinos. In fact, he opened the L.A. show.

In these discussions, emotions sometimes ran high, heightened by the fact that they were public displays. Anna has called them "fiery battles," referring at the end of the interview to our sessions in "that room." We sat on a sofa or on chairs in a dressing room backstage, surrounded by the hot, bright lights of makeup mirrors. The room was always full of people: Anna, the director, often the producers Gordon Davidson and Robert Egan, the stage managers, sometimes the production crew, assistants at the Taper. After a performance, the dramaturgs and others would give our feedback. One evening, a few days before opening, lives in memory. Anna had made a decision to cut Dan and Rudy, prompting Héctor and me to protest vehemently. Without them, *Twilight* would remain a largely black-and-white story. I argue passionately that they were critically important presences, emblematic of L.A. But I also argue that there is a responsibility we owe to the people we represent, that rightfully, "our asses are on the line with our communities." Anna's response was to invoke her obligations to the theatrical community. Héctor and I were near tears. I could scarcely look up lest my composure break. As soon as the session ended, I ran out, unable to say a word without bursting into sobs. Anna and I have since talked about the ways the people of color performed the race wars for the whites, who were the distant onlookers. Certainly, my memory of that evening was a sea of white faces looking on in pity or sympathy—observing, but not themselves experiencing the same emotions. There is, though, a happy ending to the story. The very next day, Anna reinstated both characters, and the tears of the previous night were transformed into radiant smiles. By opening night, Dan was cut in favor of Salvadoran political activist Gladys Sibrian, but this time I better understood Anna's concerns: that we not give comfort to the white audience. Dan's resonant comments about a "new racial frontier," seemingly so appropriate for the ending, had been interpreted by a prominent white critic as signifying merely that people of color should stop fighting one another, leaving whites completely unimplicated. Though I still wanted Dan to end the show, I understood the choice of Sibrian, who spoke eloquently of the uprisings as a "social explosion" and of the need for people to feel that "they can change things." Despite dramatic moments of tension, then, we worked through our differences. Anna always listened and took our perspectives seriously, and much of what I take from *Twilight* is profound respect for her sense of accountability and commitment to other people of color.

Consequently, *Twilight* embodies for me a utopian moment. This tense, painful, wonderful, and dramatic collaboration was a difficult struggle that nonetheless resulted in a production that makes American theater history. Cross-racial hostility, misunderstandings, and prejudices are never pretty or easy, but overdetermined as these conflicts might be, in *Twilight* the team managed to deal with them ways that were ultimately generative and productive. This struck Anna, too, one day when she watched her "many-hued dramaturgs" on the TV monitors backstage, in a postplay discussion with L.A. high-school students. She wrote to us:

> diversity
> un named
> is alive.
> The name
> is a waiting
> for something that is.
>
> . . .

It's real.
You are real . . .
In my life, in this moment,
you are the proof
that
'a change's gotta come'
has come
and I am so proud.
And glad
and clapping . . .

On 13 June 1993 *Twilight* had its official world premiere at the Mark Taper Forum. Ever critical, I still had some misgivings about the politics of representation, but the festive atmosphere of opening night, the warm audience reception, highlighted the historic nature of this production: an African-American woman, taking up her space, addressing politically urgent issues and performing brilliantly on the mainstage of a major regional theatre. Through her giving voice to people of different genders, ages, races, classes, all of us—a Latino lumber salesman, a Korean-American shop owner, an African-American politician, a white reporter—are authorized to take center stage, to tell our stories. *Twilight* makes a significant intervention into a mainstream theater world in which "entertainment" Andrew Lloyd Webber-style, old revivals, linear narrative, and "safe" themes predominate, and where people of color continue to be conspicuous by their absence or confined to stereotypical roles.

The first preview performance of *Twilight*'s run at the Public began on 8 March 1994, where it enjoyed critical raves and sold-out performances. On 17 April it opened at the Cort Theater on Broadway for a limited engagement.

I interviewed Anna on 24 March, the day after *Twilight* opened at the Public. We sit at the nearby Time Café, a busy scene at lunchtime. Anna points out Philip Glass to me; in the middle of the interview, Greg Tate, the music critic from the *Village Voice,* comes over to say hello. I am enthralled with this production—high praise from the most critical of the dramaturgs. I pay Anna my greatest compliment: this is the L.A. I know and love. I tell her that this version is at yet another level of sophistication from the L.A. production. "How so?" she asks, and as I try to elaborate, tears come to my eyes and I can scarcely speak. Eventually, I choke out my question, "How did it happen?" (I place a much-edited version of the response later in the interview to spare the reader the details that could be of interest only to a dramaturg.) Such is the situational frame. Clearly, I make no claims here for journalistic/academic "objectivity"—a stance I have argued elsewhere can often stand for unsympathetic distance. My interview with Anna Deavere Smith is in part a conversation between people who share a history of struggle through collaborative endeavor. I have a passionate stake in *Twilight,* as someone deeply affected by the uprisings and by the promise and possibility of Los Angeles, and as advocate, friend, and supportive critic of Anna's work.

I have edited the transcripts for redundancy and clarity, and the segments are arranged thematically rather than in linear sequence.

Theatre, Narrative, Ethnography

KONDO: I wanted to ask you about the genesis of *On the Road* because did it not arise in reaction to conventions, like the notion of having *a* part, or the convention of the well-made play? Or I'm wondering whether the interiority of the method was part of it.

SMITH: No, all of that. I mean, certainly the interiority of the method was disturbing to me. The idea of the centrality of any actor's psyche—I don't understand that. When I get interested in an interview is when I see how complicated a person is, the very moment when I think I can never capture this. And so many of the people that I taught and the way they were being taught, even if they did extroverted things, or wild improvisations, it was very packaged. "What is your technique?" They were so busy trying to develop a persona, many of them were making themselves into very, very boring people. And they were doing that because they needed this thing to perform when they went out to sell themselves. You should come with me some time when I have to speak to actors. As Hélène Cixous said to me, first of all an actor has to have a soul. That's number one. So when you go into a room and you see these young people, whether they have dreadlocks or their underwear is showing, *whatever,* if all of it's like performing themselves, I just want to start crying. Because it's a real waste. The real revolution I think that has to happen in arts training is we have to make art a civic discourse.

So what is the world around you? My father will never read this because of the journal it's in. I never had the kind of a father that gave me the psychological makeup to believe in the centrality of things, but most people do. Most people really do believe that there is one person in charge or one person who gets all of the attention, and they really invest in that. Even if they say mean things about that person and critique the person, the person is still central.

KONDO: So the notion of the single, central authority, the Law of the Father?

SMITH: Right. Even, you know, I notice a lot of aggressive political speakers are really talking to sort of one person. And I just don't believe in that.

KONDO: To me it would make sense that they would even be political speakers because it's being part of that whole type.

SMITH: Being part of that, even if it's from the outside, even if it's the outlaw, the banished.

Anna Deavere Smith as Rudy Salas. Photo by William Gibson/Martha Swope Associates.

KONDO: They want recognition.

SMITH: They want recognition. I mean, Lani [Guinier] said that. She said it to me privately, and I said, "You don't want me to repeat this, do you?" And she said, "No. Yes." So she said at the 92nd Street Y, nine hundred people. I said, "Who do you think you're talking to when you go out on talks? Who are you speaking to?" And she said, "Well, first I think I'm talking to myself, really, because I'm always trying to work through new things people are telling me. And then I'm thinking I'm talking to Bill Clinton." And of course when she said that everyone applauded. And she defined herself as banished. And it's a really amazing relationship. [California Congresswoman] Maxine Waters was talking to George Bush a lot of the time. And you develop that relationship with the community, but the community is almost like an oratorium which allows you to speak to this other person who will not give you an audience.

KONDO: And who will never recognize you the way you want to be recognized.

SMITH: Who will never! And it's something about the psychology of speaking that has to do with that.

KONDO: And the structures of authority.

SMITH: But I missed something in my development that made me—I just feel very bad when I see centrality or I see single heroes or anything like that. It's just not pleasing to me. Now there are many people who see my work, and it's very displeasing, because I do not have a central hero.

KONDO: So they're searching for it and—

SMITH: "Who *is* your favorite?"

KONDO: So they ask that? Very interesting.

SMITH: Sure, in L.A. there were lots of people who said, I mean, Jan Breslauer [theater critic for the *Los Angeles Times,* who took the production to task for not having enough "analytic" voices], I think she said in some way, "Didn't she find *anybody* who could give us a glimmer of hope? Didn't she find *anybody* who could wrap it all up? Who of all these people?"

KONDO: That's right, it was the desire for a voice of authority who would package it and give it narrative closure.

SMITH: And even Tony [Kushner] was really fighting for Maxine to close up the first act and I just said, "No!" It has to be someone from outside of this whole thing who says the same thing, and that's why I choose Jessye [Norman, the opera singer] to basically say something of what Maxine is talking about when she says, "Riot is the voice of the unheard" (162).[6]

Ethnography, Verisimilitude, Theatricality

One of the ways that Smith's "ethnographic" or "journalistic" method inevitably goes beyond these labels is through theatricality and performance. Not only are considerations of "accuracy" in representation a concern, but in order to make a point and to engage the audience, the character must engage the actress and be "performable" technically. Yet Smith clearly shares the ethnographer's misgivings about the imposition of authorial voice.

KONDO: Maybe we can move on to the performativity issues because I definitely want to get to that. There is all this stuff about the Age of Mechanical Reproduction, and L.A. as the kind of event constituted by video par excellence. So I was just wondering how you see the place of theater, what theater can bring to—

SMITH: That's very funny because now at Stanford in our faculty meetings, they have just begun to talk about virtual reality. I think I'm a disappointment in talking about that because I know so little about—I'm like living in the nineteenth century.

KONDO: But no, what is it that's special about theater? Why theater and not something else?

SMITH: I don't do media because I have this feeling that I don't *fit* in media, that I feel that I'm too big for the costumes or something. I mean literally, it's like a physical size thing. I think I'm too big.

KONDO: Does it also have to do with the notion of the bigness of the acting as well for theater as opposed to the—

SMITH: Yeah, I think that you can't be that big. I was on the set with Tom Hanks for *Philadelphia,* and I realize now that the way he worked was really perfect for film, which is, he sat to himself all the time.[7] He seemed to be very low-energy, and it was perfect for that role because the man was *dying.* So the energy of movie acting is about finding a kind of a contained energy and being very controlled with yourself. When I watch these movie actors, they seem to have a natural sense of that, of keeping themselves in complete control. And I just cannot do that; it goes against my grain. That's why I'm doing one-person stuff, even instead of being in plays. I was very uncomfortable with how much you wait around, how it's very difficult to have any idea of what is happening around you, and *doing your part.* Do you see what I'm saying? It's not even the same as *taking* part. Or it's not the same as doing your part like, "What is your piece of the pie?" It's more like, "What's my part? What are my lines?" I used to teach people at USC who would take the script—they called them bumble bee scripts—and they would black out everybody else's lines and all the stage directions and highlight their lines with a yellow marker. Like, "What are my lines? What is my part?" And in a way, you can say, well, I'm very greedy, because I took everybody's part. But it's because I want to have a feeling of the whole.

KONDO: For me, there's the desire for closure, there is what you want to say, and theatricality—and all of those things come into play, no?

SMITH: Well, theatricality is hard because—that is very hard and you and I have been through all the problems that makes, because I think about it all the time—say, like with Jessye. When I interviewed Jessye, I interviewed her on New Year's Day in her home. She was in black sweat pants and tennis shoes, sitting on an ottoman, like this, talking to me. So when we brought it into the theater, they have her sitting in the Park's [the Park family, three other characters in act 1] chair and this thing around her, it's like a stole. And I said I really don't like this. It's not working, and it's going to become a stereotype. [Smith does wear the stole in the production.] So it's this thing of how you make an identification that the audience may understand, without going so far as to do the thing that theater usually does, which is to sacrifice the complexity of a person and the unexpected for the sign. But it's all about how can we get the audience to look at different signs, and to look at contradictions.

KONDO: But also with your kind of work there is the verisimilitude thing as well, which is sort of like ethnography. So how do you represent someone, and what is the role of accuracy of representation? Because I remember, for example, at the Taper with the sound with Angela King [Rodney King's aunt] and then the hammering, remember?[8] And now that's not in at all. And so all of those complicated decisions are made, no? And you have to adjudicate them somehow.

SMITH: That's right, that's right. And they're very hard because my original goal was to say that if I repeated every utterance as it really was, I would find character. And wanting to look for a way to edit reality—by "edit" I mean not take away things, but to take a small fragment of reality in all of its detail. And that *in itself,* in what it was without my intrusion, it becomes poetic.

I have this dream that you might be interested in of—you ever heard of the actress Irene Worth? She must be like seventy now. She was a great Beckett actress, and I had this dream that she was playing in Chekhov's play *The Seagull,* the role of Mme. Arkady, an actress. And she was saying her lines like, "blah, blah, blah" [loudly] and at certain points [whispers]. So she had made this choice to say the lines that were the apparent reality one way, but those lines that Chekhov put in which were her psychic reality she would [whispers]. And in the dream, I started going, "My God, this is just absolutely brilliant!" And I thought they hadn't invented a microphone for her to do this. How will they do that? That would really be psychological realism. And in life I began to notice that people that I talked to would be sort of talking along in a sort of drone, and there would be like this real shift! And of course, in my work I am really trying to capture those shifts. But I don't really do them in their full accuracy.

KONDO: Because?

SMITH: I don't have the technique. Because I end up becoming more committed to things like telling the bigger story. And I do end up doing something which is an *impression* of them. That's different from an *impersonation.* But I would love to be able, even if it was only five minutes long, to do five minutes of absolute accuracy.

KONDO: Well, what would that consist of? What is absolute accuracy?

SMITH: As much as you can capture. You know what I mean? And the process of trying to capture it, which starts to develop a certain imagination. Because even as you and I look at this table, we see some things, we don't see other things. But it becomes this bigger historical question, which is that we look at history as these big sweeps, and we're constantly eliminating all of the inconsistencies.

KONDO: Exactly. Absolutely. So it's a narrative, and the narratives are exclusionary by definition. You can't tell a story otherwise.

SMITH: And that's really the sacrifice I'm still making, which I didn't want to do.

KONDO: Well, as you say, it's inevitable to some degree. [We talk about the pacing and some of the characters.] And I just wanted to say about Angela

King, it's fascinating for me because it reminds me of the ethnographic situation and the interview situation. She's sort of turned with her back, not sure she wants to talk to you, exactly. It's like, "You want me to tell it, right?" And then she goes into this whole kind of narrative, she's still kind of [tentative], and then clearly you asked a question or something has happened where now she's remembering the good old days. And she just starts to unfold.

SMITH: Well, that's what happened with her and me and Kishisa [Jefferson, one of Anna's assistants at the Taper], but it happened over a much longer period of time. "Do you want me to tell it?" "Yes." She starts to try to tell it to us; she bursts out crying. She goes to the thing. She comes back. She talks to us a little bit more, and she starts laughing at herself and how she cries so easily. And she tells many, many funny stories, and then she tells a story about "hand fishing" [the title of the segment]. And I love it, because I think that's the process that we all went through, particularly as children, maybe not so much anymore, when we were confused or upset. You know, that we start out in resistance and then we cry or whatever, and then we laugh. And that's what feeling better is all about. But it's condensed, you see? That's what I mean about it is no longer accurate. But it's wonderful. It's very satisfying artistically to begin to construct that type of character which I didn't start out to do. But you see what I'm saying?

KONDO: Absolutely. Because it allows you to trace that trajectory. . . .

SMITH: It allows me to put meaning in. But *I am imposing the meaning,* see, that's the thing.

Performance, Performativity

The issue of performance is a critical one. As is clear in the interview, it represents for both Smith and me a place of "escape" from complete logical/textual/academic mastery, and presents, potentially, a challenge to those modes of writing and being in the world. It is what compels me about theater and performance. For example, poststructuralist dictums about "no fixed text" come to vivid life when you see an intonation, a gesture, or a lighting change utterly transform the entire meaning of a piece.[9] Yet—the subject for another paper—performativity has been appropriated in odd ways in the academy, partially through linguistics, in a manner that remarginalizes theater and drama and reasserts the primacy of the text. The ephemerality of performance, its unrepeatability, its resistance to linearity, to the two-dimensional page, have of course been treated before. And there is a danger in allowing the "ineffability" or unrepeatability of performance to stand for some form of mystified, romantic transcendence. Yet performance, I would argue, presents some fundamental challenges to academic textual and institutional practices. Smith presents some of these challenges in a critique of the academy.

Twilight emerged through performance. As Smith emphasizes, we dramaturgs reacted to material not as it was written but as she *enacted* her interviewees before us. We heard their words and intonations, usually long before we
saw any kind of text. This was the case for Angela King, for example. I had
objected to one part of the segment vehemently in rehearsal, where Mrs. King
reminisces about Rodney as a youth, "hand fishin' ": catching a big fish with
his hands.

> I said, "boy, you sure you ain't got some African in you?"
> Ooh,
> yeah,
> I'm talkin' about them wild Africans,
> not one of them well-raised ones, like with a fish hook? (53)

At the time, I couldn't believe that no one else found it politically reprehensible,
a "self-Africanizing" statement that would surely reinforce stereotypes. Over
the course of rehearsal, I began to see that performance and context could give
even this utterance a different spin, playing up the warmth and the richness of
family memory, while showing Angela King with all her problematic prejudices. Again, simply reproducing the text cannot do justice to the quality of the
performance. It is not that the utterance ceases to be problematic or that it
ceases to invite problematic audience laughter in some instances. Yet performance adds other dimensions of meaning, giving the piece a different reso-
nance in the context of the whole.

Anna also refers in the following to Mrs. Park, part of the Park family triptych. Walter Park was shot "execution-style" by an African-American man,
which left Park partially paralyzed and lobotomized. Mrs. Park talks about her
anger at this injustice and of her devotion to her husband, but—even though I
am sure she sounded demure "in real life"—I strenuously objected to her being portrayed as too stereotypically submissive and devoted. If someone had to
embody selfless love, why did it have to be an Asian-American woman acting
out the stereotype? This typifies what was at stake in the battles over representation—knowledge that those representations have real-life consequences for
those of us who must battle them on the daily basis. Even if a representation
were accurate, what are the politics of (re)presenting that image onstage without proper contextualization? Are we thereby making our own lives worse, by
reinscribing those stereotypes? And to what degree can we control reception
anyway, given the multiplicity of possible readings from multiple subject positions, and the intentional fallacy, where authorial intention never guarantees
meaning?

KONDO: Well, Angela King is a good pivotal figure to switch the conversation a little to the performativity issue, because for me she represents my com-

ing to terms as an academic with the importance of performance. Because remember the arguments that we had about the whole hand fishing thing in the first place?

SMITH: Right, right, right, yeah. That's right, you were the one that—

KONDO: Exactly. So there's one level in which it's problematic, but it's the performance that contextualizes it and makes it something else. So I don't know how to ask the question, maybe, to academics who are so textually oriented.

SMITH: Well, let's look at this one instead, because this is another problem for you. What about Mrs. Park? My Korean teacher saw it, and she said Mrs. Park should be much more docile and humble. And I said my dramaturg in L.A. had a fit about that. And so it's like you're caught with both your political problems and her cultural problems, and to some degree your cultural problems, but you know, two different—

KONDO: Absolutely.

SMITH: And it has to do with, what can be said? What can be said? And I think in the academy, you *all* tend to take more control over what could be said. And I have very mixed feelings about that. And yet I protect my characters, too. I don't let them say things that will really murder them, usually.

KONDO: I was wondering about a way of how I can impart, maybe it's only through experience, just the power of performance and how it can utterly, utterly change meaning.

SMITH: Well, because performance is, it's like the saxophone is. There are several things going on. One is, on a level of an instrument, the human body is the instrument for the performer. So the saxophone, for example, is an instrument which is normally used in jazz, one reason being that most of the sounds have to come from the breathing. So it becomes this very personal sound that a musician makes. And breath is something that is really sort of incredible. Because of breath, no one of us could be able to ever say the same word the same way twice. And the way a word is said begins to create meaning, because all of us have a personal relationship to language and meaning comes from experience and what we've all learned individually. So if we all learn English we still impart, as we say "the word," our personal experience, it's that *saying* that makes it difficult to begin to determine what meaning is going to be the moment that the performer opens his or her mouth.

I talked to X, actually, early on. One of our earliest conversations, I asked her why so many feminists write about films but they don't write about theater? And she said, "It's because with theater you have the problem of performance." And I thought that was an amazing thing to say. And it disturbs me about the academy. What many people resisted [at a conference Smith attended] was the idea of presence and the power of presence to transform things. So there we have this great actress or dancer who performs in front of multiple thousands of people, that is a power that is not about *the* word she is singing, or *the* dance she is doing. It is about her particular charisma, and nobody else can have that. And I think that's one of the problems: it probably seems remarkably inefficient to talk about performance. Because only the performer owns the performance. And particularly the *live* performance, because the director doesn't own it, the cinematographer, the editor, nobody owns it. And that's why I'm very interested in it. Because it is the one place of real freedom and power.

KONDO: And for me as an academic, that's why I find it—I also find it a challenge. But it's totally thrilling because it *escapes* the text or it escapes the words. You can't fix it. To me films are like the new three-dimensional text. You can take it home, you can see it any time, but as you say, no word is ever pronounced [the same way] twice, no performance is ever the same. So the challenge for me, then, would be, how do you begin to talk about it? In this medium [academic prose] that's built on some other logic altogether? But I actually find that really a challenge because I think that the desire to fix is what's—

SMITH: To fix and to put it in its place. We live performers were all put in our place [at the conference]. We performed, but the day after we performed, we were all put in our place. We were all told in some kind of way by somebody on the day after our performance, "We've heard enough from you."

KONDO: "Thank you very much."

SMITH: It's really a very awful arrogance in the academy. It isn't good. I mean we had this discussion before.

KONDO: Maybe you could also comment on the new ways the performativity has somehow now become the rage of social theory.

SMITH: I don't know, you would have to tell me. I don't know. Because, see, I don't know how it is, what the performativity is. Once again, you have stolen that word from us.

KONDO: No, I absolutely think so. It's a hijacking of the term by people who don't know anything about it. Or maybe based on this linguistic notion of performative, but it's—

SMITH: Why do you think it was hijacked? I mean, first of all it just strikes me, you know, there's something very subversive about real performance. So is it that you want to participate in that subversive activity?

KONDO: Yes! It's the notion of subversion that is alluring. I think maybe it can be an important intervention in a sense, because it dislodges all that tendency toward fixity, but because it always has to be rendered in this language of high theory—this kind of academicized whatever—it ends up reprivileging the text in the funniest way and not taking into account the ephemerality. In an odd way, I think that because the academy is premised on textuality, the way it's been appropriated marginalizes performance and the kinds of interventions that it could make. And I think it also matters who is doing it and for whom. I think, for example, performance can have a really powerful impact on audiences of color, for instance, empowering in all kinds of ways. Is that so bad? Isn't that important? This has to do with all the complicated politics that we talked about before.

SMITH: See, I think that there's something very tricky about performance. I guess you know, sort of what I was learning. There's also something about performance that, and maybe this has something to do with it too. When somebody says that the problem, the *problem* of performance, you have to deal with the *problem.* There's something in the nature of how we think of performance, is that we think of it as *not* authentic and not truthful. You were saying that the performativity of gender, to me that is kind of like performance, some kind of performance. But that is not the performance that I do on stage. And, ironically, in my life I don't feel that I am a performer. I'm less of a performer than most of the people in the academy around me. So what I am doing there seems to be more real in a funny way than what I am allowed to do in life! Because what I am doing there or trying to do there, my God, it's much, much less performance than someone who's performing a certain way to get a job. It feels deeply serious to me. And the risks are enormous. And the possibility of doing something that is genuinely, humanly offensive or wrong is there: the worst kind of mistake to make, do you know? So I don't know that that is absorbed about performance. And yet I think when an academic writes an article they experience that same place, because they are doing something very creative. The difference is that in acting, we have to do that in front of a lot of people. But whatever happens, whether you're channeling, whether you're just saying your lines, whether you have stage fright, it is a *real thing* that is happening in front of *strangers.* Whatever you're creating has to be creative right there. You can't go and do it in rehearsal—or it doesn't count. You can't fix it. And so in a way, maybe what's disturbing about looking at that—the observer really is having to absorb a full human being. And we pretend that the full human being isn't there, and different ones of us stop at different levels, the level of "What is costume?" "How do you say your lines?" "Is that a stereotype you are doing?" But, say, like Al Sharpton. "Is that a stereotype I'm doing?" Frankly, I think what's more interesting to observe is, "How is she protecting her voice?" Do you see what I'm saying? That's the real thing that's going on. It's something that is technical, and maybe one night that you come there you will see that I make a different type of a connection with the man.

We talk a bit here about the ineffability of performance, and I say that theater seems to thematize that unrepeatability, something difficult for academic prose to capture. We go on to discuss the effects of the erasure of positionality from so much academic writing, even now.

SMITH: Well, I was just thinking of sitting in that room [at a conference] and being kind of horrified by some of the things that people said. And *that* disturbed *me* about academia, because it was very clear to me that people were creating theories around very personal problems that they had. And I was watching this happen before my very eyes! The people spoke from places of their own individual disempowerment, basically. And that's the truth. But it's right there! It's on the tape. I mean, it's so clear!

KONDO: But they'd never say. That's what's insidious about it. And that's why I think the fight for the move toward positioning happening in anthropology and other disciplines *minimally*—they could still be in high theoretical discourse—but at least the move to say that those positions are never from a place off in the ozone, like divorced from everyday life and your own "personal concerns." I mean, it's always from that place.

SMITH: But if you *ever* talked about it, you'd be accused of being essentialist or worse.

KONDO: Oh, essentialist or "merely personal." Especially the person of color, you can get all of this sexist stuff or be dismissed. But I think that there is more of an acceptance now, much more now than ten, twenty years ago. Because politically, also, it is important to position one's stakes and so on. Despite the fact that you could never exhaustively know yourself. But minimally some gesture toward it, so that it's not just abstract knowledge, like a disembodied brain—which I hate about academia. It's like the "big boy" voice.

The Politics of Representation

The difficulty that faced the *Twilight* production team, and that faced Anna most of all, was how to make sense of the riots and simultaneously do justice to the complexity of Los Angeles within the space of an evening, through the orchestration of the individual portrayals. For me, the Los Angeles production (though I miss some of its features, such as the beauty of the sets and lighting, the intimacy of the three-quarters thrust stage at the Taper that puts the performer closer to the audience, and in a few cases, being able to remain with a particular character at length, uninterrupted) was an instance of imposing a preliminary order onto this complexity. For Smith and for me, the more definitive work was actually realized in New York, after she had more time to reflect, write, shape the material. I include here excerpts from the first parts of our conversation, to give a sense of how the changes in the play took place.

Anna here is gracious is crediting her collaborations with others, but I think it is crucial to state that she always remained the pivot and the controlling writer of the work. Michael Feingold of the *Village Voice* best characterized her multiple skills when he mentions two of the resonant stories and characters in *Twilight:* Elvira Evers (the Panamanian woman who was shot and whose life was saved when her unborn baby caught the bullet in the elbow), and opera singer Jessye Norman. "Smith's triple ability—to evoke such statements, to recreate them so scrupulously, and to sculpt the assemblage so richly—is beyond anything else of its kind" (1994). I want to underline these triple skills given the difficulty the mainstream theater establishment and the press have had in characterizing Smith's work. Smith is in some ways enacting the kind of postmodern dispersal of authority and poststructuralist dictums of the "death of author," showing the ways we are palimpsests of voices and narrative conventions, yet this stunning enactment is rarely recognized for its subversiveness.

Indeed, acts of categorical border patrol abound. For example, this year a controversy arose among the selection committee for the Pulitzer Prizes centering around the eligibility of Tony Kushner's *Perestroika* and *Twilight*. Kushner won last year. The question was whether the prize was given simply to *Millennium Approaches,* part 1 of *Angels in America,* or to the whole play, which would include *Perestroika.* The committee decided that the award last year was bestowed upon the entire play. In Smith's case, the committee claimed that she didn't write the play, at least not in the conventional sense, and *Twilight* was disqualified—this despite the fact that *Fires in the Mirror,* based on the same technique, had been nominated the year before. Similarly, a classificatory controversy broke out for the Tony Awards for best play. Though Smith had won an Obie, an off-Broadway award for best play, some categorical confusion existed for the more mainstream Tonys, awarded to Broadway productions. Was this really a play? The classificatory confusion prompted a lengthy article in the *Los Angeles Times* calendar section, "The Tangle Over Twilight," continuing the controversy over whether Smith's work was "a play or just reportage" (Mitchell 1994). For example, the author of another Tony nominee for best play, Robert Schenkkan of *The Kentucky Cycle,* said, "From a dramaturgical point of view, it's not a work of the imagination. . . . This is not to take anything away from her performance, which is amazing. I think of it as performance art, not as a play." Clearly, this politics of reception rests on deeply embedded notions of authorship as intellectual property, creativity as the property of a central organizing consciousness operating in isolation (the myth of the individual creative genius), and the erecting of borders between imagination and reality, fiction and truth: borders that anthropologists, among others, have been problematizing for years. In this case, it is imagination that is given transcendent value.

I would argue that Smith has in essence invented a new genre that disperses authority, problematizing the boundaries between documentary and fiction, reality and imagination. Like feminist pedagogical methods or other techniques of dispersing authority and subverting genre, boundary transgression risks dismissal and/or punishment. Consequently, despite its reinscription of notions of "author-ity," I wish here to use the term *writer* quite deliberately to describe what Smith does. Though theater is always a collaborative art, it is strategically important to underline her skill as interviewer, performer, and writer, for without that triple threat, *Twilight* could not be such an epic creation.

The following excerpt is from the beginning of the interview. Two elements of difference between the two productions were striking for me. One had to do with the sheer scope of the New York production, which addressed virtually all my problems with the politics of representation. The second was the technique of quickly changing from character to character, at times intercutting them as though they were responding to one another. In the L.A. production, each character was presented singly, with the exception of the Park family, who formed a triptych. Several readings were possible of that single triptych. One was that it takes three Asians to make one other person; another is that too much time is spent with these (petit bourgeois) Korean Americans, making them too much of a point of pathos and cathexis for the white audience. All of these concerns were addressed in the New York production.

KONDO: I just wanted to talk to you about it, and ask you how [the transformation in *Twilight*] happened.

SMITH: Well, I think a lot of things happened. One, as you know, even when I was sort of struggling to write the introduction of *Twilight,* it really was about me still trying to absorb the things that you and Héctor were teaching me. But I think that something very big happened to me spiritually when I was working with the Ailey Company that I don't really have words for, about what happens when I have to take my work into another context and collaborate and having to speak the words in exact time for the dancers.[10] But because of the whole nature of Ailey, and because I love Judith [Jamison] so much, it became a real challenge and it didn't feel like a harassment. You know what I'm saying? So something really got shook up in me about performance then, and about collaboration. And then, when I started working with George [Wolfe] and Tony [Kushner], one of the first things that happened with Tony was that he really felt strongly that the show should be in two acts and that it should have an intermission, and that intermissions are very good. And once he convinced me of that, it really opened up the possibility for a longer show. The other thing that happened was that you had sent me this long fax about the show in Princeton, and Tony read it and wanted to have me read it in the show. And I said, "Well, I can't do that, Tony." And he said you should be in the show, which is what led me to interview you, because he felt that the things that you were talking about in terms of cross-cultural experiences were really important. And so what happened was, he was interested in that part of what you had to offer and George had always wanted to have some way of talking about the geography of L.A., so that section worked very well. Originally we were using something of yours which was much more complicated, which were these two sections that I called "Shifting"—"Shifting, Theoretical Version" and then "Shifting 2." And once we all read that, that really began to affect what we were thinking, in terms of looking for models of thinking and discussion that allow people to shift their points of view.[11] And we made this whole section, which was you and Homi [Bhabha] and Lani Guinier, and it made me remember my interview with Rubén Martínez. I interviewed him again this November and we sort of made this whole theory collection, but it was too hard. Your material was very dense, even for you. What I loved about it was that you were struggling with your idea, which is exactly the kind of thing I'm trying to capture. But for an audience it's tough, because it was something that even *you* were trying to reach for. And soon that whole idea of that section disintegrated, and Bill Bradley came in, and I remembered Dan [Kuramoto] came in sort of at the last minute. You were, by then, very well situated in the beginning, but we were gonna have you be there in the two places. And I think that made it kind of a wheel, to have this larger picture. Because Tony also felt that there really needed to be some theoretical base in the show, sort of like the beginning of *Fires in the Mirror.* There was really no way of escaping that. But he also felt that he could not delay the riot, so it was like we couldn't start with that, it wouldn't be like *Fires in the Mirror.* And once we realized that it should go in the second act, that becomes the center of the second act. And it's *fun,* the section that has most of the ideas is actually a *fun* section, because the people are not struggling with personal problems, and most of the people in the rest of the show are struggling with personal dilemmas.

KONDO: Another thing that was very different, obviously, was the pacing and the intercutting and how that came about—that's George and you?

SMITH: Well, George was very interested in that, but this was also something that Peter [Sellars] had said to me when he saw the show. He felt that people should reappear. And so when he said that to me, I started thinking about a lot of people in terms of reappearances. Really what I wanted to do was to be able to show people in different stages, because in a way, that's what I think identity is. It's not this one block of time. So I was listening to the interviews more in terms of how people could recur. And then George and Tony and I had a conference call and I think that's when George started talking about this idea of making the riot this chaotic thing where nobody could finish their sentences, but it was much more complex than actually what we ended up rendering. I mean, it's quite simple in the end. But we had a lot more intercutting. Paul [Parker, brother of one of the alleged Denny assailants and head of the Free the L.A. Four Plus Defense Committee] and Diane [van Iden, a white mother from upper-middle-class Brentwood] and Jessye used to be intercut. The original section that we were working on with you and Rubén [Martínez, Chicano/Salvadoran author/journalist] and Lani was *all* intercut. I should try to see if I still have a draft of that, you might be very interested to see how that was. And it was interesting to rehearse because I could—

KONDO: How was that as an actress though?

SMITH: Well, it's fun because you are—

KONDO: Because I remember one time, remember, we were talking about the through line business. So it is more fun to actually change characters quickly.

SMITH: Well, in this case, I don't have a through line, my through line is synthetic anyway. I never know what the through line is, and it takes many months of performing it to find one. The show as it was constructed in L.A. was almost an impossibility for finding any kind of an emotional through line. Absolutely impossible. And now it's very subtle, it's just beginning to develop for me, and it's very, very subtle. And it has to do with sort of echoes of things. You know, people reinforcing each other's ideas. Something in this show that's under the surface that I hadn't realized is about children and motherhood and the loss of innocence. I always felt that E. (anonymous young woman, former gang member) was very important, don't you remember, for the beginning? And I had to fight for her here too. I think on the surface it's like, "Oh, God, it's another woman talking about an abortion" or *blood!* And I kept saying no, no, no. It's about a loss of innocence. And it actually keeps happening in the show. Even Mrs. Han [a Korean-American former liquor store owner] is talking about a kind of a loss of an innocence.

KONDO: And I think for me too, for instance, remember when I talked about the Park family as the only triptych, that makes it weird, but with intercutting now it's like—

SMITH: Oh, no, not only that, George sees the whole show as trios. If you look at the show, there are many ways that it's all trios.

KONDO: It means the politics of representation are totally different. I mean even just with that.

SMITH: There's three characters, and then you're the break, and then Elaine [young Beverly Hills real estate agent] and Rudy and Suzanne [DePasse, former president of Motown] are another. Many, many times you'll see that there are three happening, there's three happening here.

Performing Race

Finally, what about race, and the position of artists of color? Race privilege was a constant feature of the process of assembling interviews and starting rehearsals for *Twilight*. The most obvious site of privilege is the way "white" remains the unmarked category, especially frustrating during the period of organizing interviews. During initial stages of interviewing, Anna received no response to repeated requests for suggestions of white people to interview about the uprisings. Without them, it would have been as though the uprisings/riots/rebellions/disturbances affected only people of color, and once again people of color would be performing for whites, while white people themselves remained unimplicated. Ultimately, this was well addressed via numerous figures in the production, but it required a struggle, and Anna's repeated and insistent requests for this to happen.

Audience and reception are also critical issues. For whom is one performing? Who finds what point of entry into the performance? Clearly, certain audiences were much more receptive than others. For example, many whites in the Los Angeles and Princeton audiences clapped for Reginald Denny, the white truck driver who was assailed by several young black men, who talked of keeping a room in his house for his mementos, all the gifts and words of good will that were sent him after the incident. He says, "I just want people to wake up. It's not a color, it's a person. So this room it's just gonna be people. It's gonna be a blast. One day, lord willing, it'll happen" (112). I was always distressed by the clapping and the problematic liberal humanist sentiments expressed thereby, for they remain blind to power relations and their own sites of privilege. In the Princeton version, Smith undercuts it with a reply from Paul Parker, brother of one of the alleged Denny assailants, who also talks of his "no justice, no peace" room, and who, I think rightfully, points out that if the victim had been Latino or African American or Asian or Indian, it would never have attracted such notice. (Indeed, there were Asian Americans and Latinos attacked at the very same intersection, but these cases received minimal publicity.) In the New York version, as we note in the interview, Denny's importance recedes. Generally, the more mainstream the audience, the more problematic the reception—certainly a problem when one takes a show to Broadway. We take up issues of race in this last excerpt, continuing our conversations about the differences between the New York and L.A. productions.

KONDO: This is extremely powerful. Lydia Ramos, I mean, that was very poignant, enacting a Latino position.

SMITH: Right. Which is something that occurred a lot in Rubén's interview, actually, is this way that Latinoness is invisible at the same time that it is the dominant culture in Los Angeles.

KONDO: Exactly. And it's the poignancy of that and the interview with Briseño [one of the so-called four white police officers, who is Latino] was very poignant.

SMITH: Yeah, I'm still working on him. I was glad to get that interview. I mean, that also made a difference, that I did go back in the field again. And I think somebody—my voice teacher—actually said that the way that the show was in L.A. and in Princeton, Reginald Denny was the center of the show.

KONDO: He was!

SMITH: And he shouldn't be.

KONDO: No, he was!

SMITH: And meeting Paul [Parker] begins to disintegrate that. Then, ultimately, it had to be a bigger disintegration.

KONDO: Yeah, very much so. No, that was wonderful, it had to do with what surrounded it, with the videos and everything. No, he was the point of cathexis for the white audience, and now it's not so clear. But because it's undercut *right* away, I think that's part of it. And it's just not enshrined in the same way. There's so much else in it [now]. This is the L.A. that I know and love.

SMITH: That's great.

KONDO: I was going to ask you about the move to Broadway and audience considerations. Maybe you can talk a little about what it's like as an artist of color to be performing in some of these mainstream theaters.

SMITH: As you know, that's a big thing with me. And I have discovered that I am, as a mission, I'm gonna have to go outside of theater to realize anything about that. I really think that right now major theater departments should have programs in audience diversity, because nobody is trained to do it. I just played in Berkeley right next door to Oakland and I probably played for fifty black people in three weeks. And it feels bad because then I start to get paranoid. I got this interview from this lady for *Time,* a black woman, and she said to me, about audience development, "Well, do you think there's a way that black people aren't interested in your work?" She was trying to say, "Are you a sellout?" I responded by saying, "Don't you think that's a dangerous question? Don't you think that's a complicated question?" But it's a real question, and it's that whole problem that I had in L.A. when I first was coming there: who is she and why is she the one who's coming. And I want to be careful about those same thoughts, because as you know, you and I have talked a lot about this issue of who could speak for whom. And I think it's very dangerous and clumsy to assume that black people or people of color don't think I can speak for them, based on the opinions of artists or others who are in privileged positions. Because my experience is that when people of color come to see my work from the general public, they are absolutely delighted to be there.

I just feel that there's so much work to be done in the area of audience development. And it's a time that it really must be done if nonprofit theater, or the mission of nonprofit theater, is going to survive. Right now the lines between nonprofit theater and for-profit theater are very slim. And most nonprofit theaters are working with goals that have to do with "making it," with sending work to Hollywood or New York, and talent is being drained. So it's almost like, what are we having nonprofit theater for? It really isn't serving the community any longer. We've also been in the period where people were funded for developing expertise and skill, and I think what we're coming upon now is, "Okay, so what?" And then on the other hand I hear, "Well, what happens to art if this is political?" And my answer is, well, now that I have something to say, my technique has to be better than ever. I have to have voice class *every day* because I have something to say now. So there is this way, I think, that we still have to be imaginative about how we combine both aesthetic goals with the *reason for speaking.* I mean it's a reexamining of what are we speaking *for?* I think in the academy you have somebody saying the issues, you know, "What am I talking about?" And if I'm talking in such a way that nobody can hear it, why am I talking? Who am I talking to? And I think it's a *big* frontier, to steal Dan's [Kuramoto, who talked about "a new racial frontier"] word again. And I think that in the next ten years—well, I'm very hopeful, actually—I think we'll see some things. Right now I'm in a climate where people are very ambivalent about this. And most producers give lip service to audience diversity, but believe me, if they think they can sell out, they're gonna sell out. They really don't care who's there. And I'm always trying to point out the importance of having an audience that can talk back to me, because I am not interested in doing presentational art. My work is unfinished. Once again, it's the call.

KONDO: Absolutely.

SMITH: But, you know I wanted to say something else about this main-stream thing, because I was on a panel with a woman named Marta Vega. She has a book out, just new. I can't think of the name of it right offhand. She is a Latina from the Caribbean, and sort of was friendly with Miguel Algarin and these people in the Nuyorican Café and so forth, and she was making this very impassioned speech about people leaving the community and being in these mainstream atmospheres and then realizing that they have to come back to their base. But before she got to the point of saying that you have to come back to your base, she was talking about how they went to the mainstream and they were coopted. I started thinking about some of the stuff you had told me about shifting, and I asked her if she felt there was anything you could gain from realizing that what you had to do is stay mobile. It's not that you go to the mainstream and they kill you. It's that you go to the mainstream, and they will suck from you what they want. That's her argument, they will suck from you what they want, so you'll come back home. But I think it's more complicated than that. I think it's that they may suck from you what you want, and you also want something from them. But the point is that your spirit can never be really killed if it's alive, and that's what leads to this shifting idea.

I mean, the way that I interpreted what you were talking about is that your spirit will keep taking you to try to get at this from a lot of different angles.

KONDO: From different positions and you're never fully—

SMITH: You should never expect, you should never expect.

KONDO: There is no pure anything.

SMITH: There is no pure anything. There isn't any community. I mean, this is the thing I think that got Lani Guinier in such trouble. I interviewed her at the 92nd Street Y on Sunday. And I was teasing my way through the book, and something that is very hard to grasp, but I think what's interesting is, it strikes me that one of the problems that we have right now is that some of the ways that we thought about community in the past no longer apply. So when she's talking about cumulative voting or when she critiques districting or when she critiques this idea of authentic leadership, I think what she's doing is claiming something that is a reality right now: it's *unclear* who the authentic leaders are. It's not just a color of a person's skin. It's *unclear* that people live in communities around like-minded people. So the question, the place for imagination, is how do we develop constituencies? How do we find leadership, and how do we have community, and how do we have democracy? That's what she's saying. If it's no longer landed. And that's the problem.

KONDO: Yes. Or this little model of homogeneity that's ultimately repressive, in fact exclusionary and built on stasis. I wondered about, in terms of being an artist of color, I mean, these are the kinds of dilemmas that we're all facing in the academy and in art, some of the ways that mainstream institutions have both enabled and disabled your work.

SMITH: I was having a conversation with somebody the other day who said—he's a funder—he said, "Well, look at you. We didn't find you in an institution." And I think I am an odd person to talk to about to about institutions. I mean, when you met me, I was in one institution, but as you know, I was doing everything in the world while I was there to fashion myself as somebody who was only there for a little bit of time. I'm constantly saying, "This isn't working, this isn't working." I want to bring *my* people in, and that is not *new.* I have never been as confrontational as I am now. But I have never belonged to *anything,* and I never will. So I'm an odd person to talk to about institutions. I've never even decorated my office. I never decorate my dressing room. Most actors do. They come in right away. Or dancers or Ailey people? Judy [Jamison]? Wherever she arrives, Judy has a whole box, a huge road box with her TV, her stereo, her CDs; she fixes everything up. They fix everything up. They have their pictures, their flowers, their towels, their things.

KONDO: So the theatrical institution is a place where you do your work, but it's not of you?

SMITH: I mean, I really don't have the temperament to set up the—

Kondo: Territoriality?

Smith: And that hurts me, too.

Here we were interrupted, and went on to another segment of the interview.

Kondo: So, any other last messages?

Smith: Well, I guess I was just thinking about that, too, which I've thought about sort of, performance for us, again, in that room in L.A. Of how, what we have touched on before when we talked of the degree to which we even performed in front of silent white people.

Kondo: Yes, we did.

Smith: And if there's something that begins to disturb me about my situation in mainstream theater it's that I am constantly in this position of performing in front of silent white people both behind the scenes, managing that behind the scenes, and managing it in front of the audience. And it has a huge spiritual toll. And we had to do that at the Taper, you and me and Héctor. [Smith goes on to refer to the session where Héctor and I were near tears as everyone else just watched.]

Kondo: Yeah I'll always remember that, too. They were like just looking at—that was one of the most horrible moments. They all looked like *so* sympathetic, but *so* distant, you know what I mean? It was like being the object of scrutiny; I mean, that was really hard.

Smith: And when were we aware of performing, and when were we not? I remember very well of the American Studies thing. You really resisted the role as of a person of color who would fix things.[12] But the question is, what do you do, though? What do you do?

Kondo: That's right.

Smith: I was upset when I went to Barnard after I performed *Fires in the Mirror* and all these kids came up to the mike, and not one kid of color came to the mike to ask me any questions. And I ran into some kid in San Francisco who had seen me there and said she'd been there, and I said, "Why didn't anybody of color come up to the mike?" And she said, "We're really tired of being the ones"—I'm sure you experienced this in your classes—kids of color who are tired of being the ones who speak out on this kind of thing. And I feel very complicated about that. All right, so you don't have to take that role, but does that mean that you play a silent—?

Kondo: No. Exactly. That's interesting because I would have read it, as in the postplay discussions, didn't it seem that the white people were asking all the questions? I read it as, who wields the power to ask something in a public place? Who feels they own the space and can ask a question? Remember, I was with Lydia [Ramos] and Rubén [Martínez, in a postplay discussion], and it was all the white men. They're the ones who feel they own the Taper. It's like, who always speaks in any situation? That's the way I read it. But I think that there could well be this other thing. When it's about race we're always the ones that have to speak.

19 April 1994

I just returned yesterday from the opening. A highly successful performance, the thousand-seat Cort Theater full, an audience full of celebrities, including visible support and representation from black artists—Harry Belafonte, Ossie Davis, and Phyllicia Rashad, among others—and other performance artists, including Lily Tomlin and Eric Bogosian. At the preview I'd attended on the fifteenth there were more Asian Americans and African Americans than I'd seen at other Broadway productions. Still, perhaps inevitably in mainstream theater, the audiences are mostly white. I hope Anna's desires for a more concerted effort at audience development and community outreach will be realized.[13] *Twilight* can potentially authorize and empower many people of color, for it gives our stories significance, affirming that we, too—even if we don't speak English well, or if our professions and class backgrounds are not the stuff of the usual Broadway play—that we, too, can take our place here.

The Broadway opening symbolizes for me a kind of closure with *Twilight.* Script in hand, memories still fresh, I write to forestall what Peggy Phelan (1993) would call a loss, in a work of mourning born of the irretrievable nature of performance, what other analysts call its ephemerality. I write in a kind of mourning that is also an affirmation, a writing into official existence, that takes its place among other such writings in this world of the academy. These are the stakes I have in this work, as documentor/historian of performances by artists of color. It has been an extraordinary ride. When Anna asked me to accept for her an award bestowed by the Los Angeles Drama Critics, I spoke of the privilege of working with her and with the production team on *Twilight,* who showed me that Los Angeles, despite its many tensions, contradictions, and conflicts, was still vibrantly alive with cultural possibility. Never simple, never easy, the struggles around *Twilight* in the end convince me that multiracial collaborations like ours must nonetheless continue, in all their difficulty *and* utopian promise.

Notes

1. For many of us in Los Angeles, the choice of terminology declares one's political affiliations and the degree to which one attributes degrees of agency and political critique to the events of April 1992. *Riots* was the term used in the media, and perhaps could be said to characterize some of the disturbances, but the "social explosion" sparked by injustice cannot necessarily be captured in that term.

2. Theater has its own special language of what critic David Román, in his forthcoming book on AIDS and performance, *Acts of Intervention,* calls arrival, or inscription

into history. Previews are actual performances, but the play is still subject to change at that point. "Opening" signifies an official entry into history; this is where the play's text, direction, and so on, are fixed, and it officially comes into being. "Press openings" may occur before the official opening, but these are aimed at reviewers; there is a tacit understanding that the version the critics will see will not be substantially changed for the opening. There is also a language of premiers, world premiers, and so on, which Román effectively analyzes in terms of inscription into history: what is foregrounded and what is effaced thereby.

3. *Fires in the Mirror,* in a truncated and rearranged version, was filmed for the American Playhouse series for PBS. George Wolfe directed. It is also advertised for educational purchase, with module/discussion guides for teachers. In other words, it has entered a canon of sorts and is marketed as a vehicle for the discussion of present-day race relations. Both *Fires in the Mirror* and *Twilight* have appeared in book form, published by Anchor.

4. The handling of the Latasha Harlins case in *Twilight* is another good example. Harlins, a young African-American woman, was shot and killed by a Korean-American store owner, Soon-ja Du, after a dispute—including physical struggles—that began with Du's accusation that Harlins had stolen a container of orange juice. Du was sentenced by white judge Joyce Karlins to a $500 fine and probation, sparking massive protests, especially in African-American communities. It is an important part of the background history of the uprisings, when Korean-American-owned stores were targeted. Héctor Tobar and I lobbied to cut it from the L.A. production, however, because it is a complicated story that continues to reverberate with racial tension and hostility, especially in Los Angeles, and at that point there seemed to be no way to tell it without heightening those tensions.

In the New York version of *Twilight,* however, the story is movingly, effectively related. Queen Malkah, a spokesperson for the Harlins family, angrily relates her account of Latasha being killed for an orange juice, "Two Dollars in Her Hand." Charles Lloyd, the African-American attorney for Soon-ja Du, replays the videotape of the shooting and argues theatrically that there was nothing out of the ordinary in the light sentence, given Du's lack of a criminal record. He proclaims that the case would have received no attention at all had Mrs. Du been black. Queen Malkah's rejoinder characterizes Lloyd as a "sellout," but she goes on to render her position problematic: "Now, it might sound very racist on my part, and I don't really care at this point if it does. Those Koreans all look alike, little bitty short women with little round faces and little short haircuts." Jay Yang, a store owner, tries to explain that, unless you are a store owner, "You Don't Understand" Mrs. Du's fear and their embattlement; the ways groups of young people orchestrate shoplifting, problematically singling out young black men. He ends by saying, "After that I really hate this country. I really hate. We are not like customer and owner, but just like enemy." In each case, the speakers have important points to make, and in each case, they are problematic. The skill displayed here, however, is that the analysis never rests at merely performing the conflict among racial groups. Rather Smith, through Yang, points to the larger society that creates this conflict. Later, Dan Kuramoto mentions the injustice of the verdict in the Harlins case and its divide-and-conquer effects.

5. The Mark Taper Forum, part of the Los Angeles Music Center (including the

Dorothy Chandler Pavilion, for opera and the symphony, and the Ahmanson Theater, for touring companies), is the most prestigious venue for new work in Los Angeles. A well-known regional theater, the Taper has premiered scores of new works, and has a reputation for fostering multiculturalism in the arts (although the upper echelons of its managerial/artistic staff is as yet lacking in racial diversity). Along with *Twilight,* which has been nominated for a Pulitzer Prize, it has within the last two years sent two other Pulitzer Prize-winning plays, *Angels in America* and *The Kentucky Cycle,* to Broadway.

6. A note on citation: quotations from the published version of *Twilight* are cited with page numbers. The New York performance version of the script I received has unnumbered pages. When these are cited, I will simply enclose with quotations. This is from Jessye Norman, who comments eloquently on the voicing of oppression in a segment called "Roar" that closes act 1:

> I mean this is how the spiritual came into being
> that in order to
> deal with this
> unbelievable
> situation
> of being transported
> from one's homeland
> and being made a slave we had to sing ourselves through that. . . .
> But I think that if I were
> a person
> already you know a teenager
> . . .
> And I felt I were being heard for the first time
> it would not be singing as we know it
> it would be a roar. . . .
> It wouldn't be words
> It would just be
> like the earth's first utterance.
> I really do feel so.

7. Smith has been in a number of films, including *Philadelphia* and *Dave.*

8. When Anna interviewed Angela King, apparently there was the sound of construction or hammering next door, which was reproduced at the Taper production. The sound actually attracted comment in the *L.A. Times,* which assured audiences that the noise was an intentional feature of the production, and not hammering overhead from backstage.

9. David Henry Hwang's *M. Butterfly* is eloquent here. Depending on the intonations of the last utterance, "Butterfly," the entire meaning of the play can change. Was this an act of revenge and mere role reversal? Could there have been love between the two men? Was there regret on the part of Chinese opera diva, Song Liling? More baldly, in terms of the politics of representation, was this another triumph of the crafty Oriental, or something more complex?

10. Smith collaborated with the Alvin Ailey company in a performance that combined spoken word and movement. She interviewed members of the company and performed interview excerpts as they danced.

11. After the Princeton performances I sent Anna a fax, after which I discussed what I would like to see in another version of *Twilight.* Mostly it has to do with the racial

cross-identifications among people of color in Los Angeles and the cultural possibilities that represents. In the interview excerpts Anna mentions I discuss the "social geography of Los Angeles," and later talk about power relations and categories as "shifting," not as essentialized, monolithic entities.

12. At the American Studies National Program Committee meetings in 1992 we were deciding upon panels to include in the fall program, the Columbus Quincentennial. It became clear that all the proposed panels on Columbus were mildly critical at best. For those of us of color, for whom the "discovery" means the advent of colonization, conquest, genocide, slavery, and labor exploitation, this seemed untenable. The people of color—Anna, José David Saldívar, Lemuel Johnson, and myself—constituted ourselves as a caucus, of which I was selected spokesperson. I brought out our concerns, but also said that it was important that the people of color not be saddled with the further burdens of organizing those panels ourselves. That is, people of color should not pay with our time and labor to rectify these oversights in the dominant perspectives on the quincentennial.

13. In fact, as I revise this article on 18 June 1994, *Twilight* will close tomorrow, a good two months early. Audience development never seemed to happen in the way Smith hoped, and *Twilight,* despite its critical acclaim, struggled at the box office, usually filling the thousand-seat theater to half its capacity or less. Had it won one of the Tony Awards for which it was nominated—best actress (given to Diana Rigg in *Medea*) and best play (given to Tony Kushner's *Perestroika*)—its life probably would have been prolonged.

References

Feingold, Michael. 1994. "Twilight's First Gleaming." *Village Voice,* 5 Apr., 97–98.
Kroll, Jack. 1993. "Fire in the City of Angels." *Newsweek,* 28 June, 62–63.
Lahr, John. 1993. "Under the Skin." *The New Yorker,* 28 June, 90–94.
Mitchell, Sean. 1994. "The Tangle over Twilight." *Los Angeles Times,* 12 June, 7.
Phelan, Peggy. 1993. *Unmarked: The Politics of Performance.* New York: Routledge.
Richards, David. 1994. "A One-Woman Riot Conjures Character Amid the Chaos." *New York Times,* 24 Mar., C13, C20.
Smith, Anna Deavere. 1994. *Twilight: Los Angeles 1992.* New York: Anchor Books.
———. *Twilight: Los Angeles 1992.* Unpublished script.

BACKWARD: CONNECTED WITH TECHNOSCIENTIFIC IMAGINARIES

PRODUCING AND MEDIATING SCIENCE
AS A WORLDVIEW IN POSTWAR AMERICA:
TWO INTERVIEWS

These two interviews are part of what we hope will be a larger project. We have begun to interview some of the people who helped set the terms in which the generation of Americans raised directly after World War II encountered science as a powerful component of contemporary culture. Although these are public figures, no strangers to media attention and often subjects of prior interviews and biographies, we consider it important to engage their thoughts in relation to a specifically anthropological project: analyzing scientific worldviews as powerfully and profoundly part of national and international cultures. This is a generation that is rapidly passing from the scene, most in their upper seventies and eighties, but they have been and often continue to be utterly crucial to and highly aware of the project of developing and diffusing science as a worldview in American culture. We are interested in contacting individuals who have played particularly creative roles in what we see as the institutional hot spots from which the social and cultural production of science emanated in the period directly following World War II and highly linked to it: government, media, education, foundations.

At the present moment, of course, the debates on the role of science and democracy include a healthy component of gender critique and multicultural initiatives, as well as a more problematic cynicism about rationally constructed knowledge. Criticisms of science as corrupting of American culture are not new. Framed as the debates between science and religion or science and superstition, they have deep roots in the nineteenth century. Recent attacks on the venality of scientists and their home institutions both evince claims about social accountability and the status of science as a public good and also play on prior narratives of "corruption." We believe that the insights of cultural activists who helped to forge the institutional channels through which a scientific worldview was promulgated in the period directly after World War II constitute a crucial contribution to understanding the current mixed interrogations of science in America (democratic and/or defensive). Most of the current debates have historical grounding in cold war politics; the growth of media links to consumer culture; the rise of the National Science Foundation, National Institutes of Health, Office of Technology Assessment, and other federal agencies which sustained and regulated scientific research; congressional support for science education; and so on. While very likely having come of age under its shadow, nonspecialists often have not given much consideration to this background. The political economy and social institution building of this period requires elucidation, especially for anthropologists and fellow travelers in cultural studies who would interpret post–World War II developments in science and technology of which their (our) own social scientific formation has been a historically embedded part.[1]

Science Studies and the Role of Anthropology
at the Present Moment

And yet, despite its relative lack of reflection in its own expansionary roots in the period directly after World War II (when scientific education and research were funded with largesse and direction), anthropology is increasingly positioned as a loyal and oppositionist discourse, interrogating emergent traditions and institutionalizations of science studies. Anthropological accounts garner increasing interest in a field well known, on the one hand, for its foundationalism—for example, histories of great scientists and philosophical and historical narratives of progress not only about specific scientific accomplishments but also about rationality itself—and, on the other hand, for its social constructivism, full of reified strong and weak programs analyzing facticity and models of agonistic behavior by scientists as if these were universal, unremarkable aspects of human behavior. "We" provide important empirical examinations of the very idea that science exists in a realm apart from the rest of its cultural matrix, breaking the frame in which laboratories become citadels and cyborgs can be viewed as revolutionary creatures.[2] Recent works by anthropologists reculturalize science and technology (Hess 1992) insist on the social co-construction of biomedical discourses by "downstream users" as well as by scientists and physicians (Layne 1992; Martin 1994a, 1994b; Rapp 1994) and track the transformation of widespread cultural norms in relation to scientific permeation (Rabinow 1992a, 1992b; Strathern 1992). Such trends are increasingly and self-consciously reviewed in relation to science studies by anthropologists as well, giving "reflexivity" a distinctively anthropological cast (Escobar 1994; Franklin 1992; Hess 1994, 1995; Traweek 1992, 1993). In other words, "we" (a rather diverse lot of field-based cultural researchers, glued rather loosely together by methodological traditions) find ourselves interpolated into a critical role in science studies. How did this positioning come about?

One way to understand our own position is to investigate the growth of scientific resources and perspectives both institutionally and as a diffuse and normative aspect of powerful sectors of post–World War II American culture. It seemed to us that after World War II there was a kind of cultural shift in the United States: those of us who went to public school during the fifties and sixties, under the shadow of Sputnik, had an infusion of science education dramatically different from what was available (and deemed necessary) for prior generations of school children. As we set out to interview some of the key figures who promulgated these transformations, we introduced our interests to them as follows:

> We are very interested in how public scientific knowledge has been developed and promulgated and how institutions—whether they are governmental or private foundations or cultural centers—have become part of how Americans understand the benefits and burdens of a scientific world view. From the late forties and throughout the fifties, it seemed to us that the language that people used to think about science was increasingly very similar to the language of scientists themselves. Yet sometime by the late seventies or early eighties, this pervasive acceptance of science as providing a beneficial worldview also began to wane. We are very interested in how the influence of science in American culture came about, and also, how it has begun to be challenged; after all, this worldview emphasizes instrumental rationality and the possibility of solving our social problems through scientific intervention. We are interested in talking to you about how such a way of viewing the world was given a boost by media, the government, private foundations, and educational institutions from World War II to the present.

We initially chose to interview Gerard Piel because he was one of the founders of *Scientific American,* the first and arguably still the most influential magazine translating scientific research for a general educated audience (see Lewenstein 1989, 1992). The interview took place on 13 February 1993.

INTERVIEWERS: We thought we might start at an earlier stage, both in your life and in this process. We were wondering how you got into science journalism and where it fit into the way science was perceived when you were a young man. We both grew up right in the post–World War II era, in which science already had a very specific role to play, but we assume it was quite different when you were growing up and coming to this perspective and your work as a science journalist.

PIEL: First of all, I'm a model product of the American educational system. I learned to hate science before I was five years old. In the classroom, I learned to hate what was called math, by the time I was five. Science got killed in high school. I had the best education America could offer. I went to

Phillips Academy at Andover, and I had a teacher named Boyce who taught physics from a little green textbook. In those days, textbooks were tiny compared to the backbreakers in student knapsacks today. One of the authors of this book was a man named Dull. You can look it up.

Pappy Boyce taught physics as a closed subject; it was like Euclid. Everything was in that book. If you applied yourself to it, you could make your own radio set, that kind of thing. Of course, you could buy one. Boyce and Dull made it clear to me that I was made for greater and larger and more significant enterprises. So I avoided science from that time on.

I managed to get through Harvard College without a single course in science. I won't go into the details of the legalistic maneuver I pulled to get away with that. The closest I came to science was to venture into sociology in my sophomore year, as a possible field of concentration.

There I had the extraordinary adventure and benefit of having Robert K. Merton, then a graduate student and part of the graduate proletariat, as my tutor. Bob gave me a total immersion in sociology. It was one of the grand experiences in my life. He showed me that I had to have an education if I was going to be a sociologist. He had me reading all the great social thinkers in the original—Karl Marx, Max Weber, and Émile Durkheim. It was an immense experience. But I could not argue with those thinkers in my ignorance of history.

So I proceeded to concentrate in history, and there I had an extraordinary advantage. Lowell had just retired as I entered college, and J. B. Conant was the new president. The momentum that Lowell had given to the tutorial system was still in force. I had Michael Karpovich, a full professor of history, as my tutor. I got an absolutely fabulous education in modern European history under his instruction. It was really like the experience in a British university. The courses that I took were appendages to the reading I did under his direction.

I meanwhile formed the ambition to be a journalist. My role model was Ralph Ingersoll, who was the glamour boy at Time, Inc. and had started *Fortune* magazine. So I never thought of going on into scholarship, but took this background in modern European history into journalism. With a clear understanding that World War II was on the verge when I graduated in 1937, I wanted to be a war correspondent. I went to work for Time, Inc. at *Life* magazine. Any graduate from the Ivy League could then get a job there. So I started as a college boy office boy. The managing editor of *Life,* John Shaw Billings, had been the managing editor of *Time;* Mr. Luce would trust no one else with the investment they were making in the new magazine.

I was proud to work for it; *Life* then was a wonderful magazine.

Time, Inc. got started by two idealistic Yale boys who decided to make a lot of money, were inspired by the notion that the Jeffersonian proposition that a well-informed citizenry is the essence of democracy, and thought every-body in the country should be able to read the *New York Times* at least once a week. So that's what *Time* was to be. Billings set out to make *Life* a picture *Time*. Instead of having one million or whatever circulation *Time* had then, they would go to five million, take it to the masses. Everything about the magazine was serious and purposeful.

Billings discovered that my A.B. from Harvard was a certificate of illit-eracy in science and made me science editor. A perfectly reasonable proposi-tion. If I could figure out what it was about, and could explain it to him, then maybe he and I could explain it to our readers. So then therewith began my education in science.

Coming to Scientific Consciousness

INTERVIEWERS: Did you have any second thoughts about Mr. Dull and what you had given up, or did you just feel like you'd forge ahead?

PIEL: It took me about a year to discover that science was an ongoing enter-prise, not a closed book. I had the great good fortune to be befriended, as I was doing my first story, by a perfectly marvelous woman named Myrtle McGraw. Myrtle was a developmental psychologist. She was studying the unfolding motor behavior in the human infant, in collaboration with a fabulous brain surgeon at P&S [Columbia University's College of Physicians and Surgeons]. She was in the babies hospital there. Their big idea was to see if they could find a relationship between the embryological development of the infant, be-cause the brain is still undergoing embryological development after birth, and the unfolding behavior. A real ambitious idea. It will come in another hundred years.

Then I met a man named T. C. Schneirla, who was at the American Mu-seum of Natural History, in animal behavior, comparative psychology. Those two people taught me what science is about. I mean, as a method, as an ap-proach to understanding. So I did a lovely story with Myrtle and a couple of stories with T. C. Schneirla on his army ants.

What happened was that when I made my first approach to scientists, they would run for cover. The symbolic, mass-circulation paper was the *American Weekly,* the Sunday supplement in all the Hearst papers. Mr. Hearst had a shine for science, but it was the kind of Jurassic Park science. He had a won-derful man named Gobin Behari Lal, an Indian, as his science correspondent. Gobin did very serious stuff. He and I became very great friends. But the *American Weekly* was razzmatazz, and reported science as new hope for you and the new cure for cancer and what it was going to do for your figure. Scientists hated to be mentioned in the popular press.

I was working for a picture magazine and because Billings and I agreed at the very outset that it would be stupid to make drawings; with photographs, we didn't have to have a barker out in front of the tent bringing the reader in. That's number one. It was a great challenge to get stories with a camera—to show with photographs how a television tube works. Because I had to get a bench scientist or an engineer willing to monkey with the tube so we could photograph, we'd tie his valuable time up for a week or two and stop work in his lab. So I had to persuade Billings to let the scientist check my copy. That's number two.

We did one fabulous story on the foundation of the performance of the battalion aid station in World War II. You know they had a 99 percent survival of kids that made it to the battalion aid station. Maybe 99 is high, but 98. It was central nervous system injuries that killed them after they got there. The wounded were saved basically because there was penicillin, and secondly there was plasma. The isolation of plasma from the rest of the blood was a piece of work done by Edwin J. Cohn at Harvard Medical School. We took over his lab for a week or two and showed how it was done.

INTERVIEWERS: In pictures?

PIEL: I had to clear every word that went under the big picture, all the little words that went under the big picture had to be right. So for the first time there was authentic and honorable coverage of science in a mass-circulation paper, and I discovered it was easier and easier for me to get the cooperation of scientists in what I was doing. The science department was a major enterprise at *Life* after a year and a half or so of this, when I finally got the hang of it. John Billings once said to me, I can count on you for the surprise I need at least once a month. I had the photographic essay once a month, the big story in four colors. I picked these up on—

INTERVIEWERS: On the street?

The Political Economy of Media and the Diffusion of Scientific Heroism

PIEL: Here's the one I want to show you, 29 June. They hid the table of contents, so the reader had to look for it in order to get him to look at the ads.

INTERVIEWERS: The *New Yorker* strategy.

PIEL: Here it is. This article was just perfectly timed to make Henry Kaiser the Paul Bunyan of World War II. Here's an example of the kind of stuff Billings depended on science for.

INTERVIEWERS: I can see. The early *Scientific American* certainly had the same format.

PIEL: Science was a spectacular department in *Life,* and I discovered that I had isolated my own public. Not that everybody didn't read the story, but the scientists of the country were my audience. It struck me that they needed much better service than I could give them in a department of *Life* magazine.

In the course of my work I came into possession of the entire story of the atomic weapon before it was set off. I didn't want to be publishing a magazine of science under Henry Luce's ownership. So I got loose from Luce in January 1945 and went to work for Henry Kaiser for a year to learn business. I told him I wanted to start a magazine, and I had to learn business. He said, why don't you come and work for me? So I was his personal assistant.

INTERVIEWERS: That's a good way to learn.

PIEL: After we got the Kaiser-Fraser automobile company launched and had raised $20 million, I had the hang of it.

INTERVIEWERS: The period you're describing, you say that you learned anti-science at school, that it killed science for you.

PIEL: Yes.

INTERVIEWERS: One of the things that has preoccupied us is thinking about all the challenges to a scientific worldview that are always emerging, certainly in America, and in other places. Did you have a sense when you were growing up that science was in some senses not a legitimate perspective, or did you see that as part of the culture?

PIEL: Not at all. It all seemed—when I was growing up, the whole notion of progress and all the rest was unquestioned, and the untoward and unanticipated consequences of technology had not yet overtaken us.

In starting *Scientific American* I was very, very concerned with the relations between science and society, science and public affairs, the war, and the bomb. All of that was what I found myself swept up into in this seven-year apprenticeship as a journalist at Time, Inc. But I was interested in science and its relationship to society, apart from the inherent interest of what it means.

In the first issue, May 1948, the lead article was on the Amazon. Every issue of the magazine had an article that made that bridge. [For example,] on the problems of arms control, I had one wonderful experience with getting Chester Barnard, who had been on the Baruch committee. The Baruch plan corrupted the Atkinson-Lilienthal proposal to internationalize the atom, a proposition the Soviets were guaranteed to reject. That was one of the opening salvos of the cold war. Barnard wrote a piece for us denouncing the Baruch plan, and spilling the beans on what had happened in that corruption.

INTERVIEWERS: At the time you started *Scientific American,* did you have a pretty substantial network by then with the practicing scientists of the thirties?

PIEL: Yes. Sure, that was a wonderful foundation on which to get the magazine launched. One of the documents that sold our financial people and our bankers was a volume of one hundred letters from scientists endorsing what we were doing, and those hundred guys were among our first authors and they helped to ratify what we were doing. That's a letter from Albert Einstein in 1950. We knew that the hydrogen bomb was being debated, and we published a whole cycle of articles on the hydrogen bomb. The issue in which we had this piece by Einstein on his general theory of gravitation got censored by the

Atomic Energy Commission. It had an article by Hans Bethe on the hydrogen bomb and how it worked and why it was the wrong thing to do, and so on. Making a long story short, we had to capitulate to the censors. We still owed our bankers $1 million. In any case, in all the history of litigation of the First Amendment, it has never come out of the courts without some kind of compromise. So we stayed out of the courts, and we insisted that the Atomic Energy Commission specify its objections—that we were going to publish the piece and they could send us to jail, but they better tell us what they were objecting to, and they finally did.

INTERVIEWERS: What was it?

PIEL: Trivial. It was Hans Bethe saying that you needed an atomic bomb to ignite the hydrogen, to produce the temperatures and pressures necessary to get the hydrogen fusion reaction going, and that was well known. There were some other trivial things like that, all of it in the public domain, and I broke the story in the *New York Times* after we published, because it suddenly occurred to me, boy, they have that information, and they could spill that to the Dyes Committee (precursor to the House Unamerican Activities Committee) or something, and say the *Scientific American* is a communist enterprise, trying to spill military secrets.

So what I did was take it to the *Times,* and instantly the press was on our side. We were heroes, and I guess it was really the making of the magazine, because up to this point it had become well known in the scientific community, where it got to 100,000 circulation, but outside the community, you know, on Madison Avenue where we had to sell advertising, they weren't paying much attention to us. But when this happened, we were suddenly heroes and by 1951, January, we were in the black with advertising revenue. So it was the crucial thing that we needed to establish our existence. Now, the magazine has always been concerned with the cold war, with the arms race, with the environment, with population, and above all with economic development. That's because I had the good fortune to know some responsible scientists, who were imbued with a vision. Freedom from want was basic to the Atlantic Charter [establishing the United Nations], and these people took it very seriously. I mean, this is the only publication you'll find in our country that has had those questions on its mind all these years.

Cosmopolitan Science?

INTERVIEWERS: So, they saw science as a means to accomplish—?

PIEL: Sure, and the technology which is its application. That was the recurring theme all through our history. We devoted our September issue to technology and economic development in 1963.

I'm very much involved with the people in the UN who are concerned with

Agenda 21. Have you heard of Agenda 21? Nobody has in this country. This was the product of what the Rio Conference on Environment and Development was about. Agenda 21 is the first international document that recognizes the demographic transition in place of Thomas Malthus.

It lays out a program for hastening economic development of the poor countries of the world and bringing their population growth [down], getting them through the demographic transition as early as possible and making the present doubling of the human race the last one, taking us to 10 to 12 billion. The UN envisions the arrival of our species now at 11.5 billion in 2150.

That is the urgency of the task, and Agenda 21 is all about that. The vision of Agenda 21 exposes the failure of the industrialized countries to meet their obligations to the human species, and just run their economies properly.

INTERVIEWERS: There is a fight on about that notion that there is an obligation between the rich and the poor in terms of mutual development. This is a position that you take and champion [in your books] with great articulateness.

PIEL: But it's also a way to make the lousy, busted, free-market industrial economies work. They've got to recognize the failure of effective demand within their own countries, as they dismantle their welfare states. Agenda 21 asks only $125 million a year of them in technology. That can be their saving. I mean, for the United States it's $45 billion. This pathetic Clinton comes up with a $16 billion stimulus package. Bob Dole was quite right when he said that's not going to affect a $6 trillion economy. $45 billion gets to be a more visible percentage, and it would be the smokestack industries in the most depressed parts of the country that would benefit.

The Cold War and the Shaping of Science

INTERVIEWERS: I read a lot of science biographies myself, and I'm particularly interested in the fifties and American culture when science really was the most prestigious, in a sense dominant, worldview around, in which primary and secondary school education was formed, and it was—and the scientists who had probably been GIs in the war and so on, or who came of age really in the thirties, had a set of values which were to some extent, I mean, fairly markedly progressive, and they were also somewhat involved in the world. Does that continue with scientists now, do they still have this view that science is something they undertake to make the world a better place?

PIEL: I'm afraid that my acquaintance with the community is with my generation. The people who run ICSU today, International Council of Scientific Unions, are solid with all of this. I mean, they are full of the great vision of the fifties. They established the first International Geophysical Year in 1954 or 1953. Now it's permanent, it's something called the International Geosphere Biosphere Project, which is a continuous picture of what the hell is happening all over the world with an increasingly rich data base. Then IIASA in Luxembourg, the International Institute of Applied Systems Analysis—

INTERVIEWERS: Because the institution of science has changed dramatically in terms of funding, I read these stories. In a biography, such a strong sense of a community of people, to some extent transcending ethnic and class boundaries, because a lot of immigrants who had moved into the sciences in the thirties in various ways. It was an unusual period, I guess.

PIEL: Yes, it was. And it was that dawn in 1945–50 when people were imbued with and confident that the world was going to be a better place, before the commitment to the cold war derailed it. We didn't really have much of a dawn before the collapse into the cold war.

INTERVIEWERS: Not so far. At the same time, in that period when that vision of science as absolutely central to human progress was really a very powerful one, were there antiscientific forces in the way there are now? Were there groups and perspectives that really opposed science?

PIEL: The scientists in popular culture were either the mad scientist or the bumbling Mr. Chips. There was the UFO crap. I'm trying to think—there was religious fundamentalism around. It wasn't taken so seriously by the press. As part of the political process in our country, when those people are financed by outfits like the Olin Foundation, you see the relationship between the oligarchy of our country and antiscience. But they didn't have that respectability then. *Scientific American* functioned as an atmospheric depollution enterprise. Jim Newman, our book review editor, did a glorious review of Herman Kahn "On Thermonuclear War." Alfred Merski outraged Julian Huxley when he blew the whistle on his Galtonian genetics in our pages. That was the kind of thing we tended to get involved in. The one time we even bothered to touch the UFO story was when our beloved friend, Edward Condon—Ed was such a wonderful man. You know his story?

It ought to be just mentioned, since his name has been mentioned. He left Princeton to go to Westinghouse; Princeton was the number one physics department in the country. He left it to go to Westinghouse because they could give him the voltages and amperages he needed for his experiments, and he was director of research at Westinghouse. So who was the man who was going to be the head of Los Alamos and run the atomic weapon development? It was Ed.

Ed had his interview with General Groves, and made it clear to General Groves that he would be boss, and in particular—Groves was always worried about the fact that people with funny accents had all our military secrets, and they were Jews, too—Ed said that he would do the hiring. If General Groves and his intelligence agents had things to report to him about the people he proposed to hire, he'd take that into account. But he'd make the decisions.

So fat man got little boy Oppenheimer to agree to his terms. Oppenheimer disgraced himself, and the reason he got in all that trouble was because he did squeal on his graduate students to the intelligence agents.

Ed was on the blacklist of the military and intelligence agencies and all the rest of them from that time on. They made his life miserable. Yet still he took on the job, for his country and for the air force, to try to help them get out of the crazy publicity jam they were in. The UFO nuts said they were concealing secret information that the public should know about UFOs, and that maybe they were part of a conspiracy with the powers of outer darkness. Ed undertook to settle the whole question by examining all the evidence and evaluating it objectively, and ending the controversy. But his own staff was infiltrated by UFO kooks, and he found himself in a tar baby situation. Every time he took a whack at it, another part of him got stuck, poor fellow. In any case, we tried to come to his rescue with a story about that.

INTERVIEWERS: Did the *Scientific American* get targeted? There was always a religious conservative movement that was hostile to science and so on.

PIEL: I always enjoyed the antiscientific cover of being scientific, so that people regarded the magazine as above politics. It was only the more alert kooks that recognized what we were up to.

I remember we refused an ad from the Consolidated Vultee Company that was printed in all the other magazines. It showed the shadow cast across the American scientist at his work, or an engineer at his work, by a big boot with a red star on it. I went out to the Consolidated Vultee plant a month or two afterward and went in to talk to the advertising manager, and found this rabid nut. We had our problems, but generally speaking, most people thought that if they saw it in *Scientific American,* it was science. I'm firmly of the belief—having been educated by Bob Merton—that science is a social enterprise and is a consensus-forming enterprise. The habit of forming consensus gets carried over into questions of value and questions of judgment about politics and the rest. The scientific community does have consensus on the big questions. There was just no question that the scientific community had a consensus on the atomic weapon. The press gives equal time to Edward Teller and to the community, so it looks as if there's a debate among experts. There *isn't* any debate. *Scientific American* never gave Teller the time of day on that or all the other questions. We found the consensus of the community, and that's what we expressed in our pages.

INTERVIEWERS: It's interesting, then, so *Scientific American* was really meant to represent a consensus that was forming, in a particular sector of American society?

PIEL: Yes, the scientific community. This takes us to a subject that is really very serious with respect to the future of science. *Scientific American* gave a lot of space and effort, including September issues, to the whole question of how science was to be financed.

I guess the last piece we published on the subject was written by Warren Weaver. Warren made the pure point that great science is done by the scientist motivated by his own curiosity, that we can be sure that if we support able people in the investigation of the things that interest them, that we're going to have good science. Therefore the funding of science ought to come from the National Science Foundation and not from the mission-oriented agencies. There was a debate about this back there in the fifties, but by the time we got to the sixties, the scientific community had been bought. I was the lone voice on this issue—outside the pages of the magazine. Nobody ever paid any attention to me, and I was regarded as an eccentric.

The National Science Foundation was getting less than 5 percent of the total flow of federal money. It was wonderful guys in the Congress like Mim Daddario and Carl Russell from the South, and Henry Reuss from Wisconsin, who were worried about what this kind of financing was doing to the universities. The man who really defined it for me was Mr. Conant. I heard him say, when he came back from Germany and resumed his presidency [at Harvard], "They came to me and asked if it was all right to take federal money. So long as it isn't classified research, I told them, go down there and get all you can, and say no more to me about it."

The model agency, the one with more bucks and with first-rate management, was the Office of Naval Research. It was in business making grants to the universities before the National Science Foundation was established. Alan Waterman, the first director of the NSF, came from the Office of Naval Research.

So physics was financed by the military, and biology was financed by the health agency. The result is that we have to feed the world now, and botany has disappeared from our universities, except the oldest and best endowed, and ones with money reserved for or restricted to botany, like Harvard and Yale. But the reason the New York Botanical Garden now has one of the world's greatest herbaria is because Columbia and everybody else dumped their herbaria into the New York Botanical Garden.

INTERVIEWERS: I had never thought about this piece, about the parts of science that get defunded as well, and what the consequences are in the long term.

PIEL: Yes, I will grant that. I was always assured by scientists that the military never tried to motivate their work, that they were most generous and wise and open about the relevance of the purest sort of research to their mission. But the fact is that, with the money coming from those two big sources, there were great big gaps in the 180-degree horizon that would have been filled with the freely motivated enterprise of scientists financed by an agency that would have respected the integrity of the university and the rest. Detler Bronk [president of the National Academy of Science in the 1950s and 1960s] was all in favor of—

INTERVIEWERS: Getting money wherever you can get it.

PIEL: But one of his successors, Philip Handler—who had gotten to be very unpopular because he had his own ideas—had in his lower left-hand drawer a piece of legislation that would have created a congressional endowment for the support of not only science, but in support of the universities. Something on the order of the British university grants committee, which really was, until Maggie Thatcher screwed it up, administered by the community and universities. They ran it on a competitive basis. They would say, it appears that the country should have better instruction in French, so we're ready to fund three departments—that sort of thing.

INTERVIEWERS: The irony is that the United States prides itself on science, but it's all imported. There hasn't been very much great homegrown science except in a couple of areas.

PIEL: There hasn't been, and the reason for it is the lousy mode of the support of science. John Pierce, who was one of the principal scientists at Bell Labs, wrote a fine piece that appeared in *Science* years ago on what had happened to the teaching of science at MIT—not only to the teaching of science, but to research. The funding of enterprises that were of interest to the exotic tastes of the military meant a real breakdown of the electrical engineering department at MIT. This country has only one manufacturer left of heavy electrical machinery. That's General Electric, and that's a busted technological enterprise. At the end of the war, a guy named Ralph Cordiner became chairman, and he broke the company up into ten profit centers. Five years later, there was no laboratory. What had been a laboratory on a par with Bell Labs was gone. And Bell Labs is gone now, with the breakup of the telephone company. It's all over. Think of what came out of there. Not only the whole computer industry, the solid state electronics revolution, but glass fibers with photons instead of electrons carrying messages. Those two fundamental developments came out of that industrial laboratory.

INTERVIEWERS: We've been speaking about *Scientific American,* which is obviously the center of your interest and the forum that you developed. But there are recently a bunch of other places where science reporting gets done, and they range very widely in quality and quantity, and the kind of audiences they're looking for. I listen to National Public Radio all the time, and always love their science blips, but there's everything from the *Utne Reader* and the *Whole Earth Catalog* on the one hand, to *Discover* and *Omni* and the talk shows even cover this stuff.

PIEL: That flurry of science magazines did not have anything to do with public interest in science, it had to do with the recognition by publishers that *Scientific American* was selling more than one thousand pages of advertising.

INTERVIEWERS: You have a very firm sense of the political economy of science, that's an absolutely crucial aspect of what supports it or doesn't support it.

PIEL: Now the National Science Foundation is getting billions, and what's it for? They've been establishing these monstrous applied science institutes at all the universities.

INTERVIEWERS: The university just develops ways to steal the money and try to divert it to whatever, but they're always suborned.

PIEL: I guess David Baltimore and Harvey Lodish and the third member of that triumvirate, those were socially responsible people with a notion of the relationship of science and the big world, and that's the generation between me and the younger ones. David Baltimore is a fine casualty of the system in the support of science—that ferocious, competitive, grant-seeking system.

The basic principle is that the university is supposed to be the institution that nurtures learning and that establishes the judgment of who is qualified for tenure, etc. Mr. Conant recognized the importance of the invisible college when he set up the ad hoc committees and insisted that the department put itself under review of its peers in other universities.

But the universities are now really thoroughly fragmented communities. Only a few people, like Richard Lewontin, will get up on his hind legs and police error in other departments. Everyone tiptoes around that: "Oh, that's their department, that's their problem, that's their work!" Lewontin has the conscience and guts to raise hell with Ed Wilson's sociobiology and Richard Hernstein's racism.

It's not a community of scholars. I don't think any university faculty can afford to walk to work, because the presence of the university raises real estate values all around it, and compensation of professors is such that they—

INTERVIEWERS: They move further and further into the suburbs in order to stay at their jobs.

PIEL: So they come in from Belmont to Cambridge now, and I guess Ken Galbraith has one of his largest assets in his house at 17 Francis Street, which he bought for maybe $1500.

Contemporary Challenges to Science?

INTERVIEWERS: We keep talking about all these challenges and the questions of antiscientific perspectives, and you named a bunch of places where it's UFOs or the Olin Foundation or the fundamentalists, but more recently there's also been a movement among some intellectuals which has been quite antiscience, or at least challenging of the universals in science.

PIEL: What's this ridiculous book from England? It was very solemnly published here, I think, by Doubleday. This is high-level intellectual crap that has been around for years. I mean, that was around when we were starting the magazine. It was that science is in charge of the means, and the humanities are in charge of the ends. That's the understanding, and that was the compromise that Darwin made with the bishops. They can be in charge of the here-after, and—

INTERVIEWERS: We'll take care of the rest. I was thinking, [challenge] comes from a lot of different places, but certainly even within the history of science there have been people who have been writing about the partial nature of scientific knowledge.

PIEL: Don't forget that Arthur Koestler was around. And I regard Kuhn as an anti-intellectual. I was able to point out to Bob Merton that there is, in the writings of Charles Sanders Peirce, a statement that the ground of the truth in science is the consensus of the people who have thought hardest and worked hardest at the question. So Mr. Kuhn takes this as "we're not really getting at the truth here"—that there is something grander out there than the consensus, which is all we have. When you triangulate on him, that's where he comes from. He's pretty arrogant, and he takes a kind of a superior position with respect to scientists. He knows what they're about because he has a more—

INTERVIEWERS: Philosophical point of view?

PIEL: Yes. From a higher level of truth. This issue has been with us, and always will continue to be with us. That's why I loved Bronowski and his writings on these questions. In his *Science and Human Values,* his first point is that it's an ethical decision to seek the truth; secondly, then, you're involved in a polity of people who are engaged in rational discourse with you, so it requires mutual respect and equality of the right to talk and so on. He builds a whole sociology, a whole political theory from it, which is splendid. So did Jacques Monod in his beautiful address to the Collège de France when he took his chair.

INTERVIEWERS: This was the first round of battle with Nietzschean skepti-cism. But at the same time, universities are almost the only place left where pursuing knowledge is admissible. The direction they've gone in is really quite unfortunate and driven by a lot of economic and political decisions, but none-theless they remain almost the only place where some kinds of relatively clear critical inquiry can take place.

PIEL: It's very hard for scientists now. There's no money in departments that are pursuing animal behavior, for example. Biology departments want molecular people, because that's where the money is. The action, that's where the genome action is.

INTERVIEWERS: But the critiques of science are actually on target about this dimension. That is, the segmentation of knowledge is driven by concerns other than those of learning about the world. They have always been artifi-cially divided up, but they are very seriously divided now in ways that—

PIEL: It's what society is doing to this enterprise. And the scientists them-selves are culpable, because they were delighted—I heard them say, "I'd rather deal with three granting agencies in Washington than with my dean."

The dean of the faculty of arts and sciences wants to steal all the overhead money. The artist at this was Mac Bundy. There's a man who just left calamity behind him everywhere he's been. Right now it's everywhere. At Harvard, as dean he used the unrestricted money that came attached to science grants, the overhead, to inflate the social science department, but not as badly as the humanities department. He was a very popular dean because anyone who came to him had his problem solved, because he had the money. Five years after he retired and went off to Washington with the Kennedy administration, there was a committee headed by a classmate of mine, a professor of history, to clean up, to cut down these departments, because just about that time— yes, it was 1967—Lyndon Johnson really brought the whole party to an end. He said, "We've got to have results." That served them right. What they had been doing was selling results to Washington. So Lyndon said, "We're going to have results."

For poor Lyndon Johnson, it was Mac Bundy who assured him, "We can have guns and butter, too."

The Mansfield Amendment kept the Pentagon from spending money on basic research; had to prove the relevance of it to their mission. This meant that the National Science Foundation got all that junk that the Pentagon had been financing prior to that. That was when the National Science Foundation began to grow, because then the Mansfield Amendment stopped the Pentagon from spending money the way it was spending it.

INTERVIEWERS: Can I ask you, what should scientific literacy look like in the coming years, say, in the year 2000?

PIEL: That's a terrible thing that happened to that Project 2061 [an AAAS project to establish scientific literacy for school children over the coming century].

You know that when you look at the total money going to the schools—this is something that people, Time, Inc. and General Electric were going to set up. They got the former head of the Federal Education Office, Francis Keppel, to head the company; they called it General Learning. They said, this country is spending (in those days) $100 billion a year on education. They didn't see that the country was spending only about $100 million on the content, and that there was no market there at all for General Learning.

A wonderful man named Jerrold Zacharias started the curriculum reform movement in the fifties. The National Science Foundation was charged by Congress with responsibility for science education, and Zacharias and his group made it real. They got money from NSF to establish the famous enterprise that brought modern science into the high schools for a few years.

Remember MACOS? "Man, a Course of Study"? That's what brought it to an end, because the fundamentalists were rampaging, that they were teaching evolution, they were teaching senilicide, they were teaching free love, wife swapping. The National Science Foundation was only too happy to get out of the business of education.

Zacharias did recognize, and his people did recognize, that you couldn't teach physics without a first-rate lab. They figured out the lowest cost type of lab you could have. What he did was to keep black boxes out of the picture. That brought the kid closer to the physical phenomena. He wasn't getting it through a black box he didn't understand.

Most of the money that was spent by the National Science Foundation in those days was spent on teacher institutes in the summer. Those were marvelous for burnout, and for reviving intellectual interest in the subjects that teachers were teaching. This is something that has to be kept going permanently. This could help our universities, to get them brigaded into doing something about public education, because that's what the whole movement was. It meant that the universities for that period of time (it was about a ten-year period) were involved in public education. Now they're not.

This AAAS project is just a catastrophe, because it hasn't touched the business of the school environment and the teaching of science and how it's done. Wonderful people tried to help the project. One was John Wilson, who had an enterprise he called "Science, a Process Approach" that had financing from the National Science Foundation. He was in the first group of advisors to that 2061 project, and they never got his message.

INTERVIEWERS: Is anything on the horizon?

PIEL: Just all making sure that students pass specified precut tests. Zacharias recognized testing as the menace that it was. His solution was to outflank it by creating a gigantic bank of test materials that could be responded to by children who were getting taught properly.

Coming to Scientific Consciousness

Our second interview was with William T. Golden, another leading figure in the post–World War II promulgation of science. Golden created the office of Science Policy Advisor under President Harry Truman, served as president of the American Museum of Natural History, and has been the long-term treasurer of the American Association for the Advancement of Science.

INTERVIEWERS: As I probably mentioned in the letter I wrote to you back last February, we're part of a larger project which is being organized by an anthropologist at Rice University named George Marcus, who has edited a series of volumes. The first two are now out, from the University of Chicago Press, thinking about themes in culture as we approach the millennium. It seemed to us, given the periods through which you have lived, that thinking about where science became important in your life would be interesting. You started with a classic liberal arts B.A. [from the University of Pennsylvania], went on to the Harvard Business School, and had a very successful career in the business world. You served in World War II. At what point did science become such a central focus?

GOLDEN: When I was a little boy, I loved tinkering with electrical things, chemical sets, erector sets—with encouragement, but no pressure, from my parents. I was born and brought up in New York City. My principal achievement was at age 13 when I got my ham radio operator's license. Station 2AEN. I don't know why, because my parents weren't especially interested in science one way or the other.

INTERVIEWERS: And the schools to which you went, did they encourage a scientific background?

GOLDEN: Well, they didn't discourage it. I was actively interested in it. They had a general science course, and I liked to hang around the lab after hours. We had a teacher there who was quite encouraging. But there was no active, particular role. I always had an interest in science on the periphery, and I thought of becoming a scientist. That's what I thought I would be. But in my senior year in college, when I had to make my mind up, at the University of Pennsylvania, I decided in the second half of my senior year. I had to decide what I was going to do. Maybe I wanted to go on to graduate school in English literature, especially Elizabethan poetry. In my junior year I was allowed to take a graduate school course in Shakespeare, and that turned me off, because that should be concerned with the beauty and the aesthetics of the poetry, but instead they were counting the commas in Shakespeare. So I ruled that out for graduate school. Biology interested me. I always thought I wanted to be a physicist. So I hadn't decided. I thought of going to law school, medical school. But I felt I wasn't going to be a first-class scientist because I really didn't like math. I wasn't bad in math, but I had no liking for it. So I thought, Well, I'll go to the Harvard Business School. I read a romantic story about Wall Street in some English course, and that seemed to be kind of interesting, so I thought, I'll go to the Harvard Business School, and then I'll go to Wall Street, and I'll be able to make some money, make some money in Wall Street to help me do other things. That's what I did, and that's the way it worked out.

I kept the interest in science always as a peripheral interest, and of course radio was a very consuming interest of mine, beginning at age eleven or twelve, anyway. I was fifteen when I discovered girls, and that diverted me from the radio.

INTERVIEWERS: Where did you go to high school?

GOLDEN: I went to the Columbia Grammar School, it's a private school in New York City, which was a boys school only at that time. Now it's coed.

I liked it at the time, although in retrospect I feel that I should have been more disciplined and required to do certain things, like pay more attention to solid geometry. I kept the interest in science all along, on the periphery. Then actively, thirty or so years ago, [I thought], I'd really like to go on with biology, and I started taking graduate school courses at Columbia, and some undergraduate courses. After quite a while, I built up a lot of credits. I noticed one day in the *Spectator* [the Columbia College newspaper] that some of the departments had relaxed their requirements to complete an M.A. in two years or one year or whatever. So I wrote a letter to Columbia, and I said, "Look at all these graduate school credits I've accumulated, how about an M.A. in biology?" Nothing happened for a month. Then, I got a letter back that said, "Send us $10 and we'll send you an M.A."

Yes. So I did, and they did. I went to commencement in 1979. It was real fun. That was forty-nine years after my bachelor's degree from the University of Pennsylvania. Anyway, I've kept an interest. When I was in the navy, I had an interest in engineering and science, the technological aspects of weaponry. And the navy had a very important influence, because heretofore I had been in small organizations. In the navy, I learned how a bureaucracy functions. I was learning about the military. It was a very influential and educational aspect of life for me, and I was at sea in the Atlantic and then in the Pacific, and in a wide variety of ships, but mostly I was in the Navy Department in Washington, the Bureau of Ordnance, which had to do with weapons, and the Chief of Naval Operations, which had to do with war plans, and I got a very broadening experience. I did have an interest in how things worked, the torpedoes and the depth charges and other such things, and in fact I invented a device to improve anti-aircraft machine guns for training gunners. It was used in World War II and I was commended for it, with a ribbon.

INTERVIEWERS: I see you had a patent.

GOLDEN: After the war, U.S. Navy officials came and asked, "Would you like a patent?" I said, "That would be nice." So they got me a patent from the U.S. Patent Office. It's very handsome, it's got a red ribbon and a gold seal on it.

INTERVIEWERS: Wonderful.

GOLDEN: Very impressive. So I framed it, gave it to my mother, and after she died, I took it back again. As you can tell, I was rather pleased.

War and Science Policy

INTERVIEWERS: But the world that emerged after World War II was one in which science became very, very important, whether you think about it in terms of security and the cold war, or you think about it in terms of education and the building of technological expertise for large numbers of people who could work in new, developing fields. You obviously started to play some sort of a role in this idea of science policy. Where did that begin?

GOLDEN: Well, certainly it was self-evident and true that science and technology were crucial elements in World War II. It was real science. The atom bomb, that was real science. The bomb itself, that was engineering, but it's quite clear that science and technology were vital elements in the conduct and winning of World War II. And I had a little part in that, in the Bureau of Ordnance of the Navy Department, but it [the importance of science] became evident to the whole public, especially through the atom bomb. The government was very well aware, and the scientific community had been very deeply involved in the war effort through the Office of Scientific Research and Development, with many ramifications. That spread to the public and to the press, and my own increasing awareness came about through my becoming one of the members of the staff of the Atomic Energy Commission, which was of course an expression of my interest in the field.

It came about through a navy connection whom I had not known in Wall Street, but I knew in the navy, who was asked to become a member of the first commission. That was Rear Admiral Lewis Strauss. He called me and asked me in a courtly way, "Bill, do you think I ought to accept this appointment? And if I do, will you come down for say three months and help us get it organized?" "Well, of course," I said, "and I would be just delighted, excited to come down." Nothing could have been more exciting at that time, in mid-1946. The Atomic Energy Commission law [the McMahon Act] had just been passed. So I went and stayed there for three years—not three months, but for three years. My wife Sibyl and I still had our little house in Georgetown, so it was very easy to do, and I got to know a large part of the scientific community, the leading scientific community, which had been very much involved in World War II war efforts. So I got to know the scientific community well, read the journals, some of them, and so on. So that gave me an exposure to the knowledge in the community, and also to the executive branch of the federal government, and to some extent the legislative branch. The executive branch, the presidential part, I got to know very well. You get on mailing lists: "Why are you calling me? You found my name on some list or in some book?" That's the way these things happen. I was asked to become a member of the American Association for the Advancement of Science's Investment and Finance Committee. Then I was asked to go on their Committee on the Public Understanding of Science. And then, when the man who had been the treasurer of the AAAS (Dr. Paul Klopsteg), who I knew, who had been the number two man in the National Science Foundation, retired at age 80, I succeeded him as treasurer. The treasurer serves at the pleasure of the board and at his own pleasure. So I've been there a long time, some twenty-five years so far.

I recall a wide range of scientists, including social scientists as well as the physical and biological sciences. Then, taking the courses at Columbia, I came to know the Columbia department faculty and some fellow graduate students very well, in the biology department and to a lesser extent in the art history department—they being of particular interest.

I probably should go on. Thus I became known in the executive branch. After I left the job of assistant to Commissioner Strauss of the AEC, the Korean War broke out in the summer of 1950, and I was called one day by an assistant director of the Bureau of the Budget. My wife and I were traveling out west for the summer, and I was told that President Truman was under pressure to consider what to do about organizing the government scientific activities in the light of the Korean War breaking out, and the memories of World War II. Would I come back to Washington and advise President Truman about what he ought to do? There were pressures from legislative sources, some of the congressmen and senators, among others. That sounded kind of interesting, and I came back and I did that, and that's when I conceived the idea of an advisor to the president and the President's Science Advisory Committee. That was a very interesting undertaking. I talked to large numbers of people from the scientific and governmental community, some of whom I'd known, and some I hadn't, but in this job I could meet anybody I wanted to. I was also asked to advise President Truman and the director of the budget on what ought to be done about the appointments and initial program for the National Science Foundation. The foundation had been enacted but had not yet been organized nor any of the people appointed, so I played a role in that.

Thus, I got more and more exposure to the federal government and to the scientific community, and my interest increased. This was further fostered by my service as treasurer on the board of directors of the American Association for the Advancement of Science, the other members being scientists.

INTERVIEWERS: When we went to public school in the fifties, the idea of what you were helping to organize at NSF was very important. NSF itself created a sense that "we're going to need a scientifically trained labor force, and that children need science education in a very big way." We imbibed that as part of our public school education, and something about the rationality of being able to solve problems this way was an uplifting orientation.

There was no question then of creationists. Or for that matter the idea that somehow our technology had so polluted the planet that we couldn't even solve our own problems with the same methods.

GOLDEN: Atomic scientists were great heroes. Robert Oppenheimer was a great hero. Now people are worried about the radiation effects, by-products. They see ghosts everywhere and worry about mysterious hazards, without adequate knowledge or ability to quantify risks.

Science as Religion, Science and Religion

INTERVIEWERS: Yes. What do you think is behind it, both the efflorescence of the scientific worldview, and also its criticism? Do you have any thoughts about that?

GOLDEN: Well, I have a feeling that it may go back to some very fundamental aspects of human nature, and the role of religion versus the role of
science. Science in a way can be looked on as one expression of the religious
gene in a romanticized way. It's much easier for people to believe in some all-
powerful god who directly or indirectly controls everything, and therefore
may be not understandable in rational terms. To believe that there's a god and
that your fate will be determined by your relationship to the principles of the
religious faith that you believe in is much easier than to understand the laws
of physics. I think it's evident that people are deeply interested in religion.
Fundamentalism in all faiths seems to be flourishing; and, in a crude kind of
way, it's easier to believe in magic than it is to believe in logic. Logic has a
relentlessness about it, but magic is believed to be a miracle and therefore
anything becomes possible. I think it's evident that only people with a high
level of education have the capacity to understand, rather than to just accept
unknowingly the findings of science; and the unknowns are greater than the
knowns. I think people would rather say a prayer than to recognize the proba-
bility or improbability that radiation will cure their cancer. I'm not saying it's
good or bad, I'm just trying to describe the behavior. I think for human beings
it's appealing to believe that there's some superior power to which one can
perhaps pray and perhaps get results, even though the results often are not
consistent with the prayers or the virtue of the prayers. Still, that hope is there,
and so I think a lot of people rely primarily on religion, even if they are fascinated by science and technology—and, in some instances, scared by it.

Certainly their lives are very greatly and increasingly affected by technology. Then there's something else: there are 5.25 billion people in the world.
How many of those do you think have had the equivalent of a college education? Suppose it's a million or several million; this is an insignificant fraction
of 1 percent. Unless one has a high level of education, one can't possibly understand the scientific principles involved, and therefore one must have re-
course only to having faith or religion or to a know-nothingism. I don't see
how one can expect more than a tiny fraction of the population of the world,
even in an advanced society like our own, to have faith in science.

INTERVIEWERS: In the fifties, it seemed that more people [had faith in sci-
ence] and the idea that you could have an impact on and instill this way of
thinking to young kids. And from there, not everybody, as you said, was going to end up as a Harvard zoology professor, but some percentage of those
people would work technically and comfortably within a worldview of science. I think that was the way we were all being trained, again speaking very
personally from within that generation, which took the benefits of the kind of
work that came in after World War II. And something has changed.

There's another side, also. There's a lot of pressure on the NSF and other
scientific funding organizations to produce less basic research but more appli-

cation, which is I think where this same battle is being fought out on another front.

GOLDEN: That may be, yes. That may well be, and for the same kind of reason that emphasizes applications rather than basic science. The Congress wants to see useful results with the money it appropriates. This gets to the whole matter of hedonism, on a short-term view that our society increasingly is moving toward. That's a topic in itself. The long-term view of things is at a great disadvantage nowadays, because people want to see promptly the results of what they're paying for. You know more about it than I do, but it seems evident why the public attitude has lessened from adulation to skepticism about science. One thing is, there have been some technological disasters, like at Three Mile Island, which wasn't actually very bad, but which gives science a bad mark in the press and with the public.

INTERVIEWERS: Compared to Chernobyl, it looks like nothing.

GOLDEN: But Chernobyl is a real thing, and so people are very much afraid, understandably, of nuclear power. Nuclear power is a wonderful thing. You get something from nothing, and we have this breeder reactor; it was a really marvelous concept. It is and was a marvelous thing. People didn't worry about it, and the Atomic Energy Commission, I think with the best of intentions and the greatest of knowledge at the time, felt that the risks were quite acceptable and very small. I think the risks are much, much smaller of a nuclear power plant than the public now fears. Some of the public also has a general idea that they have plenty to fear from low-level radiation. If you use an electric blanket, are you going to die of cancer? Nobody can be absolutely certain, being under power lines and the like, but I think a vague fear has arisen. After World War II, with the winning of the war and with the involvement of the atomic bomb, in spite of the power and the benefits that came from that, including nuclear medicine and the use of isotopes in so many beneficial ways, there came Chernobyl and the fears of a disaster, which are very real. If a nuclear power plant blows up in some way or other, however unlikely it is, lots and lots of people are going to get killed. When I say fifty thousand people a year are killed by automobiles, do you want to rule the automobiles out, or if you knew in advance that fifty thousand people a year would be killed, or probably half a million or a larger number per year are hospitalized because of the automobile, would you have prevented the automobile from being developed? Well, I don't know, but it's a good question. But there is a big difference. Fifty thousand people killed by automobiles are killed in independent accidents, and one nuclear power plant blowing up would be a concentrated disaster. So there's a real difference.

But I think what's happened is that people have begun to see some of the negative factors and develop concerns in technology, and they've also found that scientists are human, and from the competition among scientists a certain amount of scientific fraud, which hasn't been very great, but the scientists are human. There has been some fraud, and it tends to discredit the scientific community disproportionately.

INTERVIEWERS: That was one of our questions. You know there's a big debate about scientific literacy. I notice this sort of concept has really come to the fore, in the same way that science policy or public information came to the fore, and I'm sort of wondering, do you have any sense of what scientific literacy really means, either culturally or pragmatically?

GOLDEN: I would think it means some knowledge of basic scientific principles, some element of factual education. Several series of high-school textbooks that came out after World War II were very thoughtfully prepared. So I think there's available some basic knowledge, and there's also some sense of what the scientific method is, and the rational kind of thinking, thinking in terms of probabilities and not just as everything being black and white. So I think public understanding of science involves some facts, and some sense of scientific thought. Now, what has happened in the schools, I don't really know. Certainly it's clear that, from superficial observation, that there's not much science required in college courses in most places, certainly less than used to be. I think that the emphasis has dropped in the New York City school system; that's my impression, also. So one might ask why did the interest arise in the first place, and I think that's clear. I think that's clear because of the vital role that science and technology played in the winning of World War II and then there were science heroes. I think people tend to accept the idea that, for example, a particle accelerator would be a good thing, a general feeling that science is good for you. Then of course, that was quite a bit before Chernobyl. That was a dramatic example, I suppose, among other things, there's the ins and the outs, and those in the scientific community who are not on the inside and are critical of some of those who were on the inside leading edge, one might say, and that tends to sell newspapers. I'm just continuing to ramble here. Consider the UFOs. Many people believe in the UFOs; that says something about the human mind.

INTERVIEWERS: When you spoke about religion before, you spoke as if religion and science were very different worldviews, and maybe oppositional to one another, and that was certainly how I was brought up. I was brought up that there was science and there was superstition, and that's sort of in the family I came from, people were very clear about that. And yet when you look in the world, life is more complex. Many scientists are in fact religious.

GOLDEN: Yes.

INTERVIEWERS: And it's possible to be deeply practicing some aspects of certain faiths, and also be very, very involved with science and its benefits, or its burdens. So the role of religion is due for another rethinking because so much of the way we thought had to do with the way in which essentially science has replaced religion as a worldview, but in fact it coexisted in very complex and sometimes uneasy ways for a very long time. Did you think about religion in relation to worldview or science when you were growing up, or was this not an important part of your family background?

GOLDEN: I don't think I thought about the relationship between the two. I know that I had my bar mitzvah one week and passed the technical and code examinations for a ham radio transmitting license a week or so later. The latter was more important to me than the former, but I didn't question that I ought to be doing the bar mitzvah part. It didn't have a deep effect on me, going to an Orthodox synagogue, and I'm glad I have that background, because I am very strongly conscious of the Jewish cultural and ethical tradition. And I'm glad that other people observe the rituals, because somehow there's an artistic and traditional quality to it all. But ritual observance doesn't appeal to me as such.

INTERVIEWERS: I had wondered whether there was a substantial number of people in the thirties who became scientists just before World War II and just after that, but who came from very strong ethnic backgrounds, probably immigrant parents, who found in science or in scientific communities an alternative kind of American life? Does this correspond to the realities for people you knew?

GOLDEN: I'm not sure what you mean, but I think that the cosmopolitan aspect of the scientific community is very real, it's very real certainly in all the physical and biological sciences. You'd know more about the social sciences. I would conjecture that the degree of religious faith is less among scientists than among nonscientists, even though many of them maintain a religious connection, and even have a religious faith at some point, but it is less strong than in the nonscientific community.

Notes

1. While World War II may represent a particular formation of its own, it should be seen as a further inflection of the Progressive Era's emphasis on science and expertise put to their service of a new and rational American "imaginary" (Faye Ginsburg, personal communication, 18 Nov. 1994).

2. Indeed, *Cyborgs and Citadels: Anthropological Interventions into Technohumanist Culture* is the name of a forthcoming collection (Downey, Dumit, and Traweek, eds.).

References

Escobar, Arturo. 1994. "Welcome to Cyberia." *Current Anthropology* 35 (3): 211–31.

Franklin, Sarah. 1993. "Postmodern Procreation." *Science as Culture* 3, no. 17: 522–61.

Hess, David. 1992. "The New Ethnography and the Anthropology of Science and Tech-

nology." In *Knowledge and Society: The Anthropology of Science and Technology.*
Ed. David Hess and Linda Layne, 1–28. Greenwich, Conn.: JAI Press.

———. 1994. *Science and Technology in a Multicultural World.* New York: Columbia
University Press.

———. 1995. "If You're Thinking of Living in Science Studies: A Guide for Perplexed
Anthropologists." In *Cyborgs and Citadels: Anthropological Interventions into
Techno-Humanism.* Ed. Gary Downey, Joseph Dumit, and Sharon Traweek. Santa Fe:
School of American Research Press.

Layne, Linda. 1992. "Of Fetuses and Angels: Fragmentation and Integration in Narratives of Pregnancy Loss." In *Knowledge and Society: The Anthropology of Science
and Technology.* Ed. David Hess and Linda Layne, 29–58. Greenwich, Conn.: JAI
Press.

Lewenstein, Bruce V. 1989. "Magazine Publishing and Popular Science after World
War II: How Magazine Publishers Tried to Capitalize on the Public's Interest in Science and Technology." *American Journalism* 6 (Fall): 218–34.

———. 1992. "The Meaning of 'Public Understanding of Science' in the United States
after World War II." *American Journalism* 9 (Winter): 45–68.

Martin, Emily. 1994a. *Flexible Bodies: Tracking Immunology in American Culture
from the Days of Polio to the Age of AIDS.* Boston: Beacon Press.

———. 1994b. "Anthropology and the Cultural Study of Science: Citadels, Rhizomes,
and String Figures." Typescript.

Rabinow, Paul. 1992a. "Artificiality and Enlightenment: From Sociobiology to Bioso-
ciality." In *Incorporations.* Ed. Jonathan Crary and Sanford K. Winter, 234–52. New
York: Zone.

———. 1992b. "Severing the Ties: Fragmentation and Dignity in Late Modernity." In
Knowledge and Society: The Anthropology of Science and Technology. Ed. David
Hess and Linda Layne, 169–90. Greenwich, Conn.: JAI Press.

Rapp, Rayna. 1994. "Heredity, or Revising the Facts of Life." In *Naturalizing Power:
Feminist Cultural Studies.* Ed. Carol Downey and Sylvia Yanagisako. New York:
Routledge.

Strathern, Marilyn. 1992. *Reproducing Reproduction: Anthropology, Kinship, and the
New Reproductive Technologies.* Manchester: Manchester University Press.

Traweek, Sharon. 1992. "Border Crossings: Narrative Strategies in Science Studies and
among Physicists in Tsukuba Science City, Japan." In *Science as Practice and Culture.* Ed. Andrew Pickering, 429–66. Chicago: University of Chicago Press.

———. 1993. "An Introduction to Cultural and Social Studies of Sciences and Technologies." *Culture, Medicine and Psychiatry* 17 (1): 3–25.

FORWARD: MEDIATIONS
IN PERILOUS STATES

DEBI DOES DEMOCRACY:
RECOLLECTING DEMOCRATIC VOTER EDUCATION IN THE ELECTRONIC MEDIA PRIOR TO THE SOUTH AFRICAN ELECTIONS

It is March 1994. South Africans of all races are preparing to vote in the first one-person, one-vote multiparty election in the country's turbulent history. Some-where—it could be a matchbox house in Soweto, outside Johannesburg, an avant-garde apartment overlooking Cape Town's Clifton Beach, a hut perched on a hill in KwaZulu Natal—a radio plays an advertisement in any one of South Africa's eleven languages. It is an advertisement with a difference: it is not selling washing powder or margarine, it is selling the idea that democracy can build a future:

Man's voice:	I am not a young man anymore. I have seen many things. And I have many stories to tell. Sometimes, I spend more time thinking about my past than about my future. Because I have eighty years of past to think about.

(Music up)
Lyrics:

> You are the people,
> You've built this land.
> It is your time now,
> The future's in your hands.

Man's voice:	Now, I think maybe the future looks more exciting than my past. More interesting. So I think I will spend more time thinking about that. Starting with my vote.
Voice-over:	We stand at the threshold of a new land. Now it is up to us. Let every vote be a building block. Let our tolerance and goodwill cement and unite our country. On the 27th and 28th of April, as the world watches, let us build a great nation. This message is brought to you by the business community. Business stands for building a great nation.

Woman's voice: DEBI—the Democracy Education Broadcast
                   Initiative.

Introducing DEBI

DEBI—the Democracy Education Broadcast Initiative—was a voter and democracy literacy campaign conceived of as a partnership between representatives of South African civil society and the South African Broadcasting Corporation (SABC).[1] Like many groundbreaking initiatives, DEBI was born more
out of necessity than foresight. The necessity was essentially the historical lack
of credibility of the SABC. Long known as His Master's Voice for the syco-
phantic stance it took toward successive National Party governments, the
SABC, like many other structures in postapartheid South Africa, began the
painful process of "transformation" from 1990—the year in which previously
banned parties, including the African National Congress (ANC) were legal-
ized, political leaders (including Nelson Mandela) were freed, and South Africa began to claw its way back into the international family of nations.

A key moment in this transition was the appointment of a new governing
board of the SABC, a process which was the culmination of a drawn out campaign by left-wing organizations to "free the airwaves." The first fully representative board was appointed after precedent-setting public hearings on nom-
inees. I was one of the original twenty-five persons appointed, and subsequently
became a member of the board subcommittee on News and Election Coverage.
It was in this capacity that I became involved in voter education.

Despite its shortcomings, DEBI proved to have at least two redeeming qualities: it provided solid and trustworthy democracy and voter education to tens
of millions of people, and equally importantly, it forged the possibilities of
future cooperative ventures between the SABC and outside interest groups. In
this chapter I have attempted to uncover the history, motivations, purposes, and
principles of DEBI, to fairly evaluate its failures and shortcomings, and to ap-
praise (and praise) its successes.

The purpose of the work is two-fold: first, to record an enormously interesting if frustrating period in our South African history; and second, to serve as a
case study for future communication campaigns, be they voter education for
the forthcoming local elections tipped to take place in September 1995, civic
education in a more general sense, or even primary health care programs. Many
of the precepts remain the same: the lessons we learned from the interaction of
the broader "civil society" with the management of the SABC, the formats
which were successful and those that were not, and the simple logistics of
funding, can usefully be applied to "social marketing" communications in the
future.

Most of the pieces in this collection are based on single interviews. I have
chosen to do something slightly different. DEBI was at heart a communal ef-

fort. Some have identified this as its chief weakness. For me, it was its greatest achievement. For the first time, the SABC, hitherto a colossal symbol of control and authoritarianism, impenetrable to outside interest groups, joined in a partnership with disparate people representing varying interests and ideological standpoints, to produce a massive voter education campaign ahead of the April 1994 election. Hundreds of hours of radio and television material were aired, on three television channels, fourteen radio stations, in eleven different languages.

As the chairperson and coordinator of DEBI, I still feel too close to the process to assess it coherently. Instead, in an effort to recreate the story of DEBI from multiple angles, I have integrated interviews with people who were closely involved in different capacities. Much of the discussion around radio is sourced from two separate round-table encounters: one, a chat show broadcast on the independent Durban radio station, *Capital Radio,*[2] the other, an end-of-campaign assessment of DEBI undertaken by the DEBI Natal Radio Forum.[3] I transcribed both of these meetings verbatim and have blended them thematically into the present work.

"An Incredibly Cumbersome Process": Setting Up a Legitimate Structure

Nongovernmental organizations (NGOs) had begun preparation on voter education in 1993, raising most of the money from philanthropic trusts and foundations outside the country. Preeminent among these were Matla Trust, seen by many as an ANC thinktank, although they explicitly denied direct partisan ties with the latter organization. Project Vote, based in the Centre for Development Studies at the University of the Western Cape, was another important player, as was IDASA, the Institute for a Democratic Alternative in South Africa. All three of these bodies, together with a host of organizations with similar left-wing leanings, who were able to mount smaller campaigns, came together under a single umbrella organization, IFEE, the Independent Forum for Electoral Education. Voter education fell under the auspices of the media department of Matla Trust, headed by Barry Gilder, who was also the coordinator of IFEE.

Organizations concerned with voter literacy appreciated the pivotal role of the broadcast media at an early stage in their campaigns. Preliminary negotiations took place between the SABC and the IFEE in May 1993. However, it was recognized that while IFEE represented a substantial portion of organizations in the field of voter and democracy education, other groups also wanted access to the airwaves. The solution mooted was to establish an integrated structure for all organizations concerned with voter literacy in broadcasting.

As may be expected, the process wasn't as neat or straightforward as this synopsis makes it sound. In fact, it was quite turbulent and wrought with misunderstanding and mistrust. A senior television news editor, André le Roux, who was pivotal in the SABC's preparation for the election, put it this way:

I think the crisis of legitimacy had everything to do with the SABC's track record. The SABC realized, and they—particularly the TV news department—realized very early, that voter education was going to be crucial [to the election]. What happened was that at that point internal structures were developed to actually look at this. That became known outside the corporation. The immediate response from NGOs was that voter education through the SABC, given its history and its legitimacy problem, was not going to work, if it was driven by the SABC [alone]. The SABC immediately accepted that point, but was adamant that it was going to be part and parcel of that process, because first, they had a duty, a public duty to do so, and second, they had the inherent expertise and means to do so.

I asked Barry Gilder of Matla Trust what he understood as the "crisis of legitimacy" that faced the SABC at the time, and why, in his opinion, it was not possible for the SABC to "go it alone" on voter education.

Well at the time when we, as IFEE, were talking to the SABC,—it was just a few months before the new board was appointed, at that time, obviously there was a lot of concern, and not just as far as voter education was concerned, but generally, as to what role the SABC would play in the forthcoming election, given that it was still run in the old way, that is the way in which it was seen to support the previous government. There was a lot of concern at the time in voter education circles, arising from the discussions we had with the SABC up until then, that the SABC lacked the sensitivity for voter education, but were trying to go it alone. We were concerned that given the credibility, or lack of it, of the SABC, especially among the majority of people who had not voted before, that it could create problems if people saw voter education as coming from a body they couldn't trust, given the role that the SABC had previously played in trying to persuade people to participate in previous local authority elections. So it was really very tricky. Nobody knew for sure, but there was a strong feeling that the SABC didn't have the credibility to do voter education alone.

André le Roux continued his account of the early negotiations:

What happened then was that the Matla Trust, and Barry Gilder in particular, started off by approaching individual radio services and individual television channels to make airtime available at no cost for Matla Trust material.
On television they entered into a negotiation for a thirteen part dramatized series, *Kululeka.* Management in the SABC, and particularly in TNP (Television News Productions),[4] then basically said to itself, that if the SABC had a legitimacy crisis, it was going to be further exacerbated if, should what was

seen to be an ANC front was allowed to drive voter education alone in the SABC. We recommended to the group executive at the time that a much broader approach be adopted. We entered into discussions with the Matla Trust, and Barry Gilder in particular, and said to him that we cannot go with the Matla Trust alone. We had to involve other agencies and other NGOs in the process, in addition to the SABC being a fifty-percent partner in this exercise. That was resisted—heavily.

Mistakes were made on the part of the SABC where they attempted to conjure up, or find opposition in NGOs to the Matla Trust–driven voter education program. Names of institutions, particularly from the "establishment" side, were listed in opposition to the "liberation movement"–oriented NGOs. What happened again was this further brought about problems in this process. Through bad management, and through bad tactics on the part of the SABC, there had developed a situation in which there was a "them" and a "them" and "us"—a sort of triangular problem with legitimacy.

Barry Gilder, in turn, recounted the events related by André from his perspective. I asked him what he remembered about Matla and IFEE's first discussions with the SABC, prior to the establishment of DEBI.

Well, the early discussions centered around accessing airtime on radio. At that stage we were talking to Radio Active on a purely commercial basis.[5] The discussions were fairly positive. It was really only about Matla's ads on SABC, but they expected us to pay for the airtime.[6] Ourselves and our donors refused to pay for what we saw as airtime for a public service on a public broadcaster. That was really what led to the beginning of discussions with the SABC management.

At the same time we also had begun to approach CCV about *Kululeka,* and while some people were enthusiastic about it, we also found a lot of obstruction.[7] One of the responses we kept getting at a certain point, during the first part of 1993, was that the SABC was setting up a structure which was going to oversee the whole election coverage, and voter education was one leg of that structure. When we began formally to discuss with the SABC management early in 1993, right up to speaking with Wynand Harmse, their main concern, which emerged after a while, was a feeling that IFEE was biased toward the ANC's voter education project.[8] And that's really where we got stuck. The SABC's management tried—it seemed to us—to set up an alternative forum by engaging with other bodies which we felt were more sympathetic to them. And that is really where we got stuck until the new board came into being.

André le Roux's account concurs with that of Barry Gilder's:

In the end it was necessary to get the board involved. At least part of the board. A wise decision was then taken to canvass all possible NGOs on the issue, and in doing so, making it an open-ended and transparent exercise. Invitations were sent out for participation in this process.

It was as a member of the board Subcommittee on News and Election Coverage that I first became involved in the SABC's contribution to voter education. A series of advertisements on television and radio calling for NGO participation in the process was aired. Approximately one hundred and fifty responses were received. André:

Eventually the board subcommittee elected to oversee this process chose an initial forty-two NGOs from a list of about one hundred and fifty. An initial gathering of these NGOs was arranged. Even at that meeting, the split between Matla Trust family of NGOs and non-Matla Trust NGOs was evident. In order to bridge that, the SABC, through its board intervention, extended the membership so as to create an approximate balance between the "establishment" NGOs and the other "liberation-oriented" NGOs. The membership was expanded to fifty-one.

The criteria for selection onto the steering committee included absolute non-partisanship, a wide representation with a broader community, and a non-commercial interest and expertise in voter education. Part of the reason for increasing the membership of the Steering Committee was to redress the balance between religious representation. The initial applications had a fair number of Christian religious groups represented, and the board subcommittee made a point of initiating affiliation by Moslem, Hindu, and Jewish groupings. André:

It was an incredibly cumbersome process, it took an initial two-month period in effect before a structure through a steering committee and a working committee to have a system set up which legitimized itself in the process, rather by need and necessity than by design. [The committees] started getting on with the work once they realized that they were up against time, and the legitimacy problem dissipated in view of what was necessary to be done. But it was never a comfortable situation. Which made for good debate; which made for good checks and balances in the process, which in turn made for fair to good control over what went out on the air. So the legitimacy problem was dealt with in process, rather than a once-off fixing up or attempts to gerrymander a structure.

Just to sum that up, I think it is fair to say that it was crucial to arrest attempts by individual movements and NGOs who had succeeded in hogging all available financing, particularly international financing. It was crucial not only for the legitimacy of voter education, but of the election itself. There were strong indications early on that voter education on the SABC would be intensely monitored. There was even the chance that if it wasn't controlled, and if it wasn't well managed to ensure its independence and strictly educational character, that the SABC, irrespective of whether it was driven by NGOs, would have developed another credibility crisis slap-bang in the middle of the election, which could severely have hampered the election process itself.

So through providence of some design and some ham-handed management, it worked. I do think that at the end of the day, the stalling of the process by management, until such time as most people got on board, was crucial to the legitimacy of voter education by the electronic media, particularly by the SABC.

Structuring Democracy

The structure of the DEBI initiative was complex. A news and election sub-committee of the board acted as the liaison between DEBI and the SABC's board. From this body, three members were drawn: myself, as chairperson of DEBI, and two alternates: Billy Modise, of Matla Trust, and Herman Bailey, of the Rural Foundation. Both these bodies were independently accommodated on the steering committee, which represented the broad membership of "civil society." Because of its unwieldy size, a smaller executive committee, the working group, was set up and was comprised of fourteen voting members: six from the steering committee, six from the management of the SABC, together with two board members, the DEBI chairperson and an alternate. Later in the process, further groupings were added to deal with the day-to-day production and screening decisions. These were the television and radio ad hoc groups, which were made up of loosely associated individuals from both the steering committee and SABC management. Further ad hoc groups for research and publicity subsequently came into being. As their name indicate, the ad hoc groups had no formal structure or voting powers, and varied in membership at different times of the campaign. They acted as advisory groups to the working group, but in effect, much of the real work was done in these forums. To further facilitate the process, two full-time producers, one for television and one for radio, were also employed.

A good example of the preoccupation with legitimacy at this point in the campaign is illustrated by the elaborate (and acrimonious) arrangements made around the secretariat. Given the fraught birth of DEBI, independence from direct control by any member organization was seen to be an essential criterion for the legitimacy of the whole project. To this end, a separate tripartite secretariat representing both the SABC and the organizations within the NGO sector was established. The offices of DEBI were located on the twenty-eighth floor of the SABC's Radio Park, since this floor houses the offices of the SABC board, and was seen to be the symbolic locus of civil society within the corporation. A logo, letterhead, and fax cover were designed.

The SABC's telephone exchange began with the prefix 714. In order to disguise the fact that the offices were in the SABC building, separate telephone and fax lines carrying the 089 prefix, which can be used in any part of the country, were installed in place of the SABC's 714 code. Thus the telephone number was disassociated from the SABC and given an independent existence.

Beata Lipman, a long-time South African exile in London, where she had worked as a television documentary producer, returned home in 1990. On the steering committee she represented FAWO, the Film and Allied Workers Organization, which is a quasi-trade union coalition of left-wing filmmakers. Because of her television expertise, Beata was also seconded onto the television ad hoc group.

RUTH: You were involved simultaneously in a number of different areas of DEBI, and therefore you had the advantage of being able to the look at process from different angles. Do you just want kick off by talking to me a little about how you think that the process of setting up the working groups and the steering committees worked, and whether that was good idea. Should we have done it the way we did?

BEATA: I thought that the whole process of trying to involve civil society was a valuable one. The working groups clearly represented different facets of South African life, and I felt that the way we pressed to have some real powers, and not just be a sort of rubber stamp to the SABC was also useful. You know, there was an attempt to exercise some muscle, if you like. And then the idea of setting up Ad Hoc Groups which were organized to some extent on people's existing skills, was also correct.

Giving Shape to DEBI: The Principles and Targets of Democratic Education

From the outset, the purpose of the broadcast initiative was to be more than simply a vehicle for voter education. We wanted to promote education around *democracy*. Thus one of the first decisions taken by the working group was to style ourselves DEBI: the Democracy Broadcasting Education Initiative. Empowerment became a central concept in the programming.

From its inception, DEBI adopted as its main objective "the empowering of the electorate of South Africa to exercise its right to vote." Through a fairly protracted set of negotiations within the steering committee, a set of principles was drawn up.

We identified our target audience as those groups we saw as being particularly vulnerable, namely, women, youth in rural and urban areas, informal settlement dwellers, disabled people, and, later, the white right wing.

Relationship with the Independent Electoral Commission

Voter and democracy education in the broadcast media did not work in a vacuum. In preparation for the election, a matrix of statutory structures were devised. Primary among these was the Independent Electoral Commission, or IEC, which came into being as a result of extensive multiparty negotiations. The IEC was governed by an act of Parliament. Headed by a retired judge, Justice Johan Kriegler, it consisted of seven commissioners, each with their own portfolio, and a large and intricate structure beneath them. The IEC was charged with three primary duties: to prepare the logistics for the election; to provide and promote voter education; and to adjudicate as to whether the election was substantially free and fair, and, if so, declare it valid.

It was in its role as promoter of voter education that DEBI came into contact with the IEC. The relationship was a two-fold one: as the body which represented the multiparty interests of the state in the elections, the IEC was charged with financing voting education. This proved to be a very contentious point, which even at the time of writing (September 1994), remained unresolved. I will say more of this later. The second aspect related to the IEC's role in organizing the election, and laying down protocols and procedures for the actual voting process. Here, too, DEBI, in common with all other voter education bodies, experienced difficulties. I asked André le Roux how he recalled the situation:

RUTH: One of the weak areas in the whole DEBI initiative was the lack of proper cooperation and integration between what the IEC was doing, and what we were doing.

ANDRÉ: The IEC was only established two months after the SABC and DEBI had started the process of voter education. It was only established in the first week of January, literally about four months before the election, and it only got underway in the third week of January, after it had its first plenary session. It was only around the end of February before they could talk to us about voter education. And when they did talk to us—DEBI—they were fairly prescriptive from a very ignorant base. They were unable to carry out what was supposed to be a premier mandate on their part to provide voter education. The process got further stalled by their attempts to get control of a process which was already far advanced and underway, particularly as far as DEBI was concerned. What was crucial about it was that DEBI at that very point needed strong financial backing from the state—or from the ficus which was to be channelled through the IEC.

The other problem was that the IEC at a very late stage developed finality around the processes. This was not necessarily all their fault. The negotiations about how the elections should be formatted was ongoing while institutions like DEBI were trying to educate people how to vote. As a result, practical tuition on the voting process had to be stalled because DEBI and others ran the severe risk of informing people about a process which was not going to synchronize with or accurately depict the systems we eventually adopted in the voting areas, particularly in the confines of the polling stations. It was only in the last six weeks of the process that a clear, step-by-step indication of what the voting process would be was available.

This placed further pressure on DEBI and other institutions—particularly for reasons of production. The production of television programming is involved and fairly lengthy. It was only possible literally in the last three weeks of the campaign to educate people on the practical processes involved in voting.

However, DEBI in particular used the time while the IEC was trying to get its act together, and while it was trying to develop the processes through negotiation. More than anything else, this was DEBI's success, I would suggest: creating an understanding for the processes, the broad generic processes of democracy, rather than the specific practical guidance. If it wasn't for that—it would be difficult to prove it—I don't think that the specific IEC process would have been properly communicated in the short time that was available. So the broad-based democratic education, about democratic processes and about voting procedures, voter empowerment that type of thing, was well founded by the time we could start actually practically implanting the processes.

There were further problems. During the election time itself, that is, from the 26 April, literally from the word go, the IEC, as a result of its own practical problems, could not deliver the election in a way the electorate understood it was going to happen. Through the DEBI process, a culture of electoral tolerance was created—even the tolerance toward the IEC was a direct result of voter education programs. In other words, understanding the IEC's problems to a large extent could be attributed to the extent to which programs calling for electorate tolerance impacted on the public.

Commissioning and Planning Programs

The original intention of the DEBI was to act as a clearinghouse for campaigns and programs produced or commissioned by member organizations. In practice, the flow of material into DEBI, particularly on the radio side, was woefully inadequate to mount a campaign. It became clear that much of the material that was to be broadcast would have to be commissioned and produced by DEBI itself.

The guidelines that were accepted for the commissioning of the programs included the exhortation that the simple and straightforward language be used, bearing in mind the educational levels of the main target markets; that the content be scrupulously nonpartisan; that the tone of the programs be positive and future oriented, aimed at reconciliation; and that the topics, objectives, and learning points of all the programs be clear.

Faced with these objectives, it would have been very easy to fall into a didactic, boring mode of presentation. Thus it was stressed in the briefs to production houses, that both the radio and television programs should strive to capture the attention of the South African electorate through serious, well-researched voter education, enlivened with large doses of entertainment. A publicity release[9] issued in the middle of April 1994 enthused, education and entertainment "compliment one another to produce an effective message to the people of South Africa to make April 26, 27 and 28 a less painful affair and usher in and enjoy voting for a democratic new South Africa."

A guiding tenet in the initiative was that the programs would be produced at the highest creative quality. We were determined that people should *want* to watch and listen to our voter education programs. For this reason we designed the campaign around the media consumption habits of people as we found them, rather than attempting to prescribe "what was good for them." In order to be effective, voter literacy needed to be produced across formats. It also needed to fit the profile of the channel—this was particularly important on radio. Glen Masokoane, DEBI television producer, put it this way: "Soap opera is easy to get to people. In this instance we are proposing a television program that is going to be enjoyed by all South Africans regardless of color, creed, or complexion. Something the whole family can enjoy without feeling pity or not sure of where they belong within the South African image and culture."

Themes

DEBI set out to design an overall campaign structure for democracy and voter education on the electronic media of the SABC. The themes of the initiative emphasized political tolerance, the secrecy of the vote; and the importance of both the electorate and political parties of accepting the outcome of the election result. Barry Gilder reflected on how we set about identifying the campaign themes:

> Well, for me personally, and my constituency, it was a long, drawn-out process until DEBI got off the ground. From IFEE's side, we had developed fairly wide-ranging ideas as to how voter education should be conducted, including the issues and themes which should be covered. They were based not just on what we intended to do with the broadcast medium, but what we were already doing in the face-to-face voter education. So we came to the table, if you remember, with a set of ideas which were debated quite hotly—if I remember—and which, in broad terms were accepted in principle with a few changes. But really, the very first steering committee meeting of DEBI was a brainstorming session in which a lot of specific ideas were thrown around, which were later structured in subsequent working group meetings.

The campaign fell into three parts: motivation, education, and reassurance. In the first phases of the campaign, DEBI concentrated on motivating the electorate to take an interest in the election, and to interrogate the concept of democracy. The second phase was concerned with the logistics and mechanics of the practice of voting: who was eligible to vote and how to do it. The third phase identified the safeguards and precautions taken to protect the potential voter. The fourth, or postelection phase, actually began before the election took place and continued afterward. This phase concentrated on the reasonable expectations of a new order and the responsibilities which could be required of a new government.

In the television campaign, eight *macro themes* in the preparation of the voting public were identified. Each of these dealt with a number of subthemes, many of them repeated. The eight themes were arranged in a progressive narrative, starting from the most general and ending with the more specific. The eight themes were:

- Freedom of Choice

- What Is Democracy?

- Who Is Entitled to Vote?

- Meaning of the Vote

- Understanding Party Political Campaigns

- How to Vote on the Day

- Acceptance of the Results

- Postelection Concerns

It was initially planned that each theme would correspond to a core television production, as well as to a commissioned documentary, which would be featured for the two weeks of the theme. In practice, this neat symmetry went slightly awry toward to the end of the campaign. Owing to forced budgetary constraints (see below), some of the commissioned programs were curtailed, leaving us with the problem of juggling the schedule to use what was available to us. Another complicating factor was the unexpected changes in the Electoral Act, and vacillations on the part of the Independent Electoral Commission around a number of key issues in the voting procedures. Of particular importance was the late introduction of a second ballot for regional government; changes in the method of checking and marking identity documents; the extension of the voting days from one to two, and later to three; as well as uncertainty about the definition of those who were eligible for special votes. These and other uncertainties caused unexpected delays in the production of video material, and in some cases forced us to send back programs to the producers for modifications. As a result, the predetermined scheduling of programs fell out of sync, and the last four weeks took on a rather ad hoc, problem-solving approach.

Scheduling and Program Types

Much of the information in voter education was reinforced through constant repetition. Thus, in order to keep the series fresh and vibrant, DEBI commissioned inserts produced across genres and styles, featuring dramatic and documentary approaches, television formats including spots utilizing animation, puppetry, endorsements.

The core of the television campaign consisted of eight programs, produced both as five-minute-a-day serial formats and consolidated as twenty-four-minute "omnibus" programs, which when scheduled with back-and-front advertisement spots, filled a standard thirty-minute slot. This genre is discussed in some detail below. A series of twenty-six-minute instructional and documentary programs were commissioned, which were broadcast both in the evening and repeated in the day.

Each week of the campaign was labeled by a number counting backward, twenty to one, indicating the number of weeks left before the election. Thus, the week of the first DEBI broadcast was week 20 and the election week was week 1. After four weeks in which only spot adverts and commentaries emanating from member organizations were aired, the broadcasting of voter education began in earnest on 10 January, sixteen weeks before the election.

The Core Television Programs: Five-Minuters, Omnibuses

On television, each of the eight macro themes previously discussed was scheduled for two weeks. The core program format was the five-minute miniseries, broadcast on sequential weekdays. These programs were reedited to provide a twenty-four-minute omnibus program which was rebroadcast in a second language on the same channel that week. The following week the order was turned around, using the alternative language in the five-minuters and the omnibus.

By using all three television channels over a two-week period, each theme was broadcast in both the serial and consolidated in each of six languages. (A seventh language was accommodated by alternating productions in North Sotho and Tswana).[10] This scheduling pattern also ensured a fairly even spread over peak viewing times, taking into account audience-viewing patterns and preferences as far as possible. Early morning slots were valuable to the breakfast viewer, lunch-time slots were scheduled with factory and industrial workers in mind; early evening slots were highly prized "key" periods, particularly on CCV which experienced a peak viewership at this time, while the late-evening slots, although not a prime position, always found sufficient viewers to be attractive.

Illustrating Democracy in Action: **The Peace Train**

One such series of programs was *The Peace Train,* commissioned by DEBI and produced by Dave Meyerowitz, of Pegasus Productions. The series consisted of five five-minute-piece series, as well as a continuous 25-minute ver-sion. The format of the series utilized animated talking puppets interacting with live actors—a form which has been well tested as a pedagogical tool in chil-dren's programming but which was entirely innovative in application to adult viewing. The musical score was written and produced by the popular black musician Ray Phiri, a factor which was hoped would enhance the appeal of the program among alienated black youth. As Dave Meyerowitz explained, "The train is a central motif in the lives of the average black urban worker. Each day, millions of people commute from home to work and back again, often spending long hours on the rails. Trains are also notoriously dangerous, and have been the locus of much political violence in the past few years." Thus by reinterpel-lating the train as *The Peace Train,* Meyerowitz not only picked up on the everyday experiences of black people but consciously rearticulated them in a positive fashion. In his program, the steam train metaphor was used as a symbol of the nation's desire to move toward a new democracy. In this analogy, the steam train is powered by the goodwill of the nation, and the coaches attached to it are symbolic of the units making up a practical democracy. Each carriage has a thematic name— "Freedom of Choice," "Who Can Vote," and the like— and the passengers and puppets aboard that carriage carry out a little situation-scenario focusing on that theme. Meyerowitz continued:

In the first episode, passengers in the "Freedom of Choice" carriage were intimidated by a violent faction on the train, who attempted to force them into voting for a party not of their choice. The perpetrator was restrained, and free-dom of choice won the day. The following day, episode 2 took place in a car-riage called "Who Can Vote," in which an older and younger man meet at random and fall into a conversation on who is eligible to vote. This device allows all the intricacies of voting eligibility to be discussed in an entertaining and amusing manner.

Episode 3 addressed one of the most important themes stressed throughout the voter education campaign, that "Your Vote Is Your Secret." Two women aboard the train share their fears about voting for a political party of which their husbands would not approve. A fellow passenger reassures them that their vote is absolutely secret, and that they need not fear reprisals as a result of their party selection.

"Political Tolerance" was the theme of episode 4, in which an old man re-counts a parable from the animal kingdom. In his story, the animals were not united as a society because they failed to settle their differences. Through ne-gotiations and consensus, mankind, on the other hand, has control of their own destiny. The final episode was entitled "Myths and Disinformation," during which various commonly held fears surrounding the voting procedure were discussed and dispelled among the passengers.

Documentaries

In many ways, the late-evening documentaries were the most difficult part of the campaign. One reason is that they were poorly scheduled, in the later evening after prime-time viewing, with a rebroadcast to daytime audiences. They were a relatively expensive format, averaging around R3,000 per minute.

One of more innovative attempts at this slot was a docudrama, Uncle Amos, produced by Anthony de Demko, of Demko Films International. The story revolves around Uncle Amos, an old and wise man who struggled through his life to achieve democracy in South Africa. He was a visionary whose visions were a source of inspiration to many. He was widely loved and revered. He was a man who understands that his struggle was not really for himself, but for his future generations.

The recent changes in South Africa initially elated him, but then he was somewhat dismayed as he felt people appeared to be losing sight of the true meaning of freedom and democracy. Believing himself to be dying, he summons his friends and family to talk to them about democracy.

He starts out by juxtaposing images of peace, prosperity, love, and friendship against those of hate, strife, and war. He tells his friends that democracy is about freedom—freedom of opinion. He goes on to explain all the nuances of the process. The program used this narrative device to explore the following questions:

- What is democracy?

- Who can vote?

- How do I vote?

- Why is it important that I vote?

- Who can I vote for, and what do they stand for?

- Will my vote be a secret one?

- How can I avoid being intimidated, and what mechanisms are in place to protect me?

- If a party wins the election, and it's not the party I voted for, does it mean I don't have a say anymore?

- First there were negotiations, now there's the TEC, then there will be a government of National Unity, and then more elections—what does this mean?

- How will the parliament, cabinet, and president operate?

- What is the price of failure?

- How will my life change after the election?

Education as Entertainment

Democracy and voter education has a particularly pedantic ring to it. Nevertheless, the programming on television proved to be very popular, particularly the more lighthearted genres with a serious purpose: the game/quiz show *Make Your Mark* brought it up to eight thousand postcards per week, a clear indication of audience approval.[11] More scientifically, approval ratings were measured by the independently run AMPS (All Media and Product Survey), a rating system based on the Nielsen,[12] which placed two DEBI programs among the ten most popular television programmes, with *Kululeka* reaching third place on CCV, and *Make Your Mark* number eight.[13]

DEBI television producer Glen Masokoane noted:

> There is no doubt that voter education programs did not only educate but
> were also entertaining and indeed provided the much needed information
> to the electorate about the voting process. Topping the charts is not only a
> source of victory but a significant confirmation to the SABC, and the IEC and
> other donors that monies spent on DEBI programs actually ensured that the
> quality of production was not compromised in delivering a cheap product.
> Education programs and community issues deserve high production values.

Kululeku: *A Voter Soapie*

The central insight that most people who watch television and listen to the radio do so for pleasure and entertainment rather than simply education and information was the reason producer Roberta Durrant chose a comedy soap opera format for the thirteen-part voter-education saga *Kululeka:*

> People relate to things that amuse them. People want to be entertained.
> There is no question about that. People want to relax. They get mellow and
> they open out and that opens up the channels of communication. Just about
> every person I have spoken to, everyone said what they liked about *Kululeka*
> was that it was funny. It wasn't too serious and directed, and they didn't have
> to think too hard. And that came across very clearly.
>
> What made the program successful was that it was entertaining. Chat shows
> give more information. Soap operas don't give that much information, but
> what they do is create a whole mindset of what you are trying to convey. I
> honestly think entertainment is so important. I've read quite a bit about what
> has happened in soaps in South America and the education side of it—you
> know, the message is there but its not that intrusive. I think that's exactly
> right. But its a whole awareness thing, and I think that is what we are trying to
> do, to create a climate of acceptance via the program. You've got to get
> people listening, you've got to keep them entertained.

Kululeka was central nucleus to the IFEE voter education campaign. Roberta explained to me how the project came about:

When Joe Mafela and myself realized that there was going to be voter education, we approached Matla [Trust] and suggested to them that they might need a television series. Now I'm going back to September 1992. Matla simultaneously had thought that they did need something—they didn't know quite what. They had set up their communications center with Barry [Gilder] and they knew they were going to work with television, but I don't think they had at that stage any idea at all of doing a soap/comedy series.

It took a while to get the whole thing together. We worked quite a bit before we got a development contract. Then we got a development contract, but there still wasn't security of funding at all, and it was only at a later stage that we could start. We produced the program at a very equitable, minute price, knowing what it was, specifically for voter education.

There was a lot of work behind the mounting of the whole process. That took a lot of time to get the program on the go. We scripted for a long time, almost for a year. We had a team of writers on the program. It was myself and Richard Benyon, Joe Mafela, and a whole team from Matla, and we had several workshops. We would write a script, then bring it to the workshop, go back and bring it back, and in the end everyone had to be happy with it. So the scripting process was very involved.

The other thing was there was a lot we couldn't define exactly, because the processes themselves had not been defined. The IEC had not got it together. We had to get the program going—it was a soap, it wasn't a chat show—it was a complicated production with a big set. We had to get going. We had to start shooting while we were still getting the latest information.

I directed the program. First we shot in the studio and then we shot on location. We had wonderful cooperation from everyone involved, from the technical staff, and from the actors. I think everyone felt that there was a sense of purpose, and in that way it was a wonderful program to work on.

This discussion highlights a number of issues already touched on: the difficulty of working on voter education in the vacuum left by the lack of clarity over the process on the part of the IEC. More importantly though, Roberta's account emphasizes the importance of a continuous process of consultation and cooperative working.

Playing to Learn: Game Shows

One of the first full-scale programs commissioned by DEBI was the quiz show *Make Your Mark,*[14] which used the game show format to communicate information around democracy in general, the upcoming election and the voting procedures associated with it, as well as the political structure of the country, the new constitution, and associated topics. Two versions of the program were produced back-to-back, using the same set, formats, and prize allocations. CCV broadcast a version featuring English and Afrikaans contestants on adult prime time, Tuesday evenings 8:30–9:00. This followed directly after the news and *Kululeka* (see below). On Thursday evenings, NNTV broadcast a version featuring English and Afrikaans. The two shows ran for sixteen weeks, from 11 January to the end of April.

It's Your Vote[15] was another successful quiz show, this time aired at a more sophisticated audience, and broadcast on Saturdays at 11:00–11:30 P.M. The format of the show paralleled that of a real election, using the same vocabulary and role-plays. The TV compere was known as the electoral officer. The quiz contestants were "candidates," and the audiences were the electorate choosing the winning candidate. The quiz comprised a series of questions from a single "ballot," covering, for instance, the meaning of a proportional representation; what a two-ballot system was; how a ballot could be spoiled, and so on.

I asked Beata Lipman which of the different formats and genres we used in DEBI were in her opinion the successful ones. Laughingly, she told me,

> To my great surprise, I thought that the game shows. When they were care- fully researched and they came up with right answers in simple terms, they worked rather well. You know I had not been very optimistic about them. But people enjoyed that format. Obviously they were not always quite as correct as they should have been, and we tried to have a working group to have some input into that. But people liked that, and I thought that you can get a quick and easy answer in that format. As I say, I was surprised because my personal predilection is not toward game shows.

I put a similar question to André le Roux:

> RUTH: When you looked at the formats that were used—and particularly on television, because that is the area of your expertise—what do you think about those various formats? Which ones do you think worked, and which ones were a waste of money?
>
> ANDRÉ: I think that they all worked. What the spots did was even if it was directed at prime-time audiences—an audience which was probably voter lit- erate—it helped to develop an electoral awareness, it wasn't educational as such. The spots, as they grew in terms of duration on air, right through to the five-minuters and the documentaries and also the quizzes and dramas, made it possible to do a number of things: for any individual to pick a format that best suited his or her level of understanding about the process of democracy. Some people only needed a prompt, some people, at the other end of the scale, needed

virtually a formal education. And I think the different formats catered for different needs, and in particular the longer formats—because most of them were very well done—had the effect that people could pace themselves in understanding the processes that were involved.

Thinking Democratically, Acting Democratically

Part of the rationale of the DEBI project was to provide a greater degree of access to production houses which had not yet penetrated the traditional commissioning structures of the SABC. Some of these were enterprises which until recently had not chosen to tender for programs aired on the SABC channels. Thus smaller production houses, affirmative action producers, as well as the in-house production facilities of member organizations had been actively solicited to contribute.

Business Enters the Ring

Late in the campaign, a loose coalition of business interests grouped together to form the Business Election Fund (BEF). Their primary aim was to contribute to the ongoing financial stability of the country after the elections. Although they canvassed widely, and claimed significant funding, it is not possible to say how much they actually raised. I asked Larry Schwartz, press liaison officer for the United States Information Service, for his impressions of the BEF campaign:

Well, as guests in the country, as foreigners, obviously, we were just interested in facilitating the process. The business community came to us and asked for quotes from leading Americans of all races, really famous people, so we went out and obtained them. I mean, we asked some of our people in Washington to call up these people, and get a statement, a quote from them, which we obtained both on audio and print, and provided to the business initiative—the BEF—and they had some ad campaigns that they were going to put out. But in fact, none of these things ever really got off the ground. We were actually pretty disappointed, because we did a lot of work, and we went to a lot of people and asked for their brief statement on the South African elections, and encouraging people to vote. I don't think the Business Election Fund really did very much, and I don't think they had the resources to do very much. The big bucks went into Project Vote and Matla Trust and some of these other organizations that assisted with voter education. I do know that the business ad campaigns didn't seem to have a major effect.

Most of their campaign, undertaken by the multinational advertising agency, Ogilvy, Mather, Rightford, Searle-Tripp, and Markin, was aimed at outdoor billboards, taxi shades, and T-shirts. The core of their television campaign was a sixty-second epic commercial, starkly reminiscent of the British Airways International ad, with a strong exhortatory theme. Beata Lipman was skeptical of how much impact these advertisements really had:

BEATA: I thought some of the other formats also worked very well. The things I thought were least successful were the sort of vague exhortations toward peace and harmony and goodness and love our neighbor as ourselves. The sort of things that the business people started doing. I mean, I thought they just waffled.

RUTH: Okay, but towards the end, at the BEF campaign?

BEATA: I mean, I thought that whenever anything was specific, and taught people through that process on how they were going to vote, and what were the correct ways handling things, and gave them factual material but clothed in an entertaining format, those were the things that I really liked very much. When you started picking up questions about the youth and violence, it was harder. When it was very specifically geared to informing people about, not only about their rights, but how to actually to go about the process, I think that was us at our most successful.

DEBI Does Radio

Why Radio?

Radio was identified as a crucial vehicle for conveying democracy and voter education. This is because South Africa, like most third-world countries, is heavily reliant on radio to reach the deep rural areas. Radios are relatively cheap and almost ubiquitous: there are approximately 445 radio sets per thousand of the population, which is extremely high in comparison to any other comparative or third-world country, while the ownership of television sets in this country is less than 40 per thousand. More importantly, while practically none of the rural poor have access to television in their own homes, nearly all households, even in this category, own their own radios.[16] Unlike television, radio doesn't rely on electricity, an important factor when one considers that large tracts of rural and peri-urban South Africa are not connected into the national electricity grid. Battery power is also comparably inexpensive.

Radio penetration also scores higher than print media—only 5 percent of the rural poor claim to read any newspaper at all.[17] This is the combined result of a high rate of illiteracy, the poor distribution of newspapers and magazines outside the urban areas, and their relatively high cost in comparison to average wages. Finally, in South Africa, radio is broadcast in all eleven spoken languages, often on a regionalized basis, while television uses only seven. This makes messages broadcast on radio far more accessible than on television. This situation is analogous to the rest of Africa.

Structures for Democracy Education on Radio

Voter and democracy education took place on all radio stations of the SABC. Because of the regional nature of broadcasting on radio, a centralized structure was not really feasible. The radio ad hoc committee acted as the Johannesburg-Witwatersrand organizer, as well as a pivot around which regional committees were arranged. Each of the six regions set up their own regional radio forums. Each regional forum was made up of civic representatives from NGOs academic and religious organizations interested in democracy and voter education, together with representatives of the SABC management structures in those areas. The forum's chairperson was chosen from the ranks of the civic sector, while the DEBI contact person was a senior SABC employee in the region. Some of these forums worked better than others.

The regional forums were coordinated with the national effort through a weekly line conference held every Thursday morning. Representatives from each region would meet together in their local radio studio and would be electronically connected in an interregional conference. These line conferences facilitated the communication of progress reports, and provided a forum for the coordination of campaign themes and the swapping of ideas and strategies.

Regional Radio at Work: The Case of KwaZulu Natal

An account of the working of all the six regions would be too lengthy. I have therefore chosen to concentrate on one case study: Natal Broadcasting, which operates from Durban. It is a regional broadcaster wholly owned by the SABC. Three radio stations operate from this center: Radio Zulu is a full-spectrum public-service format which broadcasts in the Zulu language, and at 3.36 million listeners, boasts the largest radio audience in South Africa. Because of its large audience size, and its reach into the most inaccessible rural parts of KwaZulu Natal, DEBI had the greatest interest in broadcasting on Radio Zulu. Radio Port Natal is a top-40 commercially driven station, broadcasting in English and Afrikaans, with a listenership of 0.31 million; and Radio Lotus is a community-oriented service broadcast to South Africans of Indian extraction in English, Tamil, Hindi, and Urdu, with a listenership of 0.3 million.[18]

Zamambo Mkize is the head of Radio Zulu. She recounted the part played by the radio station:

Initially when the whole thing [democracy education on radio] was being formalized, we were asked as radio stations to give input as to what times we would be able allocate. We realized that this was a national issue, the first of this kind, and that radio, particularly Radio Zulu and the areas that we would be reaching, would be playing a critical role in this primary function of voter education. We set out the times, we even set out the formats in which those forms of voter education could take place.

As a case study, I have chosen to concentrate on the KwaZulu-Natal forum for three reasons. First, this is the region in which I live, and so I have a personal affinity for the problems, challenges, and solutions which faced the region. Second, the KwaZulu Natal DEBI Regional Radio Forum was probably the most vital and enthusiastic of the local groupings. This was a result of sound SABC infrastructure (Natal Broadcasting is well resourced and consider themselves as the most innovative of the regional broadcasters); a strong NGO presence in Durban, which provided good leadership on the civic side; and perhaps most importantly, a coincidence of hard-working and dedicated personalities from both the SABC management and the NGO/civic sector. Finally, apart from Thokoza on the East Rand, the KwaZulu Natal region was the most politically volatile area in the run-up to the elections, since it is the home base of the Inkatha Freedom Party (IFP), led by Mangosuthu Buthelezi. The IFP resisted entering the electoral process until two weeks before the election date, and IFP supporters actively harassed voter education workers, often halting their efforts completely (see Leslie Fordred's forthcoming interview with Khaba Mkize in *Late Editions 4*). In these circumstances, radio had a particularly crucial part to play in reaching those people who could not otherwise receive voter education.

Leonard Suransky is a professor of politics at the University of Durban, Westville, and was as the appointed DEBI representative for an interdenominational coalition of Jewish, Hindu, and Moslem interests. Leonard was a key member of the Durban forum, and he assessed the difficulties the imposed the Inkatha nonparticipation:

> For much of the six months that we were on the air, except for the very last few days, we were in a particularly difficult situation here in Natal, in that the IFP at that stage had not agreed to participate in the elections. That affects your job and what you had to do.

Nhlakamipho Zulu, radio announcer and producer of phone-ins and talk shows on Radio Zulu, concurred. He pointed out that not only were voter educators in the field harassed, but radio announcers also received threatening phone calls from IFP members. (In fact, the position was so serious that extra security was allocated to the homes and families of key announcers and producers.) While Nhlakamipho would not say so outright (to do so would be construed as grossly impolite), the gist of his remarks is that anyone who was seen to undertake voter education, was seen to be in a adversarial position to the IFP, and by implication, a supporter of the ANC:

> I was a bit critical about this, but I never wanted to talk about it. But otherwise I must say it really affected us greatly, because, after every given broadcast, you get the phone call from the IFP saying you never emphasized the

fact that this is voter education, and questioning who are those who intended voting, or who are the intended consumers, such that many times I was at loggerheads, with the very high profile people from the IFP, accusing us of taking sides. Because, with voter education—one must be frank about this—you were seen as on the side of the camp, you know, when you are pro-involved in voter education. So, but otherwise one was able to trade punches very well.

Ricky Naidoo was the chairperson of the DEBI KwaZulu Natal Radio Regional Forum. He represented the Multi-Party Democracy (MPD). He was seconded to the IEC during April 1994, preelection month. Here he gives his perspective on the IFP controversy:

I think there is just one point in the whole IFP situation, I don't know, I find it quite interesting, because during my month that I spent with the IEC, I spent a lot of time traveling around with the IEC vice chairperson in charge of trying to reorient the IFP into the electoral process. There were senior IFP people, you know, in these casual discussions, you know, who were actually quite impressed with the quality of the DEBI programs that came out on Radio Zulu, in terms of their content and their nonpartisan approach. So I wasn't too sure how much of the problem you have. Is this part of the politics? So they were quite impressed with the quality of the programmes, and in fact one person went to the extent of saying, "Yeah, if we had come to the process much earlier, you know, we probably would have needed their voter education campaign as well."

But I think the issues that affected them earlier, you know, our program in the region in terms of DEBI itself is one of I think the question of *violence.*

Program Genres on Radio

Programming on radio included a wide range of genres: advertisements, phone-ins, situational or minidramas, magazine programs, music programmes, soap-opera formats, panel discussions, vox pops, concerts, endorsements, and more.

Phone-ins: The Voice of the Voters

The most important program type on radio was the phone-in format. Part of the popularity of the format was that it encouraged live participation on behalf of the audience. Each week a particular theme would be announced, and the studio guest or guests would discuss the topic, after which the telephone lines would be opened to listeners queries. It was the task of the DEBI radio ad hoc group to devise the list of topics, and identify and facilitate the "expert" who would be the studio guest. An announcer from the station acted as host, but often had to do considerably more than that: he (unfortunately, it was almost never a she) would have to be well versed in both the broad political issues surrounding the election, as well as the more detailed electoral procedures. This was not only because the host had to provide intelligent questions and continuity of the speakers, but also because it occasionally happened that the speakers themselves were ill-prepared, or did not turn up at the last moment, and the station announcers had to fill in at short notice.

Nhlakamipho Zulu was a resident announcer who hosted phone-ins on Radio Zulu. He spoke of his experience in producing DEBI programming:

> I must say, I appreciated the assistance from DEBI with regard to the identification of some of the speakers that we could use. But one must also cut no bones about that. I think as South Africans we were caught up in a very crucial situation where we had to speak of election, we had to do things on our own, and with very little knowledge. And out of the speakers that we used, very few of them have been outside South Africa, just to observe how elections are run (in other countries), and to get, you know, facts about the whole thing. So it was just people who were informed in terms of their listenership (to the structures supporting the South African elections). All in all, some of the people that we used were not well informed, but otherwise we had to respect their integrity and personalities, and we used them as such. Otherwise, working in the middle you end up picking up a lot of things, and you become knowledgeable, or an expert in some areas. So you had to try be a resource person and also be an anchor, you know.

Another problem faced by the anchor was the relatively heterogeneous nature of the audience. While all Radio Zulu's listenership speak Zulu as their first language, there is a wide discrepancy in the educational levels, interests, and sophistication of the audience. Phone-ins were, however, popular across a broad spectrum of listeners. Nhlakamipho Zulu elaborated:

> And that alone was a bit of a problem because we were broadcasting for a mixed society: one part is a highly informed society, on the other, a less informed society, and then we have to try to bring those two critical factors together. It causes a problem because it would cost the credibility of the station if somebody picked it up. But otherwise I must say it went on very well; hence I ended up being the person maybe who could have been employed by DEBI today.

Phone-ins on Radio Metro

Radio Metro is produced from the Johannesburg studios of the SABC. It is a national music-format station with a relatively high talk component. As its name indicates, it is aimed primarily at the sophisticated urban sector of the South African black population, featuring local music, reggae, and other African-American genres, as well as discussion programs, live interviews, and news. Radio Metro was the first station to negotiate voter education with IFEE, ahead of the establishment of DEBI. It therefore had a headstart on other stations, particularly in terms of phone-ins and magazine programming. Based in Johannesburg, Radio Metro benefited from being close to the organizing heart of DEBI, and from having a large pool of NGO resource persons to call on. More importantly, it boasted some of the brightest, most vivacious disk jockeys and anchors. As with the regional stations, weekly themes were planned, which invited speakers would discuss, followed by open telephone lines. During week 16, for instance, Professor Vincent Maphayi led the discussion on free and fair elections:

The holding of elections in any country is a matter of importance. Elections are about power and government. It goes without saying that everybody must not only be satisfied, but must also accept the outcome of the elections. The outcome of the elections can only be accepted if the elections have been free and fair. Free and fair elections constitute the foundation of a democratic society. The experience of other countries, including our neighbors, bears testimony to the fact the nonacceptance of the election results may lead to chaos, hardship, and suffering.

International Women's Day was celebrated with a special program on "Women and the Vote" led by Miriam Titise of the Women's Development Foundation (9 March 1994). A month later, on 6 April, Sindi Sekoekle of the Young Women's Christian Association (YWCA), appeared as the guest on a phone-in concerned with the same topic. Some of the questions they dealt with included the following:

- How prepared are South African women to exercise their right to vote in the forthcoming elections?

- How can women overcome the traditional prejudices against them in African societies?

- South Africa is a religious country, and certain rights that women want seem to be in conflict with religious norms. Is this a fair observation?

- Why is it that women seem not to be fully involved in the political life of the country? How can this situation be remedied?

- What would the women of South Africa hope to see in a new democratic South Africa?

- Do women think they are sufficiently represented in the lists of political parties?

Of particular interest to American readers might be the guest appearance of actors Danny Glover and Angela Bassett, who were inspanned early in the campaign to motivate people to participate in elections. The two discussed their opinions of the significance of the forthcoming elections for South Africans, and the world in general, and talked about their own involvement with voter education. They devoted a fair amount of time to talking about the central importance of political tolerance and the acceptance of the vote, if the process was to have any validity. This particular program, which was scheduled for an hour, overran its time for another thirty minutes, a direct result of the listener enthusiasm and telephone calls.

Letters Programs: Voter Education as a Two-Way Street

An unexpected spin-off of the phone-in programs in KwaZulu Natal were the substantial numbers of letters sent in by listeners. Some of these were queries, some were accounts of their experiences with voter educators, and many outlined the concerns felt by ordinary listeners. Some of the questions included the following:

- Can prisoners vote? Why are prisoners excluded from voting when they committed their offenses as a result of apartheid laws? Will prisoners vote inside or outside the prisons?[19]

- Why is Radio Zulu emphasizing the elections when the Zulus are not voting?

- How can we stop farmworkers being prevented from getting IDs?

- Can I vote for another province if there a double ballot for national and regional elections?

- Since the Security Forces have failed to protect us against violence, how can they ensure our safety at voting stations?

- Why are ANC people killed in Natal?

To mobilize and utilize these queries effectively, a legal NGO, the Natal Forum on Education and Democracy (a regional IFEE associate), employed a group of legal students to read the letters for common themes and unusual requests for information. The results were fed back to DEBI, and to a wider network of voter educators. Radio Zulu instituted a thirty minute program on Sunday evenings, during which an IEC representative responded to questions raised in the letters. In this way, voter education became a two-way street: not only did DEBI disseminate information, but we also acted as a conduit for identifying information expressed by the voting public.

Deborah Ewing, of the Natal Forum, recounted the project from her point of view:

I think from our side, from the voter educators side, DEBI was very successful because there was cooperation between everybody: between the

SABC, Radio Zulu, People, between different members of the DEBI committee. An example was the way in which it was arranged for bilingual [Zulu-
English] students from UDW [University of Durban – Westville] to take and
read, analyze, and summarize some the issues that have been raised. Subjects
would be fed back into Radio Zulu for the letters program, and back into the
Natal Forum on Education and Democracy for voter education workshops so
that we could respond very quickly to the priority issues that were concerning
people.

This was a good example of problem solving on several levels. People
came together to look at the problem of dealing with those letters which came
from the phone-ins on Radio Zulu first. And there were also problems of not
being able to reach large numbers of people who did need voter education or
democracy information, during the period of conflict over the question of participation, when it was actually dangerous for us to do voter education in some
areas. It also was successful because it was responding directly to listeners'
needs, and wasn't just assuming what people wanted to hear: there was direct,
authenticated evidence of what was concerning people. This was done at a
very low cost; it didn't involve production costs. We did have one problem
over funding in that all we had to meet was the cost of the students and processing the whole thing, and it was due to DEBI's financial position that later
some delays were encountered.

Outside Broadcasts: Taking Radio to People

A noticeable disadvantage of the phone-in format was that it excluded people
without ready access to telephones—which in the rural areas of KwaZulu
Natal, included a substantial portion of the audience. In response to Julie Frederickse's interview on Capital Radio as to what radio genres DEBI used, I outlined the strategy of using outside broadcasting units (OBs) to cope with this
situation:

> One of the strongest criticisms that you might make about using electronic
> media for voter education is that you're really reaching the people who al-
> ready have access to information. What about all those people in the rural
> areas who don't have access to information? They have radios but they don't
> have telephones. So how do we reach them? What we do in this particular
> instance is to send outside broadcasting units to very remote areas. We have a
> program with people coming with their questions to the particular venue, put-
> ting questions to the facilitators that are there. These facilitators are made up
> of broadcasters and people from civil society; In the Far Northern Transvaal,
> for instance, they could be clinic workers, they could be social workers, any-
> body who is knowledgeable and is interested in voter education. The outside
> broadcasts become great social events to the people in the area. They bring

their food, they bring their drink, they make fires and they have a wonderful social afternoon. And so clearly, this is more than simply voter education on radio; it's providing a sense of community. I think it's a very exciting development and one which is a complete departure from the studio bound approaches that broadcasting usually takes, even in Africa.

The first radio station to undertake outside broadcasts was Radio Sesotho, operating out of Johannesburg. These programs took place on Saturday afternoons over eight weekends. Initially, the undertakings were funded by the Johannesburg radio division. In the face of enormous success, the experiment was extended to other regions, and funding for these ventures was raised from the South African Free Election Fund (SAFE). Other radio stations which did outside broadcasts were those located in the Far North Region: Radio Lebowa, Radio Venda, and Radio Tsonga. All three of these radio stations served vast, sparsely populated and often poverty-stricken rural areas in minority languages, where infrastructure was particularly poor. In view of the general lack of televisions and telephones, the impact of the OBs were significant.

In KwaZulu Natal, the problem of violence bedeviled the use of outside broadcasts. Ricky Naidoo remarked that "as the DEBI programs became more people oriented, I thought at one stage it would be great if we could mount an operation with the OBs. I think that would have made a major impact. But given the problem of the violence, obviously we couldn't implement lot of those programs." It is unfortunate that the idea of doing OBs was mooted so late in the campaign. The logistics of the exercise—arranging for the technical equipment, finding a suitable venue, and informing listeners ahead of time— were quite onerous, and really required more time than was given. This, together with fears of political instability and violence in certain areas, made OBs a less valuable part of the campaign than they should have been.

Sound Magazines: Multidimensional Sound

One of the main forms of programming were prerecorded tapes, prepared by both IDASA and IFEE. Sue Valentine, media officer and radio producer for IDASA, explained that

some of us had some experience on radio, and we decided to use the opportunity that the DEBI initiative offered. In fact, we decided to use radio in our voter education drive even prior to DEBI establishing itself properly. Radio is the way of reaching as broad as possible a number of South Africans. We decided on several different formats of radio, one being sort of straightforward community or public service announcements; the other being short, fifteen-minute magazine programs which are compiled and prerecorded with a number of different elements. It is also in an attempt to try to make things very entertaining so that it's not just a lecture for fifteen minutes but is broken up with some music, either a story or a minidrama, or an interview with a voter educator.

And then we also have recorded some music played by Mahlatini and Mahotella Queens entitled "Plant the Seed of Democracy," and the Young Bloods, a young rap group, have produced "Use Your Voice." So the idea has been to use a number of different means to try and reach people, and the same time to try and involve community-based artists and actors in the process, so we didn't just have a slick kind of advertising agency feel to it—we didn't want to reproduce that sort of sound in our program.[20]

Drama on Radio: Narrating Democracy

Soap opera on radio is a well-developed and popular genre. Funded externally, a group of Natal-based writers scripted and produced a soap opera around the theme of the election for Radio Zulu. Shortened versions of the dramas were translated and adapted by the stations in the Far North: Radio Venda, Radio Tsonga, and Radio Lebowa.

Music: Singing the News

Various tapes with music composed around voter education themes were distributed to the radio stations. The cassettes and reels came from member organizations.[21] The most important of these was a twenty-six-minute concept-type reel featuring diverse artists and hosted by local reggae hero Lucky Dube. This particular example was part of a campaign funded and driven by the Business Election Fund.[22]

Spots, Advertisements: Reinforcing the Message

A continuous bone of contention between the station programmers and the various DEBI committees was the oft-encountered inability of music-format stations to cope with the deluge of talk formats which resulted from the elections in general and DEBI in particular. Station managers felt that inappropriate genres were foisted on them, while voter educationalists felt that there was a lack of flexibility on the part of programmers.

The most difficult situation occurred in the Western Cape, in catering for the needs of first-time voters in the Afrikaans-speaking "colored" community.[23] The public service or full-spectrum station in Afrikaans is Afrikaans Stereo, but it was felt that this station, while attractive to a predominantly conservative white audience, was generally regarded as being high-brow and not appealing to the needs and tastes of most colored listeners. The latter's choice of radio station was Kontrei, a music-format station. Interviewed halfway through the campaign, Sue Valentine noted, "Certainly we have do have some problems with some of the stations here in the Western Cape, with some music-format radio stations, which have been very intransigent in terms of taking any kind of programming. So we won't succeed in that level; the only programs they will have are music tapes and spots."

The spots Sue referred to were typical social-marketing advertisements. Idasa produced a whole series, some under its own imprint, some specifically designed for DEBI. Other NGOs also produced spots: the BEF mounted a campaign around the slogan "Business stands for building a great nation," an example of which opened this chapter. IFEE commissioned a series of advertisements based on the theme of "Heal our land," which ran in tandem with their previously discussed television spots.

How Well Did DEBI Do? Assessment and Critique

In assessing the DEBI initiative, it seems best to concentrate on four areas:

- The structure of the organization entrusted with the task of voter and democracy education. This would include lines of administration and accountability, and coordination between DEBI and the rest of the SABC, specifically regional radio stations.

- The financial resources, management, and funding; including clarity on financial resources and allocation.

- The question of alleged partisanship.

- The effectiveness of the campaign, including questions surrounding the use of language and penetration, the balance between radio and television, and the overall frequency and scheduling of voter and democracy education.

Organization, Structure, Management

The DEBI structure was a complex and convoluted one, and in retrospect, not a particularly efficient way of producing a coherent campaign. The reasons behind this structure were more pragmatic than practical, and had largely to do with the crisis of legitimacy explored at the beginning of this chapter. The result was a complex web of committees, subcommittees and ad hoc committees, which in turn had to liaise with an SABC management structure—which itself was in a process of transition and transformation. I asked Beata Lipman what she felt about the committee structures that DEBI set in place:

> When you are to have an affirmation of a popular input, you have a paradox. You say you want to represent ordinary people, but at same time they didn't really have the professional skills and understanding of the technical requirements in broadcasting. So while I thought the process was indeed very

valuable, I think by the time it got to the working groups I quite frequently felt the lack of the professional background in television, which happens to be my field. I think if we are going to set up representatives of civil society again, which in a democratic terms was an excellent idea, there should be a few more people with the kind of skills which I happen to have around television, and that I'm sure other people have around radio. In other words, people who can manage in a sense to wear a couple of hats. I was there on behalf of the trade union (FAWO), but I was also there because I knew something about how to make those programs. Where possible, if a popular committee is appointed, there should be two or three representatives with technical and professional skills, because they are at that interface between the professional people at the SABC and the professionals who are going to be commissioned to make the programmes.

The Relationship between the NGOs and the SABC

DEBI suffered from the occasional lack of direct communication between the DEBI committees and the SABC management. The tension between those who interpellated themselves as civil society and those who were management was most marked at the beginning of the campaign, and tended to occupy much of the various committee's energies. The position gradually improved with time, and the setting up of the working committees in which both NGO and SABC management members were represented.

On the radio side, the integration of the SABC management and the NGOs was uneven. A constant source of misunderstanding arose from music format stations insistence on low levels of talk radio, as outlined previously. At stake here were the prerecorded "magazine" programs, which were sent directly to the stations. Local regional programmers complained that there was insufficient coordination between the supplier bodies and stations. They also complained that some of the programs were unacceptable in terms of their level of professionalism. The radio stations expressed a willingness to use the tapes but felt they should have more to say in the format and content of the tapes, so as to be able to tailor them to their audiences and schedules. Zamambo Mkize of Radio Zulu articulated it this way:

We have always been willing to give more time [for voter education]. We set out time for the magazine tapes, and said that if they were recorded they could be used. We did receive tapes and we always had a problem that we couldn't give input into the content in DEBI, especially in terms of quality. As a result, we often had announcers complaining.

Specifically, it appeared that the tapes were packaged in awkward time units, which did not fit neatly into the segmentation of the scheduling. Occasionally, the technical quality was not good enough for broadcast. Continued Zamambo, "Sometimes you can hardly hear what the person is talking about, the quality of the recording is so poor. We found that there was a lot of music in between the messages which were actually meant to be driven home to people. So now and again the announcer packaging the tape would come back to us complaining about that."

Zamambo's remarks here are reminiscent of Stuart Hall's remarks on the ethos of professionalism as a specific ideological response.[24] Her observations show not only the difference in acceptable standards between broadcasters and nonbroadcasters, but also a different sense of what was an appropriate content and context for democracy education. Sue Valentine noted earlier that when compiling the magazine programs for IDASA, she particularly went out of her way to break the mold of the slick, seamless, "professional" program, and attempted to produce a more engaging, "street-wise" version. Julie Frederickse, chat show host on Capital Radio, put the following question to her:

JULIE: Now, if you had said even two or three, four years ago, "I would like to produce something as an organization that the SABC could put on the radio," there would have been a lot of complaints about going to the right structures. They have their own production house, and they might have said the program wasn't of broadcasting quality. Was none of them an issue this time?

SUE: Well, it was. We had quite a number of headaches at the very beginning of the process and DEBI in fact was the means by which, or certainly which assisted, in things coming together. We've ended up using SABC facilities partly to make sure that the quality is their quality, but also because quite frankly they are the most reliable, and also the most affordable of the institutions around.

A more difficult situation arose when organizations which were members of DEBI unilaterally approached the stations, and made specific demands on them, instead of going through the forums set up. Zamambo Mkize again:

And also IDASA, because we found that some of the people, though they were part of DEBI they were still contacting us, because they had special things that they wanted broadcast. IDASA had a special person used as a liaison, who was doing some other talks for voter education and there was even a drama at some stage that was prepared.

There were also NGOs that were approaching us wanting to do voter education on the air, particularly on the women's programs; and at some stage we did involve some of these people. But later on we got some other people, phoning later, and we were getting confused because most of the people were represented in DEBI, but now they were coming back to us, saying, "We would like to do this on the air." We realized that particularly in the Natal situation, because of the violence, that the media was the most easily accessible form of democracy education which could be used to reach the people, so we were willing to give extra time.

Such a case happened in Durban, in which the drama became a point of contention. On the positive side, the whole DEBI initiative provided access to stakeholders who had not previously been able to penetrate the airways. Sue Valentine pointed out that particularly on the African language stations, IDASA had almost unlimited access: "But with Radio Xhosa, Radio Zulu, and Afrikaans Stereo the situation has completely turned about from what would have been expected a year or two ago."

"Everything in South Africa is Political":
Claims of Partisanship

In the beginning of April 1994, Marthinus van Schalkwyk, the director of information and media of the National Party, wrote to DEBI:

> Re: DEBI Analysis by National Party
> The results of the analysis made of some of your programmes are attached. Our conclusion is that some of the DEBI programmes definitely favour the ANC.
> Although there are elements in the DEBI programmes which we fully support, such as the emphasis on the secrecy of the vote, the examples of ANC favouritism puts a question mark over the whole DEBI initiative. The National Party fully supports voter education. We do not however support voter education programmes which claim to be neutral and then proceed to subtly (and sometimes not so subtly) favour one political party.

In its "analysis," the National Party cited three specific examples which "favored the ANC": the use of the phrases "Now is the time to vote" and "The time is now," which were said to reinforce the ANC's own advertising slogan, "The time is now, now is the time." In response we pointed out that the phrase, in all its variations, is an idiomatic expression which is in common use by all South Africans to designate a sense of urgency and potency. As such, it could not be patented, or regarded as the intellectual or ideological property of any interest group, party or political position. Not only had the ANC mobilized the wording: the Inkatha Freedom Party used it in their slogan "When the time is right . . . ," and later, "Now the time is right." The National Party itself used the phrase in a double-page print advertisement headlined "Now is the time to make the change." [25]

Among a series of short endorsements produced for DEBI, in which we used well-known nonpolitical personalities with whom large numbers of viewers would identify, was one which featured Danny Glover. Each personality delivered their own messages, in their own words, in the idiom in which they were most recognizable. The celebrities were then chromokeyed against a backdrop of moving images, depicting historical events. A central concern of the National Party appeared to be that

> The insertions which DEBI uses [as background context to voter education] only emphasised the National Party/Government history. The central message which emerges is that the NP must be replaced with a government which is not guilty of such deeds. . . . In the period of the election campaign in which the playing fields were already assumed to have been levelled, DEBI emphasises the selective past of one party [before changes were made] to the advantage of the other parties, and more specifically, the ANC.

This argument collapsed the situation in the country in a period before the "new South Africa," a situation which can best be summed up in the shorthand term *apartheid* with the history of the National Party. While it is no doubt true that the National Party was complicit in the inception, development, and elaboration of the apartheid, they alone were not responsible for apartheid. Apartheid was the continuation and elaboration of the policy of segregation, begun in the colonial era, and perpetuated by successive governments from the last quarter of the nineteenth century to the present. In this respect, the legacy of apartheid is widely shared. In looking to the past in order to move to the future, DEBI did not emphasize the National Party history, as alleged by the National Party. Rather, our central message was that in order to facilitate free, fair, and fully participatory elections, the system which existed in the past will not be able to exist in the future.

I asked Barry Gilder how he regarded the allegations of political partisanship. He responded:

> I think it was unfortunate that voter education was made a political football in the way it was. I have already said, I think it was unfortunate that we had to go through a DEBI in order to do voter education. I think the arguments, or the concerns, of the government were similar to the earlier concerns of the SABC management: that IFEE was a front of organizations for the ANC. The suspicion was there that voter education would be in favor of the ANC. When one sits back in retrospect, and one looks at it, to equate political support for democracy with support for the ANC is a bit false. Well, I mean the election showed the most people supported the ANC anyway. What we [Matla and IFEE] did was to support democracy, and broadly supported the goals of the anti-apartheid struggle of the previous decade—but without giving any support to any particular political party. We did that in principle, and I think DEBI did the same thing.

If one looks at the objections of the National Party directed at DEBI toward the end of our tenure, it is clear that they were interpreted in a party-political way. It is quite interesting when one looks at the specific accusations at programs, none of them were IFEE programs. My feeling, in retrospect, was that it was a political football situation which people still had a pro-ANC, proterrorist organization mentality. That's really the grounds for the government's reluctance.

Matla Trust, and IFEE and other organizations, had to go outside the country to bring in money for voter education in South Africa, and had to bring in a new board into the SABC to get access to the airwaves. Having done that, we still had to bring new players into voter education who were outside of IFEE. Having done that, and created a DEBI which, as I said earlier, had to negotiate every principle, down to every program, we still got accused of bias. I think that is indicative to me of the unreasonableness of the accusation of which were leveled against us.

Unreasonable or not, the accusations did have a dampening effect on the morale of DEBI. Asked whether she felt the IDASA campaigns were partisan in any way, Sue Valentine responded, "Well, I would certainly take offense at any suggestion that the material that we've produced on radio was partial. From what I've heard on radio, nothing is partisan in any way whatsoever. I think that one certainly can't pretend that the past didn't happen. But we've been pretty careful about what we said and how we said things."

Being "pretty careful about what we said and how we said things" meant in effect that the campaign was self-consciously "correct." I put it to André le Roux that one of the things that have repeatedly come up about DEBI was that it was rather doctrinaire and politically correct, and that it had a relatively narrow ideologic base. I asked him whether he felt that this was related to our definition of our target audience, or whether this was an inherent problem with the composition of the DEBI grouping:

One could argue with hindsight that we could have been more adventurous in bringing about electoral literacy. This was a historic first-time opportunity for many people. A moment of liberation. On the other hand, if the electoral process was to be undone through physical threat, this would have come from the black and white right wing. If you will, the overemphasis on neutrality, on a bland statement, took into account that possible threat. An overemphasis on the election being the result of a liberation struggle could have—and I have no doubt of that in my mind, as an Afrikaans-speaking person, or for that matter a white—could have conjured up enough emotion to present a danger to the process. And there were examples of this.

There was a direct physical threat to the SABC during the election, as a result of our coverage of the Bophuthaswana fiasco by the right wing. In this threat, constant reference was made to the DEBI programs and processes, which, even though they were stripped of emotion, were deemed to have been propagandistic toward the ANC. DEBI's acute awareness of that, also linked to the situation of violence in KwaZulu, necessitated a more politically neutral approach in the sense of judging history as a backdrop to the voter education program. So to a large extent, taking the emotion out of the voter education process made it more palatable, and kept DEBI above attack.

Had DEBI been forced to defend itself on a daily basis, and there were instances when it had to, the weight of the press, particularly the Afrikaans press, as well as conservative black newspapers like *Ilanga* and papers like that, could have necessitated a midstream severe rethink of what was going on the air. Which would have stalled the production process, which in turn would have meant that we could not maintain the necessary frequency to entrench democracy training. So the charge [of political correctness] is well taken, but I don't think DEBI had any other choice but to be as down the middle as possible. Had DEBI become a political issue, it would have sunk. That was also the editorial stance of the SABC.

Sometimes, it takes the cooler eye of an outsider to put a sense of perspective on the process. Larry Schwartz was of the opinion that while the programs themselves did not favor any specific party, the entire enterprise was steeped in politics:

> The product itself was thoroughly nonpartisan. It was the workings of the process that demonstrated that there is no such thing as a nonpolitical animal in South Africa. I'm sure there are many people who are civic minded in the classic sense of the word, and who are interested to work without political bias, but the bottom line is that in South Africa at this time, politics is so polarized and lack of trust was so replete throughout your political culture, it is hard to find a small number of civic-minded people that everyone trusts to be nonpartisan and to help build the base on which a voter education program could be constructed.

Paying the Piper: DEBI's Rocky Finances

One of the most vexed aspects of the DEBI project was that of finance. As part of its contribution to the preparation for the election, the SABC made the necessary airtime on both radio and television available on a no-charge basis. Initial estimates of budgets for production and administration indicated that the entire project would cost in the region of R 15 million, which was clearly too much. By cutting the expenditure down particularly in terms of planned television production, the costs were contained at R 8.5 million.

In September 1993, a delegation from DEBI met with a senior representative of the Department of Home Affairs, at that stage the relevant government department responsible for broadcasting. We asked for R 11 million, of which R 3 million were to be interim "bridging" finance until such time as the structures organizing the election, including the IEC, were to be put in place. Since planning and production needed to go ahead, particularly in terms of the lead time required for television programming, it was not possible to wait for the establishment of the IEC. These terms were agreed to, and the DEBI project was begun in earnest in November 1993.

In keeping with the endeavor to maintain a strict independence from all interest groups, a trust was set up and registered to administer the funds acquired and spent by DEBI. In good faith the SABC made a contribution of R 1 million to the DEBI trust. By the beginning of April 1994, no further monies had been paid into the trust, despite repeated efforts to extract the money previously promised.

The problem lay in the transitional nature of the state in the months prior to the election. Governance was shared between Parliament and the Transitional Executive Council (TEC), an all-party body mandated, among other things, to negotiate the terms of a new constitution and oversee the budget of the country. The Department of Home Affairs was no longer in charge of the election: this function had been taken over by the IEC.

In a meeting with DEBI, the chairperson of the IEC, Justice Johan Kriegler, said that the "IEC was not going to reinvent the wheel," and would not repeat voter education efforts but rather cooperate and support initiatives (including DEBI) which were already in progress. However, when representations for funding for voter education were made to the IEC, DEBI was told that this body could not make good on previous agreements with the Department of Home Affairs, and we should apply directly to the TEC. The TEC, in turn, took the view that funding voter education was the responsibility of the IEC, who in turn said they had no allocation from the TEC, and would we please go to international funders. The international funders were of the opinion that this really was the responsibility of the South African government, through the offices of the IEC—and so it went, around in circles.

Finally, through the intervention of two commissioners of the IEC, the R 3 million promised by Home Affairs as bridging finance was paid into the trust account. At the time of revising this chapter (October 1994), six months after the election, the balance of the money has not been forthcoming from the ficus and is being carried by the SABC.

I asked Barry Gilder to comment on the argument that since the IEC was a relatively autonomous body, one of whose statutory purposes was to provide voter education, the IEC should have accommodated and paid for voter education:

The IEC as whole is a different kettle of fish, which I think is quite a complicated question to answer. I'm still not sure what happened as far as the

IEC was concerned. Not just in relationship to DEBI, but also in relationship to all the other organizations involved in voter education. Because we all remember well that in discussion both with DEBI and also separately with IFEE, the IEC's voter education section, both with the commissioners and the chairperson of the IEC, we were told very clearly early on that they "did not intend to reinvent the wheel," but they seemed to spend the next few months doing just that—reinventing the wheel. I'm not sure why—whether it was internal organizational politics, whether it was attempts by certain people assigned to voter education to justify their jobs, whether it was an attitude against DEBI, or IFEE, or both.

I really don't understand what happened. It was, in a sense, illogical. You're absolutely right. The IEC should logically have supported nonpartisan voter education initiatives financially. They shouldn't have spent any money for their own voter education. They should have put whatever resources they had into existing initiatives. Unfortunately, the IEC should have been created long before DEBI came into being.

The other factor is that I don't know whether they had money. I think also the donor community played a bit of a difficult role there. Because the donor community, especially the European Union, put R 10 million into the IEC for voter education and basically said, "We've given R 20 million to IFEE already, this money is for other voter education." That created a difficult situation. I know that the IEC gave money, for example, to voter education projects which IFEE had previously turned down as duplication, so people went to the IEC who had been turned away by IFEE, and in some cases by DEBI, to try and get support. So I think it is a bit more complicated than just the political thing.

The actual monies spent on DEBI do not reflect the worth of the project in terms of either product or work. Numerous organizations—among them IFEE, IDASA, Rural Foundation, Project Vote, just to name a few—provided the initiative with ready-produced programming for both television and radio, at no charge to DEBI. The money for these efforts had been raised by the NGOs themselves, largely from foreign foundations. In addition, thousands of work-hours were voluntarily donated to the initiative. Add to this the free airtime made available by the SABC, including prime-time advertising spots, and the actual value of DEBI would be closer to three times the R 8.5 million reflected in the balance sheets. Sue Valentine makes this point:

> In terms of the funding, well, certainly IDASA raised the majority of its money for voter and democracy education itself. And so we have produced all our material with our imprint at our own expense. But there were some programs which we specifically produced at DEBI's request, in Afrikaans for Cape viewers. Certainly the work that I do as the DEBI coordinator in this

region (Western Cape), including preparing weekly talks and so on, is entirely subsidized by our organization.

As for other groups that were entirely dependent on the DEBI funding, I think it's shocking that the money is not forthcoming, because the whole DEBI initiative was agreed upon: it's a partnership between civil society and SABC and it should be supported, it's the one way in which the public can be reached through the media.

As the campaign progressed, the lack of financial resources, and the total reliance on the SABC to bankroll DEBI, had a strongly demotivating effect on all the participants of DEBI.

How Effective Was DEBI?

Speaking the Language

With the enactment of the new constitution in the wake of the April 1994 elections, all eleven languages generally spoken in South Africa were declared official.[26] African languages in South African can be roughly classified as belonging to either the family of Nguni languages, namely, Zulu and Xhosa, or the Sotho languages, which include North Sotho, South Sotho, and Tswana. Smaller percentages of home-language speakers use Venda, Tsonga, Swati, and Ndebele. The two previous official languages are English, which is the "home" language of just under half the white and "Indian" population, and the second language of other South Africans, most of whom are urban dwellers, while Afrikaans is the mother tongue of 15 percent and understood by approximately 40 percent of the whole population.

Designing a broadcast system which takes account of all these languages obviously sets an enormous challenge. Radio was relatively easy, since the different services in the various languages were tailor-made to reach their own target audience. All we had to do was to provide all our spots in eleven languages (no mean feat in itself). The local regional radio forums were charged with finding suitable discussants in the various languages to deal with the phone-in discussions. The radio magazines and minidramas were eventually produced only in the seven most popular languages, as were the IFEE advertisements.

The same seven languages were used on television, for which we devised a complicated formula for the even-handed rotation of the different languages. Nevertheless, taking into account the whole program mix, English received a greater proportion of time than any other language. This we justified in terms of the understanding that while English was mother tongue to a relatively small portion of the population, it was a common or shared language to many more.

RUTH: The one thing that I thought was very problematic, in a challenging way, and I would really like your response on this, was the whole question of using languages on television. I think we came up with some cost-effective ways of doing this by using the same program in different formats across different languages. What you think were the limitations of our approach? Would you think that we did the right thing?

BEATA: When I think of the future, and I think of eleven languages, it's quite clear there is already a bias toward two or three. I mean, I think that is understandable and natural. I think the fact that we did dub programs in a number of languages was very useful and very correct. And didn't seem to be quite as expensive as I had thought it was going to be. I mean, there is always the feeling that when you make a film and you are then going to redub it in a lot of languages, it is going to cost the absolute earth. Obviously, it is not the cheapest thing to do. But it seems to me it worked quite well.

RUTH: It seems to be that one of the sort of formats that people are experimenting with is to have multilingual programs rather than simply dubbed programs, and clearly parts of the program lost part of the audience. But on the whole, as somebody who perhaps doesn't speak that many African languages, do you find that you can follow the story line?

BEATA: Yes, absolutely. Because they were fairly simple and straightforward. And it's the clever way of doing it. I did find occasionally a little bit of a jostle in the jumble of languages that we had in some of those sitcom things; I mean, I know that can't be good in terms of language purists, but I didn't mind that so much either. And I think there is a danger here: the people are going to complain that we were presenting them with the mishmash, which isn't any language at all. I'm not sure that as a general principle, you know, forever and ever, it's something that people would approve of. I thought in that election context it was okay.

The "sitcom things" Beata referred to included the thirteen-part series *Kululeka.* Director Roberta Durrant referred to the postbroadcast evaluation of the series:

By all accounts *Kululeka* did what it set out to do. It was able to communicate its message. It seems that it was slightly less successful in the rural areas—possibility because we had the mixture of languages.

I think this is one of the most challenging aspects of having one program for everybody. It was fine in the metropolises, the metropolitan areas, where everyone understands (more or less) the different languages, certainly in a get-along kind of way. But when you get into the heavy Northern Transvaal, or the Cape, that's not the experience. For instance, the Sotho section may be lost to someone who lives in the rural KwaZulu areas. I think that was very challenging: how we were going to get across that information? In the end, we had to use five different languages. It was mainly Zulu—our research showed us that 55 percent of our target audience spoke Zulu and 35 percent spoke South Sotho. We also used Tswana, Xhosa, and English. But our research showed us very clearly the people in the Cape, for instance, were unhappy at not being able to understand. I think the project proved that you can't reach all sectors of the population with one program. But I think we went the right route in the end. Although we certainly lost the colored community in the Cape, and there were a lot of complaints about it. Had we done the whole program in English, we would certainly not have reached as many people. I personally think we would not have communicated as well.

The Debate of Radio versus Television

An on-going criticism of DEBI was the inequitable resources which were spent on television versus radio.

RUTH: We defined our target audience in the fairly narrow, and some say—and I am just bringing up what other people have said to me—in a fairly doctrinal way. It has been suggested that we actually left out perhaps not numerically large but significant parts of the electorate. Do you think that was a weakness, or do you think that was a pragmatic inevitability?

BEATA: Given the situation where just about everybody has access to radio, but when television has all the glamor and the glitz, I think we went down fairly obvious roads. The television is more expensive, and it's accessible to fewer people. Now that's a problem which is not of the SABC's doing. That's an economic problem in South Africa, plus the fact of the glamor. And so we followed a path which was inevitable, I think, given the circumstances, but which in terms of educating the mass of the population was, I felt, incorrect. I mean, we put a lot of money into television which reached, I don't know what, maybe half our target audience. But everybody would have radio available and we actually didn't spend even a third of our money on it. I wasn't on that working group, but I had the impression that not the same time, attention, and money was given to radio. It was an inverse of what we ought to have done. I understood why we were doing it.

Penetration of Voter and Democracy Education on Radio and Television

An important qualification of critique of radio versus television came from the research on the impact of voter education, commissioned by Television News Productions (TNP), which found that while radio had the greatest penetration of all forms of voter education (including print and face-to-face communication), with 82 percent of the electorate saying they heard something on radio about how to vote.[27] Radio was by far the most popular medium recalled by potential black voters, while colored respondents were more likely to remember seeing something on television. Both television and newspapers served as the primary sources of information for Indians and Whites.

Television was regarded as the most memorable of all the media, with 33 percent of the potential electorate as the most important source of voter education. Radio was mentioned by 21 percent. Both radio (26 percent) and television (24 percent) were cited about equally by potential black voters as the voter education medium most important to them. Among the rest of the population, television far exceeded the other sources in importance.

Regionally, television was judged most important to voter education efforts by residents of the Pretoria-Witwatersrand-Johannesburg area, and the Western Cape. KwaZulu Natal residents split their vote among radio and television. Potential voters in the Eastern Cape mentioned voter education organizations and television at about the same rate.

The high memorability of television can be attributed to the grammar of the medium, which incorporates a rich polysemy of words, sound, and images. This is an important observation to bear in mind when planning social advocacy messages.

Too Much Voter Education: Saturating the Audience?

One of the constant criticisms aimed at the whole area of voter education, particularly in the broadcast media, was that there was just too much election coverage. This point of view did not come from the professionals but rather from listeners and viewers. I asked André le Roux whether he felt that this might have worked against the reception of programming, or whether he felt it to be an invalid criticism:

I think it might have been the case among the more sophisticated members of the audience. Particularly the white audience, who had through years of limited democracy understood the processes of democracy and understood the process of the election. To them it became a bore. Because the content of the DEBI programs were not particularly directed at audience in the know, it was directed at the broad populace of the people and the mass audience out there who needed constant reassurances, constant grooming of the process, and I think what you sat with at the end of the day was a level of irritation among people who felt they did not need voter education but who were subjected to it because of the frequency with which it went on air. I personally think it was a very small price to pay.

Conclusion

DEBI was not a cohesive organization with a single commitment. The fifty-odd organizations represented on the steering committee embodied a wide spectrum of ideological and philosophical viewpoints. The SABC itself is a sprawling organization, with different tempos and procedural cultures in different departments. The objective of DEBI was not to meld all these contributions into a single voice but rather to orchestrate the different contributions into a harmonious chorus of voices with one message: that as many people as possible were to go the polls at the end of April 1994, and that all—both winners and losers—should accept the outcome of the election.

It is impossible to objectively assess the success of DEBI. Voter education in South Africa was so multifaceted that it is not clear whether it is appropriate or premature to credit broadcast initiative with any of the election's undoubted success. Larry Schwartz warned against such claims:

We've yet to ascertain whether these programs actually had any influence on voter turnout and voter understanding of the issues. I'm sure that given the way things work in our societies, you know, people spend money on these programs so they are going to want to see evaluation reports, which will inevitably report that they did a great job and they increased voter participation by 5 percent, or whatever it is, and that people actually understood the process. So this whole business was fraught with opportunities for people to claim credit for success in voter education. I don't know whether it will ever be proven that there was an effect, one way or the other. I personally doubt it.

Nevertheless, I am prepared to claim success. If not directly in the field of voter education—since that success was not unique to broadcast but must be shared with many other agencies working on the ground, face-to-face with voters—then at least in the area of the cooperative and democratizing potential of broadcasting.

In attempting an initiative like DEBI, the SABC was charting new territory. Not only were we treating themes and subjects not previously broached on the SABC as a state broadcaster, but we were doing so in solid cooperation and partnership with a wide constituency of organizations and interest groups. This was not an easy process. Noted Glen Masokoane,

The creation of DEBI and the many processes, stages, and moments of encounter among member organizations on the steering committee, has enriched dialogue among us at different levels as to what constitutes or what does not constitute voter education on television. The production processes with the TV ad hoc committees and within the working group has been a unique and valuable experience, a new style of education television.

Interviewees (in Order of Appearance)
It should be noted that all the interviewees spoke in their private capacity. The affiliations are indicated in order to situate them and not to suggest any official viewpoint.
Ruth Elizabeth Teer-Tomaselli: Member of the SABC Board; Chairperson of the Democratic Education Broadcasting Initiative (DEBI)

André le Roux: Acting Editor in Chief, Television News Productions

Barry Gilder: Media Officer, Matla Trust, and Voter Education Coordinator, IFEE

Beata Lipman: Steering Committee Representative for Film and Allied Workers Organization (FAWO), and member of Television Ad Hoc Group

Glen Masokoane: Television Executive Producer

Dave Meyerovitz: Television Producer, Pegasus Productions

Roberta Durrant: Television Producer, Penguin Films

Larry Schwartz: Press Liaison Officer, United States Information Services

Julie Frederickse: Radio Producer, and talk show host, Capital Radio

Zamambo Mkize: Head, Radio Zulu

Leonard Suransky: Professor of Politics, University of Durban-Westville; Member of Natal Radio Forum of DEBI

Nhlakamipho Zulu: Programme Producer and talk show host, Radio Zulu

Ricky Naidoo: Steering Committee Member representing Multi-Party Democracy; Chairperson, Natal Radio Forum of DEBI

Notes

1. For further information on both the campaigns leading up to the appointment of the SABC board, see Eric Louw, ed., *South African Media Policy: Debates of the 1990s* (Bellville: Anthropos, 1993). For a summary of the board's first year in office, see Ruth Teer-Tomaselli: "Cross the Great Divide," *The Journalist* (July 1994).

2. *Capital Radio,* 5 Apr. 1994.

3. DEBI Natal Forum Review Meeting, 19 May 1994.

4. The SABC is broken up in various business units, each with its own budget and management structure. The group executive is a management team made up of the heads of the various business units. TNP is responsible for the production of news bulletins, second-tier news programs, and at the time of elections, magazine and religious programming for all three SABC channels.

5. Radio Active is the commercial marketing arm for radio. It sells space and schedules commercials on all SABC radio stations nation wide.

6. As part of their voter education campaign, Matla produced a series of coordinated print, radio, and video (television) spot advertisements. These were eventually flighted under the banner of both IFEE and DEBI.

7. CVV is the second television channel of the SABC catering primarily to the entertainment needs of middle-class viewers. It broadcasts in English, Afrikaans, North and South Sotho, Tswana, Zulu, and Xhosa.

8. Wynand Harmse was the chief executive officer of the SABC at the time of the elections. He retired in September 1994 to make way for his successor, Zwelakhe Sisulu.

9. Publicity release, DEBI offices, 14 Apr. 1994.

10. Toward the end of the campaign, when the financial limitations became apparent, DEBI was forced to curtail the number of languages in which programs were produced, and some of the omnibus programs were only produced in four languages.

11. Minutes of the DEBI working group, 20 Jan. 1994.

12. All Media and Products Survey, AMPS is based on the Nielsen market research methodology.

13. AMPS 21–27 Feb. 1994, 28 Feb.–3 Mar. 1994. *Kululeka* was number three on CCV with 43 ARS, and *Make Your Mark* was eighth with 33 ARS on NNTV.

14. Commissioned by DEBI, produced by Ria Bonthuys for SAFRITEL, SABC, Television Center, Artillery Road, Auckland Park 2029.

15. Commissioned by DEBI, produced by Joe Shearer, Origin Pictures, P.O. Box 72053, Parkview 2122.

16. The SABC uses the Living Standards Measure (LSM) as its chief means of market/audience segmentation. The lowest category is LSM1, which is characterized, among indicators, as being predominantly rural (92.4 percent); largely unemployed (63 percent), relatively unschooled and illiterate (64 percent either have no schooling or have not completed seven years of primary schooling, and are considered to be functionally illiterate). None of these households have access to television, but 94 percent own a radio in their home. Source: CCV Consumerscope, SABC Auckland Park, 1994.

17. Source: CCV Consumerscope, SABC Auckland Park, 1994.

18. SABC Annual Report 1993, 28.

19. Questions relating to the voting rights of prisoners constituted the largest single category of inquiries, with more than a quarter of the inquiries related to prisoners' rights in the election.

20. Capital Radio interview with Julie Frederickse, 5 Apr. 1994.

21. Organizations which contributed music were IDASA, IFEE, BEF, Project Vote, and Institute for Contextual Theology (ICT).

22. Produced by the multinational advertising agency Ogilvy and Mather, Rightford Searle-Tripp and Makin.

23. Under apartheid, South Africans were classified as white, colored, Asian (or Indian), and black. The word *čolored* is used here to indicate not a specifically racial designation but rather a cultural group who identify themselves as such, share a common language (Afrikaans), and have specific cultural identities.

24. Stuart Hall, in *Culture, Society and the Media,* ed. Gurevitch, Bennett, Curran, and Woolacott, London: Methuen, 1985.

25. Published inter alia in the *Sunday Times,* 10 Apr. 1994, 11.

26. The South African Constitution (Act No. 200 of 1993) section 31 states: "Every person shall have the right to use the language of his or her choice." It further provides that conditions for the development and the promotion of the equal use and enjoyment of all official languages must be created (section 3(1)). The use of any language for purposes of exploitation, domination, or division must be prevented (section 3(9)(c)).

27. TNP (SABC): Voter Education: Polling Programme Segment. Prepared by Bill Dalbec and Craig Charney, Election Research Unit, April 1994.

APPENDIX: SELECTED EXCERPTS FROM THE COLLECTIVE EDITORIAL MEETING, 30 APRIL 1994

The following were present at the collective editorial meeting: Chris Pound, Mazyar Lotfalian, Meg McLagan, Ron Burnett, Barbara Kirshenblatt-Gimblett, Faye Ginsburg, Alexandra Juhasz, Kim Laughlin, Hamid Naficy, Sandy Stone, Lisa Cartwright, Joe Austin, Michael Fischer, Gudrun Klein, Julie Taylor, and George Marcus. Pieces by Michael Fischer, Faye Ginsburg, Gudrun Klein, Hamid Naficy, Sandy Stone, Lisa Cartwright, Julie Taylor, and Tom Wolfe could not be included in this year's annual, and will be scheduled for appearance in a later volume of Late Editions.

MEG MCLAGAN (on Mazyar Lotfalian): The author says that he was interested in studying the way that language and communication is "enframed" in the newsgroup that he started. I thought that you made some interesting observations about newsgroups and computer-mediated communication in general. But I found the theorizing to be confusing at times and not worked through and related to the conclusion. I found the use of Derrida and Barthes to be a little problematic. It signifies to me other, older debates that are really focused on the text. For me the struggle with this sort of work is to find a new way of discussing and thinking about computer-mediated communication, a new theoretical language that isn't based on textual models. I'm not sure this is possible, but this is something I've really tried to think about in my work and to think how can I move away from some of these older theorizings. I thought maybe it would be more fruitful to pursue some of the reflections on anthropology and the ethnographic method and computers. Some of your observations, I thought, were interesting. I very much liked the postings. I thought that the overlapping and the juxtaposition were very good. The cumulative effect was successful and made your point, and that sense of play and intertextuality was good.

BARBARA KIRSHENBLATT-GIMBLETT (on Lotfalian): One of the nice things about this paper is that it takes as its empirical moment the initiating of a newsgroup, and that strikes me as a good place to start because there's something very revelatory about the inception of groups in the medium. In some ways I feel that the left-hand column is a preliminary working through of ideas that I would hope in a later draft would recede. Right now, in that left-hand column there's a lot of citing of other people, and a lot of it feels to me remote from the case. And I can understand it as part of a process and a stage through which one moves toward one's goal, but I would like to see a closer fit between what's discussed in the left-hand column and what appears in the right-hand column. That's my main suggestion and, again (going along with Meg's comments) to *milk* the material more, to squeeze more from the actual case itself. I also would like to reinforce Meg's comment that you might question whether or not we need always to return to canonical positions that start with certain assumptions about writing and then move from writing out. It strikes me that this medium, particularly coming at it from an anthropological perspective, begs for some alternative way of operating, whatever it may be. So that would be my second comment. My third, and maybe this is old-fashioned, but I would like a more ethnographic sort of approach to the material itself. So, for instance, the entire use-group system in an astonishing way is one of the strangest phenomena, and it would be useful if we understood where, within that phenomenon, this particular moment comes.

MIKE FISCHER (on Lotfalian): It strikes me that there are two papers, this and Chris Pound's, that attempt to do mimetically in their texts some of what is occurring on the Net. So I'm intrigued by the fact that, Meg, you like the postings, that they work for you; and I'd like to hear a little bit more, Barbara, about what it is that this particular example might be milked for. But my sense about how these two papers work rhetorically seems somewhat different than that toward which you suggest Mazyar should revise. One of the interesting things for me in Mazyar's paper is how he uses what he suggests was an example of a kind of failure in order to understand the limits and potentials of this kind of discursive space on the Net. That is, I'm not sure that the case itself bears a whole lot more milking. More importantly, I read the paper quite differently with regard to its presuppositions about textual models of authority, canonical figures, or citations. I do not read the paper as looking to those authors as canonical; they function rather as quick takes, invoking other contemporary commentators. It is true that the left-hand column looks like a more traditional essay with a linear argument, while the right-hand side functions as illustration, as iterative mimickings of the postings, as the object of the discussion in the left-hand column. But the left-hand column also functions as a kind of posting in the form of quick takes, quick references. If the question editorially is whether or not one needs more exposition of Barthes or Derrida, I would point out that while those two are prominent, there is a long chain of such references, not only Derrida and Barthes, but Gilles Deleuze, Michael Heims, Gregory Ulmer, probably Stephen Tyler, as well as others. So it is really a chain of overlapping ideas almost as if parallel postings on a more literary form of the bulletin board. There is a tension, of course: at the same time the left-hand column also does function as the analytic argument of the piece as a whole.

JOE AUSTIN: So are you thinking that side is sort of a posting as well?

MIKE FISCHER: It's not quite fully that, but it gestures in that direction.

SANDY STONE (on Lotfalian): One of the issues that I delight in seeing you address here is how you deal with the question of representation in regard to virtual communities. The idea of the double columns is something I've seen in other contexts, and I like it here. I think it's very appropriate for what you're doing. There are problems with connecting the two, but in the sense of the disruption it produces, I think that it's appropriate here. Similar to what Mike said, I would want to see you using the left-hand column more as a kind of, what Avital Ronell called haunted writing. Where these people are coming in to do their postings, using you as ventriloquist, in a way. And thereby, you might be able to engage a more complex dialogue across the two columns. There's always trouble in doing that when you have this particular style, of finding ways to juxtapose the two in more than a random fashion. You might break up your right-hand text in ways that are a bit more formal. It doesn't have to be *too* formal, but it would only take a bit in order to create some consistent cross-links throughout.

GEORGE MARCUS: There's a really interesting issue of form in this paper. I just want to monitor something here. That we moved in the beginning of the discussion from a questioning of the form to a kind of acceptance and attempt to enhance it. So there's a really interesting tension in developing material on this particular subject that has something to do with (for or against) experiments in writing. And beyond that is the idea that these new forms of communication can or cannot be harnessed with all the assumptions thereof of our traditional languages of sociality. Everybody thinks we need new languages, but on what terms? There is a misrecognition in the use of Derridian "old textual references," but maybe they should not be understood as attempts to assimilate this new kind of communication to the text, but to use this textual theory in new ways by formal manipulation, actually, which may seem odd to people who want ethnography out of it.

CHRIS POUND (on Meg McLagan): I think that Meg's paper gets right to the core of an increasingly and extremely interesting piece of computer networks. As a native, I'll say yes, these things are happening all the time, it's not just Tibet. There are mailing lists and newsgroups for all sorts of political issues, and they spring up instantaneously anytime anything happens anywhere in the world. So, I think it's very current. I wonder if you shouldn't comment on why you characterize Barnett's work as electronic activism, despite the fact that he says that it's not. You call the work of Barnett and other senders electronic activism. Then a few lines later you say that Barnett is loathe to talk about his work in an activist context. This may lead the reader to think that you don't see the possibility of politically conscious action that isn't activist. Tseten Samdup also might position himself more as an agent of the government than as an activist. It seems like these guys are reviving a notion of doxa, which is opinion, instead of dogma, and I don't mean dogma in a bad sense—dogma is just being a more authoritative voice. And so instead of dogma, which is a word I associate with activists, it's more like doxa. So this leads me to the more general question of how political consciousness is constituted in computer networks. Barnett has some unusual things to say about the audience, he doesn't know who's reading it, stuff like that. This tends to set aside what we have traditionally understood of terms like *public* or *community* or *solidarity*. He doesn't even know who's reading this stuff, so he doesn't see a community for it. Combined with his perspective on computer networks as being subject to emotional fascism, which is true, you get a real sense for the ambiguity of computer-mediated form of political discourse that's not as clear-cut always. People don't agree about things on the Net very often. In fact, most talk.politics groups are predicated on the absence of a community or solidarity. You say *community* a couple times without going into it. It would be really interesting if you would take Barnett and Tseten Samdup's comments about monumentality and supplicating journalists to begin to *un*work the trope of collaboration between westerners and Tibetans, which are categories that you do begin to question a bit. Barnett isn't working to create any sort of solid front on the issues, and Tseten Samdup is extremely aware of the contingencies of media politics. There are several examples of that, like he understands the limitations people face, like journalists having to put out stories that aren't very good, or aren't even right. He's willing to overlook these things, which says something different than solidarity and even something different than propaganda. It's a willingness to let things get out there as long as they get out there. I think both of them have a lot of great comments in their interviews, that get away from a nonessentialist notion of community, and if you just played that up, it would be great.

KIM LAUGHLIN: All of this talk about the possibility and work of politics without conventional notions of solidarity I think is a nice way to overlay this onto the whole activist cycle. And that kind of gaming of language, doubling back on the definition of what the politics are, I think is in the activist papers also.

FAYE GINSBURG: There's a real issue about voicing in all the papers in terms of the tension between the theoretical conventional discourse of academia, and the anecdotal, intriguing way in which we feel privileged to write when we're dealing with extremely new phenomena. Because all of these papers are on the edge of these new kinds of formations, and put the author or the interlocutor in this complex position of, in a sense, advocate, promoter, and analyst.

RON BURNETT: In my own work with a lot of the activist organizations, the lack of critical discourse is sometimes profoundly alienating. The divide between the intellectual and the practitioner seems to be the key to the epistemological ground on which they base nearly all their activities—as long as it's not intellectual, at least in their terms, it's somehow activist. And that's led to an impoverishment of vision, a lack of understanding of where to go with the material. It comes across to me a lot in the lines that I read in USENET and so on. And I have a lot of serious questions about how, on the one hand, you can mythologize your own effectiveness as an activist simply because you promote yourself now more effectively because you have more places in which you can actually say that you're doing something. But on the other hand, ways of understanding, testing out, and really looking at that, and developing models and paradigms that you're comfortable with are not there.

FAYE GINSBURG: The media traditionally are incredibly parasitic on each other, and print journalism has always been the privileged form. So e-mail takes an interesting relationship to these as a new source; it's more naturalized than print journalism. I am going to string these words together and then try to come up with something cogent. Which is: activism, performance, mediation, and self-consciousness, which seem to be the linkages between these papers. When I think of Barnett, I've tried to invent this category of cultural activists who are not working in the obvious conventional domains of activism, but people who are self-consciously intervening in given social and political realities, and trying to transform them. When I read all of these things, going from performance art to e-mail self-presentation, what activists are trying to do in a naturalized sense and what the performers are trying to do in more self-conscious domain coming out of an art world starts to intersect in a way that maybe helps us get out of the old theory/practice divide and the really dead work on social movements. While the social movement model died and is languishing somewhere, all this new stuff is emerging, and it's exciting to work on it. You just have to start over and think what unites the work here—these are efforts at self-conscious mediation in various social movements. And people are using a variety of different mediating expressive forms, whatever their prior names were. So, I'm working a lot on this notion of mediation, media, mediating. My key words are *mediation, performance, activism, self-consciousness, intervention.*

KIM LAUGHLIN: One thing with this Paul Sagan interview, and especially with my first read of it, it was like, Oh, God, corporate liberalism one more time, but I found that when I went back and was cleaning up sentences and things, he is actually having to work his words pretty intensely. The question is, how do we lure readers into reading that closely with the negotiations of— you know he calls himself a journalist about nineteen times, and yet, clearly, he's not a plain old journalist. And the way in which old language is being reshaped to deal with new institutional processes, new technological operations, it really requires tight reading. I don't know how to flag the material, within this kind of context—like, should you include parts of this interview just to show it's ethnographic?—that work can be done through juxtaposition, perhaps. What do we do with this stuff?

RON BURNETT: There's a real difference between interviews, dialogue, conversation, and all of the various categories, and we're using this marvelous hybridization of all the forms of talking that we can possibly find. But I don't think that one should overvalue talk. Nor should one overvalue the profound sense that some people have that they know a lot about what they're doing. It's a really strange tension, right? You're talking to somebody and you transcribe it, you look at what they've said, you're putting it into prose, you're pulling it out of context. There's all of these various issues, that are classical issues in ethnographic research. I found it hard in my piece to include the interview material. The only way I thought I could use it was to be honest about rechannelling it through myself, as opposed to presuming that I could bring out what was happening in the conversation.

LISA CARTWRIGHT (on Barbara Kirshenblatt-Gimblett): There seem to be two main themes here, and one is that electronic communication is a distinctive medium, and the second is the thing about play. I want to pursue the first argument, that electronic communication is distinctive from forms like the phone and the fax. I want to ask why it is important to establish all electronic communications as a distinctive medium. And given the nature of the medium, might it not be more useful to talk about a kind of transmedium, in which there are various types of modalities? And the whole issue of public sphere, which is something that comes up in a couple of papers. I think that the public sphere is being used in some way as a concrete versus a virtual space, and that just might be slightly altered to think about public spheres as constructed political spaces, so that we can pluralize the concept.

HAMID NAFICY (on Kirshenblatt-Gimblett): Both sights and sites of capitalist excess, like the mega malls or five-hundred-channel television or multiplex cinemas, engender pleasure; they also engender panic. You have, I think, talked very well about the pleasure and the play of this excess, but not the panic. What does it mean to be confronted with millions of channels and avenues of information? What kinds of anxieties or chaos or panic sets in?

FAYE GINSBURG: It seems that there are two engagements—tropes, really—Ron represents one to me and Barbara the other. One is somewhat dystopic, and the other one is, "it's new, avant-garde, the cutting edge, it's utopic, full of possibility." I think what's exciting about this is we don't have to make a line saying that there's a paradigm shift or a technological shift that can divide everything we've come across into a certain era. I think what's interesting is that the conventions haven't been set yet for using these kinds of mediations. And what you talk about as play almost limits it, because we have such conventional notions of what play is. So the activism, in a certain way, is also sort of play, because the conventions haven't been set for the format and there's something very appealing about it. It gets written in American terms, like, if you read news stories on media, the guys who started Apple were these mavericks in their garage. Because the rules hadn't been set and they made them up, because the conventions weren't already established. The most interesting people in institutions that teach filmmaking or journalism are all autodidacts, because nobody taught them the rules. So there is a very important issue about cultural politics that create and define the arenas where people somehow escape conventional modes. When the computer is assimilated to work spaces, of course, there is no room for play. It's something about the line between where people feel dominated by conventions for economic, political, or intellectual reasons, or where they feel there's a space for play, whether it be sociopolitical or performative in more overtly planned ways.

LISA CARTWRIGHT (on Kirshenblatt-Gimblett): One of the points that came up for me has to do with the materiality of virtual space versus actual space. I think this piece provides a really good context for talking about the materiality of the very spaces that are constituted by the Net.

BARBARA KIRSHENBLATT-GIMBLETT (on Pound): First of all, what I really loved about it is that it's written by somebody from inside, from insider experience. That, I think, is enormously valuable. And it's an experience in the daily reality, both in terms of work and in terms of what he does on the Net outside of work. But I don't think the distinction holds up anymore. I found that that positioning distinguished it in large measure from the other papers in the subject. And that made it particularly interesting.

RON BURNETT (on Pound): It resonated for me immediately, and my take on it was the same thing that happens to me when I go into the Gopher and I'm going through endless lists and I'm trying to find out what is relevant and what is not. That is what I felt that I was doing when I entered into this. What I love about this paper is the extent to which there are millions of metaphors and none of them are actually serious, which is exactly the way the Internet works.

FAYE GINSBURG (on Laughlin-Monberg): I thought the way you could position yourself is to talk about [Paul Sagan] and to make of him an example of how the American system conceives of itself. I mean, the metaphors are there throughout. About the intrepid venture-capital creativity on the horizon. If you feel you can manage to position him as a player, as an exemplar, in a sense, a key informant about this whole system. And most of the other work is writing on the kind of margins where, you know, there's some liberty, because—he's working in an incredibly rule-bound system, despite the notion of being on the forefront. I mean, a pioneer is only on the forefront because there's an incredible apparatus of the state or the economy behind him or her. Just to call it "news on demand" and the notion of instantaneous Nielsen-type reading, when, of course, audiences are constructed and made over time.

MIKE FISCHER (on Laughlin-Monberg): What I wanted to say was it struck me that the most powerful trope in here to be explored is this notion of failure rather than futuristic language of pioneering and the utopic. Because that's what his anxiety structure seems to be all about, and its powerful way of revealing all of these disappointing mechanisms within in the institution at every level. And if you framed it that way, you then can play out, you could cut up the interview into topical units around major issues like the notion of an informed public as opposed to an activist public. What kind of public is one talking about? This is the primary disciplining matrix of the business side. I wanted to know what were those failures, what were those experiments, why did they fail, what were they learning from that? The fact that learning occurs is recuperation, but the structure is one of cutting things off. It's very much like the biotech industries, where you have to invest a huge amount of money speculatively, and there's a certain amount of burn time, burned capital that you invest before it even takes off. It's the same sort of thing here, too. And then there's all that wonderful stuff about the law, about patents, copyrights, not having contract language available for what's happening.

FAYE GINSBURG: I think indigenous media producers invite us to interrogate and rethink our own categorical imperatives. And as we get closer to a kind of more middle-class center, like even Salcedo, she accepts a certain definition that is more bounded. And these other people are more experimental—you know, wherever it works, let's try this out, let's try that out, but their goal is communication and transformation. For me, it was interesting they came from places most removed from centers in the West that are making these kind of categories that we're struggling with now. We're struggling to first make them and then escape them at the same time.

KIM LAUGHLIN: We've chosen media not because we know the boundaries of what media is, but because it's just a finegrained means to go into different contemporary spheres of ontological understanding. Media is particularly enabling precisely to understand these marginalized sites . . .

FAYE GINSBURG: Sometimes I read about these people and I feel very envious of the degree to which they're not bounded by those categories. It's this sort of absolutely incredible admiration. It provides a sort of estrangement on our categories that I find very productive.

HAMID NAFICY: We did not have translation problems in the morning [in the discussion of the Internet papers versus the afternoon discussion of perilous states papers] because most everyone was dealing with a U.S.-dominated, English-language-dominated, Western-dominated technology.

MIKE FISCHER: But we did have translation problems with technical language and common-sense language.

GEORGE MARCUS: But we were accepting that we were doing it in a totally unconventional space, so the whole assumption of what we were doing was different.

HAMID NAFICY: So I want to sort of go back on that and say that this morning we were universalizing our discourse, while that discourse is actually in many ways very ethnicized. If you look at the newsgroups you see very interesting efforts made by people who do not use Latin letters. Instead, they try and use the keyboards and its various characters in unusual ways to write in their own language or a semblance of it. And so I think there's actually quite a lot of translational multilingual effort that goes on on the Net that we elided this morning. Somehow maybe in the series, in the production, somewhere a point like this should be raised. Because both our discussion and the Net are highly Eurocentric and America-centric.

GEORGE MARCUS: Yes, that's a key point on reflection. When we were doing it, we didn't raise any of these questions. We were happy not to raise any of these things, but I don't think that we were involved in a process that denied ethnic differences which clearly play a significant role.

Contributors

Joe Austin is a graduate student in the American Studies Program at the University of Minnesota.

Ron Burnett is professor and chair of the Graduate Program in Communications, McGill University.

Alexandra Juhasz is a graduate of the Ethnographic Media Program within the Department of Anthropology, New York University.

Barbara Kirshenblatt-Gimblett teaches in the School of Performance Studies, New York University.

Dorinne Kondo teaches anthropology and women's studies at Pomona College.

Kim Laughlin is an anthropologist who teaches in the Department of Science and Technology Studies at the Rensselaer Polytechnic Institute.

Mazyar Lotfalian is a graduate student in anthropology at Rice University.

Meg McLagan is a graduate of the Ethnographic Media Program within the Department of Anthropology, New York University.

George E. Marcus is professor and chair of the Department of Anthropology, Rice University.

John Monberg is a graduate student in the Department of Science and Technology Studies, Rensselaer Polytechnic Institute.

Fred Myers is professor and chair of the Department of Anthropology, New York University.

Chris Pound is a graduate student in the Department of Anthropology, Rice University.

Rayna Rapp teaches in the Department of Anthropology, New School for Social Research.

Ruth Elizabeth Teer-Tomaselli is a researcher associated with the Center for Cultural and Media Studies, University of Natal.

INDEX